A TANGLED WEB

H Montgomery Hyde

A TANGLED WEB

SEX SCANDALS IN BRITISH POLITICS AND SOCIETY

CONSTABLE · LONDON

First published in Great Britain 1986
by Constable and Company Limited
10 Orange Street London WC2H 7EG
Copyright © 1986 by Harford Productions Ltd
Set in Linotron Plantin 11pt by
Rowland Phototypesetting Ltd
Bury St Edmunds, Suffolk
Printed in Great Britain by
St Edmundsbury Press
Bury St Edmunds, Suffolk

British Library CIP data
Hyde, H. Montgomery
A tangled web: sex scandals
in British politics and society
1. Sex customs – Great Britain – History – 18th
century   2. Sex customs – Great Britain –
History – 20th century
I. Title
306.7′0941   HQ18.G7

ISBN 0 09 466960 0

For my dearest Robbie

O what a tangled web we weave,
When first we practise to deceive!

Sir Walter Scott, *Marmion*, xvii

Contents

Illustrations

[11]

Wonersh Lodge, Eltham
10 Walsingham Terrace, Brighton
The Parnell Monument in Dublin
Sir Hari Singh (*The Mr 'A' Case*, edited by C. E. Beechofer Roberts)
Captain Charles Arthur
Mrs Maud Robinson
Mr Charles Robinson
The Hon Christabel Russell (*Christabel* by Eileen Hunter)
John Russell and his father
Christabel with the Russell baby
Geoffrey fourth Lord Ampthill
Rt Hon Jeremy Thorpe at his first wedding (*Keystone Press Agency*)
With his second wife Marion (*Associated Press*)
Norman Scott (*London Express News Service*)
Andrew Newton (*Associated Press*)
'Vote Waugh' (*Election poster*)
Tom Driberg (*Ruling passions* by Tom Driberg)
Ian Harvey (*To Fall Like Lucifer* by Ian Harvey)

Between pages 288 and 289

Victor Grayson MP (*BBC Hulton Picture Library*)
The Earl of Birkenhead (*Topical Press*)
Mona Dunn (*Courage* by Lord Beaverbrook)
Christine Keeler (*Evening Standard*)
Rt Hon John Profumo (*Epoque*)
Viscount Astor (*BBC Hulton Picture Library*)
Mandy Rice-Davies (*Mirrorpic*)
Stephen Ward (*Daily Mail*)
Christine Keeler drawing (*National Portrait Gallery*)
Captain Eugene Ivanov (*Odhams Press*)
Zina Volkova (*Salor in a Russian Frame* by Commander Anthony Courtney)
Commander Anthony Courtney (*Sailor in a Russian Frame*)
Charles Vassall (*Vassall* by Charles Vassall)
The Hon. T. G. D. Galbraith MP (*Sunday Telegraph*)
Earl Jellicoe (*BBC Hulton Picture Library*)
97 Onslow Square (*BBC Hulton Picture Library*)
Viscount Lambton (*BBC Hulton Picture Library*)
Norma Levy (*BBC Hulton Picture Library*)

Rt Hon John Stonehouse and Mrs Barbara Stonehouse (*BBC Hulton Picture Library*)

Mr Justice Eveleigh (*BBC Hulton Picture Library*)

Mrs Sheila Buckley (*BBC Hulton Picture Library*)

Rt Hon Cecil Parkinson MP (*Camera Press*)

Sara Keays and sister (*Private Eye*, 21 Oct. 1983)

Acknowledgements

The documentary and printed sources to which I am indebted in researching this book are fully set out in the notes and sources following the text.

The following individuals have rendered help in various ways and I gladly take this opportunity of expressing my gratitude to them: Commander Anthony Courtney, Marcia Lady Falkender, Mr Ian Harvey, Mr Richard Ingrams, Mr James Lees-Milne, the Marquess of Londonderry, Mr Donald McCormick, Mr Barry Penrose, Mr H. Chapman Pincher, Mr Cosmo Russell, Mr John Stonehouse, and Lord Sudeley.

Institutions and their staffs to whom I am likewise indebted include the British Museum, the British Library, the Hertfordshire County Record Office, the London Library, the National Portrait Gallery, the Registry of Births, the Public Record Office of Northern Ireland, and the Scottish Record Office.

For permission to reproduce the illustrations I am obliged to the authorities indicated in the foregoing list.

Finally I must express my warmest thanks to my publishers for their unfailing assistance at every stage; also my wife, to whom the book is dedicated, for her conscientious work in typing the draft and for her useful advice in many particulars of which I have taken advantage.

H.M.H.
Tenterden
Kent

[15]

Aristocratic Morals
in the Eighteenth Century

1

UNTIL the reign of Charles II the ecclesiastical courts in England heard cases of adultery, bigamy, incest, rape, sexual perversion, impotence and the like *in private*. In the case of peers, whether temporal or spiritual, they were tried and continued to be tried until the present century by their fellow peers in the House of Lords, the most notorious case being that of Mervyn Touchet second Earl of Castlehaven in 1633 for buggering a servant and abetting the rape of his wife by another servant: he was convicted and beheaded. Other peerage trials with sexual overtones worth mentioning were those of the Duchess of Kingston in 1776 for bigamy and John Russell second Earl Russell in 1901, also for bigamy: both were found guilty.[1]

The process of curtailing and eventually abolishing the jurisdiction of the ecclesiastical or so-called 'bawdy courts' was begun by Henry VIII after his break with Rome when, on the advice of his minister Thomas Cromwell in 1533, Parliament made sodomy and bestiality offences punishable by the criminal courts with death. Similarly, the crime of bigamy became a felony and thus a capital offence in the reign of James I. The process was completed by Charles II who abolished the criminal and most of the civil jurisdiction of the ecclesiastical courts and transferred them to the ordinary civil courts in Westminster Hall and the criminal courts at the Old Bailey and county assizes. Unlike the ecclesiastical courts, these courts sat *in public* with the publicity to be expected in the more salacious kind of case, especially suits for adultery or criminal conversation (*crim. con.*), as they were called. Publishers of pornography like the notorious Edmund Curll took advantage of the

[17]

English public's prurient interest and continued to bring out accounts of these trials until the judicial Divorce Court was established in 1857.

One subject in which the ecclesiastical courts long exercised jurisdiction was that of matrimonial relations.[2] This took two forms, validity of marriage and divorce. Marriages could be declared null and void for consanguinity within the prohibited degrees of relationship by canon law, for wilful non-consummation, physical incapacity, absence of consent and similar reasons. Such marriages were thus annulled. The ecclesiastical courts also granted divorce *a mensa et thoro* (from bed and board) on the grounds of adultery and cruelty. But such a divorce was limited in effect, being akin to a judicial separation, since as a general rule neither of the parties was free to remarry within the lifetime of the other. There was one case, that of Lord Northampton in the reign of Edward VI, where the court pronounced in favour of a second marriage. But this was exceptional. The matter was put beyond doubt in the last years of Queen Elizabeth I when it was decided that a marriage validly contracted in England could not be dissolved for any cause. It was otherwise in Scotland where power to grant absolute divorce for adultery, due largely to the influence of the presbyterian divine and reformer John Knox, was assumed by the courts in 1560 and confirmed by statute in 1573 which also introduced divorce for desertion after four years. In Ireland there was no divorce on any ground, which has continued until the present day, although actions for *crim. con.* were allowed in the civil courts. (They have recently been abolished there.) However, from the time of the Restoration in England there was a growing sense of the right to an absolute divorce for adequate cause, notwithstanding any religious views to the contrary. Eventually the matter came to a head when Parliament was moved to intervene in the case of Lord Macclesfield at the end of the seventeenth century.[3]

In 1683 Charles Gerard second Earl of Macclesfield married Anne Mason, fifteen-year-old daughter of Sir Richard Mason, Comptroller of the Royal Household. The marriage was childless and a failure almost from the beginning, husband and wife parting after eighteen months and never again living together. Macclesfield was a profligate young man, while his wife was no better, taking a lover, Richard Savage Earl Rivers, by whom she had two illegitimate children. Eventually Macclesfield began proceedings in the ecclesiastical court for a divorce *a mensa et thoro* but these failed, possibly due to the laxity of his own morals. He therefore petitioned the House of Lords in 1697 for a Private Act of Parliament, giving him an absolute divorce on the grounds

> that it would be a most unreasonable hardship upon him, that the standing law which is designed to do every man right, should, by the rigour of the letter, be to him the cause of the greatest wrong: that for his wife's fault he should be deprived of the common privilege of every freeman in the world, to have an heir of his own body to inherit what he possessed either of honour or estate, or that his own brother should lose his claim to both, and have his birthright sacrificed to Lady Macclesfield's irregular life.

Macclesfield's petition was granted and the necessary Act was passed giving him his freedom.[4] Three years later his case was followed by that of Henry Howard seventh Duke of Norfolk who had likewise been unsuccessful in obtaining a divorce *a mensa et thoro* in the ecclesiastical court. The Duke's marriage to his adulterous and childless Duchess was declared void by the House of Lords in 1700, after his grace had twice previously introduced bills of divorce which their lordships had rejected and he had sued her lover Sir John Germain, a soldier of fortune and reputed son of a Dutch inn-keeper, for *crim. con.* in the Court of King's Bench, Westminster. There he had only been awarded 100 marks (about £66) in damages and costs, although he had actually claimed £100,000. No doubt this result was due to the Duke's reputation for gallantry, a contemporary (the Earl of Dartmouth) describing him as 'notoriously a very vicious man; and besides his own example had been the original introducer of all the bad company she [the Duchess] kept to her own acquaintance.' The Duchess was born Lady Mary Mordaunt, daughter and heiress of the second Earl of Peterborough. She married Norfolk in 1677 and separated from him in 1685 when he accidently discovered her infidelity when her portrait was being painted by Simon Verelst. In 1701, the same year that Norfolk died with no direct heir, she married Germain and died four years later aged forty-six, leaving her second husband a large estate and a fortune of £70,000, which was to involve him in protracted litigation with her family.[5]

It was now possible to obtain an absolute divorce by Private Act of

Parliament, but the procedure was lengthy, cumbersome and expensive. In practice this procedure was only invoked by husbands whose wives were adulterous. Where the wife was the petitioner – and there were only four such cases prior to 1857 – it was necessary for the husband's guilt to be aggravated, for example by cruelty or bigamy. Nor was the number of male petitioners relatively large. There were only five successful petitions before the Hanoverian succession, sixty between 1715 and 1775, and seventy-four during the remaining quarter of the eighteenth century – a total in all of 139. In 1798 these proceedings by legislative process were regulated by the House of Lords which required that all applications for divorce brought before the Upper House should be supported by a divorce *a mensa et thoro* in the ecclesiastical courts and, in the case of a male petitioner, a verdict for damages for *crim. con.* against the wife's seducer in the civil courts.

One of the most sensational cases in the eighteenth century, on account of its association with the royal family, was the *crim. con.* action brought by the first Earl of Grosvenor, a notorious rake, against King George III's foolish brother, Admiral Henry Frederick Duke of Cumberland, in 1770 for having seduced the Countess.[6] This flighty lady was discovered through letters between her and the Duke which had been intercepted by her husband. As we read:

> Several of Lord Grosvenor's servants went down to St Albans with his lordship's brother, who, upon breaking open the door at the inn, found the Duke of Cumberland sitting on the bed-side along with Lady Grosvenor, with his waistcoat loose, and the lady with her dress unbuttoned and her breasts wholly exposed.

Lord Grosvenor was awarded £10,000 damages for the loss of his wife's virtue, a sum which the Duke's two brothers the King and the Duke of Gloucester had to help him to pay. Nevertheless, Grosvenor settled £1,200 a year on his errant wife. After his death in 1802 she married Lieut.-General George Porter, MP, who later became a Hungarian baron. They both died in 1828. Meanwhile Cumberland had married a widow, Mrs Anne Horton, in 1771, the year after his affair with Lady Grosvenor. He died without legitimate children in 1790 and all his honours became extinct. It was largely on account of his second

[20]

marriage, which the King considered unsuitable, that the Royal Marriages act of 1772 was passed. This important legislative enactment provided that all marriages of descendants of George II, other than the issue of princesses married into foreign families, should not be valid unless they had the consent of the King in Council, or, if the parties were aged over twenty-five, they had given twelve months notice to the Privy Council, provided that during that time both Houses of Parliament had not expressly declared disapproval of the proposed marriage. (George III's son the Duke of Sussex violated the Act when he married Lady Augusta Murray in 1793 and the marriage was consequently declared void and dissolved in the following year. On the other hand, although the King's grandson George, second Duke of Cambridge, also contravened the Act when he wed the actress Louisa Fairbrother in 1840, Queen Victoria did not invoke the Act, since the Duke's wife styled herself Mrs Fitz-George, this name also being adopted by their descendants.)

By contrast with the damages awarded in the Grosvenor case, there was the case of Sir Richard Worsley, Bart., MP, privy counsellor, Governor of the Isle of Wight and a distinguished antiquarian and art collector, who claimed £20,000 damages from a gentleman named George Bissett for having seduced his wife Seymour, who was a daughter of another baronet Sir John Fleming, of Brompton Park, Middlesex.[7] Mr Bissett, a captain in the Hampshire militia of which Worsley was colonel, was only one of Lady Worsley's lovers, who included the Earl of Peterborough, Lord Deerhurst, later seventh Earl of Coventry and the Marquess of Graham, later third Duke of Montrose. In the action for *crim. con.*, which was tried before the Lord Chief Justice, Lord Mansfield, in 1782, the jury were informed by Mr Bissett's counsel that his client could prove that at the public baths in Maidstone, where Sir Richard had a house, 'the Plaintiff had absolutely raised the Defendant upon his shoulders to view his naked wife while bathing' and 'on coming out she joined the gentlemen and they all went off merry and laughing together.' Another witness was a doctor who had attended Lady Worsley at her request and declared that he had her permission to give evidence of the truth, namely that she had 'some complaints on her' which the doctor fancied were 'the consequence of a venereal disorder' apparently acquired from the young Lord Graham.

The jury found for Sir Richard, but on account of his connivance only awarded him damages of one shilling. The case caused considerable public interest at the time and was the subject of various erotic poems and prints, enumerating Lady Worsley's many love affairs and commenting appropriately on Sir Richard's habit of displaying his naked wife to other gentlemen. She was later allowed by royal grant to style herself Lady Fleming and a month after her husband's death in 1795 she married a Frenchman named Louis Couchet with whom she appears to have been living for some time.

Another 'noble whore' of the period was Lady Anne Foley, a daughter of the sixth Earl of Coventry and a sister of Lady Worsley's lover Lord Deerhurst. She also had numerous affairs, one being with the Earl of Peterborough, another of Lady Worsley's lovers. Lady Anne was married to the Hon. Edward Foley, MP, a younger son of Lord Foley, who sued Peterborough at Hereford assizes and obtained £2,500 damages which the incautious Lothario paid. A little later, further evidence of his wife's misconduct reached Mr Foley's ears, and he brought an action for divorce *a mensa et thoro* in the ecclesiastical court in London, alleging further adultery with Peterborough in a shrubbery, against an oak tree and in the plaintiff's coach. The coachman deposed that he was able to peep through the blinds which covered the front window of the coach and 'plainly saw the sight of the Right Honourable Lady Anne Foley, lying upon the back seat of the said coach, with her naked thighs exposed, and the said Lord Peterborough lying upon her and between her naked thighs, and they were in the very act of carnal copulation and the said coach was then in motion occasioned thereby, notwithstanding the horses were standing still.'[8]

The lecherous Lady Anne was divorced by a Private Act introduced in the House of Lords in 1787. Peterborough refused to marry her, and he died unmarried and without issue when the peerage became extinct. However, she found another husband, Captain Samuel Wright, probably another of her lovers, about whom nothing further is known.

Unique as a corrupt politician, gambler and womaniser, living with his mistress as well as his wife and children, both legitimate and illegitimate, in the same house, was the peer who had the distinction of having a group of islands and a popular article of food named after him. In 1778 John Montagu fourth Earl of Sandwich was First Lord of the Admiralty when the explorer Captain Cook discovered Hawaii and called the islands by the name of his chief at the Admiralty. The

Sandwich Islands continued to be so called when they were directly ruled by local sovereigns and while they were under British protection, that is until their annexation by the United States in 1900. Lord Sandwich, who was commonly known as Jemmy Twitcher from a reference to him in *The Beggar's Opera*, was an inveterate gambler. He would often spend a whole day or a night at the tables and would bid a waiter bring him a piece of meat between two pieces of bread, which he would eat to sustain him while not stopping from play. He did this so frequently that the food soon became known as a sandwich, and so it has remained to this day. As for his administration of the Admiralty Sandwich's conduct is probably the most notorious for corruption and incapacity in British naval history.

Another notable blot on Sandwich's political career was his part in the seizing of the papers of his former friend and intimate, the radical MP John Wilkes, which included Wilkes's privately printed *Essay on Women*, an indecent parody of Pope's *Essay on Man*. Sandwich, who pretended that the work was addressed to him, brought it before the House of Lords in 1763, insisting that it constituted a breach of his privilege as a peer and proceeded to read the bawdy verses aloud to the House. Although another noble lord asked that the reading should cease, the majority of their lordships shouted to Sandwich 'Go on!' Sandwich did so, and at the end of his recitation the House resolved that the poem was 'a most scandalous, obscene and impious libel'. As a result Wilkes was convicted of publishing an obscene libel and fined £500. When he failed to appear for judgment he was outlawed and expelled from the House of Commons, but the outlawry was later reversed and he was re-elected MP. However, public opinion rightly condemned Sandwich and the others who had sacrificed the ties of friendship for mere party ends, and at a performance of *The Beggar's Opera* the audience rose to Macheath's words in the final scene, 'That Jemmy Twitcher should peach me, I own surprised me.'

Sandwich's mistress was a young actress, Martha Ray, who lived with him and his family at Hinchingbrooke, the Sandwich country house near Huntingdon, formerly owned by Oliver Cromwell. Among the visitors to Hinchingbrooke was an army recruiting officer named James Hackman, who was later ordained a priest. Unfortunately Hackman fell in love with Martha Ray and pestered her with his attentions, going so far as to propose marriage which she refused. In April 1779, the same

[23]

year as he had been ordained, the Revd Mr Hackman lay in wait for Martha who was performing in a play at Covent Garden, and as she was leaving the theatre he shot her through the head with a pistol after which he unsuccessfully tried to kill himself with another pistol which he was carrying. He was tried at the Old Bailey before Mr Justice Blackstone, found guilty and hanged at Tyburn. Before he died he asked Sandwich's forgiveness, which Sandwich conveyed to him but at the same time declared that Hackman had 'robbed him of all comfort in this world'.

James Boswell, who was present at Hackman's trial and afterwards accompanied the condemned man to Tyburn in the mourning coach, gave Dr Johnson a full account of these proceedings, which greatly interested him, particularly Hackman's dying prayer for the mercy of heaven. 'I hope he *shall* find mercy,' the doctor observed 'in a solemn and fervid tone', according to Boswell.

With the murder Sandwich had nothing whatever to do and he was extremely fond of the dead actress with whom he had been intimate for sixteen years. However, the revelation that he, a man over sixty, had a mistress little more than half his age permanently living with him, led to an outburst on the part of the public who hated him, and this eventually resulted in his resignation and retirement from public life. He died in 1792, leaving five children by his wife, the eldest of whom became the fifth Earl, and two sons by his mistress, Basil Montagu, who became the leading authority on bankruptcy and advocate of its reform, and Robert Montagu who joined the navy and ended his career as an admiral. Their father, despite his excesses in sex, gaming, politics and scandals, will always be remembered as the inventor of the sandwich.[9]

2

Not all the eighteenth-century sex cases were concerned with adultery. One of the most notorious of the others was the case of Colonel Francis Charteris, a Scotchman from Dumfries, and gambling trickster who was drummed out of the army for cheating at cards, and reprimanded on his knees at the Bar of the House of Commons for enlisting dishonest tradesmen in his military company to save them from arrest. In 1729 Charteris was arrested on a charge of raping a maid named Ann Bond in his service and was tried at the Old Bailey. Ann Bond told the court that he raped her in the dining-room on a couch near the fire, stuffing his night cap in her mouth to stifle her cries. Being asked whether the prisoner had his clothes on, she replied that he was in his night gown, and that he pulled up her petticoats before he raped her. Being asked whether she was sure and how she knew he had carnal knowledge of her, she replied she was sure he had and that he laid himself down upon her and entered her body. She was also asked how it was afterwards. She replied that there was 'a great deal of wet' and that he endeavoured to pacify her with promises of a great many fine clothes, etc. if she would hold her tongue and say nothing about it.

Since other servants confirmed Bond's testimony, Charteris was convicted and sentenced to death. This was somewhat surprising, since the rape of a servant was considered by many in the upper classes of the time to be a permissible act of gallantry rather than a crime. At all events, such was the influence of the prisoner's aristocratic friends that King George II was persuaded to pardon him after a short stay in Newgate and instead of being taken to the gallows at Tyburn he was released on the payment of a fine. He died in 1732 aged fifty-six in Scotland and on the night of his death there was a violent tempest which the populace interpreted as a token of divine vengeance. People rioted at his funeral, almost tore the body out of the coffin and threw dead dogs and offal into the grave along with it. As a notorious whore-master and seducer the gallant colonel has the unenviable distinction of figuring in the first plate of Hogarth's *The Harlot's Progress*.[10]

Homosexuality in high places also flourished in the eighteenth century to such an extent that in his picaresque and partly auto-biographical novel *Roderick Random*, first published in 1748, Tobias Smollett, who was a familiar figure in the London taverns and coffee-houses of the period, made his character Lord Strutwell declare that homosexuality 'gains ground apace and in all probability will become in a short time a more fashionable device than simple fornication.' Indeed four peers were actually involved in homosexual scandals. They were Earl Cowper; the Earl of Findlater, who was also Earl of Seafield; Viscount Courtenay, later Earl of Devon; and the Earl of Leicester, later Marquess of Townshend. Perhaps the most prominent figure in the homosexual scandals of the period was the head of an Oxford college, the Revd Robert Thistlewayte, Doctor of Divinity and Warden of Wadham, who was charged in 1739 with a 'sodomitical attempt' on an undergraduate in the college, William French. This young man told his father who promptly posted to Oxford and appealed to the Vice-Chancellor. As a result the Warden was brought before the local bench of magistrates, who committed him for trial at the next assizes but at the same time released him on bail. In due course the Grand Jury returned a true bill against him, but he failed to appear and stand his trial.

Had he done so, the Warden would almost certainly have been convicted since the depositions read to the Grand Jury included two compromising statements which had been taken from the college butler, with whom the Warden had once unwisely dined, and the barber who used to shave him. In the event the unfortunate Warden fled across the Channel having resigned all his offices – he had several livings as well as his academic post – and settled in Boulogne where he was safe from the attentions of the law. He died there several years later and, having probably expressed the wish to be buried in English soil, his remains were brought to Dover where they were appropriately laid to rest in the churchyard of St Mary the Virgin.[11]

3

Prior to the middle of the eighteenth century in England marriage was permissible at any hour, in any building without banns or licence, or even a clergyman being present, thus leading to such abuses as bigamy and the contracting of fictitious marriages for purposes of seduction or in order to obtain the fortunes of heiresses. The celebration of clandestine marriages by unscrupulous clerics in or near the Fleet prison had become such a scandal that legislative action became necessary. This was the Act of 1753, commonly known as Lord Hardwicke's Marriage Act after the Lord Chancellor who piloted it through Parliament. Henceforward no marriage in England was to be valid unless celebrated by an ordained priest of the Church of England in a parish church or public chapel according to the Anglican rite. Nor could any ceremony be performed, except by special licence from the Archbishop, unless banns had previously been called on three successive Sundays. Also a marriage register was to be kept in every church, in which a record of every marriage should be entered and confirmed by the signatures of the contracting parties and witnesses under penalty of transportation.

A later Marriage Act passed in 1836 licensed nonconformist chapels for the celebration of marriage and also provided for a civil, in addition to or in place of, a religious ceremony.[12] The law was only later applied to Ireland and did not apply at all to Scotland, where marriages could be contracted by oral declaration in front of witnesses and celebrated in the famous blacksmith's forge at Gretna Green. As we have seen, divorce in Scotland had been authorised by statute since 1573, but owing to the influence of the Roman Church it was never permitted in Ireland, although *crim. con.* actions were.

It may be asked why no action for *crim. con.* was brought by Sir William Hamilton, the British ambassador to the Neapolitan kingdom at the turn of the century, against his wife Emma's lover Admiral Lord Nelson, whose liaison is one of the most romantic and celebrated in history. The answer is that Hamilton thought it platonic, even after she had born Nelson a daughter Horatia in 1801. 'I well know the purity of Lord Nelson's friendship for Emma and me', Hamilton remarked shortly before his death two years later when they were both living with Nelson at Merton Place, his property in Surrey. By this date Nelson was already separated from his wife Frances, the daughter of a judge and widow of a doctor in the West Indian island of Nevis, whom he had married there in 1787. The cause of their separation was undoubtedly Emma Hamilton, whom Nelson called his 'own dear wife in my eyes and the face of Heaven'. If he had not been killed at Trafalgar, there is no doubt that he intended to divorce Frances and marry Emma. On the eve of the battle he added a codicil to his will, in which he set out the services he believed Emma had rendered the state when she was in Naples and he commended her and Horatia, whom he described as his adopted daughter, to his country's 'beneficence'. 'Remember,' he told his flag-captain Hardy as he lay dying on the *Victory*'s quarter-deck, 'I leave Lady Hamilton and my daughter Horatia as a legacy to my country.' The Government did not consider it politically expedient to publish the codicil on account of the references to the Queen of Naples, particularly since Nelson had been misinformed about the precise nature of Lady Hamilton's services. Nor did the younger Pitt's Government make any further financial provision for her as Nelson wished.

[27]

Neither did the fact of Nelson's affair, discreetly conducted at the time, become common knowledge until long afterwards.[13]

Although her extravagance obliged her to live in reduced circumstances and migrate to Calais, Emma Hamilton did not die there in penury, as has been commonly believed, but lived on partridges, turkeys and turbot with 'good Bordeaux wine'. As for Horatia, she was brought up by Nelson's sisters and in 1822 married the Revd Philip Ward, who became vicar of Tenterden in Kent in 1830; while the vicarage was being renovated they lived in Westwell House where these lines have been written. They had eight children. Horatia died in 1881 in her eighty-first year. While always acknowledging that Nelson was her father, to the end she kept searching for proofs that Lady Hamilton was not her mother. However, the proofs are overwhelming that Horatia was Emma Hamilton's daughter by the victor of Trafalgar.[14]

The Elgins and the Marbles

1

THOMAS BRUCE seventh Earl of Elgin and eleventh Earl of Kincardine belonged to an old Scotch family, his ancestors being related to and rewarded by the Bruce kings of Scotland. Among the Elgin family treasures was Robert the Bruce's helmet and sword. Thomas succeeded to the earldoms as a child of five following the death of his elder brother. He was educated at Harrow and St Andrews University. In 1785 he joined the army but quickly transferred to the diplomatic service, serving successively in Vienna, Brussels and Berlin. In 1799, at the age of thirty-two, he was appointed ambassador to the Sublime Porte, as the Ottoman or Turkish empire was known. Before taking up his post in Constantinople he decided to get married. As a bride he chose a beautiful twenty-one-year-old heiress Mary Nisbet, an only child, whose parents William and Mary Nisbet had an income of £18,000 a year and the estates of Dirleton, Belhaven and Biel on the south side of the Firth of Forth in East Lothian, not far from Edinburgh. They were married on 11 March 1799 by the Bishop of Edinburgh in Archerfield, the Nisbet family home at Dirleton. Elgin's ancestral property, Broomhall, was on the north side of the Forth near Dunfermline in Fife, where he had recently rebuilt the mansion house at considerable expense, incurring debts which he believed could be paid and in fact were paid with the help of a large marriage settlement. He could also look forward eventually to inheriting the substantial Nesbit fortune which was not subject to entail.[1]

Today Lord Elgin is remembered not so much for the humiliating divorce described in the following pages, but for his acquisition of the famous Greek sculptures known as the Elgin Marbles which were subsequently bought by the British government for the British Museum where they are now on public view. But now, since the establishment of independence from Turkey, for which Byron fought and died, the Greeks have demanded the return of the Marbles, a demand which successive British governments have always resisted. 'The British say they have saved the Marbles,' the present Greek Minister of Culture and former actress Melina Mercouri remarked when she saw the Marbles in the Museum in 1983. 'Well, thank you very much. Now give them back!'[2] Mrs Thatcher and her Conservative government refused, but a future Labour government may well reverse this decision. So Melina need not despair, but she and her compatriots may well have to wait a little longer.

The Elgins and the rest of the embassy set sail from Portsmouth to Constantinople, the Turkish capital, in a warship provided by the Admiralty in September 1799. Elgin's interest in Greek archaeology had been inspired by Thomas Harrison, the architect who had rebuilt Broomhall, and it received a further stimulus from Sir William Hamilton, the British ambassador to the Kingdom of the Two Sicilies in Palermo where the warship called. The ambassador had followed the court there from Naples. Mary Elgin, however, was more interested in the ambassador's wife Emma. 'She looked very handsome at dinner quite in an undress,' Mary wrote home to her parents. 'I think her manner quite vulgar. It is really humiliating to see Lord Nelson . . . as if he had no other thought than her. He told Elgin privately that he had lived a year in the house with her, and that her beauty was nothing in comparison to the goodness of her heart.'[3] At a royal gala the Elgins attended, as Mary remarked in the same letter, 'You never saw anything equal to the fuss the Queen made with Lady H; and Lord Nelson, wherever she moved, was always by her side. I am told the Queen laughs very much at her to all her Neapolitans, but says her influence with Lord N makes it worth her while making up to her. Lady H has made him do many foolish things!'[4]

The Elgins were received with every honour and many valuable gifts by the Sultan in Constantinople, Selim III, whose reforming zeal was to lead to his dethronement a few years later. The Sultan was motivated largely by his fear of the French and Napoleon Buonaparte's designs. The British ambassador had to reciprocate and his expenses for the first fortnight of his mission amounted to £7,000, which he claimed from the Foreign Office, due to the presents he had to give the Sultan and his numerous viziers. But the cost of the mission was staggering and Elgin was soon in debt. 'We have sixty people to feed every day, independent of the company at our own table that we have almost constantly,' Mary wrote to her mother after they had been in Constantinople for a few months. 'We shall go into the country as soon as I am able, and then I shall get rid of as many people as I can.'[5]

Meanwhile, Sir William Hamilton, who was noted for his collection of Etruscan vases, also now in the British Museum, encouraged Elgin to send professional artists, architects and moulders to Athens, and it was on Hamilton's advice that Elgin engaged the services of a well-known Italian landscape painter named Lusieri, who was then working at nearby Taormina and whom Elgin persuaded to take charge of his whole enterprise, including the other draughtsmen and modellers. Lusieri and the others were despatched to Athens in the following summer and they were principally employed in making drawings of the ancient monuments, but they received very little help from the local authorities. However, since Napoleon was now set upon conquering parts of the Ottoman empire such as Egypt, the British became allies of the Sultan who now gave the British ambassador permission in a firman or edict through the local Pasha in Athens, not only to fix scaffolding round the Parthenon and to mould the sculptures on its walls, but also to take away any pieces of stone with old inscriptions or figures which did not interfere with the walls.[6]

It was not the ambassador's original plan to remove the ancient marbles, but the injuries suffered by the sculptures of the Parthenon at the hands of the Turks, and the damage done to other monuments including slabs from the Athenian temple of Nike Apteros, induced Elgin and his assistants to undertake their removal. The Turks raised no objection since they were convinced that Napoleon intended to invade Greece. Admittedly there was some ambiguity about the terms of the firman and their interpretation; but, when he heard that the Turks had signed a treaty of peace with the French, Elgin, having visited Athens and seen things for himself, instructed Lusieri and his assistants to remove as much as they could before the French could put a stop to their activities.

While Elgin went on to explore the Greek islands and collect further

[31]

antiquities, he left his wife in Athens to supervise Lusieri's work. On 2 June 1802 she wrote to her parents: 'We yesterday got down the last thing we want from the Acropolis so now we may boldly bid defiance to our enemies.'[7] When an English ship arrived at the Piraeus, Mary Elgin exerted her charms with the captain to take three more cases of the sculptures on board than he wished to do. 'Female eloquence as usual succeeded and by peep of day I sent down the three cases,' she wrote to her husband who was still touring the Aegean. 'How I have fagged to get all this done, do you love me better for it, Elgin? . . . I am now satisfied of what I always thought; which is how much *more* Women can do if they set about it than Men. I will lay any bet had you been here you would not have got half so much on board as I have.'[8] Another cargo was taken on board the *Mentor*, Elgin's own vessel, but it encountered a storm and struck a rock at the entrance to the harbour of the island of Cerigo, sinking in twelve fathoms of water. It was only after three years labour and the expenditure of a large sum of money that the marbles in its hold were successfully recovered by the local divers.

In January 1803 the Elgins left Constantinople on leave. They planned a leisurely journey home, via France with which hostilities had ceased, following the peace of Amiens in the previous year. However, when they reached Lyons they learned that war had broken out again between France and Britain, and when they got to Paris they were regarded as prisoners. But since they gave their parole, they could at first come and go as they pleased. Whilst they were in Paris, Mary had her portrait painted by David's pupil François Gerard in a black velvet dress embroidered in gold and wearing a necklace with a jewelled pendant and cameos linked by chains in the style favoured by Napoleon's wife Josephine. 'It was done by the best painter here', Mary wrote to her mother, 'and he took unconscious pains about it.' This striking picture, which is reproduced in these pages, now hangs in the Scottish National Portrait Gallery.

When the English had been expelled from Paris, where they were in the summer of 1803, the Elgins went to the Pyrenees, where they stayed first at a spa, Barèges, for Elgin's health, and then at Pau. In the spring of 1805 they were allowed to return to Paris, where their son William, born a year previously, suddenly died. 'I have lost my William, my angel William', Mary wrote to her mother in anguish.

[32]

My soul doated on him, I was wrapt up in my child. From the moment of his birth to the fatal night it pleased God to call him, I have devoted myself to him. I am resigned to the Will of the Almighty, but my happiness is destroyed for ever . . . *My William, my adored William is gone . . . gone . . . and left me here* . . . Bless your Miserable Child.[9]

Mary was now pregnant with her fifth child and Elgin persuaded Napoleon, on humanitarian grounds, to allow his wife to return to Britain to bury the infant William whose body had been embalmed.

But Elgin was not allowed to accompany her as his status as a prisoner-of-war was affected by the fact that he still held a commission in the British army. However, a Scotch neighbour Robert Ferguson of Raith was among the others allowed to depart, apparently on account of his scientific achievements since he was a Fellow of the Royal Society. The Elgins had seen quite a lot of him in Paris, Mary writing home that he 'lived constantly with us'.[10] It was he who, at Elgin's wish, acted as Mary's escort on her sad journey to Britain.

A few words on the Elgins' private lives would not be out of place here. They got on together very well and Mary does not seem to have objected to her frequent pregnancies – five in four years – which she accepted as a matter of course. She worked hard helping her husband over the 'marbles' and she was plainly upset by his ill health and his detention on parole, although it was contrary to international law that an ambassador should not be allowed to return to his own country on the outbreak of hostilities. During their occasional absences from each other she clearly missed him. 'I have this moment dined and drank my beloved Elgin's health from the bottom of my heart – which I lay bet is more than you have done for your Dolly', she wrote to him in 1802. 'I am very unhappy at being separated from you . . . I want you sadly; you have no idea how deserted I feel'. Elgin for his part was just as upset: 'When I think of all you have suffered from the time we left Constantinople, my ill health and this detention, I am unable to bear myself. Our Marriage has been a continued scene of suffering to you and I can't make it up . . . God in Heaven bless my Dearest Angel, and my Dear Brats.'[11]

2

The Fergusons of Raith were a family of good standing in Fifeshire, their estate and Raith House, near Kirkaldy, being situated about eighteen miles from Broomhall. Robert, who was about thirty-five years of age at this time, was the eldest son of William Ferguson and the Raith property was entailed upon him.[12] His mother was born Jane Crauford of Restalrig, Edinburgh, and her sister Margaret was Countess of Dumfries. At the time of his departure from Paris with Lady Elgin and the infant William's remains, Elgin asked Robert Ferguson to attend to some business matters for him, such as paying the servants and looking after the horses at Broomhall, which Ferguson did. However, when he and Mary Elgin arrived in London, she was unable, probably due to her pregnancy, to attend the funeral. But Ferguson was present and saw the infant laid to rest in the Elgin family vault in Dunfermline. Meanwhile Mary Elgin, after spending a fortnight in her parents' London house in Portman Square, rented a house in Baker Street, where she spent about six months until she heard from her husband in the spring of 1806 that he had at last been released and was coming home. It was during her stay in Baker Street that Robert Ferguson became her lover. In the subsequent action for *crim. con.* brought by Elgin against Ferguson, a manservant named Robert Draper, who was employed by Lady Elgin in the Baker Street house, testified that 'Mr Ferguson's visits were very frequent, and at hours both earlier and later than those of other gentlemen, he stating that he had business of Lord Elgin to transact with her and giving and receiving letters to take to Mr Coutts the banker.' Mr Ferguson, the servant went on, 'used to express great anxiety for Lord Elgin's return from his imprisonment in France.'

At the same time Lady Elgin wrote to her husband that 'it would be absolutely necessary that the usual intercourse betwixt man and wife should cease between them.' Elgin thought that this was the result of her painful experiences during the birth of her fifth child, a daughter named Lucy. However, when Elgin returned and found that his wife had left to stay with her parents at Archerfield, he hastened north only to find that she was steadfast in her resolution and demanded that in future they should sleep in separate beds. But she did return to Broomhall with her husband for a short time. It was during this period that Ferguson wrote to her: 'You must prove and act upon your disgust.

[34]

You must exasperate him. You must consider his approach as a violation of your person.'

While Elgin was in Scotland a letter came into his hands which turned out to be from Robert Ferguson and which convinced him that Ferguson had committed adultery with his wife. The letter, dated 30 December 1805, was sent to Mary while she was living in Baker Street and read in part:

Till I breath my last, Mary, I boast of loving you with a passion never known before. Never was there such a perfect union, as in our souls, every wish, every thought is alike; yes, beloved Mary, I yet dare hope that the time of our union [will put] an end to those fetters, which, if not broken, will sink us to the grave.

Ferguson then went on to refer to his mistress's husband in far from flattering terms. 'Good God!' he wrote, 'How can you submit to that man's gross conversation? How can such language be addressed to a wife? Your husband's conversation is abhorrent, and you must break your fetters.'

In 1806, Ferguson was elected MP for Fifeshire, the constituency which included his family home Raith House and its extensive park. Before the year was ended he was sued by Elgin for *crim. con.* in London where he did not attempt to defend the action but admitted his misconduct with Lady Elgin and the jury awarded her husband £10,000 damages.[13] But this judgment and the divorce proceedings which followed did not seem to cause his constituents much concern since he was to remain a member of the House of Commons for much of his life, later representing Haddingtonshire.

3

Elgin's suit for divorce, then permissible under Scots law, took place before the Commissary Court in Edinburgh in March 1808.[14] Lady Elgin's lawyers had originally decided to defend the action, seeking among other ploys to show that Elgin had actually condoned his wife's adultery, that he had been reconciled with her and that he had obtained a substantial sum of money from her trustees (£10,000) 'for which he

[35]

said he had then urgent occasion'. Although not expressly admitted by the defence, the inference clearly was that the money was paid by Mary Elgin in return for her husband's condonation of her adultery which would have been a bar to the divorce. In the latter part of 1806 a temporary reconciliation took place after Elgin had induced his wife, who was then staying with her parents at Archerfield, to return to Broomhall, as we have seen. It was further alleged by the defence that after Elgin had intercepted several of Ferguson's letters, 'he (Elgin) not only continued to live with her on the same footing of cordiality and affection as before but took every means both by word, by writing and deed, to shew that this forgiveness and reconciliation was most complete and true . . . merely exhorting her to repentance and to a more scrupulous discharge of her domestic duties.' Also that, although they occupied separate bedrooms, Elgin repeatedly came into hers 'in an undress, both after she was in bed and before she got up and remained alone with her for many hours at a time, the marks of two persons being visible on the bed after his departure.' Finally Elgin left Broomhall for London in January 1807

after passing some time in her bedchamber and bidding her adieu with many affectionate embraces. He desired her to enquire at the same time whether it would be convenient for him to lodge at her father's house in London, and left his four children with her and entirely under her management, where indeed they were allowed to remain till this action had been several months in dependance.

It is possible that this defence was initiated by Mary Elgin's suspicion that Ferguson was having an affair with another woman. However, in the event her lawyers dropped this defence, no doubt on her instructions, when she was assured that Ferguson was faithful, so that when the case came to trial it went by default, since Mary Elgin did not attempt to deny that she had committed adultery with Robert Ferguson. The only point now of the defence was that Elgin's witnesses could be cross-examined by her lawyers if it was thought that they were not speaking the truth when examined by Elgin's counsel.

The first witness was the Right Revd Dr Daniel Sandford, Bishop of Edinburgh who deposed that he had married Lord and Lady Elgin in the episcopal chapel at Archerfield in March 1799. He could not recall the exact date, since he had not kept a written record – it was 11 March – but to his knowledge subsequent to the ceremony they were generally understood to be husband and wife. His testimony was confirmed by James Dundas, a writer to the signet, who said he knew both the parties well and that they were regarded by all and sundry as being a married couple.

They were followed by a witness, Sarah Gosling, whose evidence had been taken on commission, since she was too ill to travel from London where she lived to Edinburgh, as she suffered from the dropsy, and in fact had since died. She was a servant in the Baker Street house, and had previously been with her mistress in France. Mary Elgin objected to Gosling's testimony, but her lawyers were overruled by the Court and the contents of the commission were opened and read. Robert Draper, the manservant who had testified in the *crim. con.* action, was not called, but Gosling corroborated his evidence about the frequency of Ferguson's visits to the house. Ferguson, said this witness, often stayed until the early hours of the morning after the footmen had been told by her Ladyship that they could go to bed. Ferguson was always let out of the house either by this witness or by Mary Elgin's maid. Gosling also swore that her mistress usually changed her dress into a dressing gown which she wore during Ferguson's visits. Lady Elgin's mother Mrs Mary Nisbet once called about midnight when Ferguson was in the house, Gosling went on, and it transpired that, while Mary Elgin was talking to her mother in the drawing room, Ferguson concealed himself behind a screen.

Lady Elgin's maid Christiana Notweiler who was French, was the next witness, and she had to be interrogated through an interpreter since she spoke little English. She had been employed by Mary Elgin for four years in France before coming with her to London, she said. The witness stated that she did not know why Lady Elgin had left her father's house in Portman Square, but she thought it was 'more agreeable to her to have a house of her own.' She confirmed generally what Sarah Gosling had said, adding that she had seen Mr Ferguson admitted to the house after Lady Elgin had undressed and put on her 'loose gown'. She also spoke of the letters which she knew had passed between her and Mr Ferguson, since she had posted several of them herself and had received others from Ferguson addressed under cover

[37]

to herself and recognised the address as being in Ferguson's handwriting, since Lady Elgin had shown her Ferguson's signature on one of the letters. Somewhat naïvely she deposed that 'it was never explained to her why Lady Elgin's letters were sent under cover to her'. She also stated that in December 1806 she had accompanied Lady Elgin to Broomhall, where Lady Elgin spent some time with her husband during their brief reconciliation. The witness further said she had posted several letters for Lady Elgin at Dunfermline post office but that while at Broomhall she had received no letters for Lady Elgin under cover to herself. Also, she never received any letter notifying her that letters were to be sent to Lady Elgin under cover to her 'but that after it was said that Lord Elgin had intercepted some letters she understood from Lady Elgin that these letters should have come under cover to her the witness.'

Anne Crerar, aged twenty-two, had been a chambermaid in Fortune and Blackwell's Hotel in Edinburgh when Lady Elgin had stayed in the hotel with her friend Lady Harvey in 1806. Both had bedrooms and parlours with a communicating door. When Lady Harvey left, Mr Ferguson engaged her rooms. But the morning after Mr Ferguson arrived the chambermaid went into his bedroom and noticed that the bed had not been slept in. On the other hand, when she went into Lady Elgin's bedroom she was satisfied, she said, that two people had slept in that bedroom from the appearance of the pillows and the sheets, which were 'marked in the same manner as if a man and his wife had slept together'. She went on to say that she had asked a hotel waiter named John Fraser whether Lord Elgin had slept in his wife's bed and he replied that he had not but 'desired her to hold her tongue as she might get into a scrape,' since Lady Elgin's maid had a room on the same floor. The witness added that, when she made up Lady Elgin's bed the preceding evening, the sheets, which she had sworn were marked as described, were quite clean.

Anne Crerar's evidence was confirmed by the waiter John Fraser. He recalled that he had seen Mr Ferguson in Lady Elgin's apartments, after which he had asked whether he could be accommodated in the rooms which Lady Harvey was vacating and was told that he could. When Mr Ferguson took Lady Harvey's rooms he spent almost the whole day in Lady Elgin's, only leaving when Lady Elgin's dinner was served. He added that he 'thought it odd that Mr Ferguson should remain so long with Lady Elgin.' Next morning he said that Anne Crerar met him in the hall and expressed surprise that Mr Ferguson's bed had not been slept in. But the witness was 'not much struck with this,' he said, 'as Gentlemen who lodged in the Hotel frequently pass the night abroad, after having proposed sleeping in the hotel.' He concluded his evidence by stating that when Mr Ferguson paid his bill 'he desired that his arrival should not be put in the newspapers mentioning that from his short stay in Town he would be plagued with his acquaintances calling on him.' The witness added that Mr Ferguson, who only spent one night in the hotel, had no servant or baggage with him and he did not seem even to have a night cap.

The two following witnesses, Mary Ruper and Thomas Wiley, had been employed as servants by Lord Elgin at Broomhall, but came down from Scotland to serve Lady Elgin in Baker Street. Besides corroborating Sarah Gosling's evidence regarding the frequency and duration of Robert Ferguson's visits to the house in Baker Street when Mary Elgin was living there, Ruper specifically stated that she had mentioned to Gosling that Lady Elgin's dog had 'dirtied a green silk cushion' which was on the sofa in the small drawing room off Lady Elgin's bedroom. According to this witness, Gosling said it was not the dog and shook her head. 'It was not the dog,' Gosling repeated, 'but that rogue Mr Ferguson,' adding that it was the opinion of Gosling and herself as well as the other servants in the house that 'there was an improper connection between Mr Ferguson and Lady Elgin.' In answer to a further question, Ruper stated that Thomas Wiley, who had been Lady's Elgin's footman in Baker Street, was later dismissed by Lord Elgin for having got drunk.

In his evidence Wiley did not contradict this but stated that he was now employed by Field Marshal the Duke of Kent, Keeper of Hampton Court, who later became Queen Victoria's father. Every night Mr Ferguson was in the house the witness would carry a tray with wine, porter and other refreshments for Lady Elgin and Mr Ferguson when Lady Elgin would tell him to go to bed as Gosling or Notweiler would remove the tray. About six weeks after the birth of Lady Elgin's daughter Lucy, Wiley who had an urgent message for Lady Elgin went up to the little drawing-room, opening the door without knocking as he usually did. He saw Lady Elgin lying at full length on the sofa. He further deposed that

[39]

upon the witness's coming in both Lady Elgin and Mr Ferguson laid hold of a shawl and in general confusion threw it over her Ladyship's legs; that Mr Ferguson was then sitting on a low stool close to the sofa; that the witness could not positively say whether her Ladyship's petticoats were up, but from the hurry and confused way in which the shawl was thrown over her legs the witness was impressed with the idea that this was the case but was prevented by a little writing table which stood in front of the sofa from seeing whether her Ladyship's legs were uncovered or not before the shawl was thrown over them.

The witness went on to say that Mr Ferguson and Lady Elgin 'discovered great confusion when the witness came into the room and particularly her Ladyship, whose face was much flushed.' Mr Ferguson then got up, said Wiley, and walked towards the fire with his back to the witness, turning his head and saying, 'It's only Thomas!' From the manner in which Ferguson walked to the fire the witness could not see any part of him in front nor could he tell whether his breeches were buttoned or unbuttoned. Lady Elgin remained in the same posture while the witness was delivering his message which only took a minute or two.

This witness added that when Lady Elgin was in Baker Street she often wrote to Mr Ferguson and would give the letters to the witness to deliver to Ferguson who was living in a hotel in Jermyn Street and that Mr Ferguson would give the witness his letters for Lady Elgin and once tipped the witness a guinea for his trouble. He also accompanied Lady Elgin to Archerfield, her parents' house in East Lothian, where Lady Elgin told him to take any letters addressed to her from the postwoman and not include them with the other letters for the family, expressing displeasure whenever he failed to do this.

The last material witness was Charles Duff, who had been a member of Lord Elgin's embassy in Constantinople and had been principally employed in carrying official despatches to and from the Foreign Office. He was in London when Lady Elgin returned from France and it was at her request that he rented the house in Baker Street for her. He went on to say that he helped Lady Elgin with her packing before she left for her parents' home in East Lothian. She seemed much agitated on this occasion and said: 'Oh! Duff, I am quite miserable.' On the witness inquiring what was the matter, she replied: 'It does not signify. God forbid I should ever do any harm in this country, but if they plague me I shall go off with Ferguson.' The witness understood that by the word 'plague' Lady Elgin meant her husband and her parents. He (the witness) stated that he had replied to Lady Elgin's remark: 'God forbid that I should ever see that day, as you would be looked upon as no better than a girl of the town if you go off with Ferguson!' Duff added that he knew of the correspondence between Lady Elgin and Mr Ferguson since Lady Elgin had asked Duff's wife if she could have letters sent under cover to her but that Mrs Duff had declined on learning that the witness disapproved of this subterfuge.

A series of letters between the lovers, which Elgin had intercepted, were now put in evidence and read. In one dated 18 December 1806, when she was with her husband at Broomhall, Lady Elgin wrote:

Yesterday the Doctor went away, so E[lgin] and I had the evening alone. He was very much agitated indeed but he said nothing. After tea he got up suddenly and went into his room for a couple of hours. He coughed dreadfully which he always does when he is annoyed.

I told him my wish to go and see where my beloved William is laid, and that I wished to go alone. Friend, it was you that placed that Adored Angel there. He is happier far than us. If he can hear and know what is passing in this world, friend, he will intercede for us. There is something combined with that Infant I cannot account for, but I feel as if he was our own.

Elgin went out early this morning. I have not seen him. I must do him the justice to say he has taken upon himself to keep his promise [not to share her bed]. But I hardly think it possible he can go on with it. For your sake I hope he will not.

You know my prized resolution. I need not repeat it, need I? No power shall ever make me fail you. Friend, tho' I know you must feel desperately at this moment, yet I am convinced you have *entire* confidence in me. You know I am as much wrapped up in you as you are in me. We are united by the tenderest ties of nature; nothing but death can separate us. We know how happy we can be together . . . Ah, Friend in Heart and Soul I am never away from you – every instant of the day my thoughts are with you. You can never think of me but at the same time your Mary is thinking of you. I told Scot [Elgin's lawyer] how matters were between Elgin and me. What a

[41]

desperate horrible idea that nothing but death can make me free. I shudder when I dare think of it – and too thoroughly I feel I cannot live without you . . .

I have just got a letter from my mother wishing to send Gosling into Edinburgh . . . as the Haddington surgeon thinks she has had some hurt. I know poor soul she was hurt when the wheel came off the carriage at Pau: I driving and she holding my beloved William . . .

Friend, I cannot bear the idea that people should imagine I live with Elgin. But remember *you* never undeceived the world. I would like much to hear *how* and where I may direct to your *own name*. You know I am an economist and I cannot make you pay for my nonsense now you are MP. Friend, I love you more than ever and for ever and ever. I enclose this bit of my mother's letter. Do you not see that she hates E[lgin]? God in Heaven Bless and preserve you. Your own Mary.

On 30 December her lover responded in kind:

Yes, my own beloved Mary we were made for one another . . . I am most miserable with the thought of your being near that man. What gross, what indelicate feelings mark his conduct . . . The idea, the feeling of your being exposed, *devoted* as you are to me, to his language, indelicate and impertinent, is not bearable either to *yourself* or *me*. Yes, my Mary, well you must feel that these sentiments are those of the most perfect love; and your friend would not deserve to be that being you *doat* upon, if his ideas, feelings were not such as he has expressed. Mary, we live for one another . . .

We have but one chance now to prove that with *him* you cannot live – that your freedom must be signed, that then *coute qui coute*, you must have a small house of your own, and then we may either a little longer bear up or at once form our plans for ever.

When they had considered all the evidence including the letters, the commissaries, who were satisfied that there had been no condonation in spite of the temporary reconciliation, declared that they found Lady Elgin guilty of adultery with Robert Ferguson and pronounced Lord and Lady Elgin for that reason 'divorced and separated'.

Since he had been married and divorced under Scots law, Lord Elgin

[42]

was free to remarry without let or hindrance. However, since he was a Scottish Representative peer, he considered it prudent to have the divorce confirmed by a Private Act of Parliament, which he did, an action which involved him in additional expense which he could ill afford at this time.

4

After his divorce Elgin's life-style underwent a complete change. He got no further employment from the Foreign Office, he failed to be re-elected a Scottish Representative peer, his debts increased largely through the storage of the marbles, he suffered from a facial disfigurement which made him shy of company, and since he could no longer afford to run Broomhall on the scale on which it had been rebuilt by Thomas Harrison, much of the furniture was sold while the servants were paid off and he lived quietly and as economically as he could in one wing of the building. However, he had one comfort in his second wife whom he married in 1810. She was Elizabeth Oswald, daughter of J. T. Oswald of Dunnikeir, a neighbouring landowner and MP for Fife. Although not as interesting as the first countess, she was more stable and a great comfort to her husband in his misfortunes. She also bore him eight more children so that with the four by Mary, whose custody he now had, he found such a large family an increasing financial burden. Meanwhile Mary married her lover Robert Ferguson of Raith, who was also MP for Fife and therefore a colleague of Elgin's new father-in-law. Ferguson, who also became Lord Lieutenant of Fifeshire and from 1835 MP for Haddingtonshire, lived with his wife at Raith House, after he came into the property, but they had no children much to Ferguson's disappointment. Robert died in 1840 and was succeeded in the Raith estate by his younger brother General Sir Robert Ferguson, MP. Meanwhile Robert's widow Mary, who survived him by fifteen years, returned to Archerfield, the Nisbet family home at Dirleton, where she spent the remainder of her life.[15]

In the same year as Elgin married his second wife he co-operated in the anonymous publication of the *Memorandum on the Subject of the Earl of Elgin's Pursuits in Greece* which skilfully justified his acquisition of the marbles and defended him from the charges of vandalism, rapacity and dishonesty which had been brought against him notably by Byron in his savage satire *The Curse of Minerva*. Meanwhile the marbles were displayed to the public view in London, and on the superb merits of the Parthenon sculptures the critics were generally agreed, Canova pronouncing them 'the works of the ablest artists the world has seen'. Eventually a select committee of the House of Commons recommended their purchase for the nation and in 1816 an Act was passed giving effect to this in the sum of £35,000, at the same time justifying the ex-ambassador's claim to the ownership of the antiquities. However, since the formation of the collection and his accompanying disbursements cost Elgin more than £70,000, he was considerably out of pocket.

Although he was again elected a Scotch Representative peer, his debts dogged him for the rest of his life. Eventually Broomhall and his other assets were put into trust, and he was obliged to migrate to France to avoid his creditors. He died in Paris in 1841. His second wife, who survived him, lived on in Paris and died there nineteen years later. However, she lived to see her eldest son, the eighth Earl, created a United Kingdom peer and also appointed successively Governor of Jamaica and Governor-General of Canada. Nevertheless it took thirty years to pay off the seventh Earl's debts and they were not finally discharged until the time of the next generation.

Certainly the affair of the Elgin Marbles constituted a bitter legacy for their owner, a mass of debts and never ceasing demands by Greece for the return of the marbles to their country of origin. Worst of all was the scandal of Countess Mary, who had previously contributed so much herself to the collection and transport of the marbles to England, but also unfortunately to the blighting of her first husband's public career.

From Lady Rosebery
to Lord Melbourne

1

A CURIOUS and interesting case of *crim. con.* tried in 1816 concerned another Scottish peer who sued his wife's brother-in-law, an English baronet, for having seduced her. The peer was Archibald Primrose, fourth Earl of Rosebery and grandfather of the better known fifth Earl who achieved his three ambitions in life of marrying a rich heiress, becoming Prime Minister and winning the Derby. The fourth Earl's wife was a sister of the Earl of Radnor, having been born Harriet Bouverie, while her lover, who had been married to her elder sister Charlotte, was Sir Henry St John-Mildmay, aged thirty, and MP for Winchester, of which city he had been mayor. He was also heir through his mother to large estates in Somerset and Essex. It was in 1809 that St John-Mildmay married Harriet, Lady Rosebery's elder sister, twenty-year-old Charlotte Bouverie. Unfortunately Charlotte died after barely a year of marriage, having in this period produced a son who was eventually to succeed to the Mildmay baronetcy. Harriet was even younger when she married Lord Primrose, as the future Earl of Rosebery was then known, being only seventeen. But during the five years they were married she bore him four children, and certainly to begin with the marriage was a happy one. However, trouble developed when the widowed St John-Mildmay turned for consolation to his late wife's sister and her husband. This consolation he accepted gratefully and wrote to Primrose, as he still was, thanking him for this kindness.[1]

Early in 1814 Primrose's father, who was living in the family ancestral home Barnbougle Castle on the south shore of the Firth of Forth near Dalmeny, was taken ill, and his son and heir hastened north

[45]

to be with him in the event of his death. He was there when his father died in March. For some reason Harriet Primrose did not accompany her husband to Barnbougle but went with her mother-in-law to stay on her property in Norfolk. The fact that Mildmay's only son Henry, who was Harriet's nephew, went along with his aunt gave Mildmay an excuse for seeing Harriet frequently and it was during this period that the sympathy which Harriet extended to him turned into a romance, culminating in Mildmay becoming her lover.

It was at this time that Mildmay wrote Harriet the first of the letters which came into her husband's possession:

> Dearest of dear earthly beings! Were anything wanting to increase the misery into which my unhappy heart has plunged me, it is that you are a prey to uneasy feelings, although certainly less acute than my own. Dear object of my devoutest admiration – the English language is too weak to express my love for you – sleeping or waking, you alone engross my thoughts. I have heard with alarm that you will leave England on Friday next [for Scotland]. I entreat you to devise some means to postpone your journey. With what regret do I see, in imagination, the image of her I love, in tears; she who always had a smile from me. I have been in love before – at least I fancied so; but I never felt the all-conquering power until now.

'Yes,' commented Rosebery's counsel, the Attorney-General Sir William Garrow,* when he read out this letter in court, 'he had been in love with this lady's sister – at least he fancied so. He was married to that sister – he had a son by her. And the lady to whom he was writing those licentious letters, was the mother of four children – two boys and two girls; from whom he was endeavouring to withdraw the maternal care of their parent, thus inflicting on them the most deadly wound.'

This particular letter continued:

> I shall visit the House of Commons this evening, but I shall attend to nothing that passes there . . . You request me not to call again so early in the morning, and I shall obey you. You do not desire me to

---

* In those days law officers could have private clients and were not exclusively confined to acting for the Crown.

[46]

give the business over altogether. If you had, in that instance only could I disobey you . . . I wish you to take a walk up Buckton [Buckhurst]? Hill. I will go there; and, if I cannot see you, I must be content to kiss your dear ring, and bless the spot where you may be.

Your sincere and affectionate,

HARRY

P.S.   I have read this note over, and do not like it. It does not contain one tenth of what I could say. I would be able to say how much I love you, if my head could keep pace with my heart. But you know my heart and inmost soul. Adieu!

Cease to annoy yourself with unpleasant reflections. Are we to blame if our hearts are so closely assimilated to each other?

In the event Harriet was unable to postpone her journey to Scotland. When they next met, which was in London, the new Earl noticed that his wife's attitude towards him was noticeably cooler than it had been, and he put this down to Mildmay's attentions which he had observed, as indeed had the late Lord Rosebery. He remonstrated with her but to little effect since she continued to communicate with Mildmay, although they did not see each other. This was after Rosebery had made his principal residence at Barnbougle into which he moved with his family, including his wife and mother, the Dowager Countess, and his younger brother Lord Francis Primrose. Having tried without success to prevent Harriet Rosebery from going to Scotland, Mildmay next endeavoured to persuade her to elope with him.

'I will give up everything for you,' he wrote in one letter. 'I will leave my home, my friends, and all, if you will be the partner of my flight! With you I will roam the world! If you have resolution to accompany me, I will quit the world, and bless the hour that gave me all that is dear to me!' In another letter, which had come into Rosebery's hands and which his counsel the Attorney-General read in the *crim. con.* trial, Mildmay stated to Lady Rosebery that 'he had for some time past worn yellow garters, but that he had locked them up because his valet Hurst, if he should see them, would wonder where he got them.' Then, in tones of withering sarcasm, counsel went on to speak of 'the happiness and beatitude of those garters which had for hours, nay for whole nights,

[47]

been twined round and encircled his dear Harriet's thighs – bliss unspeakable!'

Determined that he must see her, Harry Mildmay went to Scotland where he put up at an inn near Edinburgh under the assumed name of De Grey, a colonel in the Foot Guards. Here he let his beard grow and disguised himself as a sailor, and thus disguised he managed to arrange to meet Harriet in her room in the castle. It was the habit of the Rosebery family to dine at six o'clock whether *en famille* or with invited guests. The ladies would retire to the drawing room about seven, leaving the gentlemen to their port for an hour or so. On several nights Harriet did not stay long in the drawing room but excusing herself went to her bedchamber. This aroused her mother-in-law's suspicion that 'something was going on which was not well', and on telling her son Francis 'it was conjectured it could be accounted for by no cause except that Sir Henry Mildmay was in the neighbourhood.'

On the fourth night on which Harriet left the drawing-room early, the Dowager Countess returned to the dining-room and told her sons what she suspected. As a result Francis went out and called several of the servants, some of whom he sent outside to keep watch in the grounds and others, including Rosebery's valet, he took to the Red Bed Chamber, as Harriet's room was known. Francis tried two of the doors which he found were locked. He then tried a third, which was also locked, and seizing a pair of tongs from the adjacent fireplace tried to break it open, while Rosebery's valet, Stretch, helped with a poker. The door being of oak resisted their blows for some time, but it was eventually opened by Harriet to reveal Harry Mildmay beside the bed, wearing a large blue duffle jacket with a red waistcoat and trousers, although because of his beard it took Francis Primrose a minute or two to recognise him. An hysterical scene ensued in which Harriet had to be revived with sal-volatile after which she begged Francis not to challenge Mildmay to a duel, which he said he would not do, while Mildmay knelt down, embracing Harriet's knees and begging her forgiveness. Francis then announced that the only course was for Mildmay to leave the house immediately, having noticed from the state of the bed that Mildmay and Harriet must have lain on it together. Mildmay first surrendered the pistols he was carrying, which were cocked and loaded but which Francis rendered useless by pouring water in the pans before returning them. 'Go, Sir Harry,' said Francis to the unwelcome visitor. 'I entreat you to go through the window by which you entered.' This Mildmay now did, jumping on to the terrace below.

Harriet now asked to see her children. 'Nobody shall prevent me,' she said. However, Francis replied that he could not agree to this unless her husband agreed, and he held her back as she tried to leave the room. In the event Rosebery refused to let her see her children and she left the castle next morning, as the others thought, to go to her father Bartholemew Bouverie's house. She did not do this but contrived to rejoin her lover in a nearby inn where they were recognised by some of the Barnbougle servants. Shortly afterwards, in November 1815, they sailed from Newhaven for the Continent, taking a large quantity of luggage and a carriage with them, Harriet travelling as Lady Mildmay. Meanwhile Archibald Rosebery obtained a divorce, followed by the action for *crim. con.* against his wife's lover. This Mildmay in the circumstances did not attempt to defend, so that it only remained for the jury to assess the damages, which they did at £15,000. Nor did Mildmay pay this sum since he had already left England when the verdict was returned.

The reason why Mildmay and Harriet did not stay in England, since Mildmay was a rich man and could easily have afforded to pay the damages awarded against him, was that under English law, as it then was, it was illegal for him to marry his deceased wife's sister, such a relationship being regarded at that time as incestuous and within the prohibited degrees of affinity. (The law was not altered to permit marriages of this kind until 1907.) However, such an alliance was permissible in the Germanic kingdom of Württemberg, then ruled by the Protestant sovereign Frederic II from the royal palace in the picturesque capital of Stuttgart, where, incidentally, the cream of the King's library consisted of 9,000 bibles in eighty different languages. The King gave Harry Mildmay and Harriet special permission to marry. Thus they were married in Stuttgart, where they settled and where they had three sons, Edmond, Horace and Augustus, who all became officers in the Imperial Austrian Hussars. For obvious reasons the Mildmay parents never returned to England. Harriet died in 1834 and Harry in 1848 when his son Henry by Charlotte succeeded him as fifth Baronet.

Archibald, Harriet's elder son by Rosebery, who preferred the courtesy title of Lord Dalmeny to Lord Primrose, became an MP and a junior minister. But he died before his father, so that it was his (Dalmeny's) son who became the fifth Earl and Prime Minister. Edmond, Harriet's eldest son by Harry Mildmay, left the Austrian army and became successively ADC to Frederick Adolphus first Duke of Cambridge (George III's seventh son) and to the latter's son, George William Augustus the second Duke, who was the reactionary commander-in-chief of the British army for forty years. Edmond Mildmay, who was a popular social figure of his time, died aged ninety, a year after his former chief, in 1905. But he could never forget the scandal of his parents' elopement and the reason for their being unable to get married in England.[2]

2

Sex and politics were united in two royal scandals in the first quarter of the nineteenth century. The first concerned Ernest Augustus Duke of Cumberland, George III's fifth son, and the second that monarch's eldest son, who succeeded him as George IV.

The Duke of Cumberland, who later became King of Hanover, was probably the most unpopular member of the English royal family on account of his unbending Toryism and his fanatical anti-Catholic views. On the night of 31 May 1810 the Duke was discovered in his apartments in St James's Palace with a terrible wound in his head which would have been mortal had not his attacker's weapon struck against the Duke's sword. At the same time his valet Sellis was found dead in his bed with his throat cut, Cumberland asserting that Sellis had attacked him in a fit of madness. A coroner's jury found that Sellis had committed suicide after attempting to assassinate the Duke. However, the Duke had another valet named Neale, and it was openly said that His Grace had been detected 'in an improper and unnatural situation with this Neale by the other servant Sellis, and exposure was expected.' In order to keep Sellis from talking the Duke was rumoured to have murdered him. In 1813 a journalist named Henry While was sentenced to fifteen months' imprisonment and a fine of £200 for publishing this rumour, and another pamphleteer, Joseph Phillips, got six months for repeating the story twenty years later. The truth of the affair will probably never be known. All that can be said is that the detested Cumberland, who was one of Queen Victoria's 'wicked uncles', was commonly regarded at the time as having killed Sellis in order to conceal his relations with the other valet.

The other royal scandal was George IV's unsuccessful attempt to divorce his playful, eccentric wife and cousin, born Princess Caroline of Brunswick. Their marriage, which took place in 1795, had been forced on the King when he was Prince of Wales by his father George III and only reluctantly accepted by the Prince on condition that his debts were paid. It was a failure from the beginning. However, the alliance was encouraged by the Prince's mistress Lady Jersey, who naturally did not wish to see her own charms displaced. Although he arrived in the nuptial chamber on the night of their wedding dead drunk, the Prince did sleep with his twenty-five-year-old bride at least once since she quickly became pregnant and after a long and difficult labour gave birth to a girl Charlotte, who was thus in the direct line of succession to the throne. The Prince now let it be known that he did not expect Caroline to have any more children. 'Our inclinations are not in our power,' he remarked, 'nor should either of us be held answerable to the other, because nature has not made us suitable to each other.' At the same time they were formally separated and the Prince expressed the hope that 'the rest of our lives will be passed in uninterrupted tranquillity.' This hope was not destined to be realised.

In fact Caroline was as amorously inclined as her husband. Even before her marriage she gave proof of her inclinations on the boat to England when she spent the night alone on deck with the first mate. Unwisely, she told Lady Jersey, who was her implacable enemy, about a love affair she had or was having. Though warned that such conduct was a capital offence under English law both as regards herself and her lover, she was soon openly boasting of her taste in 'bedfellows'. Shortly afterwards she appeared with an 'adopted' son of a sailmaker called William Austin, or 'Willikins', who was widely said to be her own. 'Prove it and he shall be your king' was her customary gleeful rejoinder to this charge. Her behaviour became so scandalous that in 1806 commissioners were appointed to carry out a 'delicate investigation' of her conduct. They acquitted her of having had an illegitimate child, but censured her levity and found her guilty of 'unworthy indiscretions'.

When George III's health gave way and the Prince was appointed Regent in 1811, Princess Caroline was excluded from court and not

[51]

allowed to see her daughter Charlotte despite repeated protests. In 1813 the Regent allowed her to go abroad, hoping she would stay there and keep out of the way. After briefly visiting her brother Duke Frederick William in Brunswick, she went to Milan where she engaged an Italian, Bartolomeo Bergami or Pergami as a courier, with whom she became infatuated, caressing him in public and sleeping and having baths with him on a yacht she chartered. She procured for him a Sicilian barony, a knighthood of Malta, besides several other orders, including one she had created herself, the Order of St Caroline, of which she made Bergami hereditary Grand Master. A neat epigram later went the rounds when Bergami's relations with the Princess became known.

> The Grand Master of St Caroline
> Has found promotion's path.
> He is made both (K)night Companion
> Also Commander of the Bath.

The Princess also took several of Bergami's relatives into her service and made his sister, Countess Oldi, her lady of honour.

When he heard of Caroline's behaviour, the Regent despatched a commission to Italy, the so-called Milan Commission, to collect evidence of her infidelities, particularly at the Villa d'Este near Milan where she spent much of her time with Bergami and the rest of her suite. At the same time he enlisted the help of the Foreign Minister Lord Castlereagh, who instructed his brother, Lord Stewart, the British ambassador in Vienna, to get all the help he possibly could from the Austrian Government, since northern Italy was then under Austria's rule. A mass of incriminating evidence was thus collected and put into two green bags which Stewart despatched to England for use in the divorce which the Regent had in mind when the time came. The time did come in 1820 when the mad old King George III died, and his obese and gouty son the Prince Regent at last came into his royal inheritance.

The new sovereign's change of status inevitably produced fresh complications over Caroline who was still his wife and thus now titular Queen. He now demanded a divorce from the Cabinet and, as a first step, insisted that Caroline's name should be excluded from the Church liturgy – indeed he had long been of the opinion that she was past praying for. For her part, the Queen wrote to the Prime Minister Lord Liverpool and also Lord Castlereagh, demanding that her name should be inserted in the Prayer Book and also that instructions should be given to all British ambassadors, ministers and consuls that she should be acknowledged and received as Queen of England, also that a palace should be prepared for her reception. No reply was sent to these requests. She thereupon decided to go to England and if necessary stay in London with a radical alderman named Wood, the son of a Devonshire chemist, with whom she had somehow become friendly.

The Queen arrived at Dover by the packet on 6 June 1820 and to her agreeable surprise was greeted by a salute of twenty-one guns appropriate to a crowned head. She received an enthusiastic welcome on her journey to London, and from Greenwich she rode in an open landau with the radical alderman at her side. Lord Castlereagh happened to be with the King in Carlton House when the cavalcade passed and was shocked by Wood's vulgarity in occupying such a conspicuous place of honour. Later that night, after Castlereagh had returned to his house in St James's Square, he wrote to his brother in Vienna: 'The die is cast. The Queen is at Alderman Wood's in South Audley Street, and the green bag with all the papers on the table of both Houses . . . So as now the whole proofs must be adduced, send us all the witnesses. We shall have a difficult and tedious proceeding.'

Not unnaturally the Queen became the rallying point for all the popular elements in the country, and throughout the night of her arrival and for many days and nights afterwards the London mob streamed through the streets shouting 'Long live the Queen!', and making passers-by do likewise. Castlereagh's windows in St James's Square were repeatedly broken, as were those of his aunt Lady Hertford, the King's ex-mistress, although curiously no assault was made on those of the reigning favourite Lady Conyngham. When Caroline took a house a few doors from the Foreign Minister's the mob was so ferocious that Castlereagh, fearing for his life, sent his wife to the country, removed all his plate and papers and transferred his bed to the Foreign Office.

Meanwhile the green bag was opened in the House of Lords and its contents examined by a Secret Committee, which recommended that the evidence it contained affecting the honour of the Queen was such as to require a solemn inquiry. The Cabinet, with the King's consent, drafted a Bill of Pains and Penalties designed to deprive Queen Caroline of her regal status. This measure was to be introduced in the Lords, and after its first reading, the 'inquiry' – in effect the Queen's trial on the charge of adultery with Bergami – would begin. This plan meant postponing the coronation. 'I never agreed to anything so reluctantly,' Castlereagh noted, 'lest it should appear to be a concession to the Queen and her mob. But the general feeling of our best and firmest friends was against crowning a King and trying a Queen at one and the same moment.' At the same time Castlereagh had to admit privately that the King's behaviour was nearly as bad as his consort's. 'It is lamentable', he told his brother, 'that our Royal Master, when a Bill of Divorce is pending, should be living publicly at The Cottage at Windsor with the Conynghams, and walking out every day with my lady. Never was such an unfortunate infatuation at his age and in his position.'

The Bill of Pains and Penalties was introduced in the Upper House on 21 August 1820 and the examination of the witnesses began two days later. 'What a trial we shall witness!' Princess Lieven, the Russian ambassador's wife, wrote to her lover Prince Metternich, the Austrian Chancellor. 'Those spiritual lords, how will they take the pretty things they are going to hear? Well, *mon Prince*, I am not sure that she will be found guilty. By the House of Lords, yes. But the Commons?' Meanwhile the Queen announced that she would defend herself with vigour. Her plan, according to Princess Lieven, was 'to give her own account of the relations between the King and herself, to reveal everything she knows about his behaviour, not forgetting the offspring of the unmarried Princesses.' Many strange rumours were in circulation. One was that Bergami was really a woman, and that Her Majesty would produce proofs to that effect. 'You have no idea of the ridiculous stories that are put about,' Princess Lieven told Metternich, 'and of the facility with which people tend to believe any story that exonerates the Queen.'

Unhappily for Her Majesty, the first witness for the Crown was one of her Italian servants, by name Theodore Majocchi. The unexpected appearance of one she thought she could trust so took the Queen by surprise that, at the first sight of him, she called out 'Oh! Theodore,' or, as some thought, *'Traditore'* (traitor). She thereupon rushed wildly from the Chamber. Majocchi's testimony was certainly a betrayal of his royal mistress, since he swore that while on board the polacre in the

Mediterranean she frequently had baths with Bergami in a tent on the deck. 'I have not had the heart to read the evidence,' noted Princess Lieven on the third day; 'it is too disgusting. Is the Queen really a woman? And how can the House of Lords, uniting as it does all that is most dignified and most exalted in the greatest nation in the world, lower itself by listening to such vile trash?'

The Queen, who had announced at the start that she would attend the proceedings every day so as to confound the witnesses by her presence, soon became bored. She brought a backgammon set along with her and would play in an adjoining room with Alderman Wood. Once she fell asleep in the Lords' Chamber, an occurrence which gave rise to another epigram.

> Her conduct at present no censure affords,
> She sins not with peasants, but sleeps with the Lords.

The Italian witnesses for the Crown cut sorry enough figures, and the failure of their memories under cross-examination by the Queen's lawyers soon made '*Non mi recordo*' a popular catchword. On 6 November the Lords divided on the second reading of the Bill which was moved by the Prime Minister Lord Liverpool and carried by a majority of twenty-eight. Two days later the divorce clause was carried in committee by sixty-seven. And two days after that, on the motion for the third reading, the majority fell to nine. In these circumstances the Prime Minister decided, after hastily consulting his Cabinet colleagues, to withdraw the measure, which he did by moving in the traditional formula that it be read 'this day six months'.

Shortly afterwards the Queen went to St Paul's to give thanks for her acquittal. She was received so rapturously by the crowd attending her, as her husband was surprisingly cheered when he went to Drury Lane Theatre, 'as if', remarked Princess Lieven, 'he were the most virtuous, the most fatherly, the greatest of all Kings.' The only discordant note came from a voice in the gallery which called out, 'Where's your wife, Georgy?' However, the public were beginning to tire of Caroline. Their enthusiasm waned when husbands came to realise that her conduct had not been such as they would approve in their own wives and daughters. Her stock sank lower when it was announced that she had accepted a pension from the Government of £50,000 a year, and

[55]

popular feeling was now reflected in the rhyme of an anonymous pamphleteer:

> Gracious Queen, we thee implore,
> Go away and sin no more;
> But if that effort be too great,
> Go away at any rate.

Meanwhile she quarrelled with the Whig Opposition in Parliament which had espoused her cause against the King, and she abused her legal champion Henry Brougham, whose eloquent speech in her defence had raised him to the pinnacle of his profession. Incidentally it was Brougham who was responsible for the pun which described her as 'pure innocence' (in no sense).

The unfortunate Queen Caroline lingered on in England, hoping to provide a counter-attraction to George's coronation. Although no official role was assigned to her at this ceremony, as she had requested and been denied, she nevertheless turned up at Westminster Abbey and as one final humiliation was refused admission by the door-keeper because she had no ticket. She retired amid the groans and cheers of the waiting crowd. But by this time her life was slowly ebbing away. 'What a singular close', Castlereagh wrote to his brother, 'if Providence should effect that divorce, in attempting which every human effort failed.' This was just what Providence did, since the next that Castlereagh, who was with the King in Ireland, heard of her was that she had suddenly been taken ill in Drury Lane Theatre and had died shortly afterwards. 'In doing so,' noted Princess Lieven, 'she made one last difficulty for her enemies – she upset the festivities in Dublin. And in London, what are they to do with her chaste remains? That is the only embarrassment she is from now on in a position to cause them. She did her best but her death at this moment is a mere luxury, for alive she no longer inconvenienced anyone.'

There was indeed this final embarrassment. The sight of her coffin, on which at her request she was described as 'the injured Queen of England', caused a riot as it was conveyed out of Hyde Park. The escorting troops of the Life Guards opened fire on the mob, killing two persons and wounding several others. In her will she had expressed the wish that she should be buried beside her father in her native Germany, and so eventually after a tempestuous voyage from Harwich her 'chaste remains' were laid to rest in the royal vault at Brunswick.

The monarch thus widowed, lived on for another decade with his reigning mistress. After his death countless bundles of women's love letters, women's gloves and locks of women's hair were discovered, evidence of his multitudinous intrigues. All these were destroyed by his executors as being the least reputable private effects of the scandalously dissolute and sexually sated sovereign who was called 'the first gentleman of Europe'.

3

In April 1821, the Foreign Secretary and Leader of the House of Commons Viscount Castlereagh succeeded his father as second Marquess of Londonderry, although he continued to be commonly known by the courtesy title which he had borne for the past twenty-five years. He also continued to sit in the Commons since the peerage to which he had succeeded was an Irish one. Unfortunately for him and his country, since he was a statesman of outstanding merit, he was destined to live for only sixteen more months, dying by his own hand on 12 August 1822 at the comparatively early age of fifty-three.[6]

The tragedy was the result of his mind giving way under the pressure of work and apparently other troubles and anxieties. In severing the carotid artery in his neck with a penknife at Cray Farm, his country place in Kent, he died in his doctor's arms. 'Well! This is a considerable event in point of size,' remarked his political opponent Henry Brougham, when he heard the news. 'Put all their men together in one scale, and poor Castlereagh in the other – single he plainly weighed them down . . . One cannot help feeling a little for him after being pitted against him for several years pretty regularly. It is like losing a connection. Also he was a *gentleman*. And the only one amongst them.'

A week before the end he called on Mrs Arbuthnot, wife of the Government Chief Whip, as well as the two law officers, and told them that he had received two anonymous letters from a blackmailer, in one of which the writer whose name was Jennings threatened 'to tell of his having been seen going into an improper house' with a woman, unless he was given a job. In the other the blackmailer accused him of what

Mrs Arbuthnot euphemistically described as 'a crime not to be named'. He alluded to the latter when he met the Duke of Wellington and the King a few days later.

'Have you heard the news, the terrible news?' the wild-eyed-looking Castlereagh asked His Majesty in Carlton House.

'No,' replied the King. 'What is it?'

'Police officers are searching for me to arrest me.'

'Come, come,' said the King, who thought at first that this was some kind of joke the Foreign Minister was playing on him. 'What nonsense! Why should they be!'

'Because I am accused of the same crime as the Bishop of Clogher!'

'You must be crazy.'

But Castlereagh insisted that the police were looking for him and he showed the King the two anonymous letters, making His Majesty promise not to reveal their contents to any of his colleagues. The King did so to humour him, and Castlereagh left still chattering about the Bishop of Clogher, convinced that he was a 'fugitive from justice' and must 'fly to the ends of the earth', leaving by the little gate in Carlton House garden. 'What's the matter with Londonderry?' the King whispered to an equerry. 'Either he is mad or I am.' At the same time the King insisted that his minister should see a doctor without delay and be bled.

During the previous three weeks the affair of the Bishop had made a considerable stir in London. Indeed it was a prime topic of conversation in the clubs and coffee-houses, although from the nature of the case its details were scarcely fit to be discussed in drawing rooms. Public interest was increased by the fact that the accused person was not only a high dignitary of the Church but also the member of an aristocratic family and the uncle of a peer. The Right Revd Percy Jocelyn, Bishop of Clogher, was the third son of the first Earl of Roden, a landowner whose estates were situated not far from Castlereagh's ancestral property in County Down. Although it was a suffragan bishopric, nevertheless Clogher boasted an old cathedral and a fine episcopal palace (now known as Park House), also in Ulster, which the Bishop had occupied for the past two years. He was fifty-seven years of age and unmarried.

On the night of 19 July 1822, His Lordship, who was in London on a visit from Ireland, went to a public house, The White Hart, in St Alban's Place, Westminster. There he was detected in the act of

[58]

committing a homosexual offence with a private soldier in the Guards. He was attired in his customary episcopal dress and made no attempt to conceal the nature of his calling. 'The Bishop took no precautions', noted the diarist Charles Greville at the time, 'and it was next to impossible for him not to be caught. He made a desperate resistance when taken, and if his breeches had not been down they think he would have got away.' He was then escorted along with the soldier to the watch house in Vine Street, being followed by a crowd, which shouted insulting remarks at them as they went along.

Arriving in Vine Street, the Bishop refused to give his name to the constable of the watch. But his identity was revealed by a letter, which he took out of his pocket and tore up. He threw the fragments into the fireplace, but as there was no fire burning there, they were recovered by the constable and pieced together. The letter turned out to be from his nephew Lord Roden. This was confirmed by a note which he asked the constable to send to a friend in the house where he lodged off Portman Square, in which he wrote that he was 'totally undone' and signed himself 'PC', the initial letters of his christian name and his diocese.

Next day the two delinquents were brought before the local magistrate, and after they had been formally charged they pleaded not guilty and reserved their defence. The magistrate informed them that their offences were bailable, and he fixed the amount of bail each in £500 and two sureties of £250 each, amounts for which he was subsequently criticised for making them too low. Two sureties came forward on behalf of the Bishop and entered into the necessary recognisances. The Bishop was thereupon released, though not until he had given his name and address which he did with considerable reluctance. No sureties appeared for the soldier and he was remanded in custody.

While preparations were being made to deprive the Bishop of his ecclesiastical dignities, his bail was forfeited after he had fled to Scotland, where he rightly anticipated there would be difficulties in executing any warrant for his rearrest. Here he assumed the name of Thomas Wilson and for a time, it is said, took employment as a butler – on one embarrassing occasion being recognised by a former acquaintance as he was handing round the dishes at dinner.

The one-time Bishop of Clogher died incognito in Edinburgh on 2 December 1843 and had a very different funeral from Castlereagh's impressive affair in Westminster Abbey. He was buried quietly in the new cemetery at seven o'clock in the morning, followed by only five mourners in a one-horse coach. By his directions no name appeared on his coffin, but the plate bore an inscription in Latin, which he had himself devised some years previously. The translation read: 'Here lies the remains of a great sinner, saved by grace, whose hope rests in the atoning sacrifice of Jesus Christ.'[7]

To return to Castlereagh, we have seen how he had been blackmailed by a scoundrel named Jennings, who had written him two letters threatening to expose him, and that the minister had shown the letters to the King on his last visit to Carlton House. This was confirmed by Princess Lieven who wrote to Metternich two days after Castlereagh's death about the two letters: 'One of them threatened to reveal his irregular conduct to his wife; the other concerned a more terrible subject. This second letter sent him off his head.' That Castlereagh was in fact the victim of blackmail and thought he was about to be publicly denounced as a homosexual is beyond doubt. The question remains, are there any grounds for supposing that he had committed any act of homosexuality? The answer is no. There are no such grounds, but there were suspicious circumstances in his conduct.

When Parliament was sitting and the weather was fine, Castlereagh was in the habit of walking home from the House of Commons to his house at the corner of St James's Square and King Street. From time to time he was accosted by prostitutes, and to their importunities he was, unfortunately for him, induced more than once to respond. He may have thought that he could indulge himself in this manner and remain undetected. The fact remains that his identity was soon discovered, among others by the blackmailer Jennings, as we have seen, and also by several other scoundrels who had observed his behaviour on these nocturnal walks. It is not clear whether Jennings and the others were in collusion. Probably not.

At all events, as the result of a casual encounter one night during the session of 1819, Castlereagh was taken by the individual, whom he assumed was a woman, to a certain house, where they were both shown into an apartment furnished in the conventional manner of a brothel. His companion began to undress, when to his horrified amazement Castlereagh discovered that the person who had brought him there was not a woman, as he had supposed, but a youth dressed in women's clothes and disguised to pass as a woman. Before he could decide what to do, the door was forced open and a couple of villains rushed in and accused him of being about to commit 'an act from which nature shrinks in horror' – otherwise sodomy – adding at the same time that they knew perfectly well who he was.

The purport of the accusation was palpable, and unfortunately, in the intensity of the crisis, the Marquess lost his presence of mind and his courage. He adopted the course which they suggested and gave them all the money he had about him to secure his immediate escape. This course was precisely what they had plotted to bring about. They had secured their victim, he was in their power, and they were resolved to let him know that their silence could only be obtained by full compliance with their extortionate demands.

Day after day the blackmailers stationed themselves by the railings with which the enclosure of St James's Square is surrounded opposite the windows of Castlereagh's house, and took the opportunity by signs and movements, whenever he appeared, to remind him of the scene which they had so ingeniously contrived.

Driven almost to distraction by this persecution, he made known his case, with all the circumstances to the Duke of Wellington and to another nobleman. By them he was advised to give the wretches into custody at once, avow the full facts, and extricate himself from further disgusting thraldom.

He had not the resolution to follow this advice. He shrank from the consequences which the painful disclosure of what was really to be deplored in his conduct might produce on the feelings of his wife; and in a moment of distraction adopted the desperate remedy which was to extricate him from his persecutors and himself.

The other nobleman mentioned in the above account and himself its source was the twenty-seven-year-old Richard Meade third Earl of Clanwilliam, Parliamentary Under-Secretary for Foreign Affairs at the time of Castlereagh's death, having previously been his private secretary as well as being an intimate friend. He was the first person apart from family relatives to see Castlereagh's widow on the fatal 12 August, and it was he who, at her request, made arrangements for the funeral in Westminster Abbey. To Clanwilliam was also entrusted the painful task

[61]

of breaking the news to Castlereagh's brother, Charles Stewart, the ambassador in Vienna, and now third Marquess of Londonderry, since Castlereagh died childless. This he did in a long letter, which ended on a peculiar note, which cannot be dismissed as devoid of significance, since it is evident that Clanwilliam knew something of what was going on at the back of his chief's mind. 'There is but one subject on which there remains anything to say,' Clanwilliam concluded, 'and that is the matters on which his head turned during the different moments of delirium. This I will reserve for future conversation when we meet.'

At the coroner's inquest evidence was given both by Castlereagh's doctor and the principal housemaid at Cray that the unfortunate minister was convinced that he was the victim of a conspiracy, when, for example, he saw his wife and the doctor talking together. Thus it seems clear from the testimony of these witnesses at the inquest that though the minister's mind was under a delusion as to the actual persons mentioned in evidence as being the conspirators against him, such as his wife and the doctor, the delusion was produced by the unfortunate existence of a real conspiracy which had turned his brain, and that to a certain extent there was a meaning in his madness, incomprehensible to the witnesses, but which was nevertheless acting powerfully on his mind and driving him to suicide.

The final word may be left with Philip von Neumann, the Counsellor at the Austrian Embassy in London, who was greatly puzzled by what had happened. 'The more one knew of Lord Londonderry,' he wrote at the time, 'the less one can understand what could have led him to commit such an act. Of all men he was the last from whom one would have expected anything of this kind. There is some mystery about this which perhaps time will explain; but whatever it was, it was something very serious to have led to such an act.'[8] It was indeed something very serious, and the fact that we now know the details is due to Castlereagh's Under-Secretary at the Foreign Office who divulged them generally some thirty years later.

4

Although William Lamb second Viscount Melbourne was twice Prime Minister, and proved to be an admirable mentor and trusted counsellor of the young Queen Victoria, he was a man of loose sexual morals. He was twice publicly accused of adultery and was acquitted on each occasion. Moreover, there is evidence in his correspondence with two women, who were generally regarded as his mistresses, that he showed an obsessive interest in flagellation.[9] This he may have acquired from his having been flogged at Eton where he was a pupil in the 1790s. His housemaster Dr William Langford was an ardent flogger, but he liked young Lamb so that he only beat him three times in as many years. 'I don't think he flogged me enough', Melbourne, who was a strong believer in the efficacy of corporal punishment for the young, told Queen Victoria many years later. 'It would have been better if he had flogged me more.'

William Lamb was a second son, and on his elder brother's death in 1805 he gave up the Bar, where he practised on the northern circuit, for politics in the Whig interest. In the same year he married the eccentric Lady Caroline Ponsonby, who soon became passionately infatuated with the poet Lord Byron, although she confided to her diary that he was 'mad, bad, and dangerous to know'. She wrote poetry and also three novels, but her vanity coupled with her temper and an excitability which verged on insanity led to a separation from Lamb in 1825. Three years later she died and her husband, who at this time was an MP and Chief Secretary for Ireland, hurried back to London from Dublin when he heard that she was ill and he saw her before she expired.

It was while Lamb was in Ireland that the wife of a parson who was also a peer became his mistress, or appears to have. This lady was born Elizabeth La Touche of a well-known Dublin banking family and she had married the Revd William Crosbie, a clergyman considerably older, who shortly afterwards succeeded his cousin as Lord Branden. She was a highly sexed woman, full of gaiety and good spirits, whom her husband was quite unable to satisfy physically. They never formally separated but after becoming Lord Branden he was mostly away from home in Buxton or in the south of France, having more or less given up his pastoral duties. Meanwhile his young wife was living it up in a house in Fitzwilliam Square which the La Touches had bought for her and which she made the most fashionable salon in the Irish capital. Lamb would visit her house every evening, sometimes late at night, and they went to balls and the theatre together regularly. Such conduct in Ireland amounted to the height of indiscretion on the part of both parties. But

[63]

Irish society openly tolerated their liaison. If they made love – and it seems certain that they did – it was not as frequently as Elizabeth would have liked to satisfy her desires. Occasionally Lamb would hit her when she annoyed him and once she reminded him that he had nearly broken her arm. She also reproached him for failing to satisfy her sexually or otherwise when he sat quietly with her looking stern. 'It is all a most unsatisfactory way of spending an evening, designed for better purposes,' she wrote to him, but she usually ended her letters by saying she loved him 'as much as ever'. She liked to be the centre of admiration and to be seen publicly with her lover whenever she could, and would complain vociferously if he refused to take her to the play on a cold night because he had a cough.[10]

William Lamb – or Melbourne, as we should call him, since he had succeeded to his father's peerage in July 1828 – was a warm advocate of 'discipline', particularly in the home. This seems to have begun when he suggested, after Elizabeth Branden had told him how disobedient her children were, that she should whip them more often. 'No mother really loves her children who never does it,' he commented. And again he advised her: 'All mothers and governesses should not fail to whip all refractory and disobedient children, being convinced that this would be attacking the evil at its beginning and that their insubordination arises from the disuse of that wholesome discipline.' He recalled one governess of his acquaintance who used to say, when her pupils were begging not to be whipped: 'If I hated you or were indifferent to your future welfare, I should forgive you, but as I love you dearly and am anxious for you doing well hereafter I shall whip you severely.' Upon which Melbourne observed to his mistress, 'Wasn't this admirable?'[11]

Melbourne's favourite instrument of chastisement was the birch or birch-rod with its supple twigs bound together, usually called simply the rod as it was at Eton and other schools. Girls as well as boys were regularly birched in school as well as in the home at this period, and some women – whether mothers, governesses, or schoolmistresses – were particularly fond of wielding the rod. For instance, according to Melbourne, the Duke of Leinster's daughter Letitia Lady Kinnaird 'had a positive pleasure in whipping her children when they were naughty'. In one letter to Lady Branden in 1831 when he was Home Secretary, Melbourne enclosed a letter published by the *Morning*

Chronicle. 'It is rarely that so minute and circumstantial a history of flagellation is put upon public record,' he wrote:

We live in strange times when a girl of thirteen cannot be whipped at a boarding school without it being made a subject for discussion in the newspapers. If I had a girl to educate, I should find out where this school is and send her thither. Notwithstanding Mr H.B. [the writer of the letter] calls the chastisement a slight one, I should think this young lady got it pretty well. It is a smart whipping that cures and a few *scratches* after two days. Nothing heals so rapidly as the part to which the birch is usually applied.[13]

It may be added that such was the mania for flagellation in England at that time and indeed for long afterwards that even prostitutes were inclined to administer this treatment to their clients, as appears from the birch on the wall of the prostitute's room in the third plate of Hogarth's *The Harlot's Progress*.

Melbourne's letters to Elizabeth Branden between 1828 and 1831 are full of references to flagellation, which he recommended in the case of girls and even fully grown women, finding it an erotic stimulant for both the punitive agent and the delinquent. For instance, he wrote about an idle maid whom he remembered at Lady Branden's house in Dublin.

I shall mention first what interests me the most and that is the reference in your last letter to your being left alone with that troublesome woman. I never think of her without wishing intently that I had the power to order her a birch application upon that large and extensive field of *derrière*, which is so well calculated to receive it. But these are vain wishes, and I cannot but wonder that you do not try to get rid of her and find a better.

In one letter he enclosed a coloured lithograph of a woman beating a naked child, with another older child looking on. He accompanied it with some characteristic comments.

The woman has much the air and look *d'une femme bonne*, and she is employing her right hand, which is much more usual and natural than her left. She seems quite intent and determined upon what she is doing in spite of the entreaties of the other child, and she lifts her arm with great heartiness and grace. The figure of the child is also good. It is trying to turn itself round, which children always very naturally do in such circumstances and which the left arm of the woman prevents. Upon the whole it is a very correct and lively representation of this interesting domestic occurrence.[13]

In another letter he summarised his views on whipping children, particularly young girls, as distinct from beating a dog:

It is difficult with the most violent blows to produce much effect upon the thick skin of a dog covered with hair. But a few twigs of a birch applied to naked skin of a young lady produce with very little effort a very considerable sensation. Besides in teaching animals the great difficulty is to make them understand what you wish them to do, and what for and why they are punished. Now a child learns that very well, and I remember my own experience that if once I got whipped for anything I carefully refrained from that in future. The little girl I never whipped but three times for disobedience, and she never disobeyed me any more.[14]

The 'little girl' was Melbourne's ward Susan Churchill, supposedly illegitimate, whom his wife had adopted in a moment of sentimental benevolence. She spent most of her time at Brocket Hall, the Lamb family home in Hertfordshire, where she was occasionally chastised by her guardian. Later, after she got married she wrote to Melbourne, telling him that she was following the same practice with her daughter, excusing herself for sparing her son because he was only ten months old. Nor did she bear her former guardian any ill-will for whipping her. 'I remember the *execution*,' she reminisced in a letter, 'then being thrown in a corner of a large couch there was at Brocket. You used to leave the room and I remember your coming back and saying "Well, cocky, does it smart still?", at which of course I could not help laughing instead of crying.'[15]

'There are some women from whom it delights one more to receive a letter than it does to possess another', Melbourne wrote to Lady Branden in 1831 when she was in Italy with her family. 'You are of the former description – a letter from you excites me more than the full possession of others.' The excitement seems to have been largely due to

[66]

a shared interest in flagellation, although with a few exceptions we only have Melbourne's side of their correspondence. 'You say that the English whip more than any other people,' he remarked in one letter. 'I should have thought the Irish. The French certainly less, but more to the purpose when they do it. The Germans I believe a good deal.' Whether he ever touched up Lady Branden with the rod as he did Susan Churchill we do not know. Probably not. But he certainly threatened to do so. 'So you are duller and fractious, are you?' he asked her in one letter. 'I wish I were with you. I would administer promptly what is necessary on such occasions, which I have always lamented I did not do two or three times when you were in Dublin. Letitia never did it better than I should if I had the opportunity!' And again: 'Do you mean to annoy me, or why do you not write? You cannot be terribly ill – otherwise I should hear of it. If I did not think that you were too angry to be jested with, I should say that I would certainly get a rod for you and apply it smartly the first time I see you!'[16]

Meanwhile Lord Branden had discovered some of Lord Melbourne's letters when he was still William Lamb and Chief Secretary for Ireland which left him in no doubt that she was Lamb's mistress. He thereupon wrote to her announcing his discovery and adding that he would forgive her and overlook her conduct and give her back the letters, if she could persuade the Chief Secretary to procure him a bishopric. To this unseemly communication, according to the diarist Creevey, she replied that she would 'neither degrade herself on Mr Lamb by making any such application' and that she would send on the letter to the Chief Secretary which she did. Branden responded by starting proceedings for *crim. con.* against Lamb in May 1828. He complained among other things that his wife had dined alone on several occasions with Lamb in the Chief Secretary's Lodge in Phoenix Park and he alleged that she had had a key cut to the side door of her house in Fitzwilliam Square so that her lover could visit her incognito. 'If Lord B proceeds, as I suppose he will,' Lamb, by this time Lord Melbourne, wrote to his mistress then living under an assumed name in London, in November 1828, 'I am determined to defend myself by all the means in my power and I expect your assistance and co-operation. He cannot compel anyone to come from Ireland to give evidence here unless he chooses to do so. Therefore you need not fear anyone being brought forward when it might be disagreeable.'[16]

[67]

The case came before the Lord Chief Justice Lord Tenterden in the King's Bench in the Michaelmas term, 1829, when Branden assembled several witnesses against Melbourne, designed to prove that his wife's relationship with the defendant, if not adulterous, at least showed the couple to have been guilty of the grossest indiscretion. However, only two witnesses were called by the plaintiff; one testified that Lord Melbourne had sent Lady Branden some grapes and pineapples, and the other stated that he had seen a short man, alleged to be the defendant, leaving her house in the early hours of the morning. In fact, Melbourne was unusually tall and, as his counsel the Attorney-General Sir James Scarlett remarked, 'if there was any suspicion it attached to the short gentleman.' Branden's case was so weak that the Lord Chief Justice dismissed it without hearing the defendant's counsel in reply. A similar action in the ecclesiastical court for divorce *a mensa et thoro* was withdrawn, and Melbourne appeared in the eyes of the world not guilty. But those who claimed to be in the know, liked the Lord Chief Justice's biographer Lord Campbell, claimed that the verdict 'raised a not improbable suspicion of compromise'. This was quite true, since a letter in the Royal Archives at Windsor confirms that Melbourne bought off Branden for £2,000. In his will Branden, who died in 1832, cut off his wife with a shilling, but Melbourne paid her a thousand a year for the rest of his life, after his affair with her was long since over, and this sum continued to be paid to her after his death and throughout the fourteen years by which she survived him.[17]

5

The other notable affair in Melbourne's life began in 1834, just when his passion for Elizabeth Branden was beginning to wane. The new object of his affection was one of three clever sisters, a pretty, witty Irish poetess, aged twenty-three years, the Honourable Caroline Norton. Her grandfather was the brilliant dramatist and parliamentary orator Richard Brinsley Sheridan. Her father was Tom Sheridan, poet and colonial treasurer of the Cape of Good Hope. Of her two sisters Helen married Lord Dufferin and Georgiana married Lord Seymour, later twelfth Duke of Somerset. When she was nineteen Caroline married George Norton, a younger brother of Lord Grantley and Tory MP for

Guildford, the union being possibly one of expedience rather than love since the Sheridans were in straitened circumstances financially. Norton was a barrister but he lost his parliamentary seat in the 1830 General Election, his law practice was negligible and he was now living largely on his wife's literary earnings. Caroline let it be known that she would like to meet Melbourne who was then Home Secretary in the Grey Ministry. At their first meeting in her house in London, she asked Melbourne if he could get her husband a job. Melbourne, who took a fancy to her at first sight, said he could think of nothing suitable at the moment but promised to see what he could do. He did so, and a few months later secured a metropolitan police magistracy for Norton at a salary of £1,000 a year.[18]

Melbourne began to call on her regularly, intrigued by her witty talk. The attraction was mutual and soon Caroline was addressing him in their correspondence as 'Dearest Lord' and accepting the present of a horse from him. Norton encouraged the relationship and soon people were taking it for granted that Caroline was Melbourne's mistress. Inevitably the subject of flagellation was mentioned in their letters. Caroline told Melbourne that when she was whipped as a girl she had always bitten the whipper and rushed off to commit the same offence for which she had been punished. Once when she was in Rome with her sister Helen Dufferin and the latter's husband she wrote to Melbourne:

I saw in a shop of curiosities and pictures the other day a small black cabinet inlaid with ivory etchings of birds, and in the centre (to my astonishment) your favourite subject of a woman whipping a child, (or a nymph whipping Bacchus, or some such thing, for I was not alone and could not inspect it). I had half a mind to buy it for you, but thought the difficulty of carrying a bad contraband *joke* to England and perhaps having it seized at the Custom house ought to deter me. Nor was it pretty in any way. I am sorry to say that the Italian women appear utterly to neglect this important branch of education as far as their children are concerned.[19]

Unfortunately for Caroline, her husband turned out to be a man of coarse and even brutal habits. There were continual rows between them about their three children and her literary earnings which her husband appropriated; this, as the law then was, he was entitled to do. Matters

[69]

came to a head when Norton emulated Lord Branden by bringing an action for *crim. con.* against Melbourne alleging his adultery with Caroline. At first Melbourne was more concerned than his alleged mistress. 'Since I first heard I was proceeded against,' he told Caroline, 'I have suffered more intensely than I ever did in my life. I had neither sleep nor appetite, and I attributed the whole of my illness (at least the severity of it) to the uneasiness of my mind.' He was particularly worried that his letters to her had come into Norton's possession, but he worried unnecessarily since such letters as were read out in court were brief notes and quite harmless.[20]

The trial took place in the Court of Common Pleas on 23 June 1836. It was the sensation of the season, being commented on for weeks before in the press, since there had been nothing like it since the trial of Queen Caroline. The plaintiff's counsel Sir William Follett, a former Tory Solicitor-General, was careful to make it known at the outset that he had not advised the proceedings, no doubt because he realised how weak his client's case was. As the law then stood Norton was debarred from giving evidence, while Melbourne submitted an affidavit asserting his innocence. Only three notes from Melbourne had been discovered by Norton amongst his wife's papers and these were read out in court. The first one read:

I will call about half-past-four,
Yours,
MELBOURNE

The second:

How are you? I shall not be able to come today. I shall tomorrow.

The third:

No house today. I will call after the levée. If you wish it later, let me know. I will then explain about going to Vauxhall.

Sir William Follett argued that these notes showed 'a great and unwarrantable degree of affection' because they did not begin and end with the words 'My dear Mrs Norton'. 'It seems', counsel added, 'there may be latent love like latent heat in the midst of icy coldness.'

Norton's counsel also made a great point of the fact that in his visits to Caroline's house in Storey's Gate Melbourne had entered by a 'secret door' in Prince's Court instead of using the door in Birdcage Walk. In fact this 'secret door' was actually the public one with No. 2 painted on it and the local clergyman who was called by the plaintiff testified that he had habitually used it. The other witnesses, mostly servants, were equally discredited. Two were maids who had been discharged on account of their 'indiscreet familiarities' with men in the Brigade of Guards. However, Caroline was distressed by the action of one of them, Eliza Gibson, who swore that Mrs Norton was given to 'painting' her face and to 'sinning' with various gentlemen. The evidence was entirely circumstantial and the fact that Norton had condoned his wife's relationship with the defendant for so long was another decisive factor. When Follett asked his client whether it was true that he had sometimes walked to Melbourne's house and left her there, Norton admitted that this was true, whereupon Follett told him afterwards that this admission was the end of the action. And so it was, since Melbourne's counsel the Attorney-General Sir John Campbell and Serjeant Talfourd called no witnesses for the defence, although Campbell spoke for six hours rebutting Norton's accusations with remarkable eloquence. In the event the jury returned a verdict for the defendant without leaving their box.[21]

It was a triumphant acquittal for Melbourne and a complete vindication of Caroline Norton's character. Incidentally, Charles Dickens who reported the case for the *Morning Chronicle*, got the idea from it for the celebrated trial of Bardell *v*. Pickwick in the *Pickwick Papers*, notably the speech of Serjeant Buzzfuzz which Talfourd is said to have revised for him.

Two questions remain to be answered. First, was the case a put up job by the Tory opposition in Parliament with the object of discrediting Melbourne and disabling him from holding the premiership under the expected female sovereign, Princess Victoria? The answer is possibly, but only just, although prominent Tories denied it. The second question is, was Caroline Melbourne's mistress? The answer is probably not, since her letters contain no hint of it, while Melbourne expressly denied it in private to his counsel, although if he had been guilty he might well have perjured himself in the witness-box. ('I wish it to be stated in the most clear, distinct and emphatic manner that I have never committed adultery with Mrs Norton.') And to Caroline he wrote in April, before the trial: 'You know that what is alleged (if it be alleged) is utterly false, and what is false can rarely be made true.' Melbourne's family were greatly relieved by the result of the action, since the defendant had the reputation of being a notorious philanderer. His brother, Lord Beauvale for example, wrote to his sister Lady Cowper, later Lady Palmerston: 'Don't let William think himself invulnerable for having got off this time; no man's luck can go further.'[22]

Melbourne's reputation suffered little after the trial, but Caroline Norton's character was greatly damaged in spite of her public vindication. She continued to write to Melbourne, who was dilatory in his replies, often ignoring her letters altogether. She asked him to present her to the young Queen Victoria at Windsor but this, much to her chagrin, he refused to do. However, a couple of years later, in 1839, her sister Lady Seymour, afterwards Duchess of Somerset, found that the Queen was willing to receive Caroline, and Georgiana Seymour presented her in 1839. Caroline was very nervous, a symptom noticed by the Queen, but the fact that she *was* received was regarded as a royal condonation of the irregularity of her position, since she was separated from her husband and constantly disputing with him over their three children, particularly as the Queen was very 'sensitive' about reputation and as a rule was reluctant to receive, and thus tacitly approve, anyone to whom the slightest taint attached. Furthermore, Caroline made things up with Melbourne and had the satisfaction of seeing the measure for the custody of infants by their mothers, for which she had worked hard, pass through Parliament and become law. This was the first legal recognition of married women's rights, a wife and husband having previously been regarded as one person in law and the wife's legal personality as submerged in that of her husband, so that she had no separate interest in her children and her property which automatically belonged to her husband on their marriage.[23]

Melbourne was a rich man, but he lived very extravagantly and was often in financial difficulties. Queen Victoria, who found him 'a noble, kind-hearted generous being', once lent him £10,000 at 3 per cent interest so that he could pay his broker. As we have seen, he was still paying Lady Branden a regular annual sum when he died and he also

[72]

gave Caroline Norton money and other presents. 'I dare say we shall find more debts than we reckon upon,' Brougham who was his executor wrote at the time to his co-executor. 'What a sad pillage! *Women of course.*'[24]

6

When the eighteen-year-old Princess Victoria became Queen in 1837, Melbourne was Prime Minister of a Whig government. He solved the question of who should occupy the post of the Queen's private secretary by taking on the job himself for all public business. Sir Robert Peel and the Tory Opposition as well as some of the Whig ministers feared the influence that the Premier should have with a young, untried girl sovereign. But though he had to be constantly with her, working on state papers in the morning, riding in the afternoon and dining in the evening, Melbourne's conduct was scrupulously tactful and considerate. Parliament, prompted by Melbourne, voted her a generous civil list and a personal annuity which enabled her to pay off her late father the Duke of Kent's debts. 'The Queen is as steady to us as ever,' wrote the Foreign Secretary Lord Palmerston on the eve of the coronation, 'and was in the depth of despair when she thought we were in danger of being turned out. She keeps well in health, and even in London takes long rides into the country, which have done her great good.'

Two personal scandals occurred during the remaining twelve months of the Melbourne government. The first concerned Lord Palmerston, the flamboyant Foreign Secretary, who had married the Prime Minister's sister Lady Cowper. While staying at Windsor Castle, Palmerston tried to rape one of the Queen's ladies-in-waiting Mrs Susan Brand. One night he arrived in her bedroom, having apparently mistaken her room for that of another lady who was expecting him. Palmerston locked one door, blocked the other, and advanced towards Mrs Brand's bed. The surprised lady-in-waiting managed to escape and raise the alarm. Melbourne, when appealed to, expressed himself as 'shocked beyond measure at this atrocious attempt.' He said that 'in all his experience he had *never* attempted any woman against her will', adding that he thought the matter 'could not escape detection and the result would be much damage to the character of the court and even the Queen, and the immediate break-up of the administration.'

The Prime Minister insisted that his Foreign Secretary and brother-in-law should apologise to Mrs Brand. Palmerston wrote the necessary note, the apology was accepted and the scandal hushed up. However, the Queen somehow heard of the affair and was rightly incensed by Palmerston's behaviour. But she was so much under Melbourne's influence and content to be guided by him in all things that she let him talk her out of taking any action. Thus the Melbourne administration was saved – for the time being.[25]

The other scandal concerned another lady-in-waiting, Lady Flora Hastings. Lady Flora, a somewhat acid spinster of thirty-two who wrote poetry, was the daughter of an Irish peer Lord Hastings. Her family were Tories and Queen Victoria, who disliked her, was convinced that she was a spy planted in the royal household by her mother the Duchess of Kent and her confidant Sir John Conroy, with whom the Queen thought that Lady Flora was carrying on a liaison. Early in 1839 Lady Flora showed signs of a protuberance of the stomach and the court gossips hinted that she was pregnant. Sir James Clark, the Queen's doctor, admitted that he was suspicious, and after a regrettable delay encouraged by Melbourne who also had his suspicions, Clark mentioned the reports to Lady Flora who indignantly denied them. Eventually Lady Flora was persuaded to undergo a medical examination, which she did with considerable reluctance at the hands of Sir James Clark and her family physician Sir Charles Clarke. The examination resulted in a medical certificate signed by Sir James Clark which explicitly contradicted the slander and declared that Lady Flora was not with child but was suffering from a disease of the liver.[26]

The Hastings family demanded reparation, but Melbourne brushed off their complaints with the result that they wrote letters to newspapers and published pamphlets demanding Lady Flora's public rehabilitation, so that the matter became the talk of London society and eventually a matter of national interest. Lady Flora's condition was aggravated by her mental suffering and she died at Buckingham Palace in July 1839. A post-mortem confirmed the medical report, diagnosing a tumour on the liver. Her death caused considerable public sympathy for the unfortunate Lady Flora and her family, and indignation against the Queen, Melbourne and her other advisers. Stones were thrown at

[74]

the royal carriage which accompanied Lady Flora's funeral procession, while the Duchess of Montrose and Lady Sarah Ingestre actually hissed the Queen and called her 'Mrs Melbourne' when the royal party appeared at Ascot. The Queen was furious. 'Those two abominable women ought to be flogged,' she protested to Melbourne who agreed, since he would like to have done the job himself had it been feasible.[27]

All this justified the diarist Charles Greville's comment shortly before Lady Flora's death when the scandal was at its height. 'It is inconceivable', wrote Greville, 'how Melbourne can have permitted this disgraceful and mischievous scandal which cannot fail to lower the character of the Court in the eyes of the world.'[28]

Some Victorian Sex Scandals

1

IT has frequently but erroneously been stated that divorce was originally introduced in England by the Matrimonial Causes Act of 1857. In fact this legislation did not alter the law of divorce in any way but simply made it subject to judicial process, thus making it quicker, cheaper and more widely available than the existing cumbrous procedure by Private Act of Parliament. The 1857 measure was the result of the recommendations of a Royal Commission which had been appointed under the chairmanship of Lord Campbell, Chief Justice of the Queen's Bench, seven years previously and took into account the argument that divorce had hitherto been the exclusive prerogative of the wealthy aristocracy, costing the petitioner seldom less than £800 and running into thousands when the case was contested, although in Scotland a divorce only cost £20 to £30 at the most. In spite of the strong opposition of the spiritual lords in the Upper House (with the notable exceptions of the Archbishop of Canterbury and the Bishop of London) and Mr Gladstone and others in the Commons, the Act of 1857 was passed and the new Divorce Court came into being.* The ecclesiastical courts' divorces *a mensa et thoro* were abolished and decrees for judicial separation substituted. Also civil actions for *crim. con.* in place of which

---

* The Archbishop of Canterbury was John Bird Sumner (1780–1862) and the Bishop of London Archibald Campbell Tait (1811–82) who became Archbishop of Canterbury in 1869. Palmerston in a letter to the Queen remarked that Gladstone opposed the second reading of the Divorce Bill in the Commons 'in a speech of two hours and a half, fluent, eloquent, brilliant, full of theological learning and scriptural research, but fallacious in argument, and with parts inconsistent with each other.'

the petitioner could now claim damages from the co-respondent. Generally the Court was given power to pronounce a decree of divorce for the same causes as had merited relief by Private Act of Parliament although in the husband's case adultery sufficed, whereas besides adultery a wife, in order to succeed with her petition, had to prove cruelty, desertion, rape, sodomy or bestiality. Thus, while altering the procedure for obtaining a divorce, the 1857 Act introduced no new principles.

However, it did result in the reporting of the evidence in divorce cases, often in salacious detail. This caused Queen Victoria considerable concern, and after the judicial court had been hearing divorce petitions for about two years the Queen wrote to Lord Campbell, by this time Lord Chancellor, asking whether steps could not be taken to prevent the undesirable publicity attending divorce proceedings.

These cases, which must necessarily increase when the new law becomes more and more known, fill now almost daily a large portion of the newspapers, and are of so scandalous a character that it makes it almost impossible for a paper to be trusted in the hands of a young lady or boy. None of the worst French novels from which careful parents try to protect their children can be as bad as what is daily brought and laid upon the breakfast-table of every educated family in England, and its effect must be most pernicious to the public morals of the country.

The Lord Chancellor replied that, having attempted in the last session of Parliament to introduce a measure to give effect to the Queen's wish, and having been defeated, he was powerless to prevent the evil. The situation was otherwise in Scotland where divorce cases had always been tried *in camera* and only the judgment or verdict was published, while in Ireland it did not arise, although *crim. con.* cases there continued to be reported in some detail. Hence the evidence in divorce cases in England were fully reported until after the First World War when the reports were eventually restricted to conform with the practice in Scotland.[1]

The divorce cases described here involve five MPs – the Hon. John Vivian, Sir Charles Mordaunt, Lord Colin Campbell, Sir Charles Dilke, and the Irish leader Charles Stewart Parnell. Another concerns a

[77]

member of the ducal family of Devonshire, a baronet's daughter, and a count who belonged to one of the oldest and most distinguished families in France. Finally, there is the case of another MP, who also belonged to an English ducal family (Newcastle) and was a prominent figure in a notorious homosexual scandal.

Captain George Cavendish of the Royal Household Cavalry was the son of General Henry Cavendish, also a Guards officer, a nephew of William third Duke of Devonshire and an uncle of the seventh Duke. George Cavendish was thus a first cousin of the seventh Duke and a first cousin-once-removed of 'Harty-tarty' the eighth Duke (so nicknamed from his courtesy title of Marquess of Hartington which he held from 1858 until his succession to the dukedom in 1891). He was a Liberal MP and holder of many high political offices, refusing that of prime minister no less than three times, besides having the celebrated courtesan Catherine Walters (Skittles) as his mistress. Another cousin was Harty-tarty's brother, the ill-fated Lord Frederick Cavendish MP, who was murdered in Dublin's Phoenix Park by Fenians a few hours after his arrival as Chief Secretary for Ireland in 1882.

In 1848 Captain Cavendish married Emily Rumbold, only daughter of Sir William Rumbold, third Baronet, and sister of Sir Horace Rumbold, the well-known diplomatist. Emily and her brother Horace were born in India where their father was on the staff of Lord Moira, Governor-General of Bengal. They were both sent to Paris to be educated, since they had many relations among the old French aristocracy. Their aunt, the elder Emily Rumbold, had married a Prussian nobleman Baron Ferdinand Delmar. The Delmars adopted young Emily as their daughter and she grew up in their Paris house, moving with them to England in 1847, when she was twenty-two, and later to Baden-Baden in Germany. From all accounts Emily was a beautiful and gifted young lady, being an accomplished musician and a favourite pupil of Chopin when he was living in Paris. She was also very highly sexed.

In England the Delmars took a suite of rooms in the Clarendon Hotel in Old Bond Street. This was then the largest, the most fashionable and the most expensive hotel in London, the entrance being where Cartier's now stands and the building extending to the rear in Albermarle Street, where there was another entrance and where the carriages drove up because of the traffic congestion in Bond Street. It was run by a

[78]

Frenchman called Jacquier, who had served Louis XVIII during his exile, and it was said to be the only hotel in England where a man could get a genuine French dinner.[2] Emily continued to live with the Delmars at the Clarendon, and by this time was acting as the Baron's private secretary as well as his adopted daughter. The Delmars had almost as many friends among the English aristocracy as they had among the French, and among the country houses they visited were Wynyard and Chatsworth. At Wynyard Park, which belonged to the Londonderrys, young Emily made the acquaintance of Prince Louis Napoleon, who as he told Emily, was convinced that he would become Emperor of France, which indeed he was to do shortly afterwards as Napoleon III. Meanwhile, at Chatsworth, the Devonshire family home, Emily met her future husband George Cavendish. The sixth Duke, known as Hart, who then lived at Chatsworth, was a bachelor and never married, although he had several love affairs, including one with Melbourne's wife Lady Caroline Lamb. At Chatsworth, he is particularly remembered for his patronage of the gardener Joseph Paxton, who designed the glass covered way there and later the Crystal Palace in London. The sixth Duke encouraged his kinsman's engagement to Emily Rumbold, which was in effect an 'arranged' one.[3]

George Cavendish and Emily Rumbold's marriage was a quiet affair, owing to Baron Delmar's poor health. The wedding ceremony was performed in October 1848 by the renowned preacher the Revd John Jackson, later Bishop of London, in the Delmars' drawing-room in the Clarendon Hotel. The young couple spent their honeymoon at Chiswick, which may seem an odd place for a honeymoon today being as it is a western suburb of London. But in those days it was a select residential area and among its fine villas was Chiswick House, which had been built by George Cavendish's grandfather, the first Earl of Burlington, and was one of the many properties belonging to the Devonshires. It was (and still is) a striking one-storey building with a rotunda as a centre-piece, Greek pillars, wedding cake cornices and velvet covered walls, set in a fine park of some seventy acres. After a fortnight or so there the Cavendishes moved to Brighton where they joined the Delmars, who had taken a house in Kemptown near the Duke of Devonshire's, and where Emily's brother Horace was also a guest. It was a curious ménage, George Cavendish commuting to Knightsbridge Barracks in London and Horace Rumbold doing likewise to the Foreign Office since he had joined the diplomatic service, while Emily, who soon became pregnant, resumed her work as the Baron's secretary. Her first son William Delmar Cavendish was born just twelve months after her marriage. A daughter followed a little later, but the marriage was not a happy one and Emily and her husband eventually became estranged. About 1859 she took a lover, Count Gaston de la Rochefoucauld, who was ten years younger and whom she apparently seduced. At this time the Count was an attaché at the French Embassy in Rome.

The cause of the divorce was Captain Cavendish's discovery in his wife's cabinet of a number of incriminating letters from Count de la Rochefoucauld.[4] They were written in French, a language which Emily Cavendish spoke fluently from her upbringing in Paris, and they left no doubt that Mrs Cavendish and the Count had committed adultery. The letters were in the highest degree erotic and for the most part are too obscene to be reproduced here. George Cavendish filed a petition for divorce in 1866, naming the Count as co-respondent, and the letters were put in evidence by the petitioner but as the petition was uncontested, Cavendish was granted a decree on 16 June 1866 by the divorce judge, Sir James Wilde, later Lord Penzance, who also gave the petitioner custody of his infant child. In the next law term Emily, who was then living in Baden-Baden, attempted to have the case reheard on account of the alleged negligence of her attorney. However, the judge refused her application because she was in contempt for failing to deliver the infant child to the petitioner.

Here are translations of two extracts from the letters of the young Count, who confessed that his mistress had 'picked the flower of his virginity':

I have never kissed another woman, and whatever fortune may befall it will always be an indescribable happiness for me to remember that I lost my innocence through your enchanting caresses (*par tes delices*). This is perhaps the greatest happiness and the one consolation in my life and such as cannot again be found on earth. I do not believe that he who took your innocence was a pure as I was, and if there is a greater joy than that which I know, I promise you never to seek or experience it, though I do not ask the same of you. I do not wish to hear other women spoken of: even to look at them disgusts me. You know it, and you know too that nothing in you disgusts me, but that everything that is you enchants me; and I love and worship it all. It is a kind of madness and you know it; for when you are kind you give me, at least in writing, the idea of what you would not do, if you harboured the least doubt about it.

There follow fervent descriptions of various intimate sexual activities with his beloved, such as *cunnilingus, urinam bibendi, faeces devorandi*, and *delicias omnium corporis partium*. The letter continues:

As much as the odour of women is repugnant to me in general, the more do I like it in you. I beg of you to preserve that intoxicating perfume; but you are too clean, you wash yourself too much. I have often told you so in vain. When you will be quite my own, I shall forbid you to do it too often, at most once a day; my tongue and my saliva shall do the rest.

In all these allusions a form of juvenile masochism is plainly recognisable, since it is often seen in a youth's early love-making, though not perhaps as in such an extreme form as described here. These perversions are frequently originated by older women like Emily Cavendish who seduced youths like La Rochefoucauld.

On 18 December 1877, the Queen's advocate, the law officer who then advised the Crown on divorce matters, appeared in the divorce court for the co-respondent, who, he said, had only seen the letters a few days previously since he had been abroad. He had also sworn an affidavit that the originals of these letters which were said to be in his handwriting, were not his but were forgeries, and he was 'much distressed that he should be supposed capable of writing such letters.' Also, he was only earning £200 a year in his diplomatic post. However, the renewed application for a rehearing was rejected, since it was out of time and in the judge's view both Mrs Cavendish and Count de la Rochefoucauld had done their best to delay the filing of the petition. Whether or not the letters were genuine is a matter of opinion. But Sir James Wilde, the judge, seems to have thought that they were, and he was a most experienced lawyer.[5]

So far as English society went, Emily Cavendish was ruined. But this did not worry her since she had come into the Delmars' money on the

[81]

Baroness's death, and she could afford to live comfortably abroad where she chose. Her choice was the fashionable spa of Baden-Baden at the entrance to the Black Forest where she had previously spent some time with the Delmars to whose barony she succeeded by the order of the King of Prussia in 1869. Here in due course she was joined by la Rochefoucauld, who married her in 1870 after he had given up his diplomatic career in which he had risen to the rank of Minister Plenipotentiary. They subsequently moved from Baden to Biarritz where they occupied a magnificent villa and where they were visited by Emily's brother Sir Horace Rumbold. Emily died here on 11 September 1904 aged seventy-eight, having seen both her husband and her brother heading a succession of foreign missions representing their respective countries. Count Gaston de la Rochefoucauld continued to live in the villa and died there on 28 July 1915 aged eighty-one. He and Emily had no children. The question of whether the love letters attributed to him were genuine, and whose authenticity he always denied, has never been satisfactorily resolved. It remains an intriguing mystery in the annals of erotica.

2

The short reigns of George IV and William IV and the long reign of Queen Victoria, which together covered the greater part of the nineteenth century, had their measure of society scandals with homosexual overtones. In particular, during the earlier period, two well-known figures in the literary world were involved; they also happened to be Members of Parliament and were obliged to resign their seats in consequence of the charges brought against them.

The first was the famous book collector Richard Heber, of whom it has been said that perhaps no private individual ever collected such vast accumulations of choice volumes, in more than 150,000 of which he is supposed to have invested £100,000. 'No gentleman can be without three copies of a book,' he used to say, 'one for show, one for use, and one for borrowers'. In 1822, following his election as MP for Oxford University, he received the honorary degree of Doctor of Civil Law from the university. In 1824, he was one of the founders of the Athenaeum Club and its magnificent library, which he helped to form.

Among those he met in the course of his activities as a bibliophile was a young man names Charles Hartshorne, the son of an ironmaster in Shropshire, where Heber also had property. The publication by Hartshorne, of a bibliographical essay in 1825, the same year as he graduated from Cambridge, attracted Heber's attention, and the two became intimate friends. At this time Heber was fifty-two and Hartshorne twenty-three. In the following year, a column appeared in a local newspaper in which pointed allusions were made to this intimacy. The matter might well have gone unnoticed if young Hartshorne's father had not seen fit to bring an action for libel against the newspaper. This so alarmed Heber that he fled to Brussels and immediately resigned his seat. Although no proceedings were brought against him, nevertheless Heber deemed it prudent to remain abroad for the next five years. On his return to England, in 1831, he found himself completely ostracised by society. Until his death, which occurred four years later, he lived a life of almost total seclusion either in his London or his country house, only emerging from time to time to visit the sale rooms and booksellers' shops. On the other hand, the affair does not appear to have injured Hartshorne, since he subsequently had a successful career both as a clergyman and an antiquarian, marrying the daughter of the Cambridge University librarian, and publishing among other works *The Book Rarities of the University of Cambridge*.[6]

The other parliamentarian was William John Bankes, the forty-five-year-old oriental traveller and friend of the poet Byron, who represented Cambridge University and afterwards the County of Dorset in the House of Commons. He had the reputation of being a witty conversationalist and according to Samuel Rogers he could eclipse Sydney Smith by the vigour of his table talk. In 1833, Bankes was accused of committing an act of indecency with a soldier in a public lavatory outside Westminster Abbey. At his trial, many well-known persons, including the Duke of Wellington, Samuel Rogers and Dr Butler, the Master of Harrow, came forward and testified as to his good character, with the result that he was acquitted. Some years later, however, in 1841 he was brought before a magistrate for indecently exposing himself in a public park and was set at liberty on bail pending trial. This time he forfeited his recognizances and fled to the Continent, where he died in Venice in 1855.[7]

The great homosexual scandal of the mid-Victorian period involved

[83]

another Member of Parliament, thirty-year-old Lord Arthur Clinton, third son of the fifth Duke of Newcastle who sat for Newark in the House of Commons. Living in the same lodgings as Lord Arthur were two young men, Ernest Boulton, aged twenty-two, the son of a London stockbroker, and his inseparable companion, Frederick William Park, aged twenty-three, whose father was a Master in the Court of Common Pleas. Boulton and Park were both transvestite homosexuals, who liked to play female parts in amateur theatricals and frequently appeared in public dressed as women, rouged and painted, in low cut dresses. Boulton, familiarly known as 'Stella', was an effeminate looking youth, extremely musical and the possessor of a fine soprano voice. A servant in the lodgings deposed that she thought Boulton was Lord Arthur's wife and certainly his lordship did nothing to dispel this idea; on the contrary the evidence showed that he had visiting cards printed in the name of 'Lady Arthur Clinton' and a seal engraved with the name 'Stella'. Park, who was known as Fanny, was also on terms of intimacy with Lord Arthur, as appeared from some of his letters which the police seized. 'Is the handle of my umbrella mended yet?' he asked Lord Arthur in language which caused considerable mirth when the letter was read out in court. 'If so I wish you would kindly send it to me, as the weather has turned so showery that I can't go out without a dread of my back hair coming out of curl. Ever your affectionate Fanny.'

The police, who had been watching Boulton and Park for some months, eventually arrested them as they were leaving the Strand Theatre one night in April 1870. The officer who carried out the arrests subsequently stated in evidence:

When we got to the station I saw that Boulton had on a scarlet dress and a muslin shawl over it. It was partly satin, and I believe the rest was white moire antique. Boulton had false hair and chignon of fair colour like the ordinary hair I have seen females wearing. He had ornaments – bracelets, rings and lockets. It was a very low dress and the arms were bare. He wore white kid gloves. I found afterwards that he wore white petticoats and stays, and a white skirt. He wore ladies' white boots. The bosom was padded to make it appear very full.

Park's costume consisted of a dark green satin dress, low necked, trimmed with black lace, of which material he also had a shawl round his shoulders. His hair was flaxen and in curls. He also had on a pair of white kid gloves and wore earrings.

Next morning the two men, dressed in this remarkable attire were brought before the magistrate at Bow Street and charged with frequenting the Strand Theatre with intent to commit a felony. The case was adjourned and after six further hearings both defendants were committed for trial, bail being refused.

Boulton and Park did not always appear in public in women's clothes, but, not surprisingly, when they went out dressed as men they were sometimes mistaken for women. A man named Cox, who gave evidence at the preliminary police court proceedings but died before the trial (where his deposition was read) stated that he had been introduced by a friend to Boulton and Lord Arthur Clinton, MP in a City pub. Boulton was dressed as a man, but looked like a woman, as Cox believed him to be. He (Cox) stood them a champagne lunch. ('I kissed him, she, or it, believing at the time it was a woman.') Lord Arthur appeared to be jealous, Cox went on, and left the room, whereupon Boulton presented Cox with his photograph, 'secretly as far as Lord Arthur was concerned'. Later Cox learned the sex of Boulton, and meeting the pair again at Evans's Coffee House in Covent Garden (a notorious establishment which was to serve as the prototype of 'The Cave of Harmony' in Thackeray's *The Newcomes*) exclaimed 'You damned set of infernal scoundrels, you ought to be kicked out of this place!' However, under cross-examination, Cox admitted that Boulton had never said he was a woman. ('I flirted with him believing him to be a woman.')

As drawn by the Crown lawyers, the indictment charged the defendants with conspiring to commit a felony, which was rather stronger than the charge to which they answered at the police court. Letters found in their lodgings appeared to implicate Lord Arthur Clinton, as well as two men living in Edinburgh, Louis Charles Hurt and John Safford Fiske. The latter was an American who was his country's consular representative at Leith. All three were joined in the indictment along with Boulton and Park. But before the case came to trial Lord Arthur Clinton contracted scarlet fever from which he died on 18 June 1870. However, the others eventually appeared in the dock at the Old Bailey.

[85]

The trial opened before Lord Chief Justice Cockburn on 9 May 1871 and lasted for six days. It aroused immense public interest. The Attorney-General Sir Robert Collier and the Solicitor-General Sir John Coleridge led for the prosecution and the prisoners were each defended by leading counsel of the day, Boulton by Digby Seymour, QC, and Serjeant Ballantine, and Park by Serjeant Parry. As the law of evidence then stood, the defendants were debarred from going into the witness-box to testify on their own behalf, so that, although they could be seen, they could not be heard by the jury. Unlike Boulton and Park, Hurt and Fiske were not female impersonators and they were in no way concerned with their transvestite activities; indeed they disapproved of them. 'I am sorry to hear of your going about in drag so much,' wrote Hurt to Boulton in one letter. In another letter Hurt refused to go to the Derby with Boulton if the latter were 'in drag'.

Although there could be no doubt that all the defendants were homosexuals, the prosecution was unable to prove that any of them had infringed the law. The letters seized by the police and read out in court, although most affectionate in tone, did not in any degree suggest that buggery had taken place or been attempted. Nor did the appearance of Boulton and Park in public places dressed as women and visiting the 'ladies' room' in various theatres and bars constitute proof that a felony had been committed by any of them. Much evidence was given about the numerous performances of amateur theatricals in which Boulton and Park had played women's parts, and although it was admitted that they often went to parties after the shows in their female costumes their counsel argued strongly that there was no evidence whatever of conspiracy 'beyond the mere going about as women'. In particular, the letters addressed to Park by Fiske, which appeared the most compromising, were dismissed as light-hearted notes to 'an effeminate lad, a dainty and pleasing boy, who was generally treated as a young girl'.

Whatever he may have thought of 'Stella' and 'Fanny' and their caperings, Lord Chief Justice Cockburn strongly disapproved of the form in which the case had been brought. 'We are trying the defendants for conspiracy to commit a felonious crime,' he told the jury in his summing-up, 'and the proof of it, if it amounts to anything, amounts to proof of the actual commission of crime. I am clearly of opinion that where the proof is intended to be submitted to a jury, it is not the proper course to charge the parties with conspiring to commit it, for that course

[86]

manifestly operates unfairly and unjustly and oppressively against the parties concerned.' The defendants, in the judge's view, should have been tried separately, and this would have excluded evidence against one being used to the prejudice of the other defendants. Yet so far as the Crown lawyers were concerned, the Lord Chief Justice's strictures were to go unheeded, and for nearly a century – that is until homosexual offences between consenting adults in private were abolished in 1967 – the conspiracy device was used in many homosexual trials in Britain to draw homosexuals into the net of the criminal law.

Both Boulton's mother and Park's father gave evidence of the two defendants' theatrical interests and the various lawful occasions for the possession and use of the women's dresses, in which they had been arrested. The judge was apparently convinced since he summed up strongly in their favour. 'Was there not a solution consistent with innocence?' he asked with particular reference to the letters written by 'Stella' and 'Fanny' to Lord Arthur Clinton, and the parties they attended together. 'These parties had been mixed up together in performances in which Lord Arthur continually acted with Boulton as his lover or husband, and it may have been that, half in fun at first and then habitually, they spoke of each other in that kind of way.'

It took the jury exactly fifty-three minutes to return their verdict of Not Guilty in regard to the four defendants. The verdict was greeted with loud cheers and shouts of 'Bravo!' It came as such a shock to Boulton, who had by this time grown a moustache in an effort to promote a more masculine appearance, that he fainted in the dock and had to be revived with water.

Next day *The Times* came out with a leading article which contained the following remarks:

It is not without a certain sense of relief that we record this morning the failure of a Prosecution which nothing but a strong conviction would have justified the Government in instituting. THE QUEEN *v.* BOULTON AND OTHERS is a case in which a verdict for the Crown would have been felt at home, and received abroad, as a reflection on our national morals, yet which, for that very reason, could not be hushed up after popular rumour had once invested it with so grave a complexion.

Now that justice has been satisfied and the whole story thoroughly

[87]

sifted, the verdict of the jury should be accepted as clearing all the defendants of the odious guilt imputed to them.

The following limerick, to which the case gave rise, was soon going the rounds:

> There was an old person of Sark
> Who buggered a pig in the dark;
> The swine in surprise
> Murmured: 'God blast your eyes,
> Do you take me for Boulton or Park?'

In all the circumstances, the four defendants, especially Boulton and Park, must be considered fortunate to have been exonerated as they were.[8]

3

A spectacular sensation of the Society 'season' in 1869 was the elopement of an English MP's wife with an Irish peer. The peer was the twenty-five-year-old Marquess of Waterford and the MP's wife, five years older than the Marquess, had been married since 1861 to the Honourable Captain John Cranch Walker Vivian, a younger son of the first Lord Vivian, one of the Duke of Wellington's favourite military commanders on account of his brigade's crucial support at Waterloo. Like his elder brother, later the second baron, John Vivian joined the army as a subaltern in the 11th Hussars and immediately went out with his regiment to Canada where he helped to quell the rebellions in Montreal and Toronto in 1837 designed to obtain responsible government. He was promoted to Captain but resigned his commission after marrying for the first time in 1840 and being elected Liberal MP for Penryn and Falmouth in the following year. He later sat for Bodmin and at the time of the elopement was MP for Truro, where his family property was situated. He was also a Lord of the Treasury in the first Gladstone Government, a junior ministerial post which involved his acting as Financial Secretary to the War Office.[9]

Vivian's first wife died after fifteen years of marriage during which they had no children. Six years later, in 1861, Vivian married again. His second wife was Florence Rowley, a baronet's niece whose father had been a cavalry officer in the Indian Army but had died when Florence was five years old so that the girl was brought up by her aunt the Dowager Countess of Kinnoull. John Vivian's second marriage took place in St Paul's Church, Knightsbridge, the gathering in the church and subsequent reception being one of rank and fashion, since Vivian was prominent socially as well as politically. At this date the bridegroom was forty-three, hard-working, ambitious and the rich scion of an old Cornish family, so that Florence was considered by her friends and relations to have made a good match in spite of the fact that she was twenty-five years younger than her husband.

The marriage began happily enough and the Vivians had three children, all daughters, at their first home in Belgrave Square where they lived with Lady Kinnoull in her house. Later, in 1868, when Mr Gladstone formed his first administration in which Vivian became a Lord of the Treasury, John thought that they should have a separate establishment, so that he and his wife and children moved to a house in Lowndes Street, leaving Lady Kinnoull in Belgrave Square. This suited Florence Vivian, who had begun to resent the strict eye which her aunt had kept on her activities, particularly her growing attachment to Lord Waterford.

The Vivians first met Henry Beresford Lord Waterford in 1863 when his father the fourth Marquess was still alive and he was known by the courtesy title of Earl of Tyrone. The fourth Marquess brought up Tyrone to be a figure in public life, and as soon as he came of age in 1865 he was elected MP for County Waterford. This cemented his friendship with the Vivians and he would write familiarly to John Vivian as 'My dear Johnny', sympathising with him when he did not immediately obtain the political appointment he had been expecting. John and Florence Vivian stayed with him at Curraghmore, Waterford's historic ancestral residence which boasted the finest demesne in Ireland. It was after Vivian's appointment as Lord of the Treasury, and becoming immersed in his government duties, that Florence Vivian fell in love with Waterford, who had now succeeded his father, and, it was said, she conceived such a passion for the Marquess that she could hardly bear to let him out of her sight. Both were careless with their love letters, and two – one from her and another from him to her – were somehow

[89]

acquired by an anonymous correspondent who put them in an envelope which he sent to John Vivian at the House of Commons. Vivian thereupon employed a private detective named Henry Smith to watch his wife and report on her movements. Shortly afterwards Florence Vivian left the house in Lowndes Street, on 5 March 1869, to join Waterford, and the detective reported to her husband that he had followed them from Charing Cross Station to Paris; during the journey, he said, Lord Waterford had been recognised by several fellow travellers who spoke to him but not to his companion, whom they did not recognise since she was heavily veiled. Detective Smith went on to say that he had traced the guilty couple to the Hotel Westminster, a de luxe establishment in the Rue de la Paix where they were occupying a suite.

Vivian's immediate reaction was to get in touch with his sister-in-law Mrs Emilie Knight and to ask her to go over to Paris with him which she did. On their arrival in Paris they put up at the Grand Hotel, beside the Opera House in the Boulevard des Capucines. The same afternoon Emilie drove to the Westminster, only a short distance from the Grand, and having discovered the room which her sister was occupying, entered it unannounced. Florence, who was surprised by the unexpected appearance of her elder sister, burst into tears, which continued to flow when Emilie told her that she had come to bring her back to Lowndes Street and furthermore that Captain Vivian was at hand to help her. At this Florence broke down and flatly refused to go back. However, Emilie added, John wished to see her and discuss the situation amicably.

'I daren't see him,' Florence replied. 'I'm sure he could never forgive me for the wrong I've done him.'

'You must meet him, Florence,' Emilie urged. 'Will you fling away a chance that may never occur again?'

'Don't torture me,' said Florence, still crying. Then after a little while, she calmed down, but still refused to go and see her husband.

'If you won't go to John,' said Emilie Knight, 'he will have to come to you, and I won't be responsible for what may happen if he meets Lord Waterford here.'

The prospect of an irate confrontation if the two men saw each other in the hotel was too much for Florence, and she replied that she would come to the Grand if she could first have a couple of hours rest.

[90]

'Take the night to think it over,' said her sister. 'You are not in a fit condition to see anyone. Come tomorrow afternoon, say about three o'clock.' To this Florence agreed.

Next day John and Emilie waited uneasily, fearing that Florence would not turn up, since they thought she probably felt unable to face the ordeal of meeting. However, she appeared at three o'clock, looking deathly pale and trembling violently. Emilie left the two together, going out of the room immediately after Florence had been shown in.

Husband and wife spent the next hour and a half together, John doing most of the talking. He pointed out that the elopement was still a secret and he implored her to give up Waterford if only for the sake of the children and come back with him, pointing out that otherwise, if he was compelled to divorce her, she would lose the children, and her lover would probably not marry her, owing to the difference in their ages and the pressure the Beresfords would certainly bring to bear on him against her. Unfortunately she was so besotted by her passion for the Marquess that the most she would agree to was to think it over and let him have her answer as soon as possible the same day.

She then returned to the Westminster where she saw Waterford, whose enthusiasm for his mistress was not as great as hers was for him. He advised her to go back to London with her husband since he was evidently prepared to forgive her. But she persuaded her lover that she loved him too much to do this, and Waterford, true to the tradition that the Beresfords never let a woman down, amiably consented to continue their liaison.

Towards six the same evening a special messenger arrived at the Grand Hotel and handed Vivian a letter addressed to him in his wife's familiar handwriting. Vivian tore it open and read the following unsigned note:

Five o'clock

I cannot go. I have tried and tried to give him up, and, against his own urgent advice, I shall stay. For God's sake, don't think too hardly of me or I shall do myself some harm. I am going to my ruin, I know, but it is impossible for me to go back. Try and forgive me in your heart. I could not look at those poor children after what I have done, and do not send for me for Heaven's sake.

[91]

Sadly, Captain John Vivian, MP, returned to London and filed a petition for divorce, citing John Henry de la Poer Beresford Marquess of Waterford as co-respondent.[10]

The case was heard in the Divorce Court by Lord Penzance and a jury on 5 August 1869, but since it was virtually undefended it only lasted part of one day. Waterford's family insisted that he should be represented by counsel whose sole contribution was to object successfully to the admission as evidence of the two letters which had been sent anonymously to the petitioner. The petitioner tendered the letters in evidence, but as no objection was raised to the allegation that Lord Waterford lived with Mrs Vivian at the Hotel Westminster in Paris the letters were withdrawn and not read. On the other hand, the petitioner was able to put in the short letter which he had received from his wife at the Grand Hotel to the effect that she could not give up her lover. The respondent's sister Mrs Emilie Knight described her meetings with Florence at the Westminster and how she had begged her sister to go back to Lowndes Street and the children, but Florence refused to leave the Marquess. 'She has since never returned to England,' the witness added.

The petitioner testified that the first intimation he had received of his wife's infidelity was in the two letters sent to him anonymously, and he further testified to his meetings with Florence and her sister in Paris. The other witnesses included the detective, Lady Kinnoull and Vivian's brother-in-law the Hon. Henry Foley. Lady Kinnoull related how affectionate her niece and the petitioner were when they lived with her in Belgrave Square, while Henry Foley told how very much distressed the petitioner was when his wife left him. Finally, Detective Smith described to the judge's satisfaction how Mrs Vivian and Lord Waterford shared a suite of rooms in the Westminster Hotel in Paris.

'The adultery is plainly proved,' Lord Penzance declared in a brief judgment. 'I pronounce a decree *nisi* with costs against the co-respondent.'

It was generally expected after the regulation six months, when the decree would normally have been made absolute on the petitioner's application and both Vivian and his wife would be free to remarry, that Florence would immediately become the Marchioness of Waterford. However, as John Vivian had correctly foretold, Waterford's family strongly objected to the Marquess marrying Florence Vivian, particularly Colonel Charles Leslie of Glaslough, Co. Monaghan, whose sister had married Waterford's father the fourth Marquess. The Colonel believed, quite wrongly, that the divorce had been deliberately arranged by the Vivians and his nephew, and he took the extreme course of applying to the Queen's Proctor, who represented the Crown in divorce cases, to intervene and declare the divorce invalid. This the Queen's Proctor quite rightly refused to do and Colonel Leslie withdrew his application, having admitted to the divorce judge that there was no justification whatever for it. Owing to the delay occasioned by Colonel Leslie's action, Vivian did not get his decree absolute until June 1870. Colonel Leslie continued the struggle and after his death in 1871 it was carried on by his brother Sir John Leslie, Bart. Waterford was implored to have nothing more to do with Florence and induced to offer her a considerable sum of money if she would give him up. But the only compensation Florence would accept was marriage, and when she fell ill, which she did in August 1872, Waterford hastened to her side in London. Shortly afterwards they were married at a civil ceremony in the St George's Register Office in Hanover Square.

Unfortunately Florence's career as a marchioness was short-lived. In the following summer she told her husband, with whom she was very happy, that she was pregnant. In the event she gave birth to a son at Waterford's town house, 27 Chesham Place on 29 March 1873. But the baby was still-born and, worse still, Florence got puerperal fever from which she died less than a week later. She was only thirty-three at the time.[11]

The divorce case in which Lord Waterford was involved did not affect him adversely, since unlike John Vivian he had no political ambitions. On 21 July 1874, fifteen months after Florence's death, he married Lady Blanche Somerset, the youngest child and only daughter of the eighth Duke of Beaufort, who invented the game of badminton, so-called after his Gloucestershire home, and who was also well known as a sportsman and philanderer. Waterford's marriage took place at St Michael's Church, Badminton, and was a much more stylish affair than his first wedding in a London register office. The second Lady Waterford, whom her husband first met in the hunting field, was a beautiful, gifted and loyal woman. (Her elder brother Lord Arthur Somerset was the central figure in the Cleveland Street homosexual brothel scandal.)[12] She was devoted to her husband and bore him four children, a son who eventually became sixth Marquess, and three daughters. As for Waterford, although he was a Conservative and Chairman of the Irish Landlords Committee, he was very popular with his tenants at a difficult period. The Liberal Chief Secretary for Ireland John Morley described him as 'thoroughly able, direct, frank, a masculine mind, with a good deal of liberality and breadth of apprehension.' Unfortunately both he and his wife became invalids, Waterford as the result of a gate blown against him by a gust of wind while out hunting, thus damaging his spine so much that he could only stand up with the greatest difficulty; for this reason he was allowed to speak in the House of Lords while seated.

Blanche Waterford developed cancer. The combination of watching her suffering, while himself in constant pain aggravated by a stone in the kidney, proved too much for her husband, who took his life by shooting himself at Curraghmore in 1895. He was fifty-one when he died, while his wife, who survived him was only forty when she died on 22 February 1897, not knowing the nature of the disease which killed her as her doctor would not tell her. 'Mother would have been forty-one on the following 26th of March but I never realised that she was young to die,' wrote her youngest daughter Clodagh Anson many years later. 'I suppose no one has ever really believed that one's father or mother was ever young like oneself. I was seventeen at the time, and very old for my age after all we had gone through but I remember quite well thinking it was very sad for us that Mother should die; still, I supposed it was inevitable that people must die when they get old, and it was only when I actually became forty-one myself that it came home to me how hard it was for her . . . It is impossible to convey how delightful and ridiculous they both were, so quick-witted that nobody ever had to explain anything, no pretence of affectation, and absolutely free from all hypocrisy . . .'[13]

Divorce, even for the innocent party, was now a bar to political advancement, so strongly did Queen Victoria feel on the subject, aided by Mr Gladstone and the growing Nonconformist conscience in the Liberal party. Thus John Vivian realised that he could never rise higher than the junior ministerial post he occupied. 'Always pleasant, always genial', he was described in a contemporary article in *Vanity Fair* which accompanied his cartoon, 'he would, we venture to think, be doing better service, in administering the Government of one of our colonies, or one of the Indian Presidencies, than in vain endeavours as Financial Secretary, to make pleasant the sham economies of the disorganised-organisation in Pall Mall [the War Office].'[14] But an overseas governorship was barred to him as well as higher political office because of his divorce. However, Gladstone did not scruple to make use of Vivian's knowledge of army affairs, and in 1871, probably at the War Minister's suggestion, the position of Permanent Under-Secretary for War, in other words the senior civil servant in the ministry, was offered to him. Vivian wisely accepted it and gave up his seat in the House of Commons. In 1878 he resigned his office for health reasons.

Meanwhile, he had married, for the third time, his third wife being a London widow by whom, like his first wife, he had no children. A few months after his retirement from the War Office he died aged sixty at his Surrey home in Richmond and was buried in the Vivian family vault in St Mary's Church (now Cathedral), Truro. His widow, who survived him by forty-five years, died at Lyme Regis in 1924.[15] However agreeably *Vanity Fair* wrote about him, Captain John Vivian could never live down the scandal of his second wife's elopement.

4

In 1866 Sir Charles Mordaunt, thirty-year-old English baronet and Conservative MP for South Warwickshire, married Harriet Moncreiffe, seventeen-year-old daughter of the Scottish baronet Sir Thomas Moncreiffe of that Ilk, and brought her home to Walton Hall, his property near Warwick. Harriet was one of eight sisters, known as 'the beautiful Moncreiffes' who all married well. At first the Mordaunt marriage prospered. The initial difference occurred when Sir Charles saw his wife reading a letter from the Prince of Wales, the future King Edward VII. 'I don't approve of your friendship with the Prince,' her husband remarked. Harriet, who had known the Prince before her marriage, tossed the letter across the table to him. It was a harmless one dated October 1867 from Dunrobin where the Prince was staying with the Duke of Sutherland. He named the other guests, regretted that he had not seen her when he was recently in London, and hoped that they might meet before he and Princess Alexandra went abroad.

Charles Mordaunt liked to fish in Norway every year and in 1868 he was annoyed when Harriet refused to accompany him. However, she was pregnant at the time and naturally perhaps preferred to remain at home, since in addition to Walton Hall her husband had a town house in Chesham Place. It was at Walton Hall that her only child, a daughter named Violet, was born in February 1869.

If he was disappointed that the child was not a boy, Charles Mordaunt did not show it. Indeed he treated his wife most tenderly. A few days after she had given birth, Harriet clutched her husband by the hand as he was leaving her bedside. 'Charley,' she whispered to him hoarsely, 'I have deceived you. The child is not yours. It is Lord Cole's.'

A glance at his wife's pallid cheeks and eyes convinced Mordaunt that his wife must be raving. 'There, there, dear,' he said soothingly, 'you must not upset yourself. You'll be all right soon.' However, she persisted that she had been unfaithful, not only with Lord Cole but with various others including Sir Frederic Johnstone, the Crimean War hero Lord Lucan, and the Prince of Wales himself 'often and in open day'. In view of these repeated admissions, Charles Mordaunt felt that his only course now was to file a petition for divorce. This he did. A tragic element in the case was that little Violet was born almost blind, and Harriet Mordaunt hinted that this was due to a venereal infection which she had contracted from Viscount Cole, who was the son of the third Earl of Enniskillen, an Irish peer.

In the course of his inquiries, prior to the divorce hearing, Charles Mordaunt prised open his wife's escritoire, where he found her diary in addition to about a dozen letters from the Prince of Wales to Harriet as well as a handkerchief of the Prince's and a valentine, besides letters from Lord Lucan and hotel bills made out to the Prince's friend Sir Frederic Johnstone, Bart. Meanwhile Harriet Mordaunt went to stay in her father's house in Perthshire. Here she was examined by several doctors, one of whom, the well-known Sir James Simpson, declared positively that Harriet was out of her mind, although there was no evidence that she had ever been syphilitic. Armed with this information Sir Thomas Moncreiffe of that Ilk applied to the divorce court to rule that his daughter could not be sued because of her mental condition. Although Mordaunt's counsel argued that Harriet was feigning madness to save herself from public disgrace, on 27 July 1869 the Divorce Court judge Lord Penzance appointed Moncreiffe guardian of his

'Sir Richard Worse-than-sly
Exposing his Wife's Bottom: O fye!'

The Worsley scandal at Maidstone public baths

Sir Richard Worsley MP: 'My fair Seymour, Bisset is going to get up to
look at you.' Captain Bisset: 'A charming view of her back and bottom,
Sir Richard.' Baths attendant: 'Good luck, my Lady, the Captain will
see all for nothing.'

From a print published after the *Worsley* v *Bisset* trial in 1782

Thomas Bruce seventh Earl of Elgin who transported the Elgin Marbles from Athens to England where they are now in the British Museum. He was helped by his wife Mary whom he subsequently divorced for adultery in scandalous circumstances.

One of the Elgin Marbles which forms part of the west frieze of the Parthenon in Athens and shows two riders in the procession at the Great Panathenaic festival c. 440 BC

Mary Countess of Elgin, first wife of the seventh Earl. After her divorce she married her lover John Ferguson MP of Raith. From the portrait by François Gerard

John Ferguson MP of Raith. From the portrait by Sir Henry Raeburn

King George IV

Robert Stewart Viscount Castlereagh
and second Marquess of
Londonderry. Foreign Secretary and
Leader of the House of Commons.
His suicide in 1822 was the result of
blackmail.

Princess Caroline of Brunswick, Princess of Wales and wife of the Prince Regent later King George IV. From the portrait by Sir Thomas Lawrence

Bartolomeo Bergami, Princess Caroline's courier and lover. From a lithograph by G. Engelmann

The Villa d'Este Lake Como. From a contemporary engraving

The Trial of Queen Caroline in the House of Lords. The Queen is seated beside her counsel, Henry Brougham, Stephen Lushington and her Solicitor-General Thomas Denman. The future Prime Minister, Earl Grey, is speaking in favour of the Queen and against the divorce bill. From the painting by Sir George Hayter

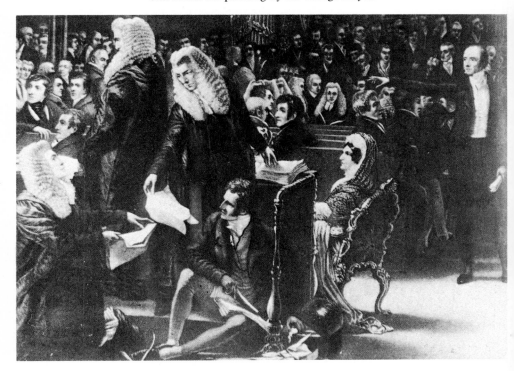

William Lamb Viscount Melbourne.
From the portrait by Sir Thomas Lawrence

The Hon Caroline Norton.
From the portrait by Frank Stone

Lithograph enclosed in Melbourne's
letter of 8 March 1830 to Lady
Branden. Melbourne had an obsessive
interest in flagellation and was a firm
believer in domestic 'discipline'.

The Hon John Vivian, MP. Cartoon
by Carlos Pellegrini in *Vanity Fair*
(*above left*)

George Marquess of Blandford, later
eighth Duke of Marlborough.
Cartoon in *Vanity Fair* (*above right*)

Harmony in White and Ivory. Lady
Colin Campbell. From the painting
by James McNeill Whistler
subsequently destroyed.

daughter and ordered the question of her sanity to be investigated by a special jury. Thus the trial, which opened on 16 February 1870, was really not to settle her guilt or innocence but to determine whether she was sane or mad, although Sir Charles Mordaunt's petition remained on the file. At the same time Harriet Mordaunt's lawyers served the Prince of Wales with a subpoena as a witness for her as respondent.

The Prince immediately informed his wife and mother who were both sympathetic, although Queen Victoria was appalled at the idea of the heir to the throne having to give evidence in a filthy divorce court. In the hope of getting him excused, the Queen consulted the Lord Chancellor Lord Hatherly. She wrote to him:

> The fact of the Prince of Wales's intimate acquaintanceship with a young married woman being publicly proclaimed will show an amount of imprudence, which cannot but damage him in the eyes of the middle and lower classes, which is to be most deeply lamented, in these days when the higher classes, in their frivolous, selfish and pleasure-seeking lives, do more to increase the spirit of democracy than anything else.

While the Lord Chancellor agreed, he was adamant that no question of privilege could excuse the Prince. Hatherly's opinion was endorsed by the soliticor Sir George Lewis whom the Prince consulted. 'You must go into the witness-box,' Lewis told the Prince. 'This is the only way to clear your name.'

At the trial, which took place before Lord Penzance and a special jury, Serjeant Ballantine led for the petitioner and William Deane, QC, for the respondent (represented by her father), while Sir John Karslake appeared for Sir Frederic Johnstone, who had been cited as a co-respondent along with Lord Cole and 'some persons' not mentioned by name but generally considered to include the Prince of Wales. The defence was that Harriet Mordaunt, who had been certified as insane, was unfit to plead, and in view of the judge's previous ruling Dr Deane opened the proceedings for his client. Harriet Mordaunt's insane behaviour was confirmed by a mass of witnesses, who testified that she would walk about the house at night dressed only in stockings and a cloak and would try to break into the butler's room with a hammer. She would also put her head out of her carriage window and scream for

[97]

several minutes without a pause; she would repeatedly try to throw herself out of the carriage and she also threatened to kill her child. She would smear herself with excrement and 'performed the offices of nature without a utensil'. At the end of this rigmarole, Serjeant Ballantine rose to his feet. 'In view of the evidence we have heard,' he announced, 'we cannot any longer deny that Lady Mordaunt is insane.'

This announcement caused a sensation in the court room. Dr Deane protested that he had not finished, while Frederic Johnstone's counsel stated that he wished to ventilate his client's grievance. In the event, Lord Penzance ruled that the case should proceed. Various chambermaids and footmen testified as to Lady Mordaunt's comings and goings. An entry in her diary was read out dated 5 April 1869. It ran: '280 days from 27 June.' This referred, suggested Serjeant Ballantine, to the fact that she had conceived a child by Lord Cole on 27 June 1868 while her husband was away fishing in Norway.

The high point in the trial was when the Prince of Wales was called and stepped into the witness-box. He was examined by Dr Deane, whose questions were few and simple. The Prince, whose age was then twenty-nine, stated that he had known the Moncreiffe family for several years before Lady Mordaunt's marriage. When she married he sent her some wedding presents. He also confirmed that Harriet had visited his London residence Marlborough House before her marriage when the Princess of Wales was there. The Prince added that he saw a good deal of her in 1867 and he met her occasionally in 1868, including once at a pigeon-shooting match at Hurlingham, when Sir Charles Mordaunt and the witness were captains of the opposing sides and Lady Mordaunt scored for both.

'I will only ask Your Royal Highness one more question', Dr Deane concluded. 'Has there ever been any improper familiarity or criminal act between yourself and Lady Mordaunt?'

'There has not,' the Prince answered emphatically.

The Prince's denial that he had committed adultery with Lady Mordaunt was greeted with applause by the spectators in court, and it was increased when Serjeant Ballantine said he had no questions to ask in cross-examination.

Sir Frederic Johnstone now asked through his counsel if he could likewise deny the charge of adultery. This was allowed. It appeared from his examination-in-chief that Charles Mordaunt had told his wife that Johnstone, who was in his twenty-eighth year, had never married because he had *repeatedly suffered from venereal disease*. 'A more unfounded statement was never made behind a man's back,' Johnstone protested. 'It is perfectly untrue.'

'You do not mean to imply that you have never suffered?' Serjeant Ballantine asked the witness sweetly.

'Certainly not!' Sir Frederic replied. 'I have had youthful indiscretions.'*

The Prince's letters were put in evidence and read at the end of the fifth day. However, the letters had been published shortly before the beginning of the trial in a Birmingham paper, having no doubt been deliberately 'leaked' with the Prince's connivance. Their publication by the provincial daily amounted to a contempt of court, but Lord Penzance let the matter pass, since their harmless nature did more than anything else to exonerate the Prince, although his suggestion in one of them that he should call on Lady Mordaunt in Chesham Place on a Sunday when her husband was absent offended sabbatarians in the community and others who sniped at the 'Marlborough House set'.

In his summing-up the judge confined himself strictly to the legal issue of Lady Mordaunt's mental state and scarcely troubled to mention Sir Charles's allegations of his wife's misconduct which were mainly based on her confession. After an absence of less than ten minutes the jury found that Lady Mordaunt was 'utterly unfit' to plead and 'to instruct her attorney for her defence.'

Poor Harriet was ruined socially, she lost her good looks and grew fat, and was the butt of crude rhymes of which the following is an example:

> This lady's appetite
> It really is enormous,
> But whether right or wrong,
> The papers will inform us.
> She is fond of veal and ham,
> To feed she is a glutton.
> She got tired of Charley's lamb,
> And longed for royal mutton.

* Sir Frederic Johnstone (1841–1913) sat as Conservative MP for Weymouth from 1874 to 1885. In 1899 he married the widow of the fourth Earl of Wilton, but they had no children. His baronetcy descended to a nephew.

However, Charley did not give up. He immediately appealed against the verdict. The third trial came on in the following April when three judges in the Court of Appeal reserved their judgment. It was delivered on the 2 June 1870. Only Chief Baron Kelly was in favour of the appellant, while his two judicial brethren Lord Penzance and Mr Justice Keatings supported the trial jury's verdict.

Sir Charles Mordaunt now changed his tactics. He admitted his wife's insanity, but applied to the court claiming that her mental state did not debar her from being sued for divorce or disqualify him from obtaining it. The application was heard four years later by five judges, who held by a majority of three to two that a respondent's insanity was no bar to divorce.[17] In March 1875 Mordaunt filed a fresh petition, this time citing only one co-respondent – Lord Cole. Since the petition was undefended, the proceedings were largely formal. Thus on 11 March 1875, after five trials, Sir Charles Mordaunt at last secured his divorce, the decree *nisi* being made absolute six months later, as was then the law.[18]

The successful petitioner married again, this time a parson's daughter. She presented him with a male heir named Osbert who succeeded him as eleventh baronet on his death in 1897. His daughter Violet by Harriet recovered her eyesight and married the fifth Marquess of Bath K.G., by whom she had five children. Still insane, the unfortunate Harriet died in 1906.

Apart from the fact that the future King Edward VII was a witness, the Mordaunt case is unique as being the most protracted and most expensive in the annals of the English divorce court.

5

One morning in September 1880, the twenty-seven-year-old Lord Colin Campbell, Liberal MP for Argyllshire, and youngest son of the Duke of Argyll, left his ancestral home Inverary Castle to go shooting from the family's nearby shooting box. On the way he met a friend who asked him casually whether he would care to meet an interesting Irish girl named Gertrude Blood, whose friends, a family named Clarke, had taken a shooting box near the Duke's on the Inverary estate and she was with the Clarkes. Lord Colin, little knowing to what the proposed introduction would lead, amiably agreed. From the moment he met Gertrude he was obsessed by her dark gypsy-like beauty, her intoxicating voice, and her trim athletic figure. He contrived to meet her again two days later and on this occasion he proposed marriage to her. She did not immediately accept as she had to consult her parents. Also Lord Colin had been ordered to take a sea voyage for health reasons by his doctor, so that it was agreed that they should meet again on his return when the question could be settled.

Educated at Cambridge where he graduated in law, Lord Colin was called to the English Bar, but he practised little if at all, preferring politics, so that the Argyll family influence secured him the local county seat which he had represented since 1878. His delicate state of health which necessitated the sea voyage was due to the fact that he had contracted syphilis, a fairly common complaint among the aristocracy in those days before the discovery in 1910 by the German bacteriologist Paul Ehrlich of the arsenical compound salvarsan which could completely cure the disease.

Gertrude's father was Edmund Blood, an Irish landowner, of Brickhill, County Clare, but he and his wife and children spent much of their time in Florence and also in Paris, where Gertrude grew up with the result that she spoke Italian and French fluently. On Lord Colin's return he again proposed to Gertrude and was accepted since the Bloods were delighted at their daughter's conquest, although her fiancé did not reveal the nature of his complaint. On the other hand, the Duke of Argyll, a nobleman of immense wealth and power, who was Lord Privy Seal in the Gladstone government, and whose eldest son the Marquess of Lorne was Governor-General of Canada, and was married to Queen Victoria's daughter Princess Louise, strenuously opposed the match since he did not think that Gertrude Blood was good enough for his youngest son, although the Bloods belonged to an old and eminently respectable Irish landowning family and Edmund Blood had been High Sheriff of County Clare in 1867. However, so bewitched was Lord Colin by Gertrude's beauty and personality, that he persisted. He told his fiancée that on account of his illness it would be necessary for them to occupy separate bedrooms for a time. (He did not tell her the nature of his illness and that he had been operated on for it by the famous urinary surgeon Sir Henry Thompson.)

[101]

'Do you mind marrying me under those circumstances?' he asked her.

'Not in the least,' she replied.

On 21 July 1881 Lord Colin Campbell and Miss Gertrude Elizabeth Blood were married in the Chapel Royal, Savoy. The Bloods were present at the ceremony but none of the bridegroom's ducal family appeared. An unusual feature of the melancholy honeymoon – five days in the Isle of Wight – was that a nursing sister had to travel with the bridal pair, in order to administer mercurial treatment to the bridegroom, mercury then being the remedy, and an inadequate one, for Lord Colin's complaint. Indeed he was so ravaged by syphilis that he was practically an invalid. On their return they spent a few weeks in London and then travelled to Scotland, so that Lord Colin could visit his constituency. In October they went to Bournemouth, and it was there that the marriage was consummated, the result being that Gertrude was infected by her husband's syphilis. This necessitated the attendance of a surgeon, Thomas Bird, who operated on her. Lord and Lady Colin Campbell were then living in the husband's London house at 79 Cadogan Place.

The marriage was doomed from the outset. Lord Colin was constantly ill, and although his wife helped to nurse him, she led a busy social life and also worked in an East London mission for the poor. She was interested in music, painting and literature. In 1883 she admitted that, while she had no desire to separate from Lord Colin, 'to live with him as a wife had become intolerable to her.' In a letter she wrote to her husband at the time she stated that she wished to continue as a friend and nurse but not as a wife. Lord Colin subsequently declared that he never received her letter. Eventually after a meeting with her parents and brother Neptune in their London house in Thurloe Square she decided to apply for a decree of judicial separation, equivalent to divorce *a mensa et thoro*.

Her case, which her husband defended, came before the President of the Divorce Court Sir James Hannen in March 1884. Because of the nature of the medical evidence Lady Colin's counsel asked for the case to be heard *in camera* and as Lord Colin's counsel raised no objection the judge agreed. There is therefore no publicly available record of the proceedings which Lady Colin brought on the ground of her husband's cruelty in the form of the venereal disease with which he infected her.

This was a sufficient ground for a judicial separation which the judge granted.[19]

Shortly after this Lady Colin went to see the well-known society solicitor George Lewis and told him the sad history of her marriage. He immediately advised her to file a petition for divorce, charging her husband with cruelty (already proved) and also adultery with a house-maid named Amelia Watson, cruelty as well as adultery then being necessary for a wife to establish if she was to obtain a divorce. Lord Colin, who got wind of this, thereupon determined to cross-petition on the grounds of his wife's adultery with four named co-respondents. The cynics remarked that Lady Colin's lovers had been selected from every walk of life – the Duke of Marlborough, owner of Blenheim Palace; Captain Eyre Massey Shaw, the chief of the London Fire Brigade; Thomas Bird, the well-known surgeon; and General Sir William Butler, a distinguished Irish soldier and author. Lewis sent a confidential clerk to file Lady Colin's petition in the Law Courts which the clerk duly did, arriving just before the clerk employed by Lord Colin's solicitors. These tactics on Lewis's part were designed to ensure that his client's counsel had the first word with the jury.[20]

The case began before Mr Justice Butt and a special jury on 26 November 1886 and lasted for eighteen days.[21] The parties were represented by the leading Queen's Counsel of the day. The Attorney-General Sir Charles Russell (later Lord Chief Justice) led for Lady Colin Campbell; Robert Finlay (later Lord Chancellor) for Lord Colin; Sir Frank Lockwood (a future Solicitor-General) for Captain Shaw; Sir Edward Clarke (a former Solicitor-General) for the surgeon Mr Bird; and Sir Richard Webster (a former Attorney-General) for the Duke of Marlborough. Sir William Butler was not represented and did not attend the trial, conduct for which he was subsequently censured by the jury. At the outset, in spite of Finlay's objections, the judge ruled that Lady Colin's case must have priority, so that Russell was the first to open for his client.

This the Attorney-General did with consummate skill as he related the story of the unfortunate marriage. It was not long before Lady Colin realised that she had made a mistake, Russell told the jury. To begin with, she believed that her husband's bad health affected her, devotedly as she nursed him. Then she was such a brilliant success in London society that she was often not with him, and of course he grumbled. She went everywhere, even to houses where her husband was not known, but this was because she did so in a professional capacity – she had a splendid singing voice – and her object was to earn money, since Lord Colin was relatively poor. The marriage settlement only amounted to £10,000, of which she and her parents contributed £6,000. Besides singing she contributed regularly to weekly and monthly reviews, and she had written a book on fishing. Thus in one way or another she had achieved a position for herself quite distinct from being a duke's daughter-in-law.

The trouble over the heal+h question, Russell went on, was intensified by Lord Colin's suspicion that she was too familiar with certain of her friends such as the Duke of Marlborough, or the Marquess of Blandford, as he then was. Lord Colin disliked what he considered her Bohemian ways, which paved the way to the judicial separation. His client would have left it at that, said Russell, but when she received positive information about her husband's relations with Amelia Watson she had no alternative but to bring her suit for divorce.

Lady Colin's principal witness was her cousin Lady Miles of Leigh Court, Bristol, whose husband Sir Philip Miles was MP for East Somerset. Frances Miles described various acts of familiarity which she had seen between Lord Colin and Amelia Watson and swore that on one occasion she saw the maid sitting on Lord Colin's bed with both arms round his neck. The witness went on to relate an incident which had occurred when both Lord and Lady Colin Campbell were staying at Leigh Court.

One day her Ladyship was ill. Mr Bird was called in and remained for some time. The next time I saw Lord Colin he told me that Lady Colin had had a miscarriage. I did not believe it and said he was only slandering his wife. Lord Colin remained convinced of it and believed that Mr Bird only wanted to conceal the fact . . . On this I questioned Mr Bird, who swore on his word of honour that there was no possibility of a miscarriage with her Ladyship; she was suffering from a venereal disease and would never be blessed with children.

'Gonorrhoea or syphilis?' asked the judge.
'Syphilis,' was the prompt reply.
The witness continued:

[104]

On June 7th 1883, at a dinner at 79 Cadogan Place, Lord Colin suddenly complained of pains in his stomach. I told Amelia Watson to make compresses for him, but got the rude answer: 'Make the bloody things yourself!' When Lord Colin heard it, he laughed and said: 'The little vixen is jealous of you.' 'What! jealous of me!' 'Yes, of course.' Amelia Watson laughed at me when I was making the compress. When I asked Lord Colin to reprimand her, he praised her and said she was a pretty poisonous little vixen! Which was an insult to me.

Finlay failed to shake Lady Miles in cross-examination, and although she occasionally contradicted herself most spectators in court believed that Russell had established his client's case for Lord Colin's adultery. However, a surprise was in store for them.

Russell now put his client in the box. Lady Colin was a convincing witness. She described her literary and charitable work and how she contributed to journals such as the *Saturday Review*. Her defence was unusual. She could not possibly have committed adultery, she said, because she simply had no time to do so. What Shakespeare called the 'act of darkness' (in *King Lear*) would have taken too long to have been fitted in at any point in her day. She had to manage her house in Cadogan Place; act as hostess for her husband, who was a Member of Parliament; deal with extensive correspondence; teach working girls at night school; and help run a soup kitchen at the Stepney mission. She had also sung in fifty concerts. What time was there for adultery in such a busy day?

Finlay now opened the case for Lord Colin: 'Whatever opinion you may have formed with regard to the story of Amelia Watson,' he told the jury, 'we must all recollect that it is seldom that a case is brought into court founded on such miserably weak evidence as there is in this case – the unsupported evidence of Lady Miles. The charge is absolutely and wholly untrue. It will be sworn to be false by Amelia Watson herself, and by Lord Colin. Feeling certain that this was an infamous conspiracy concocted by two women, Lady Miles and Lady Colin, to injure Lord Colin, we took the unusual course of asking Amelia Watson to consent to a medical examination. She consented, and she was examined this morning by two medical men of eminence, and they will tell you that Amelia Watson, without the possibility of doubt, is a virgin.'

The sensation which this statement caused can be imagined, and it was confirmed when the two medical men in question, Drs Godson and

Gibbons, swore to it on oath. What was not made clear was that Amelia Watson's virginity did not necessarily mean that sexual intercourse between her and Lord Colin had not taken place. Nevertheless, this medical evidence knocked the bottom out of Gertrude Campbell's case against her husband, the offensive passing to the other side, and the trial now resolved itself into a battle for Lady Colin's reputation.

Evidence followed from maids and footmen. Rosa Baer, a lady's maid, said she used to dress and undress Lady Colin. She referred specifically to the fact that she dressed her one evening when she was going out with the Duke of Marlborough. On her return she undressed her but noticed that the dress had been taken off while Lady Colin was out since some of the fastenings and buttons on the back were in a different position from the time she dressed her. Rosa further testified that Lady Colin and the Duke had been guests at a country house party where Lady Colin slept in a double bed and next morning there were signs of two people having occupied it. But Rosa, who had since been dismissed by Lady Colin for some reason, was quite possibly an unreliable and vindictive witness. She admitted, in cross-examination by Charles Russell, that she had agreed to give evidence in the case at Lord Colin's request 'without knowing what it was all about'. Nor at that time had she ever heard of a divorce suit, she said.

A footman of Lord Colin's named O'Neil swore that he once peeped through the keyhole of the drawing-room door in the house in Cadogan Place and saw Lady Colin lying on the floor with the Fire Brigade Chief Captain Shaw. The popular Captain (later Sir) Massey Shaw, a Cork man, who was an old friend of Lady Colin's family in Ireland and whose daughter was one of Lady Colin's bridesmaids at her wedding in 1881, had been immortalised the same year in one of the most romantic melodies in the Gilbert and Sullivan comic opera *Iolanthe* when the Queen of the Fairies, spotting the Captain in the front row of the stalls on the opening night, made this impassioned appeal to him with outstretched arms:

> Oh Captain Shaw
> Type of true love kept under!
>   Can thy Brigade
>   With cold cascade
> Quench my great love, I wonder!

[106]

No doubt this verse was recalled at the Campbell trial, but in the event, whatever love Captain Shaw had for Lady Colin, the jury were to believe that it had indeed been 'kept under'. Finlay also called the head waiter at the hotel in Purfleet in which the Duke of Marlborough (then Lord Blandford) had stayed with a lady. It was also alleged that Blandford had been to Paris with Lady Colin and under French law an aggrieved husband would have an erring wife arrested if found in the company of her lover and put in prison. But although Lord Colin went to Paris when his wife was staying there with her parents, there was no sign of Blandford.

Lord Colin, in his evidence, admitted that he objected to his wife's friendship with the Duke. 'I do not know Lord Blandford,' he told his wife on one occasion when Blandford called and they talked together alone. Lady Colin assured her husband that the association was quite innocent. 'We have only been having a talk about Gladstone,' she declared. The Duke of Marlborough confirmed this when he swore that he was never guilty of adultery with Lady Colin. As for his visit to Purfleet he admitted that he had spent a week-end there but his companion on this occasion was a certain Mrs Perry, 'a woman about town'. Writing to a friend on 15 December, Oscar Wilde remarked that he had had a long talk with George Lewis the previous night about the case: 'He is very nervous about Marlborough's cross-examination.' The solicitor's nervousness was due to the Duke's reputation as a woman-iser, and in particular his having been divorced and also cited as the co-respondent when Lord Aylesford, a friend of the Prince of Wales, had unsuccessfully petitioned for a divorce from his wife, who was the daughter of an MP.[22] Lewis's fears turned out to be unjustified, and although Finlay elicited the details of Marlborough's affair with Lady Aylesford, including the fact that he had settled £10,000 on the child whose father he was alleged to be by her, this was cross-examination as to credit and could not incriminate Lady Colin Campbell. In fact Marlborough pointed out that his friendship with Lady Colin was due to their common interest in literature. There were not many good books in Lord Colin's house, he said, and he had lent Lady Colin such works as Greene's *History of the English People*, Lecky's *Rise and Influence of Rationalism in Europe*, and Motley's *History of the Dutch Republic*. Lady Colin, he went on, was 'a person of undeniable literary attainments' who had written more than one book and contributed to the Press.

[107]

When he came to the case of the surgeon Thomas Bird, Finlay made great play with the allegation that Lord Colin had discovered him asleep in Lady Colin's bedroom. Bird's counsel Sir Edward Clarke made light of this: 'Mr Finlay seems to believe that if a man is found alone with a woman it implies that adultery has taken place. . . . I do not think there is much in that to prove improper conduct here. Had Lord Colin found him *awake* the case might have been stronger.'

Many contemporaries, including his official biographer, considered this to be Charles Russell's best case. In his concluding speech to the jury, he discredited the notion that his client and her family were determined to bring about her marriage. He derided Lord Colin's pretensions to be a somebody, although he was an MP, and pointed out that Lord Colin was merely a younger son with very little money. 'True he was a Campbell of Argyllshire', said Russell in a humorous interlude, 'and my learned friend Mr Finlay, who is a Scotsman, appears to think with another Campbell, who exclaimed on the marriage of one of the family with a southerner: "Eh, mon, the Queen must be a proud lady this day!"' (Russell was, of course, referring to HRH Princess Louise's marriage to the Duke of Argyll's eldest son Lord Lorne.)

Here is a part of Russell's peroration:

> I have little more to say. Your verdict of guilty or acquittal will close this sad controversy. It is important for Lord Colin; it is infinitely more important for his wife. To her it may mean lifelong condemnation, loss of friends, a dark and cheerless future. She is as much upon her trial today as if she sat in the shadow of the criminal dock; and just as it would be your duty to weigh the evidence carefully, so it is your duty now. A serious and solemn duty lies before you . . .
>
> I make no appeal for mercy. I ask for justice, justice, which forbids life or fame to be sacrificed save on evidence at once credible and cogent. Gentlemen, Lady Colin Campbell's life – nay, something dearer than life – is in your hands: and with an earnest heart and with a spirit of reverence I would humbly pray that your minds and your judgments may be inclined to give in this case a just and honest deliverance.[23]

Mr Justice Butt summed up the evidence at considerable length but with conspicuous fairness. In particular, he warned the jury, in

[108]

considering the evidence of and about the Duke of Marlborough, not to allow themselves to be influenced by the fact that His Grace had been divorced on his wife's petition and accused of adultery and cited as a co-respondent in the Aylesford case. The jury then retired but first asked the judge whether they could visit Lord Colin's house in Cadogan Place to ascertain just how much could be seen through the keyhole of Lady Colin's drawing-room. Their request was granted. After more than three hours and twice coming back to court and informing the judge that they could not agree on a verdict, they eventually returned with their finding that Lady Colin had not committed adultery with the Duke of Marlborough or with any of the other three co-respondents. At the same time, in the cross-petition the jury found that Lord Colin had not committed adultery with Amelia Watson. Lord Colin was also ordered to pay the cost of the proceedings which amounted to £15,000.

Although Sir Charles Russell had by his eloquence saved Gertrude Campbell's honour, it was an inconclusive and unsatisfactory verdict, since the Campbells remained man and wife, although judicially separated. He died less than six months after the verdict from the effects of his syphilis. Gertrude survived him by sixteen years. She died in 1911, having written a novel and an autobiography, besides some excellent articles in journals like *The Artist* and *The Queen* where she had a column in which she advised readers on such questions of social etiquette as the correct use of visiting cards when making calls, how to handle fish knives and finger bowls, and how to address titled personages. In *The World*, of which she was art critic, she extolled the virtues of the Italian spa Salso Maggiore as a cure for arthritis from which she suffered in later years.

Gertrude Campbell has been described, perhaps with some justification, as a glamorous nymphomaniac. There is little if any doubt that she was the eighth Duke of Marlborough's mistress and that he was very much in love with her from the time of his divorce in 1883, despite his remarrying a rich American widow five years later. In his will – he died in 1892 aged 48 – Marlborough left Gertrude £20,000 'as a proof of my friendship and esteem', whereas his former mistress Lady Aylesford got nothing. Whistler called her his 'lovely leopard' and she posed for his striking picture 'Harmony in White and Ivory' which was later destroyed supposedly by an outraged Mrs Whistler.[24] The novelist Robert Hichens saw a good deal of her towards the end of his life,

[109]

particularly at concerts and exhibitions when they were both contributing to *The World*. 'She was a clever woman and a woman of spirit,
and I should think a stoic', Hichens wrote in his autobiography.

Her divorce case, of course, with its ugly details and scandalous
accusations against her had made her very notorious, and she had to
turn a brave face to the curious world, which whispered about her
wherever she went. But she was always perfectly self-possessed and
seemed to have a thorough-going contempt for the scandal-mongers.
Eventually I knew her, though not intimately, and found her well
worth knowing.[25]

A just and fair tribute to a remarkable woman in a sensational scandal.

Dilke and Parnell

1

THE two most distinguished politicians to be involved in sex scandals
during the last years of Queen Victoria's reign were Charles Wentworth
Dilke and Charles Stewart Parnell. The divorce suits in which they were
cited as co-respondents cost each the leadership of his political party
and caused irreparable damage to their reputations. Indeed Parnell
survived the scandal of his divorce by only eighteen months. Yet each
case differed widely from the other. While there cannot be any question
of Parnell's adultery, the similar matrimonial offence with which Dilke
was charged has always been a matter of some doubt in spite of his
repeated protestations of innocence.

Sir Charles Dilke, Bart., a privy counsellor and Liberal MP for
Chelsea, was forty-three at the time of his fall and was the acknowledged
leader of the radical section of the Liberal party.[1] He had been a
member of Gladstone's second government, first as Under-Secretary
for Foreign Affairs from 1880 to 1882 when he had to answer for the
Foreign Office in the Commons, since the Secretary of State was in the
Lords, and secondly, as President of the Local Government Board from
1882 until the Government was defeated in June 1885, during which
period he had a seat in the Cabinet. Although the Queen disliked him on
account of his one-time republican views, and it was said only agreed to
him becoming a Cabinet minister and a Privy Counsellor with considerable reluctance, he discharged the duties of both the political offices
which he held with outstanding ability. In particular, he carried the bill
for the redistribution of parliamentary seats through the Commons with
exceptional skill. He also presided over the royal commission for the

housing of the working classes, of which the Prince of Wales, Lord Salisbury and Cardinal Manning were members.

Outside Parliament, both in aristocratic circles and lower down the social scale, Charles Dilke was greatly esteemed. His first wife had died in 1874 while giving birth to their only son, who was eventually to succeed him in the baronetcy. In 1884 he became secretly engaged to Emilia Pattison, the French art historian and widow of the Revd Mark Pattison, Rector of Lincoln College, Oxford. She and Pattison were generally assumed by their contemporaries to be the originals of the characters Dorothea Brooke and Mr Casaubon in George Eliot's novel *Middlemarch*.[2]

At the end of a busy week in July 1885 in which he presided at the royal commission, went to parties at Lady Salisbury's, the Austrian Embassy and the Duchess of Westminster's, besides giving a large dinner at his house, 76 Sloane Street, he was, on the Saturday evening, the guest of honour at a banquet in the Reform Club for his achievement in passing the Redistribution Bill. He returned home around midnight with the intention of spending a quiet Sunday on the river at Taplow since his fiancée was abroad in India. But it was not to be a quiet Sunday. The reason was that his private secretary J. E. C. Bodley, who had waited up for his return to Sloane Street, handed him an envelope marked 'Private and Confidential'. Dilke slit it open to find a note inside from Mrs Rogerson, a neighbour and family friend, asking him to call on her immediately since she had some 'grave information' to impart to him. Since it was too late to go and speak to her at that moment, he went next morning to her house in nearby Hans Place. Mrs Rogerson's news was devastating. It was to the effect that a Scottish lawyer, shortly to become a fellow MP, Mr Donald Crawford, aged forty, had learned from his wife Virginia that shortly after their marriage in 1881 Dilke had become her lover and that consequently Crawford intended to petition for a divorce, naming Dilke as co-respondent.

Mrs Rogerson's role in the story was ambiguous, possibly even conspiratorial. In his early days, when Dilke was something of a womaniser, she had been his mistress, among other ladies who included Virginia Crawford's mother Mrs Eustace Smith. Christina Rogerson had married an amiable alcoholic much older than herself, who had died in 1884, and she had hoped that Dilke would marry her. She was on intimate terms with Virginia Crawford and facilitated Virginia's liaison

[112]

with a certain Captain Henry Forster, an officer in the Duke of Cornwall's Light Infantry. Hence Christina Rogerson had a foot in both camps. When she discovered that Dilke was in love with Emilia Pattison and intended to marry her, she may well have conspired with Virginia Crawford to ruin Dilke. Dilke certainly believed that he was the victim of a conspiracy. 'In my belief the conspiracy comes from a woman who wanted to marry me', he wrote to Mrs Pattison in India.[3] Emilia Pattison's immediate reaction on learning the news of the impending divorce was to telegraph *The Times* in London informing that journal of her forthcoming marriage to Dilke. An announcement to this effect was duly published in August 1885.

The American novelist and critic Henry James, who was fascinated by the political and still more the sexual mores of the period, outlined the Dilke situation in a characteristic letter to his friend Grace Norton in the United States:

Dilke's private life won't (I imagine) bear looking into, and the vengeful Crawford will do his best to lay it bare . . . For a man who has had such a passion for keeping up appearances and appealing to the middle class, he [Dilke] has, in reality, been strangely, incredibly reckless. His long double liaison with Mrs Pattison and the other lady [Mrs Rogerson] of a nature to make it a duty of honour to marry *both* (!!) when they should become free, and the death of each husband at the same time – with the public watching to see *which* he *would* marry – and he meanwhile 'going on' with poor little Mrs Crawford, who is a kind of infant – the whole thing is a theme for the novelist – or at least for *a* novelist.[4]

James, who knew Christina Rogerson quite well, described her as compensating for her 'homeliness' by her dark skirts, white shirts of the finest linen with stiff cuffs and links, and Highland shoes with large silver buckles. 'If she had been beautiful and sane,' he added perceptively, 'she would have been one of the world's great wicked women.'[5] As for the twenty-three-year-old Virginia Crawford, she was called 'pretty but hardly beautiful', having 'milk-maid looks' (her own description) and fine white skin which she had inherited from her mother Ellen, who had married a rich north country shipbuilder Eustace

[113]

Smith, Liberal MP for Tynemouth. Like her elder sister Helen's husband, a rich stockbroker named Robert Harrison, Virginia's husband was much older than herself – in fact Donald Crawford was more than twice her age. Both sisters got married primarily in order to get away from their garrulous and overbearing mother, and in the result their husbands failed to satisfy them sexually. Another sister Maye married Sir Charles Dilke's younger brother Ashton who died in 1883. Charles Dilke was at first against this marriage since he disliked the idea of his only brother, to whom he was devoted, marrying the daughter of his former mistress. But he accepted it since it was a love match and a success, and after Ashton's death he became joint guardian with Maye of his sister-in-law's three children. However, when it came to the point, Maye Dilke ranged herself strongly on the side of her sister Virginia.

Meanwhile Emilia Pattison had returned from India, and she and Charles were married in Chelsea Old Church on 3 October 1885. Emilia was given away by her brother Captain Henry Strong, while her husband was supported by his eleven-year-old son, his private secretary, J. E. C. Bodley, and his closest political colleague Joseph Chamberlain who was best man.[6]

Shortly after the wedding Mrs Rogerson called on the Dilkes and met Emilia. She asked them to dinner at her house and the invitation was accepted. As Lady Dilke was leaving and putting on her wraps in Christina Rogerson's bedroom, her hostess assured Emilia that she had done right to come back from India and marry Charles. 'I know that he is worthy to be the husband of a good woman like yourself,' she told Emilia. 'Whatever may have been the faults of his youth, I am certain that for the last five or six years he has led a life such that any woman might be proud to bear his name.' She went on to declare that she was innocent of having any hand in implicating Charles in the Crawford divorce. 'If you can't believe me, we had better not meet. Can't you believe me?' To which Emilia Dilke replied: 'If I knew you to be guilty of this, Mrs Rogerson, I should not be here.' During the ensuing weeks they kept in touch, visiting each other, since Christina was friendly with the Crawfords and for this reason it was necessary that the Dilkes should keep in with her. However, Christina was not always truthful; also she had had one nervous breakdown and as the hearing of the divorce approached she became so mentally unbalanced that she was unable to respond to the subpoena with which she had been served by Dilke's solicitor as a witness.

Another caller on the newly weds was Mrs Ashton (Maye) Dilke. Emilia asked her if she could not get Virginia to withdraw the charge against her husband, since Virginia was known to have other lovers who might be cited as co-respondents. 'I must think only of my sister,' said Maye. 'I think it is best for my sister that things have gone so far that she should get her divorce against Charles, as I know if she changes two other suits will be immediately commenced against her.' 'Do you mean to say', Lady Dilke replied, 'that you wish to screen your sister at the expense of an innocent man?' 'Oh!' was Maye's laughing retort. 'Innocent people can take care of themselves.' This remark so infuriated Emilia by its cynicism that she immediately requested Maye to leave the house, which she did. The next time they met was in public, when Emilia ostentatiously cut her dead.[7]

2

If Christina Rogerson did not always tell the truth, Virginia Crawford was an egregious liar. Her husband had suspected her of infidelity for some time, notably with Captain Forster, and had had her watched by detectives. His suspicions were aggravated by anonymous letters he received, alternatively attributed to Virginia's mother and Christina Rogerson. In one of these Donald Crawford was advised to 'Beware the Member for Chelsea' (i.e. the Rt. Hon. Sir Charles Dilke). The last of the four anonymous letters which reached Crawford read: 'Fool, looking for the cuckoo when he has flown, having defiled your nest. You have been vilely deceived, but you dare not touch the real traitor.' Immediately on its receipt Crawford went into his wife's bedroom, holding the letter in his hand. After reading its contents, he said: 'Virginia, is it true that you have defiled my bed? I have been a faithful husband to you.'

'Yes, it is true,' Virginia replied. 'It is time that you should know the truth. You have always been on the wrong track, suspecting people who are innocent, and you have never suspected the person who was guilty.'

'I have never suspected anybody except Captain Forster,' Donald Crawford retorted.

[115]

'It was not Captain Forster,' Virginia rejoined. 'The man who ruined me was Charles Dilke.'

Virginia went on to describe the details of her liaison with Dilke. Shortly after her marriage, when she was eighteen, and staying with her husband at Bailey's Hotel in Gloucester Road, Dilke called when Crawford was out and made 'amorous proposals' to her and kissed her, she said, and that was as far as it went on this occasion. She did not meet Dilke again for some months since the Crawfords were away in Scotland. However, in February 1882, she said, Dilke met her in a house 'off the Tottenham Court Road' (in fact in Warren Street) where she became his mistress. Their relationship continued for two-and-a-half years, Virginia went on, during which time they met intermittently at various places besides Warren Street, notably Dilke's house in Sloane Street, where she spent two nights, also in a house which the Crawfords had rented in Young Street, Kensington, during the sessions of 1883 and 1884. In the late summer of 1884 Dilke tired of her and their clandestine meetings ceased, although they continued to meet socially. She described how she was dressed in Sloane Street by a maid named Sarah Gray, who had been a former mistress of Dilke's. Another servant named Fanny, who was Sarah's younger sister and about Virginia's own age, Virginia said, was persuaded to meet her when she was in Dilke's bedroom and they all three got into bed together. 'He taught me every French vice,' Virginia told her husband. 'He used to say that I knew more than most women of thirty.' As for Captain Forster, she added, he was not and never had been her lover, although she admitted to having been 'too familiar' with him and others. But she solemnly denied that she had committed adultery with anyone other than Charles Dilke.

There is little doubt that Virginia Crawford was lying. For one thing Dilke had a house full of servants, not to mention a private secretary, who would have noticed anything untoward in the way of a visit from Mrs Crawford. In particular, Bodley was positive that Dilke always slept alone until his marriage to Mrs Pattison, and that he (Bodley) must have known if anyone else had gone up to Dilke's bedroom at night besides its normal occupant. It was Captain Forster who had been Virginia's lover, as he had also been Helen Harrison's: both sisters hunted in couples, Forster had taken them singly and together to a house of assignation in Hill Street, Knightsbridge, (now Trevor Street), and when he took them both they shared a bed, this being the

[116]

origin of Virginia's three-in-a-bed story which she repeated in her 'confession'.

Crawford's divorce suit was due to be heard in February 1886. On 30 January Gladstone became Prime Minister for the third time, following a General Election at which Dilke's constituents in Chelsea had again returned him as their Member and Crawford had been returned for the first time as MP for North Lanarkshire. However, there was no place for Dilke in the new administration, the Prime Minister expressing his 'profound regret' in a private letter to the Member for Chelsea that 'the circumstances of the moment' should deprive him of the opportunity of enlisting on behalf of the new Government 'the great capacity' which Dilke had 'proved in a variety of spheres and forms.' Dilke accepted the letter with good grace, but the marked exclusion was damaging not only to his political prospects but also to his private reputation. As Roy Jenkins has remarked in his admirable life of Dilke, 'it created in the public mind a greater presumption of his guilt than had hitherto existed; and he can hardly have failed to reflect on the mischance that the formation of the Government could not have been delayed for two weeks. Had this been so, and had he in the interval secured even a formal verdict in his favour, it would have been much more difficult to exclude him.'[8] Incidentally Joseph Chamberlain was given Dilke's old post in the Local Government Board.

The case of *Crawford v. Crawford and Dilke* came before Mr Justice Butt and a jury in the Divorce Court on 12 February 1886.[9] F. A. Inderwick, QC, led for the petitioner, while Mrs Crawford was represented by Frank Lockwood, QC, MP, although he had nothing to do since the case was undefended by Mrs Crawford. The Attorney-General Sir Charles Russell and Sir Henry James (no relation to the novelist) a former Attorney, led for the co-respondent. Dilke's friend Joseph Chamberlain was in court but Virginia Crawford was not. Neither were Mrs Rogerson who was ill, nor Fanny Gray. In his examination-in-chief the petitioner was taken through the details of his wife's confession, but as she did not give evidence she could not be cross-examined on it. There were only two other witnesses besides Donald Crawford. One was Anne Jamieson, a parlourmaid in the Crawfords' London house, who swore that Mrs Crawford had spent two nights away from the house during her husband's absence. According to her, Mrs Crawford received visits from both Dilke and Forster. However, in cross-examination she admitted that Mrs Crawford had told her to tell Donald Crawford all she (the witness) knew about Dilke. The other witness was Helen Harrison's butler George Ball who was called to rebut Virginia Crawford's statement about being two nights away from home. He was not cross-examined.

That was the petitioner's case. The co-respondent's counsel were now faced with the difficult decision of whether to put their client in the witness-box to deny on oath the uncorroborated story which Virginia Crawford had related to her husband. As the judge said in his summing up, he could not see any case whatever against Dilke: 'By the law of England, a statement made by one party in the suit – a statement made not in the presence of the other – cannot be evidence against the other.' After considering the question during the luncheon break, Dilke's counsel advised him not to give evidence, and their client – unwisely as it turned out – agreed with them, since he thought that his past life might be raked up against him in cross-examination, notably his relations with Virginia's mother Ellen Smith, although such evidence would almost certainly have been ruled inadmissible by the judge. Nevertheless, Mr Justice Butt agreed with the advice of Dilke's counsel for the reason he had already given, namely that there was no case against Dilke. The judge thereupon dismissed the case against the co-respondent and ordered the petitioner to pay the costs of the trial while at the same time granting him a decree *nisi*.

What the verdict amounted to was that Mrs Crawford had committed adultery with Sir Charles Dilke, but that he had not done so with her. While accepted by the legal profession, this paradoxical distinction was not appreciated by the lay-public who did not understand it. It was assumed to be an admission of Dilke's guilt, an assumption accepted by the press, notably the *Pall Mall Gazette*, whose editor W. T. Stead, with his Puritan conscience and obsession with sex in all its manifestations, consistently harped. What Dilke's counsel and his friend Joseph Chamberlain failed to foresee was that the public might not endorse the judge's decision in this case. And the public did not, arguing that the failure of Dilke's counsel to put him in the witness-box must mean that they did not believe him to be innocent and that they took advantage of a legal technicality to protect him, so that he could resume his political career.

3

Although Dilke received a friendly reception when he took his seat in the new Parliament after the trial, the newspapers displayed varying degrees of hostility, generally condemning him for not having gone into the witness-box. In the *Pall Mall Gazette*, W. T. Stead went so far as to blame Joseph Chamberlain for advising Dilke to do what turned out to be the wrong thing, hinting that Chamberlain wished to wreck his colleague's political career. Chamberlain was upset by this insinuation and urged Dilke to go into the witness-box and state the true facts of his case, either in an action for libel or else through the intervention of the Queen's Proctor. In fact the Queen's Proctor was actually making up his mind to intervene due in great part to press comment on the divorce. At first Dilke was not very favourably disposed to this course, apparently because he was not clear exactly what the role of the Queen's Proctor was, namely to show whether material facts had not been disclosed to the court which would consequently be grounds for not making the decree *nisi* absolute. However, Dilke eventually welcomed the intervention by the Queen's Proctor in the mistaken belief that he would be a party in the second trial and that he would be represented by counsel with full right to cross-examine. He did not realise – and it is extraordinary that neither Russell nor James disillusioned him – that he had been dismissed from the case by the verdict in the first trial and that he could only appear as a witness in the second one unrepresented by counsel. 'If I had known that I should not be allowed to be represented at the intervention,' he wrote afterwards, 'I could not have faced it. The hardships of the course taken proved too great. But no one, of all these great lawyers, foresaw this.'

The second trial opened before the President of the Divorce Court, Sir James Hannen, and a special jury on 16 July 1886.[10] It lasted for six days. The Queen's Proctor was represented by Sir Walter Phillimore, a noted ecclesiastical lawyer who had little or no experience of divorce proceedings. Phillimore's junior counsel was a young man of strikingly handsome presence who had only recently been called to the Bar. His name was Edward Marshall Hall, destined to become the most brilliant and fashionable advocate of his day. It was the Queen's Proctor's case which first brought his name before the public, although his role was quite minor. Inderwick, who had led for Crawford in the first trial was now led by another QC, Henry Matthews, a robust cross-examiner, a Tory and a Catholic, who bore Dilke no love as he was to show. Mrs Crawford was represented as before by Frank Lockwood. Russell and James sat in court with Dilke, but they could take no part in the proceedings. Mrs Rogerson was present but not Fanny Gray, who had recently married a man named Stock. The special jury, mostly City men with property qualifications, could hardly be expected to display much sympathy for a radical like Dilke. The odds were further weighted against him by the equally unsympathetic judge.

Phillimore began by asking the judge whether he could call Mrs Crawford before Dilke, since the natural course would have been for Mrs Crawford to specify her charges and for Dilke to answer them. But the judge refused this request, so that Dilke was called first and he had to seek to controvert Mrs Crawford's story, while the lady herself could sit in court and listen to his evidence, so that she could fabricate the details of her story when she took the stand.

Unfortunately Dilke proved to be a very bad witness. Instead of giving a straight affirmative or negative answer to counsel's questions, his method of denying a fact was to launch into a long explanation as to why it was inherently improbable. Phillimore's examination-in-chief was directed to meeting the points put forward by Mrs Crawford in her proof. Briefly, these were, first, Dilke's degree of acquaintanceship with Mrs Crawford; secondly, the house off the Tottenham Court Road where Mrs Crawford alleged that Dilke had taken her or met her; third, Dilke's domestic activities in 76 Sloane Street, his fencing exercise, working on Foreign Office telegrams, when he went to the office, and how long he stayed there; fourth, his movements on 23 February 1882, when Mrs Crawford had accused him of first seducing her in Warren Street; fifth, his movements on 13 and 14 February 1883 when she alleged that she spent each night at 76 Sloane Street; and last, Dilke's relations with Sarah Gray and her sister Fanny. These could be summarised in Phillimore's final question and Dilke's answer.

'Have you ever committed adultery with Mrs Crawford?'

'Certainly not!'

Matthews's cross-examination was hostile and skilful. Asked whether he believed that Mrs Crawford had any motive for asking a confession about him if it was untrue, Dilke replied: 'Finding that she was near discovery in the course of adultery with other persons, I

[120]

believe that she desired to fix upon a person already agreed between her and others for this purpose.' Pressed to say who the others were, he mentioned Captain Forster, Mrs Crawford's mother Mrs Smith, and the author of the anonymous letters, whose identity he did not know, with whom Mrs Crawford conspired. Asked to name anyone to whom Mrs Crawford had confided her alleged relations with him, Dilke answered, 'Mrs Rogerson'. Matthews then suggested that in view of this it was most improper for Dilke not to have gone into the witness-box at the previous trial.

'Is it true or untrue', Matthews persisted, 'that there are acts of indiscretion in your life which you desired not to disclose on cross-examination?'

'Acts which came to an end eleven and a half years ago,' Dilke admitted.

'Then it is true?'

'Yes.'

Reverting to this next day, *à propos* of Mrs Crawford, Matthews asked: 'Was it true that you were her mother's lover?'

'I was yesterday asked a question of a somewhat similar kind, and I replied to it. I must decline to answer that question.'

Matthews went on to make much play with Dilke's habit of cutting pieces out of his engagement diary, but of this there was a perfectly innocent explanation to the effect that he did so when an engagement was cancelled and in any case there was always a duplicate entry.

As for Mrs Crawford's occasional visits to his house, Dilke stated that he regarded her as more or less one of his family since his brother Ashton had been married to her sister. It appeared that she thought that Dilke might help her husband to get a post in the Lord Advocate's office which in fact he did. Dilke also stated that he thought that Captain Forster had been Mrs Crawford's lover but the only person with whom he had discussed this was his sister-in-law Mrs Ashton Dilke. Finally, the witness admitted that he had spent several months in France between 1876 and 1880 when he had bought a property in the south, and his familiarity with French habits and ways no doubt constituted a black mark against him in the jury's eyes.

It is unnecessary to consider the particulars of all the evidence with their odious details. But besides Mrs Crawford two handwriting experts may be mentioned, one of whom thought the anonymous letters had been written by Mrs Rogerson and the other by Mrs Crawford herself. Of the twenty-three other witnesses called by Phillimore, Mrs Rogerson tended to support Mrs Crawford's statement that she had confessed to her about her alleged relations with Dilke. She also said that she had seen Donald Crawford and had tried to make him agree to a quiet judicial separation so that the matter should not become public. After that she became mentally ill and consequently was not available to testify at the first trial and in fact had only just left a nursing home. Bodley and Emilia Dilke, who were likewise called, strongly defended Charles Dilke.

With the conclusion of the case for the Queen's Proctor by Phillimore, Matthews immediately put Virginia Crawford in the witness-box, where her examination-in-chief was conducted by the judge. Was she willing to give evidence? Had she read her husband's evidence at the last trial? Was it true? In particular, had she committed adultery with Sir Charles Dilke? When she confidently answered 'yes' to each of these questions, Matthews rose to cross-examine. The questions were thorough but much less gruelling than those put to Dilke. Her self-confidence was remarkable. When asked to draw a plan of the inside of the house in Warren Street, she did so immediately and it was passed to the jury. In fact it was wildly inaccurate but no one knew or noticed this at the time. Her most significant admission was that Captain Forster had been her lover, although she had denied this at the previous trial. Her relations with him began in 1884, she said, and at Easter in the following year she had gone over to Dublin to see Forster, telling her husband that she was staying with Mrs Rogerson. Incidentally Forster had syphilis and there are grounds for believing that he infected Mrs Crawford with the disease, since she was medically treated for it and her health suffered from its effects. The dates of her adulterous relations were the evidence in her diary where the individuals were described by their initials on the relevant dates – C. W. D. (Dilke), H. F. (Henry Forster) and so on.

Matthews also questioned the witness about Dilke's alleged admissions to her about his other mistresses.

'Let me see, he told you Fanny was his mistress; he told you about your mother, and he told you about Mrs Rogerson, and did he tell you about Sarah – that Sarah had been his mistress?'

'Yes.'

[122]

'And Sarah, who had been his mistress, was dressing you on every occasion when you went to his house, and bringing you tea and letting you out on those occasions when you slept there?'

'Yes.'

'And Mrs Rogerson, who was his mistress, was meeting you,' counsel went on, 'and you were making statements to her?'

'Mrs Rogerson always denied it to me,' the witness replied. 'Of course I was bound to believe Mrs Rogerson.'

Mrs Crawford also informed the court of her understanding that, in the spring of 1885, Dilke had asked Mrs Rogerson to marry him, but that Mrs Rogerson had refused.

Matthews's last witness was Captain Forster who stated that he had been to Hill Street, Knightsbridge, with Mrs Crawford and admitted that he presumed the place was 'a house of ill-fame'.

In his summing-up Mr Justice Hannen put the matter squarely to the jury.

Mrs Crawford has come into court and asserted upon oath that her confession to her husband was a true confession. Sir Charles Dilke has sworn to the contrary, and substantially you have to determine which of these two persons, who have been brought face to face with you is telling the truth, and which is telling what is false.

Generally the judge was unfavourable to Dilke, for example over Mrs Crawford's three-in-a-bed story. 'That is a most revolting subject, gentlemen, and one would be glad to believe untrue,' Mr Justice Hannen remarked sententiously. 'But the question for you in regard to that is do you think Mrs Crawford invented the story? . . . Which is the more probable, that a man should do such things or that a woman should invent them of him?' Finally, the judge reminded the jury that at the first trial it was for Crawford to prove that his wife had committed adultery with Dilke. But on this occasion it was for the Queen's Proctor to prove that Mrs Crawford did not commit adultery with Dilke. 'The onus is on the Queen's Proctor,' he emphasised.

After an absence of fifteen minutes, the jury found that the decree *nisi* was not pronounced contrary to the justice of the case by reason of material facts not being brought to the knowledge of the court. Public opinion for the most part took this to be a verdict against Dilke and regarded it as just. Dilke, however, always maintained his innocence and in this he was supported by his wife and the majority of his friends. He refused to resign his privy counsellorship as Queen Victoria wished him to do, since he considered such an action tantamount to an admission of guilt. In the General Election the same month he suffered a further blow when he was defeated in Chelsea, which he had represented for the past eighteen years. Nevertheless, he was to return to public life in 1892 when he was elected Liberal MP for the Forest of Dean for which he was to sit until his death in 1911 and where the electors indicated their belief in his innocence by returning him at five elections, two being without a contest. But he never again held political office. Although Gladstone had written to him in 1886 explaining why he could not include him in the Government, Dilke resigned himself to a long spell as a back bencher, but he took advantage of his precedence as a privy counsellor to speak on a variety of subjects of which he had detailed knowledge and the House always listened to him with attention. For the rest he consoled himself in writing and travel with his wife who never wavered in her steadfast belief in his innocence so far as Mrs Crawford was concerned.

'*Of course*, Dilke was innocent,' Marshall Hall told his biographer Edward Marjoribanks many years later. 'I have read papers which *prove* it.'[11] The document in question which Marjoribanks found among Marshall Hall's papers was a copy of a statement by Fanny Stock, formerly Gray, taken by Dilke's solicitors Humbert & Co. on 10 April 1886 before the second trial. According to Marjoribanks, she was the one witness who might have saved Dilke, since her statement consisted of a categorical denial that she had had any immoral relations with him. She had been approached by a detective before the case and was frightened, she stated, and as she was very anxious not to be called as a witness she disappeared. In December 1885 she had married Stock and her husband was also opposed to her testifying. After making her statement she again disappeared and the fact that she was not available as a witness must have prejudiced Dilke's case considerably. Had the jury believed her word against Mrs Crawford's, Marjoribanks thought, Dilke would have been in all probability cleared. What Fanny said in her statement could not, of course, have been given in evidence. Here is what she said:

[124]

I certainly never saw Mrs Crawford at Sloane Street or any other lady. I did not even see Sir Charles Dilke. I never heard of Mrs Crawford till the commencement of this case, and I should not know her if I saw her. The reason why I decline to say where I was during part of 1883 and 1884 has nothing to do with Mrs Crawford or Sir Charles Dilke.

The detective told me that I knew I had seen Mrs Crawford at Sir Charles Dilke's house. I told him it was not true, but he told me that he did not believe me, and that if I did not admit it I should be prosecuted. I told Mr Humbert this, and that I was too frightened to go into the witness-box, and felt I could not stop at home after what the detective said, but should go away somewhere. My husband was very anxious that I should not be a witness. We agreed not to let anyone know where we were.

The subsequent careers of the other participants in the Dilke drama may be briefly summarised. Virginia Crawford, who had enough money to live on, dwelt for many years in a flat in Oxford and Cambridge Mansions in Marylebone Road. About 1888 she was introduced by W. T. Stead to Cardinal Manning and under his influence was received into the Roman Catholic Church, making a general confession to the ageing Cardinal. Her conversion meant much to her and she was associated with various religious bodies, being a founder member of the Catholic Social Guild. She was also a member of her local Board of Guardians for many years and in 1919 was elected to the Marylebone Borough Council as its first Labour member. In 1931 she moved to Kensington and spent her remaining years in a house on Campden Hill. She also wrote extensively on literary and religious subjects. She died aged eighty-five, on 19 October 1948.

Unlike her ex-husband Virginia never remarried. But Donald Crawford did, his second wife being the Hon. Susan Moncrieff, daughter of the third Lord Moncrieff. However, it is significant that he made no reference to his first marriage in the entry which he wrote for *Who's Who*. From 1895, when he ceased to be MP for North Lanarkshire, until his death in 1919 he was Sheriff for Aberdeen, Kincardine and Banff, a post corresponding to that of County Court judge in England. Emilia Lady Dilke, historian of French art and pioneer women's trade unionist died in 1904, thus predeceasing her second husband by seven years. They had no children.

[125]

Dilke left his papers to Emilia's niece Gertrude Tuckwell, who was later to write his official biography. Sir Shane Leslie, Manning's literary executor and biographer, told Miss Tuckwell that he had plenty of proof that the Cardinal believed in Dilke's innocence. Unfortunately, he did not produce it in his book on Manning.[12] However, the sum of all the available evidence is that, although Sir Charles Dilke as a young man was the lover of Virginia Crawford's mother, he did not commit adultery with Mrs Crawford, despite the scandal of the divorce which blasted his political career.

4

Like Sir Charles Dilke, the Irish Nationalist leader Charles Stewart Parnell was co-respondent in a sensational divorce case, but whereas Dilke was almost certainly innocent of committing the adultery with which he was charged, Parnell was unquestionably guilty in his case in which the petitioner was a fellow Nationalist MP whose election was due to the co-respondent's influence. However, unlike Dilke who was re-elected for another seat and remained in the House of Commons for a further nineteen years, Parnell's health as well as his political career was ruined and he only survived the scandal of the divorce by eighteen months. In common with other historic nationalist figures in Ireland, Parnell was a Protestant. His family on his father's side had lived in Ireland since the reign of Charles II, having migrated from Cheshire. Parnell's great-grandfather Sir John Parnell had been Chancellor of the Exchequer in the old Irish Parliament in Dublin, and both his grandfather and his father had nationalist sympathies which Charles shared. His mother was an American with strong anti-British feelings.[13]

At Magdalene College, Cambridge, where he spent four years and left without a degree, Parnell appeared a diffident youth and gave no promise of his remarkable future. He began by leading the life of a retiring country gentleman at his family home Avondale, near Rathdrum, in County Wicklow.[14] Then in 1875 he entered the House of Commons as Member for County Meath and five years later, when he exchanged this seat for Cork city, he was chosen as chairman of the Irish Home Rule party at Westminster, having already become President of the Irish Land League pledged to transfer the land to its rack-rented

[126]

tenants. His rise to political power was thus meteoric. During the decade of his political leadership, it has been said that he exerted over his parliamentary supporters a sway unparalleled in parliamentary annals. He initiated it by sponsoring the system of 'boycotting', so called from a certain Captain Charles Boycott to whom it was first applied, the victims being those who took over the farms of evicted tenants.[15]

Parnell was imprisoned in Kilmainham Gaol in Dublin for his incendiary speeches, which sparked off a series of terrorist outrages for which he was blamed. Nevertheless, his popularity outside as well as with his followers inside Parliament was immense and he came to be known as the uncrowned king of Ireland. His major achievement was his conversion of W. E. Gladstone, the Liberal Prime Minister, to the cause of Home Rule for Ireland. His popularity reached its height after he had been accused of conniving at terrorism, such as the Phoenix Park murders, in a series of articles entitled 'Parnellism and Crime' which appeared in *The Times*, and included an incriminating letter purporting to be signed by Parnell. This, along with others exposed as forgeries in 1889, was the work of an Irish journalist named Richard Pigott who subsequently fled to Madrid where he killed himself in a hotel room.

At the General Election of 1880, which returned Gladstone and the Liberals to power, two Irish Home Rulers were returned for County Clare. One was the octogenarian commonly known as The O'Gorman Mahon; the other was the forty-year-old Captain William (Willie) O'Shea, late of the 18th Hussars. O'Shea's parents were Catholics and he was brought up in their faith. His father was a Limerick pawnbroker who later became a Dublin solicitor, while his mother, a Tipperary lady named Catherine Quinland, was created a papal countess on account of her devoutness and services to the Roman Catholic Church. Willie was a tall, handsome, rather cynical man, who cultivated an English upper class accent and pronounced his surname *O'Shee* in preference to *O'Shay* as it would normally be in Ireland. (Incidentally the Irish always accentuated the second vowel in Parnell rather than the first which the English did.) In 1867 Willie O'Shea married Katharine (Katie), the sixth and youngest daughter of the Revd Sir John Page Wood, Bt. Katie had a rich aunt Anna Maria Wood known as Aunt Ben. At Katie's request Aunt Ben paid the election expenses of Willie and The O'Gorman Mahon, who introduced Willie O'Shea to Parnell at this time.

[127]

Willie and Katie were in the habit of giving political dinners at Thomas's Hotel in Berkeley Square and Willie suggested that his wife should invite Parnell which Katie did on several occasions, the invitations being invariably ignored, although he accepted one and failed to turn up. On this particular occasion one of the guests pointed at Parnell's empty chair and defied Katie to fill it. Katie acknowledged the challenge by replying, 'The Uncrowned King of Ireland shall sit in that chair at the next dinner party I give.' To this end she and her sister Anna Steele called at the House of Commons one summer afternoon in 1880 and sent in a card to Parnell asking if he would come out and speak to them in their carriage in Palace Yard.[16]

Normally Parnell disregarded such cards unless he knew the individuals, but on this occasion he decided to come out. Katharine and her sister introduced themselves and then Katharine asked Parnell why he had ignored her invitations and what she could do to persuade him to attend her next dinner party. Parnell excused himself by saying that he had not opened his mail for days – indeed he would sometimes leave it unopened for weeks at a time and then go into the Commons library and open the letters *en masse*. However, Parnell promised to accept Mrs O'Shea's next invitation if at all possible. 'He looked straight at me smiling,' she afterwards recorded her impression of their first meeting, 'and his curiously burning eyes looked into mine with a wonderful intentness that threw into my brain the sudden thought: "This man is wonderful – and different."' As the two sisters were leaving Palace Yard, Katharine leant out of the carriage to say goodbye and the rose attached to her bodice fell off. Parnell picked it up, kissed it lightly and put it in his button-hole. When the rose had withered, he did not throw it away but put it in an envelope on which he wrote Katharine's name and the date. Soon he was writing to her about 'the powerful attractions which have been tending to seduce me from my duty towards my country in the direction of Thomas's Hotel.' About a fortnight later he came to a small dinner at the hotel, and afterwards the party went to the Gaiety theatre since Katharine thought that Parnell would find the entertainment a welcome change from his parliamentary exertions. They sat together at the back of the box while the others sat in front. Thus began their romance which was to have fateful consequences.

During the following weeks Parnell contrived on several occasions to meet Katie, whose delicate vivacious features and merry eyes captivated the lonely bachelor. They had lunch and tea together at the Cannon Street Hotel, and once, when she missed her train home, Parnell hired a cab and drove her to Eltham where she lived at Wonersh Lodge through the benevolence of Aunt Ben who had a house nearby. Willie O'Shea was away at this time and Parnell wished to stay but Katie would not let him do so. But they arranged to meet again whenever possible. With the prorogation of Parliament in September Parnell had to go to Ireland to see to constituency matters and address Land League meetings. But he could not keep his mind off Katie for long. On 5 October he wrote to her from Dublin saying he was leaving Ireland and would meet her anywhere she wished in London. He began this letter 'My dear Mrs O'Shea'. No doubt it was during this visit that they became lovers, since Parnell's next letter to her dated 17 October from Dublin began 'My own love'. No doubt too it was at Wonersh Lodge that Katie became Parnell's mistress. Shortly afterwards Parnell more or less moved in to the house, being given a bedroom at the top of the stairs which was conveniently connected with Katharine's via her dressing room. Willie was away from the place more and more, mostly in Spain where he had an interest in a sulphur mine, and although he initially welcomed Parnell's visits he expressed the view that Parnell should not come when he was absent. However, Willie had ceased to have sexual relations with Katie and he showed little interest in the education of their three children, Gerard, Carmen and Norah, who were brought up as Catholics, although their mother, who was an Anglican, refused to be converted. As regards her sexual relations with Parnell, she was coy and reticent. But one gathers that they were passionate, since she spoke of Parnell's fiery kisses and his masterful behaviour, on one occasion throwing her over his shoulder and carrying her into her bedroom. In November 1880, when he was in danger of being arrested for his Land League activities she hid him for a fortnight in her dressing room at Wonersh Lodge, where he spent the time eating larger meals than usual and reading *Alice in Wonderland*.

Willie's suspicions of his wife's intimacy with Parnell culminated in his challenging the Irish leader to a duel after he had found Parnell's suitcase in the house, taken it with him by train to London and flung it on to the platform at Charing Cross Station. 'My dear Mrs O'Shea', wrote Parnell plaintively on 7 January 1881, 'Will you kindly ask Captain O'Shea where he left my luggage? I inquired at both the parcel

[129]

office, cloakroom, and this hotel at Charing Cross today, and they were not to be found.' However the affair was smoothed over by Katharine who wished to avoid a public scandal. Indeed Willie appears to have accepted the situation from an early date and become a *mari complaisant*, since, with regard to the divorce proceedings he spoke of initiating, Katharine kept him quiet by threatening to reveal publicly his own adulterous liaisons of which she had ample evidence. They quarrelled after Parnell had spent ten days in the summer of 1881 with Katie and the children in Brighton and she discovered that she was pregnant by Parnell, although she subsequently persuaded Willie that he was responsible for the pregnancy after resuming sexual relations with him for a short time.

In October 1881 Parnell and other Land League agitators were arrested in Dublin and confined in the notorious Kilmainham Gaol. Four months later, in February 1882, Katie was delivered of a baby girl at Wonersh Lodge after a long and difficult labour. The child at Willie's insistence was baptised a Catholic in the drawing-room at Wonersh Lodge since the little girl called Claude Sophie was too weak to be taken to church. Parnell was distraught that he could not be with his darling 'Wifie' or 'Queenie' as he affectionately called her, but he was not released as he expected for the opening of Parliament. However, he was allowed out on parole in April and made straight for Wonersh Lodge where the infant died two days later after a brief life of six weeks. Meanwhile Willie, who was also at Eltham, was with Parnell's knowledge to see Gladstone, Joseph Chamberlain and other members of the Liberal Government, and negotiate the so-called Kilmainham 'treaty', by which Parnell if released undertook to discourage lawlessness in Ireland in return for the promise of a government bill which would put an end to the eviction of Irish peasants from their holdings for non-payment of arrears of rent. Parnell had to return to Kilmainham since he was on parole, so that he missed Claude Sophie's funeral and burial in the Catholic cemetery at Chislehurst. Parnell was eventually released at the beginning of May. Asked how his 'no rent' campaign was going he replied, 'All I can say is that my own tenants at Avondale are living up to it!'

Shortly afterwards, Katie made an agreement with her husband to the effect that she would pay him £600 a year from the money she was receiving from Aunt Ben on condition that Willie would not interfere with her life but leave her to behave as she thought fit. Parnell naturally approved of this arrangement. 'It will be too intolerable having him about always,' he wrote from Kilmainham when he was back there from parole and the agreement was being considered. Its implication was that Willie, with his additional income, would do nothing provided Katie and Parnell were discreet and Willie's own political career prospered. Prosper it did through his close relationship with Joseph Chamberlain who promised that in the event of his coming to power O'Shea would be appointed Chief Secretary for Ireland. News was now leaking out that Willie's wife was Parnell's mistress, a fact known to Gladstone's government as well as to some of the leading Irish Nationalists. Sir Charles Dilke, who was a member of the Cabinet at this time, recorded that the Home Secretary Sir William Harcourt had 'informed the Cabinet that he knew that in 1881 O'Shea had threatened Parnell with divorce proceedings, and that it was only Mrs O'Shea's discovery of adulterous relations of her husband which put him in her power; that he had shut his eyes and made the best of it'.

In August 1884 Captain O'Shea wrote again to Parnell about Parnell's relations with Katie, since he feared that if they became public knowledge his own political career would be adversely affected. 'You have behaved very badly to me,' wrote Willie. 'While I have often told you that you were welcome to stay at Eltham whenever I was there, I begged of you not to do so during my absence, since it would be sure, at the least, sooner or later, to cause a scandal.'

'I do not know of any scandal, or any ground for one,' Parnell replied unyieldingly, 'and can only suppose that you have misunderstood the drift of some statements that may have been made about me.' At the time of this exchange of letters, Katie was pregnant by her lover for the third time.

Meanwhile Parnell established himself more or less permanently at Wonersh Lodge to which Katie had an annexe built on as a workshop for him. She also bore him two more children, both girls, Clare in the early part of 1883 and Frances Katie in the autumn of 1884. As with Claude Sophie, Katie had both the births registered, the paternity being ascribed in each case to William Henry O'Shea, Member of Parliament for County Clare. It is significant that she does not refer to any of these births in her memoirs, but no doubt this was because the memoirs were edited by her and Willie's son Gerard who was anxious to conceal the

[131]

fact that the children, though registered as his father's, were really Parnell's.

During this period, which culminated in Gladstone's conversion to Home Rule and his introduction of the first Home Rule Bill in 1886, Katharine O'Shea acted as an intermediary between Parnell and the Liberal Prime Minister both by interviews and correspondence in which she would enclose important letters from Parnell. At times she was the only real link between them, and her assurance that Parnell trusted and confided in her and her alone was accepted by Gladstone as accurate; otherwise the Liberal party leader would not have written to her so frequently and at such length as he did. 'I have not, and never had had any desire to push myself forward as a means of communication,' she told Gladstone in one letter. 'I have nothing to gain by it except the hope that some good may come of the interchange of ideas and views for the common good.'

In November 1885 Gladstone became Prime Minister for the third time following the General Election at which the Liberals had a majority, and he began with Parnell's encouragement to draft the Home Rule measure which he intended to introduce.

There now occurred an episode which has been described as the most discreditable in Parnell's career. Willie O'Shea, having failed to secure the support of his constituency party in County Clare, had stood as a Liberal at the General Election for the Exchange division of Liverpool and been defeated. Katie was anxious to find him another seat and the possibility emerged when the Nationalist T. P. O'Connor, who had been returned for both Galway and the Scotland division of Liverpool, chose the Liverpool seat, thus leaving Galway vacant. Katie pressed Willie's nomination for the vacant seat on Parnell, but at first the latter hesitated, since Willie O'Shea refused to take the pledge to support Home Rule. However, Willie went over to Galway and offered himself as the Nationalist candidate. His action was countered by the leading Nationalists Tim Healy and Joseph Biggar who proposed to nominate a local man, Michael Lynch. 'All hope is gone unless you come at once,' O'Shea telegraphed Parnell. 'Things have gone so far that the presence of anyone except yourself would not save the situation.' At the same time Biggar, with remarkable foresight, also sent Parnell a telegram: 'The O'Sheas will be your ruin.'

'It is no matter, Queenie,' was Parnell's reaction to Katie. 'I'll run

[132]

him for Galway and I'll get him returned. I'll force him down their throats, and he can never again claim that I have promised and not performed. It will cost me the confidence of the party, but that much he shall have.' If Ireland wanted Home Rule, she would have it, he added, and 'what would be, would be.'

Once in Galway Parnell quickly re-established his authority which had been challenged by Healy and Biggar. 'I have Home Rule in the hollow of my hand,' he declared. 'The man who strikes at my hand strikes at the hopes of the Irish nation! If my candidate is defeated, the news will spread round the universe that a disaster has overwhelmed. The world will say "Parnell is beaten. Ireland no longer has a leader."' The result was that Michael Lynch withdrew, O'Shea was chosen almost unanimously as the Nationalist candidate, and in the ensuing election was returned by an overwhelming majority (942 to 54). The rumours assiduously spread around by Healy and Biggar (himself a man of the loosest sexual morals) that the successful candidate's wife was Parnell's mistress were dismissed by Willie O'Shea as malicious gossip; indeed he swore to the local bishop that there was no truth in the allegation.

Significantly, Captain O'Shea gave no pledges on the Home Rule question during the election, and he abstained on the vote on the second reading of the Home Rule Bill on 7 June 1886, when the Government was defeated through the secession of Joseph Chamberlain, Lord Hartington and other so-called Liberal Unionists. It was the shortest Parliament in Victorian times, being dissolved three weeks later, and in the ensuing General Election the Tories were returned to power under Lord Salisbury. On the day after the crucial vote Captain O'Shea resigned his seat for Galway, since his conduct over the Bill resulted in threats from Irish Nationalist quarters which made him fear for his life.

Because of the rumours of his wife's infidelity, O'Shea endeavoured without success to persuade Katie to give up seeing Parnell. This she refused to do, although she subsequently wrote two letters to her son Gerard in which she agreed to have no further communication with Parnell and that she was surrendering the lease of the stables at Eltham where Parnell kept his horses. However, O'Shea took no steps to ascertain whether Katie was implementing her promise. Although he had threatened divorce proceedings if she refused to comply, in the event he took no action since he hoped that *The Times* articles,

[133]

subsequently exposed as forgeries, would ruin Parnell's career. There was also the question of money since he was financially dependent on his wife's bounty through Aunt Ben, who had changed her will leaving Katie much more money than she originally intended – about £150,000 in addition to real estate – and as she was ninety-five she could not expect to live very much longer. Later the Wood family tried to prove that she was insane but their lunacy petition failed, as did their subsequent action to invalidate the will.

There followed the publication of *The Times* articles with the letters attributed to Parnell being proved forgeries by the Special Commission. Although no one accused that newspaper of having known the incriminating letters to have been forged, *The Times* was considered by many to have acted recklessly without doing more to check the authenticity of the letters. Public opinion swung strongly in Parnell's favour, he became the hero of the hour, being given a standing ovation in the House of Commons and invited to numerous dinners and receptions, most of which he refused as he felt he could not take Katie with him. Incidentally at the Special Commission Willie O'Shea had been called as a witness who was familiar with Parnell's handwriting and, after examining one of the letters, said after a momentary hesitation that he thought the signature was that of the Irish Home Rule leader.

The Commission was still sitting in May 1889 when Aunt Ben died and Katie sold Wonersh Lodge, which was then hers. Shortly afterwards, she and Parnell moved to a rented house in Brighton, 10 Walsingham Terrace, a four-storey building, the end house of a short terrace at the Hove end of the town to which they added the adjoining house to give them more room for their three children, servants and horses and dogs. This suited Parnell as there was an excellent train service between Brighton and London and the open country towards Shoreham was good for riding.

In the autumn of this year Parnell was at the summit of his political power. Gladstone was friendly and invited him to stay at Hawarden which he did. They discussed and agreed on the principles of Home Rule, including the thorny question as to whether the Irish MPs should continue to be represented at Westminster besides having their local Parliament in Dublin. Although his health was giving him trouble – Gladstone's daughter in her diary commented upon how ill he looked – he had recurrent attacks of bronchitis – Parnell's spirits were high and he was happy with Katie and the children. There was every prospect of the Liberals being returned to power at the next General Election and Home Rule would form a major feature of the party manifesto. For Parnell political victory was in sight. Then, suddenly and unexpectedly, the blow fell. On Christmas Eve 1889, Captain O'Shea filed a petition for divorce, citing Charles Stewart Parnell as co-respondent.

5

What made Willie O'Shea choose this moment to launch his time bomb? The Wood family proposed to contest Aunt Ben's will in Katie's favour in the action which Katie had initiated in the Probate Court but which had not yet come on. Aunt Ben never had any idea of her niece's adulterous relationship with Parnell, and Willie determined to exploit the situation, since if he could show that Katie had been deceiving Aunt Ben the case for declaring the will invalid would be strengthened on the assumption that the old lady would not have changed her previous will if she had known of Katie's relationship with the 'uncrowned king of Ireland'.

It appears that the Woods thought they might be able to persuade O'Shea to withdraw his petition in return for Katie agreeing to split the money with them out of court. They sent Katie's sister Anna Steele to see Katie and try this ploy. However, it failed because Katie considered that she was entitled to Aunt Ben's entire fortune under the terms of the will. On the other hand, Willie O'Shea, as always indigent and greedy for money, was apparently still amenable to withdrawal if Katie would come up with £90,000. But the probate suit had not yet been heard and she was unable to persuade anyone to lend her this sum. The reason which Willie gave Joseph Chamberlain at the time for proceeding with the divorce petition was that he and Gerard went down to Brighton the week before Christmas. Gerard called at 10 Walsingham Terrace and to his surprise found 'a lot of Mr Parnell's things, some of which he chucked out of the window'. According to his father a violent scene took place between Gerard and his mother with the result that, in Willie's words, 'on our return to London we went to the lawyers and settled that an action should be taken immediately.'

Katie continued to think that she could bribe her husband. But unfortunately for her the wherewithal to do so was not forthcoming. George Lewis, whom she employed for a time as her solicitor, might have helped if he and Katie had not quarrelled and he passed her on to another firm. 'I wish you joy of your client,' was Lewis's comment to her next solicitor. 'I don't know how long you will keep her. She's a very charming lady but an impossible one. However I hope you have better luck.'[17]

Meanwhile Parnell was confident that he would emerge triumphant from the case as he had done before the Special Commission, 'without a stain on his character or reputation', as he told the Irish Nationalist Michael Davitt. In April Parnell filed his answer to the charge of adultery with a simple denial. Katie did nothing for about three months when she likewise denied the adultery, but went on to file a counter-petition charging Willie O'Shea with connivance and condonation of her adultery, neglect, cruelty, adultery on seventeen occasions, and unreasonable delay in filing his petition. One of his alleged adulteries she stated was with her own sister Anna Steele.

O'Shea's solicitor had briefed the Solicitor-General Sir Edward Clarke, who later stated that he considered Katie's defence extremely puzzling. 'Who could have advised this step or why Mr Parnell permitted it, was and is a mystery,' he wrote in his autobiography. 'The charge against Mrs Steele was utterly baseless and wanton; while of course the plea of connivance was in effect an admission of the adultery alleged against herself.'[18] The answer seems to be that Katie took nobody's advice but acted on her own initiative, with which Parnell went along, hoping to bribe or frighten Willie O'Shea into abandoning the suit. This had been set down for hearing on 15 November 1880. Two days before, John Morley told Gladstone that Parnell was going to be triumphantly acquitted. Indeed Parnell had given him that assurance. Morley had asked Parnell whether there was any chance of the divorce proceedings leading to his disappearance from the political scene. 'Oh, no,' Parnell had replied reassuringly 'nothing in the least leading to my disappearance will come out of the legal proceedings. The other side don't know what a broken-kneed horse they are riding.'

On the day before the trial Katie and Parnell went to London and saw Frank Lockwood, QC, MP, who had been retained for Katie's defence. According to Katie, Lockwood begged her to persuade Parnell to let him fight the whole case on her behalf, to which she responded by doubting her ability to do this. When she and Parnell left Lockwood's chambers, the question was undecided. However, they promised him that they would telegraph him one way or the other next morning by eight o'clock. This was certainly cutting things fine since the court was due to meet at 10 a.m. the same day.

When they got home to Walsingham Terrace, Parnell put Katie to bed, and gave her scraps of food washed down with sparkling Moselle which she had been recommended for her neuralgia. She kept wondering about her defence and whether she should not tell Lockwood to abandon it. 'We have been longing for this freedom all these years, and now you are afraid!' Parnell reproached her, assuring her that she had been his salvation, and that his private life belonged to her. There was a characteristic strain of fatalism in what he then said, a feeling of *che sera sera*. 'If they turn from me, my Queen, it matters not at all in the end,' he told her. 'What the ultimate government of Ireland will be is settled, and it will be so, and what my share in the work has been and is to be, also.' However, Katie spoke about going up to London for the hearing, but she did not ask to be wakened early which she might well have done if she was really determined to appear in court and not to let her defence go by default as Parnell wished. When she eventually awoke in the morning, it was too late. Parnell was at her bedside with a cup of tea and some buttered toast. When she asked what time it was, Parnell laughed and said: 'I've done you this time, Queenie. I sent the telegram long ago, and they must be enjoying themselves in court by now.'[19]

The case opened on Saturday 15 November 1890 before Mr Justice Butt and a special jury in Court Number One of the Royal Courts of Justice, which by a coincidence was the same court room where the Special Commission had sat in the previous year and cleared Parnell of the charge of approving terrorism on the basis of Pigott's forged letters. As on the previous occasion the court was packed to the doors. The proceedings began with a brief statement by Lockwood who said that he represented the respondent Mrs O'Shea, but would not be calling any witnesses or cross-examining. Parnell, the co-respondent, was unrepresented by counsel. Thus the petitioner's case was in effect undefended, but the fact that the respondent had entered a counter-petition which was read in court, accusing her husband of connivance, condonation and cruelty besides implicating her sister Anna Steele, enabled O'Shea's counsel Sir Edward Clarke to introduce some damning

[137]

evidence in his client's favour, which he could not have done had the suit been entirely undefended as it was by Parnell.

The proceedings were mercifully short, although they had been expected by the newspapers to last a week. Clarke had thirty witnesses available to refute any defence the co-respondent might make, but since he made none, it was only necessary for Clarke to call a few of them. Parnell had been subpoenaed by Katie's solicitors as a witness in the counter-petition, but he failed to appear and Clarke persuaded the judge that in the circumstances identification by photograph was acceptable. After Clarke's relatively brief opening, the petitioner took the stand. In his testimony he dwelt on his happy relations with his wife before she met the co-respondent, and he did not suspect her of adultery until 1887 when his suspicions were allayed by his wife's letters to their son Gerard that she would cease all communication with Parnell. It was not until December 1889, he went on, that he received information that his wife was living with Parnell in Brighton when he consulted his solicitors and filed his divorce petition. Finally, when asked about his relations with Mrs Anna Steele, he replied that there was not the slightest truth in the allegation that he had committed adultery with her or indeed in any of his wife's counter-charges. Asked by Mrs Steele's counsel whether there was a great deal of ill feeling between the two sisters in the previous summer 'owing to a pending probate action', the witness agreed that this was true, thus implanting the idea in the jury's minds that Katie had acted wantonly after a family row over money. Of course, he was not cross-examined, although he was later asked by a juror why he was not at Wonersh Lodge every night seeing that it was only an hour's journey from London. Willie agreed that he was not there constantly but that his diaries had been put in evidence and these showed what a kind husband and father he was.

Perhaps the most damaging witness called for the petitioner was Mrs Caroline Pethers, the cook who had been employed at the house in Medina Terrace in Brighton, which had been rented towards the end of 1883. She swore that Parnell, whom she knew as 'Mr Stewart' and identified by his photograph, first visited the house with the petitioner but later came alone and frequently slept there in Captain O'Shea's absence. She went on to relate how on one occasion, when Parnell and Mrs O'Shea were in the upstairs drawing-room, Captain O'Shea rang the front door bell and was admitted. Ten minutes later the front door

[138]

bell rang again, and on opening the door the witness saw Parnell who requested to see Captain O'Shea. Asked how Parnell had managed to make such a dramatic appearance on the door step so soon after he had been in the drawing-room, Mrs Pethers replied that there was a rope fire escape which Parnell had used since he certainly did not leave by the stairs. The incident of the fire escape created a sensation and was the subject of jokes in the clubs and music halls.

At this point the judge told Clarke that he would be prepared to sum up to the jury if the Solicitor-General would close his case. However, Clarke wished to call Mrs Steele who was not in court since she did not think her evidence would be required so soon. In these circumstances Mr Justice Butt adjourned the hearing until the following Monday when Mrs Steele went into the witness-box and swore that she had not committed adultery with the petitioner in 1881 or at any other time. There followed the judge's summing-up in which Mr Justice Butt, while indicating the difficulty of only having heard one side of the case, told the jury that the question of Mrs O'Shea's adultery with Parnell seemed to him to have been proved without the shadow of a doubt, at the same time making it clear that in the petitioner's evidence on oath there was no connivance or condonation on his part worthy of belief. The judge went on to stress the damage done to the co-respondent's reputation by the respondent's unsubstantiated counter-petition:

> If it had appeared that the husband was really a consenting party and accessory to his wife's guilt, Mr Parnell, although the issue of adultery might have been found against him, would still have stood in a better position than he does at present, because although it is an immoral, improper and reprehensible thing to indulge in intimacy of this kind with a married woman, whether her husband is a consenting party or not, nevertheless the man who stands in that position is to some extent not so guilty or blameworthy as the man who takes advantage of the hospitality offered to him by the husband to debauch the wife.

As regards the allegation in the cross-petition of Captain O'Shea's adultery with Mrs Steele, the judge stated in his view that it should never have been made.

The result of the trial was a foregone conclusion. The jury had no hesitation in finding the respondent Katharine O'Shea guilty of adultery with the co-respondent Charles Stewart Parnell, and that the petitioner had not connived at the adultery. Mr Justice Butt thereupon gave Captain O'Shea his decree *nisi*, awarding costs against Parnell and reserving them against Mrs O'Shea until it was known whether she had a separate estate. Lockwood then broke his silence to ask for a similar reservation in the case of the two younger children, who were undoubtedly Parnell's. But Mr Justice Butt said that usually custody was awarded to the innocent party, so that Willie O'Shea obtained the legal custody of Clare and Frances Katie, although in the event he did not choose to enforce it. Thus ended what *The Times* described as 'a story of dull and ignoble infidelity, untouched so far as can be seen by a single ray of sentiment or a single flash of passion and comparable only to the dreary monotony of French middle-class vice, over which M. Zola's scalpel so lovingly lingers.' On the other hand, the *New York Times* expressed the view followed by other American papers that it was 'impossible to find a man of the world who does not believe that O'Shea was guilty of connivance'. At least to any intelligent observer it was difficult if not impossible to accept that for ten years Captain O'Shea was unaware that Parnell was sleeping with his wife at Wonersh Lodge, Brighton and other places.

6

A week after the verdict in the divorce suit, Gladstone, who had to reckon with the Nonconformist conscience in the Liberal party, published an open letter to John Morley in which he stated that, 'Notwithstanding the splendid public services rendered by Mr Parnell to his country, his continuance at the present moment in the leadership would be productive of consequences disastrous in the highest degree to the cause of Ireland.' Parnell retorted indignantly in his *Manifesto to the Irish People*, in which he appealed to Irishmen 'to save me from the English wolves who are howling for my destruction' and warned his countrymen that a postponement of Home Rule was preferable to such sacrifice to Irishmen's independence as was implied by the acceptance of Gladstone's dictation on the question of leadership.

In accordance with a requisition signed by a majority of his followers,

Parnell called a meeting of the Irish party in Committee Room 15 of the House of Commons on 1 December to consider the situation. Parnell took the chair – he was still nominally leader – and adroitly ruled all motions for his deposition out of order, while diverting the discussion to a consideration of Gladstone's views on Home Rule. When one of Parnell's supporters declared that if the party rejected Parnell it would in effect be placing itself under Gladstone's leadership, an anti-Parnellite named Arthur O'Connor asserted that Gladstone was not a member of the Irish party. Parnell's chief supporter John Redmond thereupon interposed with the declaration to the accompaniment of cheers that Gladstone was 'the master of the party'. At which Tim Healy inquired, 'Who is to be the mistress of the party?' This impertinent question was greeted by cries of 'shame' and other expressions indistinguishable in the accompanying uproar. Finally Arthur O'Connor said, 'I appeal to my friend the chairman.' 'Better appeal to your own friends,' replied the infuriated Parnell, pointing at Healy. 'Better appeal to that cowardly little scoundrel there, who dares in an assembly of Irishmen to insult a woman.' Healy said nothing more, 'being contented', as he afterwards told his wife 'with the thrust which will stick as long as his cry about Gladstone's "dictation" continues.' Eventually a leading anti-Parnellite Justin McCarthy suggested that, since there was no further use in carrying on the discussion, 'all who think with me in this grave crisis should withdraw with me from this room.' He then departed with forty-four of his colleagues, who held another meeting which declared Parnell's leadership at an end. Twenty-five members headed by Redmond remained faithful to the leader. But the Irish Nationalists were split into two camps – the Parnellites and the anti-Parnellites – and it was not for another ten years that Redmond succeeded in healing the rift between them, long after Parnell's death, and reuniting the party.

Meanwhile Parnell had been repudiated by the Irish Catholic hierarchy, and although he went to Ireland repeatedly during the ensuing months it was to fight a losing battle. At the same time his health rapidly deteriorated under the strain of his exertions. Three Parnellite candidates for whom he spoke at by-elections were defeated, largely as the result of ecclesiastical influence. He further offended the priests by marrying Katie after her husband's decree *nisi* had been made absolute. Incidentally it was at this time that, owing to some

[141]

inexplicable quirk, she came to be known as 'Kitty', although her Christian name was Katharine, abbreviated to Katie, as she always signed herself in her letters even when writing to Gladstone.

The wedding ceremony took place at 8.30 a.m. on 25 June 1891 in the local registry office, which was at Steyning, about nine miles from Brighton. They both wished to be married in an Anglican church, but no Brighton vicar would agree to marry the world's most notorious divorcee and her lover. So they contented themselves with the registry office ceremony, hoping to have the union later solemnised in London where there were apparently some amenable clergy willing to officiate. It was a happy day for the bridal pair, Katie wearing a lace shawl over a black silk brocade dress and a hat decorated with pink roses. 'Queenie,' exclaimed the bridegroom when he first saw her that morning, 'you look lovely in that lace stuff with the beautiful hat with the roses. I am so proud of you!' After the ceremony they returned to Walsingham Terrace where Parnell told the waiting reporters that it was the happiest day in his life and that he and his wife hoped to be married later in a church in London. In the afternoon they sat in the sunshine on the beach at Shoreham and talked of the future, when Parnell had won Home Rule for Ireland and he could retire from politics and they could live together happily in some quiet retreat in a warmer climate than the English.

Two days later Parnell had to return to Ireland for the Carlow by-election in which his candidate was defeated by an anti-Parnellite who secured more than twice the number of the Parnellite's votes. This was due in part to Tim Healy's bitter campaign in his paper the *National Press*, in which Healy referred to Parnell as 'Mrs O'Shea's husband' and denounced the 'legalised concubinage' of 'the hero of the fire escape' which would do him no good in Holy Mother Ireland. The influential *Freeman's Journal* now deserted the Parnellite cause, but Parnell responded by launching a new paper the *Irish Daily Independent* to champion his interests. During the summer he paid several more visits to his native country, speaking wherever he could but showing signs of increasing strain. He had financial worries too. In August he wrote to 'Queenie' from Avondale asking if she could arrange with his solicitors to defer payment of the costs awarded against him in the divorce until the end of the year when he thought he would be in a position to settle them. On his return to Brighton in the middle of September Katie was

[142]

alarmed about his health and begged him to see the specialist Dr Henry Thompson, but he refused on account of the cost. On 25 September he left again on another tiring journey to Ireland, as was his custom kissing the white rose Katie had given him for his button-hole as he drove off to Brighton station.

He had arranged to speak at Creggs, a remote village in Galway, but on his arrival in Dublin one of his most devoted supporters, a medical man, begged him not to go to such an unimportant meeting. But every meeting, however small, was now important to him. He began his speech haltingly but soon braced himself to tell the audience that he would continue to fight because he was fighting not for a faction but for Ireland's freedom. It was pouring with rain and he stood bareheaded in the downpour, afterwards unable to change his soaking clothes since the bag which Katie had packed with dry shoes, socks and other clothing was mislaid. He was suffering from acute rheumatism and by the time he arrived back at Walsingham Terrace on Thursday 1 October he was so weak that Katie had to help him out of the carriage. Although the weather was very warm, he complained of the cold and Katie lit a blazing fire, beside which they sat, with her head nestling on his lap while he stroked her hair. Finally she put him to bed, having to undress him as he was unable to take off his clothes. He still refused to see Dr Henry Thompson as 'the fee would be enormous at this distance', tossed restlessly during the night and spoke of rheumatism as the disease from which thousands of Irish peasants had died. By Sunday morning his condition had worsened and he was feverish, running a high temperature. Katie called in a local doctor, but there was little he could do apart from prescribing some medicines and hoping that he would get over the fever. But the fever did not abate and by Tuesday he was delirious. In the early evening he was calmer, smiling at Katie when she touched him and begging her not to send the dogs out of the room, at least not Grouse, his favourite.

While Katie and Grouse sat by the bedside a storm blew up in the English Channel, rain lashing the windows, and waves crashing on the rocks on the nearby beach. Late in the evening the dying Parnell opened his eyes and said: 'Kiss me, sweet wifie, and I will try to sleep a little.' She did so and as she pressed her lips to his she was startled by 'the fire in them, fierce beyond anything I had felt, even in his most loving moods.' He then lapsed into unconsciousness from which he never recovered. It was shortly before midnight on 6 October 1891 that his breathing ceased and the 'lost leader' was dead, the cause of death being officially certified as inflammation of the lungs. He was forty-five.

The body was placed in an unusually large coffin, and as she took a last look at her beloved King, Katie placed on his breast a withered flower. It was all that remained of the rose which had fallen from her bodice on that July afternoon in 1880 in Palace Yard, Westminster, when he had entered her life.

It was raining in Brighton as it was in Dublin when the funeral hearse arrived at the City Hall where there was a brief lying-in-state, during which thirty thousand people filed past the coffin before it was transferred to its last resting place in Glasnevin cemetery. The grave was later marked by a large boulder of Wicklow granite on which was inscribed the single word PARNELL.

The distraught Katie advisedly did not attend the funeral. Indeed she nursed her grief for a month in Walsingham Terrace without once leaving the house.

Although the probate action was settled out of court with Katie getting approximately half Aunt Ben's fortune and the remainder going to the Wood family, she suffered an additional blow due to her and Parnell's ignorance of the law. Parnell had wished that Avondale and his Irish estate should go to Katie and should eventually pass to their children, and he made a will to this effect. But neither he nor Katie realised that under the law the will was invalidated by his marriage and that his intentions should have been expressed in a fresh will. The result was that Avondale was inherited by his brother John, who was then living in America. John Parnell returned to claim his inheritance, but he discovered to his chagrin that Parnell had left debts of over £50,000. After denuding the demesne forest of any saleable timber which he disposed of, he sold the house and remainder of the property to a Dublin butcher for £8,000. The place is now lovingly cared for by the Irish Forestry Commission.[20]

Nor did Katie ever visit Parnell's native land, although every year on the anniversary of his death she sent a wreath to be placed on his grave in Glasnevin. She died in February 1921 so that she lived to see the passage by the Westminster Parliament in the previous year of the Act which granted a measure of Home Rule to Ireland, of which twenty-six counties became the Irish Free State, now the Republic of

Ireland. Under the new dispensation it was natural that many of the southern capital's streets and squares which bore the names of former viceroys in the days of British rule, should be changed to those of great patriots and pioneers of independence. Sackville Street, the city's main thoroughfare, thus became O'Connell Street, while Rutland Square was renamed Parnell Square. At the junction of Parnell Square with O'Connell Street, there stands the Parnell Monument, commemorating the Home Rule leader by a bronze statue fronting a slab of Galway granite on which are inscribed the famous words from Parnell's speech in Cork on 21 January 1883:

> No man has the right to fix the boundary of the march of a nation; no man has the right to say to his country – thus far shalt thou go and no further. We have never attempted to fix the *ne plus ultra* to the progress of Ireland's nationhood and we never shall.

The Mr 'A' Case

1

OF the victory balls celebrating the first anniversary of the Armistice, which ended the fighting in the Great War, probably the largest was the one in the Royal Albert Hall in London on 11 November 1919. Many of those who attended took boxes from which they could watch the dancers and accompanying festivities. Among the boxholders was an English-speaking Indian prince, twenty-four-year-old Lieut.-General Sir Hari Singh, nephew and heir-presumptive to the elderly and eccentric Maharajah Pratab Singh of the Himalayan State of Kashmir to the command of whose military forces the young prince had been appointed three years previously.[1] It was young Hari's first visit to Europe and on the evening in question he was accompanied by various members of his suite including his Indian secretary who had the curious name of Maboob. The box had been engaged by the prince's ADC Captain Charles William Augustus Arthur, who belonged to an old Irish landed family and who had served with the City of Limerick Artillery in the Great War, having been recommended for his position with the prince by the India Office. In fact, Captain Arthur was not present on this occasion, but thinking to please his master and his native retinue he had engaged an adjoining box for two attractive and good-looking women, Mrs Maud Robinson and her friend Mrs Lilian Bevan.

During the evening some of the prince's suite got into conversation with the two ladies, as might be expected on such a gala occasion, but they did not include the prince, although he noted their attractions. A few days later, Mrs Robinson was leaving the Savoy hotel where she and Mrs Bevan had been lunching, and someone in the prince's suite who happened to be there recognised them as they were waiting for a taxi and offered to drive them home. They accepted with pleasure and when they arrived at Mrs Robinson's house in Chapel Street, Belgravia, she invited the Indian in for a coffee and liqueur. The Indian suggested that they should meet the prince who was anxious to make their acquaintance. Accordingly they both went to tea with the prince at the Curzon Hotel where the prince and his suite were staying. On this occasion Captain Arthur was present. The prince was greatly taken with the vivacious Mrs Robinson, who had been in India; she proved a most congenial guest as did her companion Mrs Bevan, to whom the Indian secretary Mr Maboob also took a strong fancy. Maud Robinson and the prince arranged to meet again and during the next fortnight or so they saw a lot of each other, going to dinner parties and dances. Eventually, about the beginning of December, Mrs Robinson became the prince's mistress in her house in Chapel Street. At this time her relations with her husband Charles Robinson, a bookmaker, were strained and he seldom appeared at Chapel Street, where Mrs Bevan, who was a widow, lived with Mrs Robinson as a companion.

Before she met the prince, Mrs Robinson planned to go to Mentone in the south of France about the middle of January 1920. When she informed the prince of her plan, he suggested that they should meet in Paris since it was on her way to the Riviera and that she should bring Mrs Bevan with her for his secretary's delectation. This proposal was quite agreeable to both ladies and they accordingly arrived in Paris on 20 December 1919. They booked or were booked into the Hotel Brighton in a suite which was also occupied by Captain Arthur, who arrived the next day with the prince and the Indian secretary. The ladies were there for two nights when they received a message from Captain Arthur that they should move to the nearby St James and Albany Hotel on the flimsy pretext that the ADC did not wish to compromise them if they stayed together in the same suite. Consequently the ladies were transferred to the St James and Albany where a large suite of rooms had been engaged for them. On Christmas night the prince, the ADC and the secretary dined with Mrs Robinson and Mrs Bevan and did not get back to the hotel until six o'clock on the morning of Boxing Day. Mrs Robinson went to her bedroom in the suite with the prince, while Mrs Bevan went to hers with the secretary.

About 8 a.m. the same morning there was a knock at the door of Mrs

Robinson's room. She thought it was Mrs Bevan and called out, 'Is that you Lilian?', while she got up and unlocked the door. To her utter astonishment she saw a man named Montagu Newton standing there. Newton, who had once been Mrs Robinson's lover, pushed past her, saying 'I have got *you* at last.' He then went over to the prince who was in bed and said to him 'You will hear more of this.' At which the prince turned to his mistress and said to her, 'Go and get the secretary.' Newton, who was posing as Mrs Robinson's husband, thereupon left, and Mrs Robinson rushed off to her friend Mrs Bevan who was in bed with Mr Maboob. The two ladies arranged to return to London immediately, since Maud Robinson was naturally anxious to reach her husband before her ex-lover did so. She and Lilian Bevan left Paris by the afternoon train, being seen off at the station by Captain Arthur. Back in London it took Maud Robinson several days to find her husband, whom she eventually tracked down at the Royal Automobile Club. When she saw him, it was obvious that Newton had reached him first, since he was in a bad temper. 'I don't want anything more to do with you,' he told her. 'I am going to take divorce proceedings against you.'

Meanwhile Captain Arthur had immediately warned his master that Mr Robinson would certainly institute divorce proceedings on the ground of his wife's adultery, naming the prince and claiming heavy damages from him. The resultant scandal, Arthur went on, would undoubtedly jeopardise the prince's succession to his uncle's throne. Naturally Hari Singh was horrified, and at his ADC's suggestion he signed two cheques, each for £150,000, and sent Arthur to London with them to do his best to buy off the injured husband. The place for the name of the payee was left blank in each case, and the reason why there were two cheques was that the prince had not sufficient funds in England to meet the entire demand, although this was a mere formality since he was extremely rich and only had to make the necessary arrangements with his bankers.

The truth was that there was a conspiracy to defraud the prince, the participants being Captain Arthur, Newton, and an equally dishonest solicitor's managing clerk named William Cooper Hobbs, an old crony of Newton's, to whom Newton sent Robinson for the purpose of commencing the divorce proceedings against his wife, on the ground that she was 'carrying on with a nigger in Paris.' The principal

[148]

conspirator was the ADC, who had arranged with Newton to pose as Mrs Robinson's husband as already described. Further, the reason for Maud Robinson and Lilian Bevan to move to the St James and Albany was because unlike the Brighton, this hotel had two entrances so that Newton could leave by the rear entrance in the Rue St Honoré without attracting the attention of the hall porter at the front entrance in the Rue de Rivoli through which he came in. When Mr Robinson met Hobbs, he told him that he found it difficult to believe in his wife's infidelity. 'There's no question, Robinson, about her guilt,' said Hobbs, adding untruthfully that the prince's solicitors had already admitted their client's adultery.

A week later Robinson saw Hobbs again and was informed that the prince was prepared to pay £25,000 if the divorce proceedings were dropped, since he 'did not want an exposure', particularly since he was married. Robinson at first told Hobbs that he did not want the money, but a little later he had second thoughts, and he again saw Hobbs, this time with his wife, and he gave a signed undertaking for the prince's solicitors not to proceed with the divorce and to accept £25,000 in settlement. Hobbs then went into another room and returned with a large parcel of banknotes which he said amounted to the £25,000 he had received from the prince's solicitors. Robinson thereupon declared that he did not wish to have the money and told Hobbs to give it to his wife Maud. He then left Hobbs's office, his wife remaining behind. The same day Robinson received a letter from his wife enclosing £3,000 and asking him to place £2,000 of the amount to the credit of her business in ointments and pills and to use the remaining £1,000 to pay sundry debts which she owed as she was going abroad. He carried out this request, but after the payment of his wife's debts there was £650 left over which he used for his own living expenses. Incidentally Hobbs retained £4,000 of the £25,000 as a fee for his services. He had cashed the first cheque for £150,000, but had parted with only £21,000 to the Robinsons, while Captain Arthur and Newton each got about £40,000. Furthermore, as soon as Mrs Robinson had reached the hotel where she was temporarily staying in London, Newton went into her room and took £10,000 of her money by force.

Meanwhile Sir Hari Singh had come to England with Captain Arthur, and the prince saw his solicitors, telling them what had happened, with the result that the second cheque was stopped. Sir Hari then returned to France with his suite, followed by Mrs Robinson and Mrs Bevan, who still hoped to make their way to Kashmir with their lovers. What exactly happened now is unclear, but when the two ladies reached Nice where they had arranged to meet the prince and his Indian secretary, they were interviewed by the French police and obliged to return to England, while Sir Hari and his entourage went on to Kashmir. The next thing that happened was that Newton with characteristic effrontery followed the prince to Kashmir hoping to persuade him to honour the second cheque. However, he was disappointed as the prince's wife died at this time and in accordance with custom the prince had to remain incommunicado for the protracted period of mourning.

When Sir Hari again became accessible, the blackmailing demands might have continued. But fortunately for him and the Kashmir treasury, the thieves quarrelled among themselves. Apparently Newton lost his share of the loot by injudicious speculation in coffee. However, he recouped himself to some extent from Captain Arthur who was now no longer in the prince's service, having no doubt come under suspicion. Arthur, who had lost money to Newton through gambling, now sued Newton for £1,700, his claim being for 'money lent' but he prudently settled out of court for £1,000. Arthur then tried to get more money out of Hobbs. Next, in July 1923, Newton sought out Robinson and revealed to him that Sir Hari Singh's price for dropping the divorce proceedings was not £25,000 as Hobbs led Robinson to believe, but six times that amount. Robinson thereupon consulted his regular solicitors and instructed them to issue a writ against Hobbs and his firm Appleton & Co., claiming £129,000, being £150,000 less the £21,000 Robinson and his wife had received. Hobbs's defence was that the plaintiff had entered into a scheme with another man (namely Montagu Newton) to pass himself off as Charles Robinson, the husband of Mrs Maud Robinson, at the same time claiming to be indemnified by Newton against any liability in respect of Robinson's threatened action.

As a result of enquiries made by Robinson and his solicitor, they called on the manager of the Kingsway branch of the Midland Bank, from whom they discovered that Hobbs had opened an account there for a 'Mr C. Robinson' with Sir Hari Singh's first cheque for £150,000 and that the whole of this amount had been drawn out by Hobbs with cheques singed 'C. Robinson'. Seeing that it was unlikely that Hobbs could pay the £129,000 claimed by Robinson, Robinson's solicitor, reinforced by counsel's advice, felt that his client had a strong case against the Midland Bank. If a bank is indiscreet enough to pay out a customer's money to an unauthorised person without proper investigation, they argued, then the customer was entitled to restitution by the bank. Also there was nothing illegal in receiving money as a condition for dropping divorce proceedings. In the result Robinson issued a writ against the Midland Bank claiming £150,000 less the £25,000 he and Hobbs had shared.

2

The civil action of *Robinson v. The Midland Bank* opened before Lord Darling and a special jury at the Law Courts in the Strand on 19 November 1924 and lasted for nine days. Actually Darling had retired from the High Court bench after twenty-six years' service but had been brought back as an additional judge to cope with the heavy backlog of work. Lord Halsbury, KC led for the plaintiff, and Sir John Simon, KC, MP, a former attorney-general and later Lord Chancellor, led for the defendant Bank. At the request of the India Office it was agreed that Sir Hari Singh, although he was not a party to the proceedings but was to figure prominently in them, should be referred to throughout as 'Mr A', while Captain Arthur should be similarly referred to as 'the ADC'.

In opening the plaintiff's case to the jury, Lord Halsbury remarked that the defendant Bank had set up 'the most hideous case of a blackmailing conspiracy of which you have probably ever heard.' The Bank must prove the conspiracy if they could, he said; it was no part of his client's case. But undoubtedly the question on which the jury had to decide was whether Robinson had anything to do with it. Halsbury's first witness was his client who deposed that as a boy he had emigrated with his parents to Australia where he was in his family business of wholesale butchers and then became a bookmaker. In 1898 he returned to England where he carried on as a bookmaker, and he had twice been made bankrupt. In 1908 he married his wife, he being thirty-four and she twenty-one. The marriage was quite a happy one at first, but later became strained. Nevertheless he more or less lived on his wife and was paid a salary for managing her pharmaceutical business, while they inhabited a big house with three acres of grounds and five or six servants including a groom and two gardeners. Shown the various cheques signed 'C. Robinson' which had been cashed at the Bank the witness denied that the signature was his. He admitted to having met Newton but he also denied that he had agreed with Newton that he should pose as himself (the witness) in the hotel in Paris where Mr 'A' was found with Mrs Robinson. Cross-examined by Sir John Simon, the witness agreed that Hobbs, Newton and 'the ADC' had conspired to trap Mr 'A' but he insisted that he was wholly innocent of any part in the conspiracy – indeed his main purpose in bringing the action, he said, was to prove his wife's innocence as well as his own.

Cross-examined by Sir John Simon, Robinson was obliged to admit that his career had not been particularly creditable. When he declared that he had once given a 'dud' cheque to someone at cards, the witness said the game was crooked so that the cheque was appropriate to the occasion. Questioned about the drawings from his wife's business, Robinson asserted that these were perfectly legitimate and rebutted Simon's suggestion that this was the channel through which he had received his share of Mr 'A's money.

Robinson was followed into the witness-box by his wife who described her unhappy experiences with Newton, who, she said, had seduced her and whose mistress she was for some time until he became supercilious and insulting. The reason why she asked Mrs Bevan to live with her at Chapel Street was that she was frightened of Newton, who had once threatened to tell her husband of their relations, and Mrs Bevan's presence in the house would prevent Newton from seeing her again alone. She swore that there was no collusion with Newton in Paris and that she did not know that he was there until he entered her bedroom when she was in bed with Mr 'A'. She later described what had happened with the money in Hobbs's office when she was given £21,000 and how Newton subsequently called at her hotel, and came into her room where he picked up a large packet of banknotes on the bed, and when she tried to stop him flung her across the room. She added that she had given her mother £3,000, the same amount to her husband, and something between £2,000 and £3,000 to Mrs Bevan because 'she had not got anything and I had been the means of upsetting a perfectly happy future for her.'

Cross-examined by Simon, Mrs Robinson insisted that the payments to her husband which appeared in her passbook related to her ointment business known as Grasshopper. Questioned about her Christmas visit to Paris in 1919 and why she and the others had moved from the Brighton Hotel to the St James and Albany, Simon suggested that it was Newton's idea so that he could use both entrances. No, Mrs Robinson asserted, it was Mr 'A's wish that they should move since he did not wish to compromise the ladies in the eyes of Captain Arthur who might report the affair to the India Office. She added that she had not the slightest idea how Newton knew which door led to her bedroom or how he managed to enter the suite. 'I have been wondering for the last five years,' she said, and went on to deny that she had unlocked the door so that he could enter. She also denied that the whole affair was pre-arranged with her husband and Newton, as Simon suggested, nor had she told Mr 'A' that Newton was her husband, although the prince first thought that he was. On the contrary, said Mrs Robinson, she told her lover that she must hurry back to London 'before that brute reaches my husband'.

At this point defence counsel turned to the judge. 'I have to ask this lady a question, my lord,' he said. 'It is a very painful thing to do, but I have to ask a question which is an intimate question, and I think I shall best consult her feelings if I just hand it to her written on a piece of paper.' Lord Darling agreed, provided he could see it. The plaintiff's counsel also asked to see it, and this too was agreed, although Lord Halsbury appears to have thought that if he were to deal with it the women on the jury – there were two – would be embarrassed. 'I can't help there being women on the jury, Lord Halsbury,' the judge interjected. 'The law was altered at their own wish, and there they are. They cannot leave the jury at a certain moment and then come back again.' However, Lord Darling said he would be willing that the women could do so provided the case went on with the remaining ten male jurors, but the two women could not return. Neither Halsbury nor Simon would agree to this, and so the trial continued as before.[2]

In fact there were four secret questions and although they were not published in the official account of the trial it is not difficult to reconstruct them, or their sense. The questions and Mrs Robinson's replies went something like this. Did you use an instrument? Yes. What was it? A safety razor. What was its purpose? To shave off my pubic hair. Why was this necessary? Because Mr 'A', in accordance with

[153]

oriental tastes, liked his ladies to remove any superfluous hair on their bodies. This practice was confirmed when plaintiff's counsel called a doctor who was secretly questioned and replied on paper as Mrs Robinson had done.

There was some difficulty with Hobbs, since neither side wished to call him as a witness although he had been served with a subpoena to produce cheques and other relevant documents. The judge therefore called him into the box, where he surprised everyone by saying that his office had been burgled and some of its contents stolen. Lord Darling told him to make another search, but when he was recalled he refused to produce the cheques, saying that he had never had them in his possession. Nor could he produce his passbook with the Paris branch of the Bank of South America recording that he had paid £120,000 of the blackmailing money into an account he had opened there. He cavilled when it was suggested that he should telephone Paris, so that Lord Darling told him that with all the money he had collected he ought to be able to afford a telephone call to France. He turned up next morning and gave an account of his difficulties in telephoning Paris and was generally unhelpful. Halsbury then called an accountant of the Bank of South America to prove that Hobbs had paid the money into the Paris branch in £1,000 notes and bought French bonds with them, of which roughly one third (£40,000) was transferred to Newton and another third to the ADC.

When the plaintiff's case was closed, Simon submitted to the judge that there was no case to go to the jury since there was no proof that the Bank ever undertook to be answerable for £150,000 or any other amount to *this* 'C. Robinson', i.e., the plaintiff, and moreover it was clear from the plaintiff's own story that the money still belonged to Mr 'A' since it had been obtained illegally from him by menaces. Secondly, the plaintiff's claim, if he had one, was against Appleton & Co. and not against the Bank. Thirdly, it was obvious that Hobbs never intended to transfer the money to the plaintiff and consequently he had no title to it. On reflection Lord Darling ruled that he could not give a decision on these arguments immediately and it would be better to postpone doing so until he had heard the defendant Bank's evidence.

In opening the case for the defence Sir John Simon naturally followed the lines of his cross-examination of the plaintiff and his wife. He ended his speech with a touch of drama. The Bank, said counsel, had learned

[154]

that Newton was willing to tell the whole truth about the affair, but he wished that his evidence could be taken on commission in Paris where he was staying, being understandably unwilling to place himself within the jurisdiction of the British courts and police who might well order his arrest for conspiracy and fraud. However, the plaintiff's legal advisers objected to this, as they were entitled to do so, and they insisted that if Newton were to testify, he must appear in person. 'The question was, could we get him here?' Simon asked, and himself answered, 'Well, Mr Newton, after some reflection with which we had nothing to do, decided that he was prepared to run the risk – and it is a very serious risk – of coming abroad to this country if he was promised a certain payment. We promised him £3,000.' Thereupon Sir John turned round and, pointing to a well-dressed man sitting behind him, exclaimed: 'Here *is* Mr Newton! And I call him into the witness-box.'

Neat, dapper and self-assured, Newton began by identifying Mrs Robinson in court and went on to describe her and her husband as old acquaintances as a result of business dealings he had had with her. His own share in the conspiracy began when Mrs Robinson telephoned him at his Mayfair flat in November 1919, he said, and asked him to visit her in Chapel Street.

'When you saw Mrs Robinson in Chapel Street in answer to her invitation, what did she tell you?' Simon asked him.

'She told me that she had met the ADC attached to Mr A,' Newton replied.

'Did she say anything about Mr A's position or resources?'

'That he was a man of great wealth.'

'She said that he was a man of great wealth?' queried the judge.

'A man of great wealth,' the witness repeated. 'She also said that the ADC was very dissatisfied with the way he was treated by Mr A – on account of his meanness – and it was suggested that money should be got from Mr A.'

'Did she say how?' asked Simon.

'Yes, she did,' the witness answered.

'How?'

'That she was to be discovered in bed with Mr A.'

'Yes, go on.'

'And she then suggested that I should take the part of her husband.'

[155]

'Did she give any reason?'

'Yes, she did.'

'Give it to me.'

'The reason she gave was that her husband did not look like the husband of a society lady.'

'Were you willing to contemplate this proposal?'

'Yes, I agreed to it. She, that is Mrs Robinson, then said, "I must have the approval of the ADC."'

'Was anything said as to how many people would be sharing the proceeds?' Simon went on.

'Well,' replied Newton, 'there were to be five people in it – herself, her husband, Mrs Bevan, the ADC and myself.'

'You said the ADC had to approve. What happened?'

'I met the ADC the following day in Chapel Street.'

'Was Mrs Robinson there?'

'Yes.'

'Had you seen the ADC before?'

'No, that was the first time I met him.'

'You knew the purpose of the meeting?'

'Yes, the ADC had to approve as to whether I would do for the husband.'

'Did he approve?'

'Yes, he thought I would be all right.'

Originally, Newton continued, the trap was to be sprung in Chapel Street, but difficulties arose, not least of which was Newton's rheumatism which troubled him, and he disliked having to wait outside the Chapel Street house in the cold since it was uncertain when Mr 'A' would appear, so the conspirators decided on Paris as a more comfortable location. When the ADC suggested that a solicitor would be required to arrange the matter in its final stages, the plaintiff suggested Hobbs, according to Newton. Asked about Mr 'A's reaction when he walked into the bedroom and found him in Mrs Robinson's bed, Newton declared, 'If it is possible for a coloured gentleman to turn green, he did.'

Later Newton was asked about his hearing what the state of affairs was between Mrs Robinson and Mr 'A'. 'Oh, yes,' he said, 'Mrs Robinson used to tell me everything. That he was getting very keen, but the longer she held him off the keener he would get. And then she

[156]

told me that at last it had happened. That was before they went to Paris.'

'Did she tell you, or did you learn, of an intimate matter connected with it?'

'Yes.'

The witness was then asked to write down on a piece of paper what he had learned, which he did. Sir John Simon then asked him another question. 'I am confident that the members of the Press will not report this question and answer: it is only relevant in order that the jury may follow. I want you further to write down the answer to this question. "Did you learn anything about the instrument used and did you yourself subsequently take any action having regard to the instrument used?"' This was the first open reference to the safety razor. Presumably what he wrote was the nature of the instrument and that his subsequent action was that he had got a respectable firm of jewellers to enamel a representation of a safety-razor on a match box which he gave to Hobbs as a souvenir of their coup. Incidentally it was due to a member of the firm who testified as to what the secret instrument was that it became publicly known.

Finally Newton denied that he had ever seduced Mrs Robinson, alleging that it was physically impossible for him to do so because she had had a hysterectomy.

Halsbury's cross-examination of this witness was directed as to credit, so that Newton was obliged to admit all the offences of which he had been convicted, blackmail, forgery, and so on. But he did not contradict himself and answered quite truthfully about his various villainies. The judge summed up strongly against the plaintiff and in favour of the finding of a conspiracy which he suggested could not be doubted on the evidence. He mentioned the secret instrument in passing.

We now know the thing was a razor, and I am very glad that it has been brought out, because it must have been very embarrassing to a respectable well-known firm to have it supposed that they would have anything to do with anything at all which it was not perfectly legitimate to deal with . . . They asked no questions. If you want a matchbox and if you want a safety-razor enamelled on it, it shall be done. There is no harm in that. And he [Newton] gave it to Hobbs.[3]

[157]

Finally Lord Darling put six questions to the jury. These were with the jury's answers:

1. Was there a conspiracy to entrap Mr 'A'?   Yes
2. Was the plaintiff a party to it?   No
3. Was Mrs Robinson a party to it?   No
4. Was Mr 'A' induced to pay through fear?   Yes
5. Did the Bank in paying out the £150,000 obey the mandate
   they had received?   Yes
6. Did Hobbs, in drawing out, purport to act under the same
   authority as in paying in?   Yes

On the last day of the trial Halsbury and Simon both asked for judgment to be entered for their respective clients. Halsbury yielded to Sir John who submitted that in view of the answers which the jury had returned to the judge's questions, the Bank was entitled to succeed. Lord Darling agreed with this argument, even though the jury had declared that both the Robinsons were innocent of the conspiracy charge. He also ordered that Mr 'A's cheque and other relevant documents should be sent to the Director of Public Prosecutions for possible action against Hobbs. Judgment was accordingly entered for the Midland Bank, with costs for what it was worth.

'The King's Bench Division has been called from earliest times to be the guardian of good faith,' Lord Darling declared in regard to the question of costs. 'Is it good faith for the plaintiff to make profit out of his wife's adultery? This is an action which should never have been brought, and which could not have been brought by a man whose mind was not thoroughly debased. The plaintiff will have no costs in this action.'

Robinson thereupon appealed, but he fared no better before the Court of Appeal than he had done in the lower court. He lost his appeal and in the result was ordered to pay all the costs of the further proceedings, so that in theory at least he ended up worse off than before.

3

Three months later, following Lord Darling's direction that the documents in the case in which he was the trial judge should be sent to the Director of Public Prosecutions, William Cooper Hobbs was prosecuted at the Old Bailey on charges of conspiring with Arthur and Newton to steal from Mr 'A' (whose real name like that of the ADC was now publicly revealed) and to defraud him, also with receiving two cheques signed by the accused knowing them to have been stolen. Hobbs had been arrested at Gravesend, as he was about to board a Dutch ship for Rotterdam in the company of another confidence trickster. He was taken back to London where he came up before the Bow Street magistrate who remanded him in custody. His trial began at the Old Bailey on 2 March 1925 before Mr Justice Avory, a much sterner judge than Darling, and lasted for nine days.[4] Travers Humphreys, the senior Treasury counsel, led for the prosecution, while the defence was led by Sir Henry Curtis-Bennett, KC, a leading practitioner at the criminal Bar, although Hobbs would have preferred Marshall Hall, but he was not available.

In opening the case for the prosecution Travers Humphreys began by summarising the events in the Mr 'A' case which have just been described. He went on to stress that, as the jury in the civil action had acquitted the Robinsons of any share in the conspiracy to blackmail Sir Hari Singh, he would conduct his case on this assumption. However, the judge remarked that the verdict of a jury in a civil case was not binding upon a jury empanelled at the Old Bailey and he repeated this several times in the course of the trial. The first prosecution witness was Newton, whom Humphreys said he would have greatly preferred to see in the dock beside the prisoner, were it not unfortunately that Hobbs's guilt could not be established without Newton's evidence, he having what is called turned King's evidence, that is although himself incriminated he agreed to testify for the prosecution in return for not being himself proceeded against. Humphreys also expressed regret that Captain Arthur, the third conspirator, had fled to France where the French authorities refused to extradite him on the grounds that in his case extradition was out of time.

Newton repeated his story that Arthur and Mrs Robinson suggested the blackmailing of Sir Hari Singh, and he now added that he went to consult Hobbs about the best way to carry out their plot. He was cross-examined vigorously by Curtis-Bennett about the details of his unsavoury past, but the witness made it clear that he was not and had never claimed to be a model of moral rectitude, agreeing that he had passed under many names in the course of his nefarious career. Incidentally he admitted that when he went to India after the Paris episode, he travelled under a passport in the name of Robinson but with his own photograph in it, and he took with him the second of Sir Hari's cheques which he hoped the prince would honour.

Sir Henry Curtis-Bennett, opening the defence, began by submitting that there was no evidence that Sir Hari Singh's two cheques had been stolen from him, so that count 1 (which charged Hobbs with conspiring with Arthur and Newton to steal them) and counts 3 and 4 (which accused him of receiving them, knowing them to have been stolen) should be withdrawn from the jury; likewise counts 5 and 6 (which charged him with having received the cheques, knowing them to have been unlawfully obtained). As for count 2 (which charged Hobbs with conspiring to defraud Sir Hari Singh), counsel submitted that there had been no such fraud so far as the prince was concerned in so far as he had parted with the cheques willingly. The judge agreed with Sir Henry as to counts 1, 3 and 4 and they were accordingly withdrawn from the jury, but he ruled that the other counts must be left to the jury and the defence must deal with them.

Hobbs was called into the witness-box and allowed to give his evidence seated, since he was obviously unwell and while in the dock had several times to receive medical attention. Briefly his story was that he had been misled by Newton, who posed as Robinson, into believing that Mrs Robinson was Newton's wife and the real Robinson was her brother, and that he had acted in good faith in negotiating with Captain Arthur for compensation to be paid to the injured husband, whoever he might be.

'It is your case', Humphreys began his cross-examination, 'that there was no conspiracy to defraud Sir Hari Singh?'

'It seems to me now that there was,' Hobbs answered, 'But I was no party to it.' The witness repeated what, he said, he honestly thought, namely that Newton was Mrs Robinson's husband. But Humphreys forced him to admit that he had been a witness to Newton's marriage. Hobbs countered this by asserting that the marriage in question was to another lady. In general counsel's questions demonstrated that Hobbs was much too shrewd a man to be easily deceived, especially by Newton whom he had known intimately over a long period.

Curtis-Bennett did his best for his client, arguing that the prosecution's case was too weak to justify a conviction since it rested on the evidence of 'the unspeakable Newton'. Curtis-Bennett begged the jury not to let Hobbs, whom he described as 'an honest, if foolish man', be made a scapegoat for the crimes of Newton and Captain Arthur, both of whom ought to be in the dock instead of the prisoner. Counsel also asked why had not Sir Hari Singh been called as a witness. To which Humphreys replied that there was no reason to do so, since the prince had never set eyes on Hobbs and so could provide no evidence of any value, whereas evidence of the Paris episode had already been given by Newton.

It did not take the jury long to find Hobbs guilty on the receiving and fraud counts which had been left to them. Curtis-Bennett thereupon asked the judge to confine his sentence to the fraud count and ignore the receiving counts, pleading that his client had only been brought into the conspiracy at a comparatively late stage and was also in poor health. Humphreys raised no objection to this, and in the event Mr Justice Avory sentenced Hobbs to two years' imprisonment, the maximum penalty for conspiracy, but much less than for the other counts on which he could have been given a long term of penal servitude.

This was not the last to be heard of Hobbs. On the day after his conviction, a number of newspapers published articles about him and his disreputable life story, and he sued several of them for libel when he came out of prison at the end of 1926. Some settled and others paid small sums of money into court, but in no case settled out of court did Hobbs obtain an apology or a withdrawal of the charges. He has the distinction of giving his name to a leading case in the law of libel on the question of the admissibility of evidence of bad reputation in mitigation of damages.[5] In 1938 he again appeared at the Old Bailey on a charge of forging the will of the well-known theatrical costumier and wig-maker Willie Clarkson who died suddenly and mysteriously. The only words in the will which were genuine were Clarkson's signature which had been written on a paper the contents of which had been obliterated by chemicals and the faked will largely in Hobbs's favour superimposed. For this he got five years' penal servitude, while his confederate, a solicitor named Edmond O'Connor, got seven. With his death in 1945, there passed away one of the most notorious figures in the criminal world of this century.

The subsequent history of the other figures in the Mr 'A' drama may be retailed briefly. Montagu Newton went abroad where he lived happily until after the Second World War. Captain Arthur, who was tried by a French court for his part in the conspiracy since it mostly took place on French territory, was sentenced to thirteen months' imprisonment, but as he had been in custody for almost the whole of that period he was released shortly afterwards. He too went abroad and died in the West Indies in 1939.[6] Mrs Robinson and Mrs Bevan, who remarried, vanished altogether from the scene, while Charles Robinson died in poverty and obscurity in 1946.

There remains the controversial figure of Mr 'A' himself. On 23 September 1925, Lieut.-General Sir Hari Singh succeeded his uncle as Maharajah of Jammu and Kashmir, comprising some 84,000 square miles. Like his predecessors, the new ruler was a Hindu, although the majority of his subjects were Muslims, and since they practised polygamy they would not have objected to His Highness's affair with Mrs Robinson even if they ever heard of it. He was not unpopular with his subjects, although he was not a particularly strong ruler. His personal life-style was lavish. He once had an aeroplane coated with silver, and he was a noted big-game hunter, racehorse owner and polo player. His visits to England included two India Office conferences and the Silver Jubilee celebrations of King George V and Queen Mary in 1935 when he arrived with a couple of dozen polo ponies, as well as carrying an umbrella and a mackintosh. But he could afford these luxuries since he had an annual income of two million pounds. During the Second World War he showed his loyalty to the British Raj by handing over the whole supply of his country's walnut for the manufacture of rifles. But the weakness he had shown in not defying Captain Arthur and the other blackmailers in the early 1920s was repeated when India and Pakistan were granted independence in 1947 and he vacillated on the question whether to adhere to India or Pakistan, the former being like himself predominantly Hindu in religion and the latter like most of his subjects Muslim. Consequently there was a Muslim revolt, supported by tribesmen from Pakistan. Sir Hari Singh abdicated in favour of his son Karan and fled to Delhi where he signed an agreement placing Kashmir under the dominion of India. Indian troops were despatched to Srinagar, the Kashmir capital, where they were opposed by Pakistan which backed the rebels. The matter was referred to the United Nations, and eventually the fighting was ended by a cease-fire in 1949, when the territory was divided between India and Kashmir along the cease-fire line, India gaining the major part constituting the Srinagar region along with Jammu.

Meanwhile Sir Hari Singh retired to Bombay where he was allowed to retain the title of Maharajah and given a share of Kashmir's privy purse. He died in Bombay on 26 April 1961.[7] His former palace in Srinagar is now a hotel which belongs to the Oberoi group. Few of the many tourists, who stay there in the Palace Hotel overlooking the beautiful Dal Lake and floating gardens, today recall that it was once the home of a Maharajah who was the central figure in a most sensational trial in London's Law Courts over sixty years ago. Nor are they aware for the most part that the activities of Sir Hari Singh and his ADC form the basis of one of AEW Mason's most successful novels.[8]

Who's Baby?
A Matter of Paternity

1

'MATERNITY is a matter of fact, but paternity is a matter of opinion.' So wrote the Roman jurist Gaius in the second century AD. The jurist's dictum can rarely have been so remarkably exemplified as in the famous divorce suit of *Russell v. Russell*, which by reason of the evidence given was the immediate cause of legislation being passed by Parliament to prohibit the publication of details of divorce proceedings in England and Wales. In fact, the case, which began in 1922 and caused enormous public interest at the time, involved two trials and two appeals, and it eventually led to a hearing before the Committee of Privileges in the House of Lords. The petitioner was the Hon. John Hugo Russell, eldest son and heir of the second Baron Ampthill, to whom he was to succeed as the third Lord Ampthill in 1935. In the divorce proceedings the petitioner charged his wife with committing adultery with three named men and one of unknown identity. The petitioner also denied that he was the father of the baby born to Mrs Russell during the period of their marriage.[1]

John Russell's childhood was spent in India where his father was governor of Madras and interim acting viceroy. After going through the Royal Naval College at Dartmouth, he joined the navy as a midshipman in 1912. Nicknamed 'Stilts' on account of his height (six foot six) John Russell was from the outset a dedicated sailor and popular with superiors and subordinates alike. He served throughout the Great War, qualifying as a submarine officer and taking part in numerous underwater patrols in the North Sea. In 1915 he first met his wife, Christabel Hart, who was then living with her widowed mother in Sussex, her father, a colonel in the Leinster Regiment, having died some years before. At this time John Russell was nineteen and his bride-to-be a year older. Two years later he proposed marriage and to his surprise he was rejected. Christabel thought she was in love with Gilbert Bradley who was a shipmate of John Russell's and together they went off to Scotland with the intention of getting married at Gretna Green; but unexpected difficulties arose, probably due to the necessary residence qualification, and they returned to England single.

Then in October 1918, Christabel wrote to John Russell agreeing to marry him if he still wanted her. He telegraphed his acceptance and they were married later that month in St Jude's Church, Kensington, by special licence, the ceremony being attended by the bride's mother but not by the bridegroom's parents who disapproved of the match. The day before the ceremony Christabel told John that she did not wish to have children 'to begin with' and he agreed. The first part of their honeymoon was spent at Harwich where the husband was stationed at the submarine base there. On their wedding night they went to bed together and John immediately rolled over and went to sleep without kissing his wife. They both woke up at three o'clock, and Christabel said: 'Is this all that marriage means?' Her husband reminded her of the promise he had given her about not having children immediately, and she kissed him and said she understood. There was no marital inter-course that night. The second part of the honeymoon was spent at Oakley, the Ampthill family home in Bedfordshire. The Ampthills now decided to accept their son's wife. However, Christabel took a dislike to her mother-in-law, who was a Lady of the Bedchamber to Queen Mary and who, Christabel rightly felt, considered that her son might have done very much better for himself in the way of marriage, perhaps even allying himself with a member of the royal family.

At Christmas 1918, John had ten days leave and during that time he and his wife became quite affectionate, Christabel submitting to her husband's kisses and embraces, although she disliked the physical results which followed in the form of incomplete sexual intercourse, when he would ejaculate between her legs. (She described this be-haviour as 'Hunish'). Meanwhile her husband gave her a copy of *Married Love*, the classic work on family planning by Marie Stopes which was first published at this time.

John Russell left the navy shortly afterwards and got a job with

[165]

Vickers, while Christabel and her mother opened a dress shop in Curzon Street, which proved very successful. Meanwhile Christabel hunted and danced with a variety of men including Gilbert Bradley. During the next two years she admitted that she only dined twice with her husband, who shared neither her bedroom nor her passion for hunting and dancing at both of which she excelled. While it is true that Christabel had numerous young men friends, there is no evidence that she misconducted herself with any of them. On the other hand, she felt that these extra-marital associations might induce her husband to petition for divorce for adultery or annulment on the ground of non-consummation of the marriage.

In an undated letter from the flat above the shop in Curzon Street which she shared with her mother, Christabel wrote to a woman friend, Miss Maud Acton, whom she had known for some years:

> Of course Stilts can make up a thousand things against me without going an inch out of his way. Every week-end I have spent with George Cross, and Gilbert [Bradley] (I stayed one night at Gilbert's flat and G. had to phone Stilts to bring my clothes so that I could get home again) and various others. All this John knows about in the fullest details, so he has only got to bring any of these facts against me and he has all the evidence he requires . . . I have been so frightfully indiscreet all my life that he has enough evidence to divorce me about once a week.[2]

In June 1921 Christabel Russell consulted a *clairvoyante*, who told her, much to her surprise, that she was going to have a baby. This prognostication was confirmed by her doctor and gynaecologist who informed her that she was seven-and-a-half months pregnant, but that she appeared to be a virgin. 'It is really extraordinary,' Christabel told her husband on 23 June. 'I suppose I must be another Virgin Mary!' At all events, the baby, a son named Geoffrey, was born four months later, on 15 October 1921 in a London nursing home in Devonshire Street.

Whoever was the father, said John Russell, he certainly was not, since there had been no form of affection between him and his wife after July or August 1920.

Here he was mistaken, since there had been on two nights in December 1920 when they were staying with the Ampthills in Bedfordshire and according to her account John Russell evinced the greatest delight over the child and even spoke of his kinsman the Duke of Bedford being a godfather. Then he suddenly changed his mind and decided to sue Christabel for divorce.

In filing his petition, the husband accused his wife of committing adultery with a man unknown. He also cited two other co-respondents, his former shipmate Gilbert Bradley, and Lieutenant Cross, an artillery officer stationed on Salisbury Plain who had trained a horse for her. Christabel was alleged, as already noted, to have spent a night with Bradley at his flat, and also to have visited hotels in Salisbury and Paris with Cross.

2

The trial opened before Lord Merrivale, formerly Sir Henry Duke, the President of the Divorce Court, and a special jury, on 7 July 1922. It lasted for ten days, Sir John Simon, KC, MP, led for the petitioner with two other 'silks', Mr Douglas Hogg, KC, MP, (later Lord Hailsham) and Mr R. F. Bayford, KC, and the Hon. Victor Russell, Mr Patrick Hastings, KC, and Mr Digby Cotes-Preedy, (later County Court judge) appeared for the respondent wife, while the co-respondents Bradley and Cross were represented by Mr Ellis Hume-Williams, KC, and Mr Bush James.

Sir John Simon opened the case for the petitioner, but left his client's examination-in-chief to Mr Douglas Hogg. In the witness-box Mr Russell described an interview which he had with his wife on 23 June 1921, when she told him for the first time that she was pregnant.

'You desired to be the father of a child in June 1921?'

'I did.'

'Did you read in *The Times* of the birth of a child to the respondent on 15 October 1921?'

'I did.'

'Were you the father of that child?'

'No.'

Hastings then began his cross-examination of the petitioner.

'When did you first come to the conclusion that your wife had committed adultery?'

'After she made the extraordinary statement to me on 23 June.'

'When did you first communicate with your lawyers?'

'After she made the statement to me. I had no idea with whom she had committed adultery, but as she was going to have a child I came to the conclusion that she had committed adultery.'

'If I proved in this Court that the child is yours, would you be glad or sorry?'

'You never could.'

'Answer my question,' said Hastings sharply. 'Would you be glad or sorry?'

'The child is not mine,' insisted the witness. Then, after a moment's pause, he added: 'I should be sorry.'

'Supposing that I am able to prove that in June 1921 your wife was a virgin,' Hastings continued, 'would that affect your view?'

'Not in the least.'

Mr Russell then described how his wife had spent the night in Bradley's flat after a dance, when she had lost the key of their own flat in Curzon Street, and how she telephoned for some day clothes which he brought round.

'When you found her in Mr Bradley's flat and you brought her clothes, you did not accuse her of adultery?'

'I believed my wife. But since she has had a child –'

'Then it all goes back to the child,' Hastings interrupted. 'Would you believe that she had committed adultery if she had not had a child?'

'I accepted her story at first,' said Mr Russell. 'If she had a child and I was not the father of it, it is quite obvious she has committed adultery.'

'Obvious?' queried Hastings. 'And you cannot discover who is the father of the child?'

'No.'

It must be admitted that the petitioner gave his evidence admirably. He was simple, manly and quite obviously speaking what he believed to be the truth, and it was clear that he had made a favourable impression on the jury. Hastings's task was not going to be easy.

In opening the case for Mrs Russell, her counsel began by saying that everything turned on what happened between the husband and wife on one or two nights during the latter half of December 1920. As the petitioner's case had been presented, the impression left on the jury's minds must have been that Mr Russell had done nothing which could

[168]

have resulted in the birth of a child. 'The truth is that not once but scores of times Mr Russell had partial intercourse with his wife which might have resulted in the birth of a child,' said Hastings. 'He did not know that it might so result, and she did not, but it now appears that the risk of conception was very great.' Hastings went on to point out to the jury that Mr Russell had not dared to call one doctor to say that what had happened between them could not have resulted in the birth of a child.

Mrs Russell then went into the witness box, where she gave her evidence with all the fire and determination of a woman who felt that she had been wrongly accused of a matrimonial offence. She began by describing her free and easy student life in the Latin Quarter of Paris, where young men and women were accustomed to go about together with little or no supervision. She also spoke of her war-work at a munitions factory where she had 2,000 people under her. On the question of the compact with her husband about children she did not want them at first as she wished to go on with her work. There had, however, been no agreement that they should never have children. At the time of her marriage, she emphasised, she was very devoted to her husband.

'Was there any reason except affection why you should marry him?' asked Hastings.

'Well,' she replied, 'I thought it would be nice to be no longer pestered by men to marry them. I thought it would be peaceful!'

About three days after their marriage, she went on in answer to her counsel's questions, her husband had attempted incomplete intercourse, and this incomplete intercourse took place frequently afterwards. She never thought it could result in the birth of a child. Her feelings of affection for her husband gradually decreased.

Mrs Russell went on to say that she often went out dancing in the evenings. She realised that her behaviour had been indiscreet, but everyone always knew everything she did. She admitted having been three times to Bradley's flat and to have gone to Paris twice with Cross, where they had rooms on separate floors. But she strenuously denied that she had been guilty of adultery with either, and this denial was repeated by each of the men in turn when they came to give evidence.

After a searching cross-examination by Sir John Simon, from which

[169]

she emerged completely unshaken, Hastings applied for the baby to be produced for inspection by the jury. After some argument the judge agreed and ordered the baby to be brought to the jury room during the luncheon interval.

Considerable expert medical testimony followed on the question of the possible limits of the duration of pregnancy and the variations in the period of gestation. The consensus of gynaecological opinion was that, assuming relations had taken place on 18 December, there was nothing inconsistent with the child's being born on 15 October of the following year.

After deliberating for five hours the jury found that neither Bradley nor Cross had committed adultery with Mrs Russell, but they could not agree on the question of adultery with the man unknown. Since there was no possibility of agreement on this point and since the parties refused to accept a majority verdict, the trial ended inconclusively with the discharge of the jury.

3

The second trial, which opened before Mr Justice Hill on 28 February 1923, lasted for eleven days, one day longer than the first trial.[4] Besides the alleged unknown adulterer there was another co-respondent called Edgar Mayer, who had helped Christabel to form her dressmaking company and for a time was a director. By this date Douglas Hogg had become Attorney-General and was debarred from accepting a brief in a private case, while Sir John Simon was otherwise engaged. The petitioner's solicitors went to see Hogg and asked his advice on whom they should now employ as their client's leading counsel. 'Well,' said Hogg, 'John Simon and I both failed where two co-respondents were cited. Now there's only one. There's only one man at the Bar who might pull it off for you. He might win you a brilliant victory, or he might make a terrible mess of it. But I really believe he's the only man who could do it – Marshall Hall.'[5]

Sir Edward Marshall Hall was very unwilling to accept the brief. 'I do not like to take a brief which has been hawked round the Temple', he told Russell's solicitors, saying he would think it over and let them know. He intended to refuse the brief, but Russell's mother Lady

[170]

Ampthill came round to his chambers and begged him to accept it. She was very distressed, according to Marshall Hall's biographer, and he was on the point of refusing, when he saw in Lady Ampthill a resemblance to his own mother. His emotional nature was touched and he accepted. 'I am going to do Simon's brief,' he wrote to his friend the playwright Sir Arthur Pinero, adding, 'I don't like doing cases after they have been tried once.' As in the first trial Patrick Hastings led for Christabel Russell and now Sir Ellis Hume-Williams led for the co-respondent Mayer.

There were three women members of the jury, of whom one was unmarried and the judge offered to excuse her from serving. 'The lady is unmarried,' said Marshall Hall, 'and it would save her hearing very unpleasant details.' 'I am inclined to agree', echoed Ellis Hume-Williams. 'I think the details will be found rather shocking to an unmarried lady. For a married one it would be different.'

'It is for you to decide rather than me,' said Mr Justice Hill, addressing the unmarried lady.

'I think I should be better employed elsewhere,' the lady in question replied.

'I am sure we all here think the same,' the judge rejoined, to the accompaniment of some laughter. Another male juror was then sworn.

This little interlude at the outset of the trial is mentioned as showing how people thought sixty odd years ago on sex matters. It would be unlikely to occur in the permissive age of today.

In his opening speech to the jury Marshall Hall quoted what Christabel had said to a friend on 27 June 1921 when she knew that she was pregnant: 'I have never done anything to be ashamed of in my life. I don't mind having an illegitimate child. I would rather it was anyone but John's, but as a matter of fact it is his. He behaved like a Hun. John walked in his sleep, and I found him in his pyjamas in the street sleep-walking. Is it not curious? That is how it happened.' Evidently she seems to have thought that conception had taken place after her husband had walked in his sleep and returned to bed still unconscious. But this was not so, since conception was due to incomplete intercourse, what is medically termed *fecundatio ab extra*.

Much of the evidence followed that given at the first trial, and it is unnecessary to repeat it. However, a significant incident occurred at an early stage in the hearing which must be mentioned, since it formed the

[171]

legal crux of the whole case. In the course of the petitioner's examination-in-chief by Marshall Hall, Mr Russell began to give evidence of
the cessation of all relations between himself and his wife in July 1920
when Hastings rose to his feet and objected that this evidence was
inadmissible. It was clearly established law, argued Hastings, that
evidence was not admissible, either by the husband or by the wife, to
prove the illegitimacy of a child born in wedlock and that marital
relations had not taken place when the opportunity for intercourse was
admitted to have existed.

'Do you say that rule applies to divorce proceedings, as well as to
petitions for declarations of legitimacy?' the judge asked counsel.

'Yes, my Lord,' said Hastings.

After considering the point, Mr Justice Hill ruled that the evidence
was admissible, and the trial proceeded on this assumption, which was
later to be overruled by a majority of the House of Lords.

The petitioner was again cross-examined by Hastings.

'During your married life you made frequent attempts to consummate your marriage?'

'I had incomplete relations.'

'Were you satisfied that they could not result in the birth of a child?'

'Yes.'

'Was your wife equally convinced that they could not?'

'Yes.'

'You now know that they might have resulted in the birth of a child?'

'Yes. I understand that it is barely possible.'

Mrs Russell then went into the witness-box for a second time.

'I must ask you what took place on the nights of 18 December and 19
December 1920,' said Hastings. 'Did you and your husband occupy the
same bed?'

'Yes,' replied the respondent. 'I remember that I threatened to kick
him out of bed unless he would leave me alone.'

'What was it that took place?'

'Relations of the same kind as had happened before.'

'Did you ever know that what had taken place would result in the
birth of a child?'

'No. I thought it impossible.'

'Have you ever committed adultery?'

'No.'

[172]

'Or has any other man had any relations with you of the kind your husband had?'

'No.'

'Would you have permitted any such thing?'

'No, and no man ever suggested such a thing.'

As for the named co-respondent, Mrs Russell stated that Mayer was purely a business friend; he had never attempted to make love to her or even to hold her hand.[6]

Marshall Hall's cross-examination of the respondent lasted for four hours and was a gruelling one; but Christabel stood up to him brilliantly as he questioned her about the most intimate details of her private life.

'Did you hear Lady Ampthill say that you had told her that you had taken the marital oath with reservations?' Marshall Hall began.

'It is not true,' replied Christabel. 'I told the clergyman I refused to obey any man, and if he made me say it I would make a mental reservation, and he said it was not necessary for me to say it.'

Later she said that she had spent two winters studying in Paris in the Latin Quarter and led the life of a student. 'That is what is called Bohemian life?' counsel asked.

'Yes,' the witness agreed. 'Very free and easy.'

'Were you an ignorant woman on sex matters when you married?' Marshall Hall continued.

'I knew absolutely nothing about them.'

'You were twenty-three years of age?'

'I was.'

'Did you believe Mr Russell loved you?'

'As much as I believe in the love of any man.'

'Did you ever ask your mother about sex relations?'

'I asked her why a wedding ring made women have babies.'

'Did you ever tell your mother that you believed if you kissed a man you would have a baby?'

'Not until long afterwards.'

At one point counsel asked her about the tears which had come into her eyes on one occasion when she had parted from her husband. 'Did they come genuinely to your eyes?'

'I do not know any other way of bringing tears to your eyes except by smelling onions.'

[173]

'Do you think our great actresses smell onions on the stage to produce tears?' asked Marshall Hall.

'I am not an actress,' the witness replied smartly.

'Are you not?' counsel retorted. 'I suggest you are, Mrs Russell, and were throughout the whole of your maried life.'

Questioned about her husband's statement that August 1920 was the last time he attempted physical relations with her, she replied: 'That most assuredly is a lie. My relations with my husband continued until we parted in April 1921.'

'You had been doing odd things about this time,' Marshall Hall continued. 'Your sleeping in Bradley's bachelor flat while he slept in the adjoining room was risky, was it not?'

'In view of events it might be considered so,' the witness admitted.

'Although you were riding a heavy motor-cycle, horse riding, and playing tennis a great deal, you say you never knew you were about to become a mother?'

'I did not until June 1921, when I went to the *clairvoyante*.'

In reply to Marshall Hall's question as to why she did not tell her husband she was going to have a child as soon as she met him in June 1921, Christabel Russell answered characteristically: 'You can't roar out in Dover Street, "I am going to have a baby". You can't even whisper it, and I am afraid I am not a sentimental type who says, "Stilts, old thing, I am going to have a baby."'

'You are not acting, are you now?' counsel asked the witness.

'No,' she replied, raising a loud laugh. 'I was only imitating you.'

'You have heard Mr Russell say on oath that he does not believe he is the father of the child?' Marshall Hall persisted.

'Doesn't believe it.' said the witness with contempt. 'He knows it!'

'You have indeed married a bad man?' was counsel's final query.

'I married a fool,' Christabel Russell replied with a defiant toss of her head.

After a long hearing in which the child itself was produced in the judge's room for the jury to see whether it looked like the petitioner, and various doctors and domestic servants were called to testify, Marshall Hall addressed the jury with characteristic passion. 'I ask you,' he concluded, 'to find a verdict in favour of John Russell, and free him from the tie which he once hoped would be a tie of love, but which is now a rusty chain that burns into his soul.'

In his closing speech to the jury, Hastings expressed deep regret on behalf of Mrs Russell that Mayer should have been dragged into court. 'Someone on this front bench where I sit lives in Curzon Street, and he is grateful that he has not been dragged into this case as a co-respondent,' said Hastings amid laughter. (It was realised that Hastings was referring to himself since he lived in Curzon Street.) 'I don't suppose there is a single male acquaintance of Mrs Russell who does not thank God he has not been made a party to this suit.' The real issue in the case, he went on, was the legitimacy of the baby. On that point an adverse decision by the jury would not indeed decide the question of succession, but 'it would send the little fellow out into the world with no father, a cast-off, whose mother had been divorced.'

In his summing-up, Mr Justice Hill put it to the jury that, if Mr Russell had satisfied them that he had had no sort of sexual relations with his wife in or about December 1920, then they ought to find that the child was not begotten by him and that Mrs Russell was guilty of adultery.

After an absence of nearly four hours the jury found Mrs Russell guilty of adultery with a man unknown, but not guilty of adultery with Mayer. The judge accordingly dismissed this co-respondent from the suit and, on the application of Sir Edward Marshall Hall, granted Mr Russell a decree *nisi*.

4

On her counsel's advice Mrs Russell appealed to the Court of Appeal, and several months later, on 23 and 24 July 1923, Patrick Hastings argued the appeal on her behalf with Marshall Hall against him, the Appeal Court consisting of the Master of the Rolls Lord Sterndale, Lord Justice Warrington and Lord Justice Scrutton. In the appellant's submission by her leading counsel, the rule laid down in numerous cases was that it was not permissible for a husband or wife to give evidence of non-intercourse in their marital relations so as to prove that a child so born, as in this case, was not the child of one of them. That rule, Hastings argued, applied to non-intercourse where access was admitted or proved, and naturally not to evidence of non-access, such as by absence abroad.

[175]

This argument was rejected, and the Court unanimously dismissed the appeal. In thus supporting Mr Justice Hill's ruling in the court below, Lord Sterndale held that, in a husband's suit for divorce on the ground of his wife's adultery, evidence of the husband that there was no intercourse where the parties admittedly occupied the same bed was admissible. Lord Justice Warrington added that in the Russell case there certainly was evidence upon which the jury could come to the conclusion that they did.[8]

Since such an important and controversial question of law was involved in this case, Hastings advised that it should finally be decided by the House of Lords. This was done; but by the time the case reached the supreme appellate tribunal, Hastings had become Attorney-General in the first Labour Government and he consequently could take no part in these further proceedings. The law lords, who heard the appeal, which began on 21 March 1924, were the Earl of Birkenhead, who as an ex-Lord Chancellor presided, and Lords Finlay, Dunedin, Sumner and Carson.[9] Hastings's place as leader for the appellant wife was taken by Stuart Bevan, KC, while Sir Douglas Hogg, who had returned to private practice following the defeat of the Conservative Government in the 1923 election, led Marshall Hall for the respondent husband. Marshall Hall, who had never argued a case in the House of Lords before, asked Hogg to do this, as he doubted his own abilities to lead in such a case in the highest court in the land.[10]

Stuart Bevan began by stating that the appeal rested on three grounds – first, that the verdict in the court of first instance was against the weight of the evidence. As to the first point, Hogg submitted that it was not open to the appellant since it had been abandoned by her counsel in the Court of Appeal, and was so treated by the Court. Birkenhead on behalf of himself and the other law lords agreed that it had been so abandoned, but ruled that nevertheless it could be raised after the other points had been dealt with. Their lordships similarly intimated that no case for misdirection had been made out, so that the only point which remained to be argued was that of the admissibility of evidence tending to bastardise a child born in wedlock.

The appeal lasted for four days, Bevan's argument taking three days and Hogg's followed by a brief reply from Marshall Hall on the fourth. Birkenhead said afterwards that the legal argument between Bevan and Hogg was the finest he had ever heard, and as Hogg sat down Birkenhead whispered to Dunedin: 'How can that possibly be wrong?' Birkenhead then said that the House would take time to consider it. Their judgments were delivered on 30 May 1924, when the appeal was allowed by the narrow majority of three to two, Birkenhead, Finlay and Dunedin forming the majority, with Sumner and Carson dissenting. Thus the verdict in the court of first instance was set aside and a new trial ordered.[11]

'My own impression may be stated at once,' said Lord Birkenhead in delivering the majority judgment, 'that unless the evidence given by the husband, the petitioner, was in law receivable there was no evidence to go to the jury at all. . . . I have formed the clear opinion that such evidence is not receivable.' He based his opinion on a number of authorities, the most important going back to the eighteenth century when it was laid down by Lord Mansfield that 'it is a rule founded on decency, morality and policy that they (that is the spouses) shall not be permitted to say after marriage that they had no connection and that therefore the offspring is spurious.' The rule's application to legitimacy proceedings was everywhere conceded, said Birkenhead. 'Our task, therefore,' he went on, 'is to determine whether evidence inadmissible in such proceedings is admissible in divorce.' In view of the authorities which he cited at length, he concluded that it was not, adding that if this was considered to be an intolerable inconvenience, it was up to Parliament to provide a remedy by changing the law. This is precisely what Parliament was to do twenty-five years later.*

The case now went back to Mr Justice Hill in the Divorce Division of the High Court with a view to a new trial. The matter came before this judge on 27 June 1924 when Marshall Hall informed him that the petitioner could not afford a new trial, particularly as he was now debarred by the judgment of the House of Lords from giving evidence of non-access such as he had given in the previous trial. There was also the question of costs, John Russell having already paid his wife's solicitors £8,640 as her taxed costs, and he still had to pay the costs of the proceedings in the House of Lords besides his own costs of

---

* The principle of the House of Lords decision, known as the rule in *Russell v. Russell*, remained law until 1949, when it was abolished by the Law Reform (Matrimonial Causes) Act. This statute was re-enacted by the Matrimonial Causes Act, 1950, with the result that such evidence of access as that given by the petitioner in this case is now admissible.

[177]

the two trials and the appeals, estimated altogether as more than £30,000.

In reply to Stuart Bevan, who appeared for Christabel Russell, Mr Justice Hill rescinded the decree *nisi* and made the judgment of the House of Lords an order of the High Court. Thus by implication Christabel was not an adulteress and her child was legitimate.[12] Two years later, on 29 July 1926, formal effect was given to this implication by Mr Justice Swift when a declaration of legitimacy was sought by the child's maternal grandmother and guardian *ad litem* Mrs Blanche Hart, and this judge formally declared Geoffrey Denis Erskine Russell to be 'the lawful child of his parents, the Hon. John Russell and Christabel Hulme Russell.' Incidentally Christabel, who gave evidence at this hearing, stated that her husband had never contributed to the support of their son, nor had he ever recognised the child as his. In fact he never even once saw him in the flesh.[13]

Thereafter the Russell baby case, as it was commonly known, was only occasionally mentioned in the press. Once was on the death of the second Lord Ampthill on 7 July 1935, when John succeeded to his father's title and Christabel became Lady Ampthill. Another occasion was in 1937 when Christabel divorced her husband, the suit being undefended. The third occasion was in 1973 when John died after a successful career as a director of Gallaher's, the tobacco manufacturing company in Belfast. The question now arose, who was to succeed him? After Christabel divorced him he had remarried twice, his second wife dying childless and his third wife having a son and a daughter by him, the son John being born in 1950.

Geoffrey Russell's claim to succeed his father in the Ampthill title and sit in the Upper House was contested by young John. The matter was considered for four days in February 1976 by the Committee of Privileges in the House of Lords, comprising nine peers, laymen and law lords. The Committee pronounced its findings on the following 26 April, but by this date the indomitable Christabel was dead, so that she never knew that Geoffrey, by this time a successful theatrical impresario and the father of a family, was officially confirmed the lawful heir and the fourth Lord Ampthill.[14] One of the law lords, Lord Russell of Killowen, who was not related to the Ampthill Russells, stated that in essence young John's case amounted to an attempt to appeal fifty years out of time from the 1926 declaration of Mr Justice Swift. Furthermore there had been important legal and scientific changes since then. The Birkenhead ruling on the inadmissibility of a spouse's evidence to bastardise his or her issue had long since been abrogated by statute, and new techniques such as blood tests had come to be used in proving or disproving paternity. Incidentally Geoffrey Russell, through his counsel Sir John Foster, QC, refused to make available the blood tests carried out on him and his mother. 'It would be putting Geoffrey in an Agatha Christie position,' said Foster. 'Someone could have substituted the blood samples, or mixed them up in the laboratory. There were lots of opportunities for something criminal being done, not necessarily by someone in the case.'

While displaying sympathy for the twenty-six-year-old John Russell, Lord Wilberforce, the chairman of the Committee of Privileges, came down strongly on the side of Geoffrey.

Declared the lawful son of his parents in 1926, treated, as documents show, for the purpose of family settlements as legitimate, having married and founded his own family on the assumption of legitimacy, he is now, after fifty years, when both his parents, and probably other contemporaries of his birth, are dead, to have his status questioned, to be graded as some kind of fictional issue which cannot rank as lawful issue, or qualify as such under the terms of the barony. This cannot be the law. If ever there was a case for closing the chapter in a family's history, the case for closing this in 1926, after the distressing revelations over so many years, must be one.

A few final words about Christabel. She brought up her son Geoffrey with marked affection and gave him all the comforts she could afford. Fortunately she made money from her business activities and this enabled her to send the boy to Stowe, a top public school, whence he was able to join the army in the Second World War and to secure a commission in the Irish Guards. After the war she settled in Ireland where the hunting was very much to her taste with packs like the Galway Blazers and the Ballymacad in County Meath, of which she was Joint Master for three years. She always rode side-saddle and was impeccably turned out as was her mount wherever she hunted. Eventually she bought an old castle called Dunguaire, a sixteenth-century building at Kinvara on an outlet of Galway Bay which had previously been acquired by the Irish surgeon and poet Oliver St John Gogarty to save it from demolition. This place with its superb view over the bay to the Connemara mountains she cleverly restored with the help of a friendly architect who liked her and the place so much that he charged her nothing for repairing the roof.

It was at a lunch party in the home of Gogarty's daughter Brenda Williams nearby that the present writer met Christabel Lady Ampthill for the first and only time. I remember we talked a lot about hunting for which I shared her enthusiasm, and I particularly liked her story of the huntsman she knew who died and was buried as he wished, not lying down, but upright in the earth, so that even in death (as he hoped) he might hear the hounds giving tongue as they passed over his head. She invited me to lunch at Dunguaire, an invitation which for personal reasons I declined, but looking back now regret that I did so. She continued to ride and hunt well into her seventies.

In 1972, wanting a change of scene, she disposed of Dunguaire Castle to the Irish Tourist Board, which now uses it as a showpiece for medieval banquets and the like. 'Taking herself to Australia, she rode across most of this continent on a horse, bought a van and drove home, alone, at the age of seventy-eight. Arriving spick and span in London three months later, it emerged that the van was unlicensed and un-insured and she had mislaid her driving licence. But her character and personality had, as usual, triumphed.'[15] She died on 16 February 1976, in hospital in Galway, aged eighty. Had she lived a few months longer, she would have had the satisfaction of seeing her son Geoffrey take his seat in the House of Lords. As she told her friend and biographer Eileen Hunter on one of the rare occasions on which they discussed the Russell baby case, 'I knew I would win *eventually* . . . Besides right always triumphs in the end.'[16]

When the Kissing Had to Stop

1

THERE has been a considerable number of cases involving the kissing or attempted fondling of girls in public parks, notably Hyde Park, and also in railway trains, particularly in the days when there were no through corridors and the coaches consisted of separate carriages. Most of the kissers have been ordinary folk charged with improper behaviour or indecent assault as the result of their actions. But there were two cases in the past hundred years or so involving men in public life, both writers. The first individual, in 1875, was a British army officer, Colonel Valentine Baker of the 10th Hussars. The second, in 1928 and again in 1933, was an ex-MP and Liberal government minister Sir Leo Chiozza Money. Only the latter's career was permanently blighted after the second case, in which he was convicted. On the other hand, Colonel Baker began a new career in the Turkish army where he was known as Baker Pasha and in which he served with such distinction that while fighting the Arab rebels in the Sudan he was temporarily taken on to the staff of his old regiment, since Egypt was then under British occupation.[1]

Valentine Baker's father was a successful West India merchant who possessed property in Jamaica and Mauritius as well as in Gloucestershire. His elder brother was the explorer Sir Samuel Baker, whose discovery of Lake Albert Nyanza revealed the source of the Nile. Valentine, who shared his brother's interest in exploring, accompanied him on an exploratory expedition to Ceylon where he joined the Ceylon Rifles as an ensign. His military rise was rapid and after the Crimean War in which he fought he was appointed to the command of the 10th

Hussars. This position he held for thirteen years, during which period he gained a reputation as an authority on cavalry tactics. In 1873 he travelled on a reconnaissance mission to Persia where he spent about nine months, and although he failed to reach Khiva he collected a quantity of valuable information which was later published in book form as *Clouds in the East*. This work and his political and strategical reports were perhaps the most important attempt of its kind to draw public attention to the advance of Russia in Central Asia which was a threat to India. In 1874, after his return from St Petersburg where his mission terminated, he was appointed Assistant Quarter-Master-General of the Army at Aldershot. It was in the summer of the following year that the episode in the railway train occurred.

During the afternoon of 17 June 1875, a young and attractive lady of good family, Miss Rebecca Kate Dickenson, was travelling alone in a first-class railway carriage from Midhurst to London. At Liphook a middle-aged gentleman entered her compartment and took a seat opposite to her. He began to talk to her on a variety of subjects, and, discovering that they had some interests in common, she reciprocated. The gentleman, who was wearing civilian clothes, was Colonel Baker. On leaving Woking, he suddenly suggested that she should correspond with him. On her refusal, according to her, his manner changed and, crossing over to the seat beside her, sat down, putting his arm round her waist and kissing her repeatedly. This conduct so terrified her that she screamed for help, opened the carriage door and tried to jump out. The passengers in the adjoining compartment, hearing her cries, looking out of the window and seeing her standing on the footboard, stopped the train by pulling the communication cord. As the guard arrived to find out what had happened, Colonel Baker, who had not told her who he was, endeavoured to reassure her. 'Don't say anything', he begged her. 'If you do, you don't know what trouble you will get me into. Just tell him you were frightened.'

However, the guard, seeing that she was in a state bordering on collapse and suspecting that something was amiss, asked a clergyman among the passengers to attend her, which he did. On reaching Waterloo, Colonel Baker was escorted to the railway police superintendent's office, where he gave his name and his address as the Army and Navy Club, Pall Mall. But he refused to give any explanation of his conduct, beyond declaring that Miss Dickenson 'had reported the case incorrectly'. The colonel's name and address being verified, he was allowed to return to Aldershot. There he was arrested next morning by the Deputy Chief Constable of Surrey on a warrant charging him with 'indecent assault'. Incidentally Baker had been married for ten years and had two daughters.

Colonel Baker appeared at Guildford police court and was committed for trial at the next county assizes at Croydon, being granted bail in his own recognizances of £2,000 and two sureties of £1,000 each, which were furnished by his brother Sir Samuel Baker and Viscount Valentia, a fellow officer in the 10th Hussars. When the summer assizes opened on 30 July before Mr Justice Brett, afterwards Lord Esher, the grand jury returned a true bill. Baker's counsel asked for an adjournment to the next spring assizes and also that a special jury might be empanelled. The prosecution opposed this application and the judge agreed, further ordering that the accused's bail should be doubled until the trial which had been set down for 2 August.

Baker was defended by Henry Hawkins, QC, afterwards Lord Brampton, one of the most brilliant advocates of his time. He pleaded not guilty, but as the law then was he could not go into the witness-box and give evidence in his own defence, whereas of course his accuser was able to do so. After Miss Dickenson had told her story in the witness-box she should in the normal course have been cross-examined by Baker's leading counsel. But from a rare sense of chivalry Baker refused to allow him to do this. 'I was debarred by his express instructions from putting a single question,' Hawkins said afterwards. All Hawkins could do was to suggest to the jury that the gravity of the charge had been exaggerated. But to no avail. It only took the jury a quarter of an hour to find the accused guilty.

'You have attained a high rank and reputation,' said the judge in passing sentence. 'I cannot forget that for your distinguished services in the past your country is indebted to you . . . I hope that some future day you may be allowed, by some brilliant service of which you are capable, to wipe out the injury you have done to yourself and the dishonour you have done to your country. Yet I must pass a severe sentence upon you, and that sentence is that you be imprisoned for twelve months in the common gaol, that you pay a fine of £500, and that you also pay all the costs of the prosecution, and be further imprisoned for three months until they are paid.' He was consequently dismissed from the army, in

[183]

the words of the *London Gazette*, 'Her Majesty having no further use for his services.'[2]

'I say to his honour', said his counsel recalling the case some years later

> that, as a gentleman and a British officer, he preferred to take to himself the ruin of his own character, the forfeiture of his commission in the army, the loss of his social status, and all that would make life worth having, to casting even a doubt on the lady's veracity in the witness-box . . . The manliness of his defence showed him naturally to be a man of honour, who, having been guilty of serious misconduct, did all he could to amend the wrong he had done: and so he won my sympathy in his sad misfortune and misery.

On the other hand, some members of the public considered the sentence was one of 'excessive leniency' and that 'favouritism' had been shown towards him. However, the novelist and dramatist Charles Reade took a contrary view, assessing that, if the accused in this case had been a navvy, he would have got off with a month's hard labour at the most.

Baker served his sentence in the gloomy old Horsemonger Lane Gaol, along with numbers of robbers, thieves and pickpockets, which must have been a sore trial to a man of his habits and temperament. On his release he went to Constantinople where he learned that because of the strained relations between Turkey and Russia war was likely to break out between these two powers. The Sultan Abdul Hamid II accepted his services and appointed him a major-general in the gendarmerie. During the ensuing Russo-Turkish war he was given the command of a division in Bulgaria. Here he acquitted himself so well against the Russians that he was promoted to the rank of lieutenant-general. Commonly known as Baker Pasha he continued in the Sultan's service and after the conclusion of the war he was commissioned to superintend the carrying out of the proposed Turkish reforms in Armenia. In 1882 he was offered the command of the newly formed Egyptian army which he accepted, but on arriving in Cairo he found that the offer had been withdrawn and instead he was appointed Chief of Police. Making the best of a bad job, Baker Pasha transformed the Egyptian police into a para-military force of gendarmerie acting in conjunction with the native troops. In February 1884, when the Sudan War broke out, he led a body of 3,500 troops and gendarmerie against the Arab rebels. He was attacked by an enemy force of barely a thousand at El Teb. Unfortunately the bulk of his men threw down their arms in a panic and fled, allowing themselves to be slaughtered indiscriminately without putting up the slightest resistance. However, Baker Pasha and a few of his officers succeeded in fighting their way out, and shortly afterwards British troops of the 10th Hussars arrived in Suakin under the command of Sir Gerald Graham, who appointed Baker to the intelligence staff of his old regiment. Baker Pasha guided the British force to the scene of his defeat and at the desperately fought second battle of El Teb, in which Baker was wounded, the British force was victorious.

In recognition of his personal gallantry at El Teb, strong efforts were made by Valentine Baker's friends to reinstate him in the British Army. The Prince of Wales (later King Edward VII), who had served under him at the Curragh in Ireland, the army Commander-in-Chief the Duke of Cambridge, the Adjutant-General Lord Wolseley and Sir Evelyn Baring (later Lord Cromer), the British Resident in Cairo, warmly supported the proposal. But Queen Victoria was adamant. Rules were rules, and in her opinion an officer who had once lost his commission, especially for misconduct, could never regain it.

Baker Pasha thus remained in command of the Egyptian police until his death from heart disease at Tel-el-Kebir in 1887. He was buried with full military honours in the English cemetery at Cairo. Four years later, his only surviving child Sybil married Sir John Carden, the fifth baronet, of Templemore, County Tipperary.[3]

2

Leo George Chiozza Money was the son of an Italian father Joseph Chiozza and English mother Gwendolen Stevenson, and he was born in Genoa. As a young man he came to England where he became a journalist, editing a city journal on commercial intelligence and assuming the additional surname of Money. In 1906 he entered the House of Commons as Liberal Member for North Paddington, transferring to East Northants in 1910 which he represented for the following eight years. On the outbreak of the Great War he served on committees dealing with war trade and restriction of enemy supplies, in which capacity he attracted the attention of Mr Lloyd George, whose parliamentary private secretary he became in 1915 when Lloyd George was Minister of Munitions. In the same year he was knighted for his public service. As Parliamentary Secretary to the Ministry of Shipping in 1917 his most conspicuous achievement was to propose the successful Atlantic concentration of ships' convoys to counter the attacks of enemy submarines. At the end of the war he resigned from the Liberal party and joined Labour, but he failed to win a seat at the General Election of 1918 under his new party political colours. Thereafter he devoted himself mainly to writing, poetry as well as prose, editing among other literary ventures the economic, industrial, financial, engineering and sociological sections of the 14th edition of the *Encyclopedia Britannica*, originally published in 1929. He was fifty-eight years old at this time and was married with a grown-up daughter.[4]

About 9.45 on the evening of 23 April 1928, Sir Leo and a young woman, Miss Irene Savidge, who was engaged to be married and worked for the Standard Telephone Company, were sitting on two chairs under a tree near the Albion Gate entrance to Hyde Park, talking and smoking cigarettes, when they were suddenly arrested by two police officers in plain clothes who informed them that they would be charged with indecent behaviour contrary to the Parks Regulation Acts. 'You must be mad,' Sir Leo exclaimed. 'We have done nothing wrong and nothing improper. We are most respectable people.' However, they were both taken to Hyde Park police station, Sir Leo putting up a struggle on the way. A man who had seen Sir Leo leave his umbrella by his seat ran after them, but the police constables did not ask the man for his name and address but simply took the umbrella which was returned to Sir Leo. At the police station the two constables repeated the charge to the sergeant on duty, and the two alleged delinquents were released on bail and instructed to appear at Great Marlborough Street Police Court next morning. Sir Leo then asked if he could telephone the Home Secretary and was told that he could telephone anyone he liked. Sir Leo then called the minister at his house but he was out. Next morning Sir Leo and Miss Savidge duly appeared at Great Marlborough Street and were remanded on bail for a week. During this period Miss Savidge was medically examined and found to be a virgin.

At the next hearing Sir Leo Money, who was defended by the popular advocate Sir Henry Curtis-Bennett, KC, went into the witness-box and repeated his denial of the charge. He had been introduced to Miss Savidge by a mutual friend, Miss Marie Egan, he said, and he had met Irene Savidge seven or eight times either alone or with Miss Egan. Irene's parents knew of her friendship, the witness went on, and he would usually take her to a cinema and then for dinner at a restaurant. This was what happened on the evening of their arrest. As for his struggle with the police on the way to the station he had only struggled when the police refused to let him get the man with his umbrella as a witness, since, as the magistrate remarked, this individual must have been pretty close to the couple at the time of their arrest.

As Miss Savidge was about to leave the dock for the witness-box, the presiding magistrate, old Etonian Henry Chancellor, made a dramatic intervention. 'After hearing the case so far and the positive denial Sir Leo has given,' he observed, 'I have heard enough and have come to the conclusion that both defendants are not guilty.' He therefore dismissed the charge against them with costs of ten guineas against the police. In doing so the magistrate stated that he did not think that anything would be gained by exposing Miss Savidge to the ordeal of going into the witness-box. At the same time the magistrate criticised the police on two grounds: first, for not taking the opportunity they had of obtaining corroborative evidence of the man with the umbrella, and secondly, for not sending their reports immediately to Scotland Yard so that the Metropolitan Police Commissioner might, if he thought fit, proceed by summons instead of the accused being charged straight away and taking them to the police court next morning. 'If that had been done in this case,' said the magistrate, 'I am certain that this case would not have been brought and a great deal of pain and a most unpleasant ordeal would have been avoided.'[5]

Interviewed after the case by the popular Sunday newspaper *News of the World*, Miss Savidge, who was described as 'an attractive blonde, with fair, wavy hair, who lives with her father, mother and two brothers', was said to be 'naturally upset by the unpleasant publicity' which she had received. The interview continued:

She stated that she and Sir Leo were discussing matters of industrial economics, in which she had been for a long time interested, when they were confronted by the police. 'When those men came up to us in Hyde Park,' she related, 'I thought they were robbers, and I was going to call out for the police. I thought they were going to take us to some quiet spot and try to blackmail us. Even when we went into the police station I did not quite understand what had happened. It was not till we were at the police court next day that the seriousness of the situation began to dawn upon me.

Lady Money was perfectly sweet to me the whole time, as was her daughter. After the case was dismissed, she congratulated me, and asked me to have tea with her. I rushed off, however, to my fiancé's place of business to tell him what had happened. He has been splendid about it, and never doubted me for a moment.'

The fiancé, who was described as a tall, handsome young man, declared, 'I have absolute faith in her, and I told her that whatever the verdict I would stick to her.' Miss Savidge had a similar welcome from her fellow workers when she went back to the Standard Telephone Company's factory at New Southgate. 'It was simply splendid,' she said afterwards. 'Everyone crowded round and congratulated me on having cleared my character and they made me feel quite happy again.'

Sir Leo Money, who told the Press that he reckoned the defence would cost him something in the region of £200, much more than the paltry sum awarded by the magistrate, immediately got busy through his parliamentary connections. A few days later the matter was raised in the House of Commons, when it was suggested that the police evidence was perjured. The Home Secretary, Sir William Joynson-Hicks, familiarly known as 'Jix', was asked in view of the results of recent prosecutions in such cases as that of Sir Leo Money and Miss Savidge, whether he was 'satisfied that sufficient care is taken to establish the trustworthiness of the evidence before the charge is made.' The Home Secretary replied that he would have to consider with the appropriate authorities whether the police officers concerned in this most recent case were guilty of perjury or other breach of duty. He added, in language which caused considerable amusement, both inside and outside Parliament, that, in view of the suggestion that Sir Leo had been discovered kissing, as alleged by the police, 'it is not illegal for any young member of the community to take any equally young lady to

Hyde Park to sit in the Park, and it is not illegal to salute her with a chaste embrace.' Cartoons appeared in the newspapers showing the embrace taking place, with 'Jix' in the guise of Cupid making a careful inspection assisted by two constables with flashlights.[6]

The Home Secretary now instructed the Director of Public Prosecutions to make a full investigation into the possibility of perjury by the two police constables. The Director was also asked to ascertain, if he could, not only what were the character and reputations of Sir Leo Money and Miss Savidge, but also the whole circumstances of their association, since if they were not considered potentially reliable witnesses for the prosecution, it would be useless to prosecute the two constables. The Director accordingly asked the Metropolitan Police Commissioner to recommend an experienced CID officer to undertake the investigation, and the Commissioner recommended Chief Inspector Collins who was instructed, after reporting on the police constables' record, to see Miss Savidge, Miss Egan, who had introduced Miss Savidge to Sir Leo Money, and finally Sir Leo himself, in that order.

Next day, 15 May 1928, two policemen and a policewoman Wpc Wyles called at Miss Savidge's place of work in the Standard Telephone Company's New Southgate factory where she was employed in testing radio valves, and they took her to Scotland Yard for questioning telling her that they wished 'to clear up a few points about the Leo Money case,' although she told them that she thought the case was finished. What happened there was raised two days later by Thomas Johnston, Labour MP for Dundee, in the House of Commons on a motion for the adjournment.[7] Mr Johnston alleged that during a five-hour interrogation by Chief Inspector Collins Miss Savidge had been subjected to 'third degree' treatment, and allegations of familiarity on the part of the police officers present were supported by an affidavit sworn by Miss Savidge to her solicitors, part of which was quoted by Mr Johnston.

I was then requested to give full particulars of the clothes I was wearing and what Sir Leo was wearing. They first requested me to stand up so that they could see the length of my clothes, which I did. I gave them full particulars of the clothes I was wearing. There was no woman present. They inquired whether I wore a petticoat, and, if so, what colour, and they made the statement that it was a very short petticoat I was wearing.

[189]

According to Miss Savidge, Inspector Collins said to her: 'Now you are a really good girl, and you have never had a man, have you? But there are several things you could do without real sin. Don't be afraid to tell us, as we are looking after you.' The officer then sat down beside Miss Savidge and asked for a demonstration of what had happened in Hyde Park, saying 'When we were young, we had a good time ourselves. We are only making these inquiries, you know, for the sake of the police officers whose conduct is being inquired into.' The Inspector then put his arm round Miss Savidge's waist to show how, possibly, Sir Leo might have behaved. Her affidavit continued:

> The officer said, 'Now perhaps you can't remember, but he may have put his hand on your knee', and at the same time he placed his hand on my knee. He said, 'Are you sure he did not put his hand up your clothes?' I told them that no such act or anything approaching such an act had taken place. The officer said to me, 'As you and Sir Leo were sitting with your arms linked, is it not possible that he took your hand and put it somewhere without you having noticed?'

'Then', said Mr Johnstone, 'proceeded what, I suppose, is called a practical demonstration of where the hand might have been placed. The inspector put one of the girl's hands on his thigh by way of suggesting where the girl might have put her hand during the alleged incident in Hyde Park. She was asked whether she could remember whether or not her legs were crossed . . . After five hours of this treatment without any opportunity given her of being assisted by legal advisers, without even a woman police chaperone being present, that girl was released from what I can only describe as a third degree examination. She was taken home in a car. She was questioned in the car about her father's income and her fiancé's income . . . When she got home she collapsed. 'The officers', she said in her affidavit 'repeatedly warned me that I was not to say a word to anybody that I had been at Scotland Yard or that I had made a statement, and I would never hear any more of this matter, and this was repeated to me after my arrival home.' Later the same night Sir Leo Money called there and told her there was no need for her to have gone to Scotland Yard. He found her hysterical.

In response to Mr Johnstone's request for an inquiry into the proceedings at Scotland Yard, supported by other Members, the Home

Secretary promised that the fullest inquiry should be held. Shortly afterwards Joynson-Hicks appointed a tribunal consisting of Sir John Eldon Bankes, a former Lord Justice of Appeal as Chairman and two others, one Conservative MP Mr J. J. Withers, and one Opposition Labour MP Mr H. B. Lees-Smith. The Tribunal commenced its public sittings in the Law Courts on 6 June, Norman Birkett leading for the police and Patrick Hastings and Henry Curtis-Bennett representing Miss Savidge. Sir Leo Money declined to appear before the tribunal and testify.[8]

It is unnecessary to recapitulate the evidence given before the tribunal since much of it has already been indicated. But one passage in Norman Birkett's cross-examination of Miss Savidge is worth summarising. Answering his questions, she admitted that she had gone out to the theatre with Sir Leo Money on a number of occasions, knowing that he was a married man with a daughter, and that she had sometimes arrived home at midnight. In this respect she agreed that she had deceived the young man to whom she was engaged, but after all, she said, she was 'an independent sort of girl' and 'perfectly able to look after herself.' She also insisted that Sir Leo had kissed her only once in the park and not several times as the police alleged, but she averred that she had said this after the inspector had told her that there was no harm in kissing. 'It was just a peck at that,' she added, 'not a passionate kiss.' As for the statement about Sir Leo's hand resting on her left knee, she denied that this had in fact happened, but the inspector had suggested it and she had let it go as she was 'fed up' by that time and felt 'awful' and would have signed 'anything to get away'. Otherwise Birkett was unable to shake her evidence in any material particular.

In his concluding speech for the police Norman Birkett submitted that she was willing to go to Scotland Yard and that she made no request that was not complied with. His principal contention was that the whole situation was changed when Sir Leo Money arrived at her home the same night. 'If Sir Leo Money had gone into the witness-box', said Birkett,

he would have shed a great deal of light on the conversation which took place when he saw Miss Savidge at midnight on that day, the conversation at her solicitor's office next day and the why and wherefore of it all . . . . It is plain that Sir Leo Money wanted to let the

[191]

matter drop. Up till the moment he went to her house that night, Miss Savidge never thought for one single moment that she had been subjected to any treatment which she resented in the smallest degree.

It was not until she went to the solicitor's office on the following day, Birkett went on, that she swore that certain things were put down in her statement to the police which she had not said, all of which were matters affecting Sir Leo Money.

In his speech Sir Patrick Hastings began by saying that, although in one sense he was appearing for Miss Savidge, the value of the inquiry was of far greater significance, and in that regard he was appearing for anyone who under the present system might be put in Miss Savidge's position. 'The question is whether a system which permitted or even encouraged an examination such as that to which Miss Savidge was subjected is tolerable', he went on.

In the clearest possible terms I desire to put my view before the Tribunal that it is absolutely intolerable. The method by which Miss Savidge was got to Scotland Yard was an outrage. The police knew perfectly well that, if she had been told what she was wanted for, they would not have got her there at all. This inquiry is useful in this respect, that the police will never get another girl to Scotland Yard in this way. We boast of the fairness of our police, who adopt no 'third degree' methods. If this is the exception, they should be the first to stop it and see that it never happened again.

The Tribunal's findings, which were announced some weeks later, were not unanimous, since a sharp difference of opinion between the members arose on the credibility of Miss Savidge's evidence, which resulted in the publication of a majority report and a minority report. The majority report, which appeared over the signatures of Sir John Bankes and Mr J. J. Withers, completely exonerated the police and did not accept Hastings's submissions of what had happened. Miss Savidge, according to the majority findings, was not intimidated into answering questions and was treated with no lack of propriety at Scotland Yard; the alleged 'demonstration' did not take place nor was the alleged remark about her being 'a good girl' made by Chief

Rt Hon Sir Charles Dilke Bt, MP.
President of the Local Government
Board. Cited as co-respondent in the
Crawford divorce petition.

Mrs Virginia Crawford. Confessed to
having committed adultery with Sir
Charles Dilke and was divorced by
her husband Donald Crawford, MP.

Charles Stewart Parnell, MP. As photographed by his mistress Katharine (Katie) O'Shea at Won Lodge, Eltham.

Mrs Katharine O'Shea. From a photograph of the picture which Parnell always had with him.

Wonersh Lodge. Katie O'Shea's house in Eltham.

10 Walsingham Terrace, Brighton. The house where Parnell lived with Mrs O'Shea before and after their marriage and where he died.

The Parnell Monument in Dublin

Lt-Gen Sir Hari Singh (Mr 'A')
heir to the Maharajah of Kashmir

Capt Charles Arthur
ADC to Sir Hari Singh

Mrs Maud Robinson

Mr Charles Robinson

The Hon Christabel Russell,
later Lady Ampthill

Christabel's husband John ('Stilts')
later Lord Ampthill with his father the
second Baron (right)

Christabel with the Russell baby

Geoffrey fourth Baron Ampthill

Rt Hon Jeremy Thorpe MP, Liberal Party Leader, at his wedding to his first wife Caroline Allpass in 1968, with David Holmes, best man and Liberal Party Treasurer (*above*)

With his second wife Marion, former Countess of Harewood, whom he married in 1973.

Norman Scott, the horse trainer and male model with whom Jeremy Thorpe was alleged to have had a homosexual relationship.

Andrew Newton the airline pilot who killed Scott's dog Rinka and tried to kill Scott.

A BETTER DEAL FOR YOUR DOG

VOTE WAUGH

Auberon Waugh's poster for the Dog Lovers' Party at the 1979 General Election at which he stood and polled 79 votes, losing his deposit.

Tom Driberg (Lord Bradwell)
who got away with it.

Ian Harvey
who did not.

Inspector Collins; neither were Miss Savidge's answers, which she approved at the time, misconstrued or improperly recorded.

We are unable therefore to accept Miss Savidge's statements on the material matters as to which there was a conflict of evidence between her and Chief Inspector Collins, and we acquit him of any improper conduct during the taking of Miss Savidge's statement. We are satisfied that the interrogation followed the lines indicated to him by the Director of Public Prosecutions and was not unduly extended.

In his minority report, Mr Lees-Smith, who agreed with Sir Patrick Hastings, blamed the police, and in particular Chief Inspector Collins, for the method by which Miss Savidge's presence was secured at Scotland Yard. The Inspector also incurred censure for having sent Miss Wyles away, particularly as her presence in the car had been used as an inducement to Miss Savidge to come to Scotland Yard. As to what happened after she arrived, there was a clear contradiction between the two versions of what occurred, and little corroboration could be obtained of the story told by either side. 'The test is the credibility of Miss Savidge on the one side, and the two police officers on the other,' observed Mr Lees-Smith.

My conclusion is that Miss Savidge is the more credible witness. The impression that she made in the witness-box was that of a frank, simple and somewhat child-like witness, whose evidence remained unshaken under cross-examination. The police officers did not give the impression that they were equally frank in their evidence, but denied both the probable and improbable with equal force. The mechanical precision with which the chief police witnesses corroborated every detail of each other's statements casts suspicion upon their evidence . . . I, therefore, give the preference to Miss Savidge's credibility, and conclude that she was asked a number of questions that she ought not to have been asked, and that certain of her replies were forced into a form that misrepresented what she wished to say.

For this, in Mr Lees-Smith's view, the responsibility rested with Chief Inspector Collins.

[193]

This momentous inquiry had the effect of introducing three important changes in police methods in interrogating persons who might be witnesses or even defendants in subsequent criminal proceedings. These changes, which had the support of the whole Tribunal, were, first, that the person to be interrogated should in future be clearly informed beforehand of the nature of the statement and the possible consequences involved in making it; second, that the statement should be normally taken at the person's home and not at his or her place of employment; and third, that in cases in which a statement to be taken from a woman by the police 'involves matters intimately affecting her morals', a woman should always be present unless the woman being interrogated expressed a desire to the contrary.

3

The second case of kissing, in which Sir Leo Money was involved, occurred in a railway train five years after the Irene Savidge affair.[9] On 11 September 1933 he was charged at Epsom police court in Surrey with regard to an incident which was alleged to have taken place on the previous 16 August on a train between North Dorking and Ewell. There were two summonses, the first taken out by the Southern Railway against the defendant for wilfully interfering with a passenger contrary to the railway company's by-laws, and the second taken out by the passenger herself, a thirty-year-old shop assistant, Miss Ivy Ruxton, against Sir Leo for assaulting her by kissing her in the carriage in which they were both travelling.

The Chairman of the Bench of Magistrates, which included one woman, was His Honour Judge Tudor Rees, a former county court judge and like Sir Leo Money a former Liberal MP. Sir Henry Curtis-Bennett, KC, with Mr Walter Frampton appeared for the defendant, and Mr F. W. Wallace prosecuted.

It appeared that Miss Ruxton had gone to visit her sister at Shere on the morning of 16 August and had left her sister's carrying two suitcases and took a bus to Dorking to catch the London train. The prosecution's case was that Sir Leo travelled on the same bus, having got in at Abinger Hammer, and, according to the complainant, was wearing a light coloured suit and a Panama hat and 'appeared to be a man of foreign appearance'. She said that he got into conversation with her while they were waiting for the 7.19 p.m. London train at North Dorking station. He followed her into her compartment, where he again began to talk to her. During the journey he was alleged to have kissed her passionately on the face and neck, and to have forced her head back against the cushions above her seat. When the train stopped at Ewell, she got out and complained to the guard and also to a porter. As a result Sir Leo was identified when he alighted at Waterloo terminus and asked to go to the police office. There he made a statement to the effect that he told Miss Ruxton that he liked nice hands and with her permission had kissed her fingers but nothing more. He supplemented this with a further statement the following day that if he had done anything to offend the lady he would like to apologise and asked for her name and address. She spoke of a man who had misused her or let her down, Sir Leo went on, and she added that she did not like men. Sir Leo said he replied that men were not to be judged by one single bad example.

Giving evidence Miss Ruxton described how, when the train arrived at North Dorking, Sir Leo opened a carriage door and gestured to her to get in. 'I am not going into that carriage,' Miss Ruxton stated she told him. 'I always travel in the one behind the guard.' She then walked towards the end of the train carrying her cases and got into the last carriage, the door being open, and Sir Leo followed her. She went on to say that Sir Leo asked her if she went to the cinema but she replied that she was usually too tired after business – she worked in a draper's shop – and generally stayed at home. According to her, Sir Leo looked at her hands and said, 'How astonishing that a young lady with tiny hands should have to work so hard for a living.' He called her 'My dear' and asked her whether she had any objection to his doing so. 'A habit of yours, perhaps?' she asked him. 'Are you accustomed to calling your lady friends "My dear"?' 'Yes, if I like them,' Sir Leo was said to have replied. 'My life is centred among the ladies. I could not live without them.' She continued:

Just as we were going to enter the tunnel between Box Hill and Leatherhead, he said, 'Lay your hand on mine.' I said, 'No, I don't want to.' With that he reached over and took my hand. As we were running into the tunnel I found there were no lights. He took my right hand and then my left, and in the tunnel I could feel him kissing

[195]

my hands alternately. I drew my hands away and sat back in the corner.

Asked by the prosecuting counsel whether she felt happy in that situation, she replied: 'No, I was very nervous. I did not know where he was. As the train came out of the tunnel he was leaning over kissing my coat on my knees. I told him to sit back, and not to be so stupid and to leave me alone. He said, "That was lovely: I felt a thrill. Didn't you feel a thrill?" I replied, "No, I don't know what you mean."' She went on:

I told him that I did not like men and that I hated to be fussed and kissed. Then he said, 'Dark eyes speak to dark eyes.' I said, 'Yours do not speak to me, and I am sure mine do not speak to you.' He looked at his hands and said, 'I too have small hands. In fact, I have two nice parts about my body. Do you know what they are?' I said, 'No.' He said, 'My hands and my feet. My feet are as nice as my hands.' As an after-thought he added, 'A third, my lips. Wouldn't you like to try them?' I said, 'No, I would not.' He said, 'You don't know what you are missing in life.' I said, 'Perhaps I don't.'

Asked why she had not pulled the communication cord, she said that she was too short to reach it. She went on to say that Sir Leo had forced her head against the cushion, after he had got up and moved her cases and sat down beside her. He kissed her face and neck, she said, adding 'He kissed me on the mouth in a most horrible manner.'

'Do you remember how many times he kissed you?' prosecuting counsel asked her.

'Quite a lot,' she replied.

'Was it done deliberately?'

'It was done very harshly.'

Miss Ruxton went on to say that she managed to move her arms and get away from him. She told him that she was getting out at Ewell, the next station. 'Darling, darling,' Sir Leo said, 'I thought you were going to Waterloo.' She admitted that when they got to Ewell, Sir Leo helped her out with her cases, but she turned to him and said brusquely, 'I can manage.'

A porter at Ewell said that, when he saw Miss Ruxton as she got off the train, she was very agitated and trembling. However, the guard stated that he twice passed the compartment where Miss Ruxton and Sir Leo were and he noticed nothing wrong. He added, in reply to a question from the chairman of the Bench, that there would be no difficulty if any lady in distress wished to attract his attention.

Sir Henry Curtis-Bennett called Sir Leo as the only witness for the defence.

'Did you touch her at all going through the tunnel?' Sir Henry asked him.

'No, I sat perfectly still as one usually does in tunnels,' the witness answered.

'Did she tell you that some man in her life had let her down badly and that it had put her against men?'

'Yes. She said that she had no further use for them.'

'We are accused at times of being too insular in our habits,' defence counsel went on, 'but are you in the habit of talking to people when you are travelling with them?'

'Not in the habit,' replied the witness. 'I like it and I indulge in it.'

'You gain a good deal of knowledge by discussing matters with all and sundry?'

'Yes. It is my province.'

'You spoke of marriage, the question of modern girls, business and so on. Did you notice her hands?'

'Yes. I always do notice hands.'

'Did you say anything to her about them?'

'Yes. I remarked that they were nice hands and it was remarkable that such small hands had done so much work. I then jestingly referred to my own hands and remarked that they were small and that they in their time had done a great deal of work.'

'Then what happened?' Curtis-Bennett went on.

'Her remarks with regard to her devotion to business and disappointment at not being married made me sympathetic,' replied Sir Leo, 'and I felt very sorry for her. I put out my hands and placed them over hers. The gesture was very simple.'

'Did she say anything?'

'Not at all. Nor did she withdraw her hands and say "Don't do that."'

'Did you in fact kiss the ends of her fingers?'

'Yes. I kissed the back of her hands.'

[197]

'Is there any truth in the story that she has told us that you took her in your arms, kissed her passionately, throwing her head back and kissing her upon the lips?'

'It is not true,' the witness answered emphatically.

'Did you call her darling?'

'It is not true,' the witness repeated.

'And did you say, "It is a lovely night for two"?'

'There is no truth whatever in that.'

'May you have used the expression in the course of conversation, "Well, my dear"?'

'It is quite possible.'

Sir Leo added that when the train approached Ewell Miss Ruxton said that was her station and she would be getting out. He helped her with her cases.

'Have you told us all that happened between you and her in the train?' was Curtis-Bennett's final question.

'I have told the truth and nothing but the truth,' Sir Leo replied.

Prosecuting counsel began his cross-examination: 'You are sixty-three years of age, are you not?' To which the witness agreed.

'You have and still have some position in the public life of this country?'

'I suppose that is so,' Sir Leo again agreed.

'This girl was a shop girl?' counsel continued.

'Yes,' Sir Leo said, adding 'and obviously a respectable young lady.'

'A lady who until that evening you had never set eyes upon in your life?'

'Never,' the witness again agreed.

'And within half an hour of meeting this total stranger you admit you were kissing her hands in a railway compartment?'

'I made that statement voluntarily.'

'Did you say, "Dark eyes speak to dark eyes"?'

'No.'

'Did you speak about your beautiful hands and your beautiful feet?'

'I did not use the word beautiful. I did say that I had small hands and small feet.'

'Did you ask her what she did in the evenings, if she liked to go out to the pictures or to flirt?'

[198]

'Certainly not,' the witness replied with some emphasis. 'Our conversation was a perfectly proper conversation and contained no such remark. Indeed the seriousness of the conversation precluded any such remark.'

Sir Leo declared that he did not leave his seat, and neither did Miss Ruxton during the whole of the journey. Her bags, too, were never moved from the time she got into the train until he handed them to her when she got out at Ewell.

'When that young lady says you put your arm around her and kissed her harshly and passionately, was that an illusion?' prosecuting counsel went on to ask.

'I can only describe it as imaginative,' the defendant replied. However, he admitted that he did kiss Miss Ruxton's hands, adding by way of explanation, 'It is a common gesture with me.'

'When you are alone in carriages with young ladies?'

'No, but when I am in deep sympathy with a person and I am leaving them I often kiss their hands.'

'But you were not leaving this young woman when you kissed her hands?' counsel persisted.

'And not always when I am leaving,' the witness hastened to add.

Sir Leo went on to say that it was pure imagination to allege that he had pushed Miss Ruxton's head against the carriage cushions and kissed her. He agreed with counsel that it was a very serious complaint to make against anyone.

'Can you explain why this strange woman, not knowing who you are, should tell a complete lie and plaster you in a public Court?'

'I can only suggest her state of mind which she herself has described in this box.' Sir Leo added that he did not suggest that Miss Ruxton's complaint was made out of spitefulness against him. It was based on her view of life and men.

Sir Henry Curtis-Bennett, addressing the Bench, said that instead of there being corroboration from the one person from whom they would expect it – the guard – they got precisely the reverse. The charges were such as were easily made but extremely difficult to counter, and they could only be met by the sworn testimony of the person accused and by the common sense of the court looking at all the circumstances of the case.

[199]

'I am not saying a word against the girl's morality,' Sir Henry continued:

She is a girl one seldom comes across in these days, a girl who is terribly nervous, full of suspicion of what may happen if she finds herself in a railway carriage with a man. There are many women who will not travel alone in a railway carriage with men, and there are an equal number of men who will not travel alone in a railway carriage with women.

I think this will be a lesson to us not to speak to people to whom we have not been introduced. I have no doubt this highly nervous, sensitive girl got frightened and thought that something might be going to happen. Later she quite persuaded herself that something did happen.

4

The Chairman, giving the decision of the Bench, said the case raised several matters of considerable public importance.

While it is our duty to protect so far as we can any individual woman from any unwelcome attention or molestation from fellow passengers, it is none the less our duty to see that no man is humiliated or disgraced, or in circumstances which may easily be conceived, subjected to unfounded accusations that might be made against him. It seems to us that in a case of this sort, in the absence of the greatest circumspection, a grave injustice might be caused by the institution of proceedings by mischievously disposed persons.

The Chairman went on to say that in such a case the difficulty was the difficulty or impossibility of getting corroboration. There had been some corroborative evidence in this case, and to that, of course, they had given their closest attention.

'On the admission of the defendant himself,' Judge Tudor Rees concluded, 'we have come to the unanimous conclusion that the conduct of the defendant was such as to bring him within the charges preferred against him, and there must therefore be a conviction in this case.'

[200]

On inquiring whether the defendant had any previous convictions and being told by a police officer in attendance that there were not, the Chairman said in that case Sir Leo would be fined £2 for the common assault and forty shillings in respect of the breach of the railway's by-laws. He would also have to pay five guineas towards the costs of the prosecution as well as the costs of the witnesses. It was a very much more lenient sentence than that passed on Valentine Baker for a similar offence fifty-eight years previously.

Sir Henry Curtis-Bennett then rose to say he wished to give formal notice of appeal, to which the Chairman agreed, allowing Sir Leo recognisances in £25 pending the appeal. However, on subsequent reflection and no doubt on legal advice Sir Leo decided not to appeal, since he was unlikely to succeed before the King's Bench Divisional Court which might well increase the fine with further unpleasant publicity.

Socially the case caused Sir Leo Money an immense amount of harm, particularly as his involvement in the case of Irene Savidge, whom he had also admitted kissing, was recalled by many people. He was ostracised by former friends and acquaintances and he constantly worried over the second case. Finally, in desperation he wrote from his home to Lord Carson, whom no doubt he had met when Carson was First Lord of the Admiralty in 1917 and Sir Leo was Parliamentary Secretary to the Ministry of Shipping and Chairman of the National Maritime Board.

The Old Quarry, Bramley, Surrey. 18th September 1935. Many years ago you championed young Archer-Shee and vindicated him through a Petition of Right. I am wondering whether I could avail myself of the same method in respect of my conviction in 1933 for assaulting a woman by kissing her; no criminal assault or verbal insult being even alleged.

The fine was small and the conviction, I am legally assured, only 'technical'. However that may be, the injury has been almost beyond endurance.[10]

It is unlikely that Carson answered this letter, since he was seriously ill at this time and in fact died a few weeks later.

Sir Leo Chiozza Money himself died towards the end of the Second

World War at his Surrey home aged seventy-four. Despite his outstanding record as a politician, a poet and an economist, he is remembered today, when he is remembered, for his extra-marital kissing of two young women rather than for his invention of wartime shipping convoys, his most distinguished public achievement.

5

This seems an appropriate place to mention another affair 'where the kissing had to stop'. It may be regarded as a scandal, albeit a suppressed one, although it was well known in political circles at the time. The individuals involved were F. E. Smith, Earl of Birkenhead and Lord Chancellor, and Mona Dunn, a beautiful and vivacious girl, who was the daughter of Lord Beaverbrook's great friend and fellow Canadian millionaire Sir James Dunn. Birkenhead first met Mona in 1919 during the Peace Conference in Paris, where she was a pupil at the same finishing school as Birkenhead's daughter Eleanor. At this time Birkenhead was forty-seven and Mona Dunn was seventeen, the same age as Eleanor, so that there was thirty years difference between them. Birkenhead, the youngest occupant of the Woolsack in modern times, attended the Peace Conference as a Cabinet minister in Lloyd George's Coalition Government and when he was there he liked to show off his daughter and Mona in Parisian society, taking them to Versailles and the other show places. When 'F.E.' and Mona became lovers which they did during the next twelve months or so, Eleanor was understandably put out by her father's liaison with her school friend, in much the same way as Lloyd George's daughter Megan was when her ex-coach Frances Stevenson became her father's mistress as well as his private secretary.

That 'F.E.' seduced Mona is no doubt true but she was also no doubt a willing bedfellow. However, the details of their affair are unclear and for the most part depend on the testimony of Beaverbrook, who may well have provided the lovers with opportunities for surreptitious meetings at his house in Fulham. In August 1923, when the affair was still flourishing Frances Stevenson wrote to Lloyd George who was in Wales that she had had a most interesting gossipy talk with Beaverbrook in the train while travelling down from Scotland: 'He told me many things about the F.E.–Mona affair which I will tell you when we meet, though you may have heard them already.'[11] The affair was evidently known to the Conservative leader Stanley Baldwin who used it as a pretext for excluding Birkenhead from his first government when he succeeded Bonar Law in the same year. 'We are a Cabinet of faithful husbands,' the new Tory Prime Minister remarked at the time, 'and I think we will remain so.'[12]

If Eleanor Smith's friend Alannah Harper is to be believed, Mona was besotted with 'F.E.', while the latter was much less seriously smitten on his side, merely enjoying going to bed with a charming and intelligent girl when he felt like it. Nor was there apparently any question of Birkenhead leaving his wife Margaret, although according to some gossips 'F.E.' did think of doing so but was dissuaded by friends since there had been no precedent for a Lord Chancellor ever having had a divorce. That 'F.E.' and Mona loved each other is indisputable, besides which they had a common interest in horses, since Mona had been a good rider since childhood. 'Mona Dunn was a most unusual girl,' wrote Beaverbrook, 'cast in her father's image and sharing his love of life and gaiety to a highly unusual degree. . . . The more vivid a personality, the harder it is to put down in words. How then describe Mona's genius? It took the form of an intense originality of view poured out in a rich flow of talk – coruscating, inexhaustible. Yet hers was a mind essentially sympathetic and receptive'.[13] Some idea of her youthful beauty may be seen from Sir William Orpen's portrait of her with her golden hair hanging below her shoulders, painted about the time she met 'F.E.' in 1919.

The affair seems to have petered out after Birkenhead had gone over to the Conservative camp, which led to his becoming Secretary of State for India in the second Baldwin administration. At all events, in February 1925, Mona married a man nearer her own age, Edmund Tattersall, a twenty-eight-year-old ex-Guards officer and a member of a well-known sporting family with a distinguished war record, who had been invalided out of the army in 1922. The wedding, which 'F.E.' did not attend, took place in Paris, where Mona had many friends. She may possibly have married on the rebound from her affair with Birkenhead and may not have really been in love with Tattersall. Anyhow by 1927, she was living with her father at Sutton Place, near Guildford, which Sir James Dunn had leased from the Duke of Sutherland – it was later the

[203]

home of Paul Getty – although she was pregnant at the time and gave birth to a daughter Monica in May of that year. Whatever her difference with her husband may have been – he was probably a difficult man to live with since he was divorced from his two subsequent wives and may well have got a divorce from Mona had she lived – it seems certain that Tattersall was the father of her child, and not 'F.E.' as has been suggested, her affair with him being long since over, although 'F.E.' retained a strong affection for her. Nor, when her sudden death occurred following an operation in a private nursing home at Auteuil in December 1928, was this the result of an abortion caused by her carrying Birkenhead's child as has also been suggested. The cause of her death was peritonitis. She was buried on Christmas Eve in Putney Vale cemetery in London. The fact that the inscription on her gravestone, like that of Oscar Wilde's wife in Genoa, contained no reference to her husband cannot have been accidental.[14] It read simply:

Mona, much beloved daughter of Sir James Dunn, Bart., and Gertrude, Lady Dunn, who died in Paris, 19th December, 1928, at the age of 26 years.

Birkenhead confessed to Beaverbrook that he was 'deeply upset' by the news of Mona's death. He was unable to be present at the funeral service since he was on his way by sea to Madeira, but he sent Beaverbrook a moving obituary poem for possible publication unsigned in Beaverbrook's paper the *Sunday Express*. The third and last stanza was as follows:

Loyal in friendship; prodigal in trust;
 Of valiant fibre: ever quick to give,
She smiled and loved; and trod the road she must:
 And died as those shall die who dare too vividly
  to live.

Beaverbrook did not publish Birkenhead's poem in the *Sunday Express*, but he did so thirty years later in his life of her father, without however giving any explanation of why 'F.E.' should have been so affected by Mona's death.[15] Instead Beaverbrook, who was godfather to Mona's daughter Monica wrote his own brief obituary in the *Sunday*

Express: 'She has not left a single enemy or critic behind her. And of how many people of genius can this be said?' Birkenhead himself had only two more years to live, but Mona's memory surely remained with him to his dying day.

Homosexuality

1

IN September 1892 Oscar Wilde's friend Lord Alfred Douglas, who had just come down from Oxford and was staying with Oscar and Constance Wilde and their children on holiday in Norfolk, wrote a poem which he called *Two Loves*. The first of these loves was heterosexual. ('I am true Love, I fill the hearts of boy and girl with mutual flame.') The other was homosexual. ('I am the love that dare not speak its name.') Although at his trial Wilde claimed that the other love in his friend's poem was misunderstood, being in fact 'such a great affection of an elder for a younger man as there was between David and Jonathan, such as Plato made the basis of his philosophy, and such as you find in the sonnets of Michelangelo and Shakespeare', and moreover that there was 'nothing unnatural about it', Wilde could not deny that this love was essentially homosexual in character, even if it did not involve any physical relationship.[1] The poem was published two years later in the first and only issue of *The Chameleon*, an Oxford undergraduate magazine, to which Wilde contributed his epigrammatic *Phrases and Philosophies for the Use of the Young* and which unfortunately contained a blatantly homosexual short story by the editor entitled 'The Priest and the Acolyte', which was to do Wilde a great deal of harm although he was unaware at the time of its inclusion in the magazine with his own contribution until it appeared.[2]

In an article which he wrote for a French journal in 1896, while Wilde was in prison, Douglas declared that the decision to prosecute Wilde a second time, after the jury had disagreed in the first trial, was the result of a political intrigue. Douglas alleged that Lord Rosebery, who had succeeded Gladstone as Prime Minister, had told the Home Secretary, then Mr Asquith, that, if the Wilde prosecution was dropped following the jury's disagreement, this would create a most damaging impression among the voters at the next General Election and that this would undoubtedly result in the defeat of the Liberals at the polls. Hence the decision to instruct the Solicitor-General to prosecute at the last trial and so make sure that Wilde would be convicted. According to Douglas in the same article, the Liberal party at this period contained a number of homosexuals, and the 'maniacs of virtue' threatened to launch further actions unless the case against Wilde went on. 'If Oscar Wilde was found guilty the matter would be hushed up,' Douglas wrote.

> This was the cause of the second trial and the verdict of guilty. It was a degrading *coup d'état* – the sacrifice of a great poet to save a degraded band of politicians. The conviction of Oscar Wilde was one of the last acts of this disgraceful and discredited Liberal Party which is now in an exceptional minority in the House of Commons.[3]*

There is no evidence to substantiate Douglas's charge, although it may conceivably have some substance. Nor is it possible to say how many members of the Liberal party were homosexual. However, the Prime Minister himself Lord Rosebery was suspected of being homosexual or at least bisexual. He took a great fancy to Douglas's eldest brother Lord Drumlanrig, whom he made his private secretary and then an English peer and a junior minister so that he could answer on occasion for the Government in the Upper House. In October 1894 Drumlanrig, when a guest at a shooting party in Somerset, was found dead from a gunshot wound. It looked on the face of it like an accident, and this was confirmed by the verdict of 'accidental death' returned by the coroner's jury at the inquest. Nevertheless there were rumours at the time that Drumlanrig was implicated in a homosexual affair with Lord Rosebery, then Foreign Secretary, and that he committed suicide rather than face a public scandal which he evidently thought possible at the time.[4]

---

* There were only 177 Liberals in the 1895 Parliament, in which 340 Conservatives under the premiership of Lord Salisbury formed a majority of 152 over the combined opposition parties. The House of Commons numbered 675 in those days.

[207]

Wilde was prosecuted to conviction under the Criminal Law Amendment Act, 1885, section 11, which made homosexual acts between consenting males a criminal offence whether committed in public or *in private*, the section in question having been proposed by Henry Labouchere, editor of *Truth*, and agreed to in a thinly attended House in the small hours of an August morning on the eve of the parliamentary summer recess. A judge at the time, not without good reason, dubbed it 'The Blackmailer's Charter', as subsequent cases were to demonstrate until the obnoxious section was repealed eighty-two years later, a period which was to witness many 'monstrous martyrdoms' as Wilde described them.[5]

The first monstrous martyrdom of a politician under the new law was remarkably enough that of an Irish MP named de Cobain, one of the Belfast members. Edward Samuel Wesley de Cobain was the son of a Methodist minister in Belfast and as a young man had entered the service of the City Corporation, where he became cashier. Here he acquired a detailed knowledge of local affairs; at the same time, like other Conservatives in politics, he joined the Orange Order, eventually becoming Grand Master for Ireland. At the General Election of 1885, when he was in his middle forties, he challenged the local party caucus in East Belfast, standing as an Independent or 'Democratic Conservative' and defeating the official nominee by over a thousand votes. He was again returned, at the Election in the following year, after the rejection of Gladstone's first Home Rule Bill for Ireland. The Bill's rejection led to rioting in Belfast and a commission of inquiry sat at which de Cobain gave evidence, boldly denouncing police brutality in connection with the riots. He thus incurred the enmity of the police force as well as that of the Conservative party caucus, whose power he had successfully challenged. His undoing seems to have been the work of a blackmailer, convicted forger and embezzler named Heggie, with whom he admitted that he had 'swapped a handkerchief once or twice because he admired the perfume on it'. There seems little doubt that de Cobain was a homosexual, but it is equally clear that he was the target of a blackmailing conspiracy engineered by Heggie. The atmosphere was poisoned against him, the East Belfast Member declared, 'by the babbling of the police and his enemies in the city.' In May 1891, while he was in London attending to his parliamentary duties, he received a telegram from a friend in Belfast advising him to take a trip abroad for the benefit of his health. De Cobain thereupon crossed the Channel to Boulogne.

Afterwards the unfortunate MP said somewhat implausibly that he thought the telegram was really sent in the interests of his health, though he must have quickly been disabused of this idea when he read in the local papers that a warrant had been issued for his arrest. While at Boulogne he also received a summons from the Speaker of the House of Commons to return to Westminster and explain his conduct. It appears that he was suffering from some kind of nervous breakdown, since he was confined to bed when the Speaker's summons was served upon him. However, when he recovered he did not immediately return to England but went instead to America, where he remained for the next eighteen months. Meanwhile, since he had ignored a resolution of the House of Commons to appear in his place and answer the charges which had been brought against him, he was expelled. Eventually he returned to Belfast early in 1893 and after a delay of five weeks, during which the authorities were making up their minds what to do, he was arrested and charged on ten counts with the commission of acts of gross indecency with five persons in Belfast during 1887 and the three succeeding years. He was tried at the next Belfast assizes in March before Mr Justice Johnson, convicted and sentenced to twelve months' imprisonment with hard labour.[6]

In the Liberal party two young Liberal contemporaries of Lord Rosebery, who reached Cabinet rank, were subsequently involved in homosexual affairs. One was Lewis ('Lulu') Harcourt, later Viscount Harcourt, son of Sir William Harcourt, the Leader of the House of Commons, whose private secretary he was. At the same time, Harcourt was active in the party organisation and afterwards served in the 1906 Liberal Government as First Commissioner of Works, in which capacity he did much to improve the amenities of the Houses of Parliament, where there is a room named after him. One February morning in 1922 he was found dead in bed by his valet in his London home in Brook Street (now the Savile Club), from the effects of an overdose of bromide, a sleeping draught which he had taken, so it was said, to avoid arrest on a homosexual charge. On the other hand, when asked by the coroner at the inquest whether he was in any trouble, his widow said no, adding that 'he was most cheerful'. The coroner's jury returned a verdict of 'death by misadventure'.[7] The object of his homosexual

[209]

affection was generally believed to be a wealthy young Etonian, Edward James, whose mother Mrs Willie James, a leading Edwardian hostess, was *reputed* to be a natural daughter of King Edward VII. At all events she left her son 150 letters to her from the King which were all very paternal and began 'My dear child'.[8] Also the King was her son's godfather. Incidentally Harcourt was an avid antiquarian collector, particularly of books about Eton. According to Edward James in his autobiography, Lord Harcourt tried hard to seduce him when he and his mother were spending a weekend at Nuneham Courtney, Harcourt's country place near Oxford. ('He was a hideous and horrible old man.') On being pressed young James admitted as much to his mother, who gossiped about it to all her women friends in London. When the boy met Lady Harcourt shortly afterwards, she was very dignified and tried to greet Edward James as if nothing had happened. 'But she must have known, poor Lady Harcourt', wrote James, 'because the whole of London was talking about it, and not long afterwards Lord Harcourt committed suicide.'[9]

The other young Liberal contemporary of Rosebery's, who besides obtaining Cabinet office eventually became party Leader in the House of Lords, was William (Lygon) Earl Beauchamp. In 1931 he suddenly resigned his offices and went to live abroad, at the insistence, so it was said, of King George V, who otherwise wished him to be prosecuted. One of his offices was that of Lord Warden of the Cinque Ports, and it was alleged that he had misconducted himself with various youths, fishermen and the like, at Walmer Castle, the Lord Warden's official residence. He was also in the habit of inviting his homosexual friends to visit him at Walmer. Lady Aberconway recalls in her memoirs calling on Lord Beauchamp there with her husband and Sir William Jowitt, then Attorney-General, one Sunday afternoon. On their arrival they were shown into a garden surrounding a grass tennis court. To her surprise Lady Aberconway saw the actor Ernest Thesiger 'nude to the waist and covered with pearls: he explained that he had the right type of skin to heal pearls'. Her ladyship also met two or three other young men, including 'a nice young man whom Lord Beauchamp introduced as his tennis coach', although it turned out that he could not even pat a ball over the net. Some time later Lady Aberconway read in a newspaper that the Lord Warden had gone abroad 'to have mud baths'. Somewhat naïvely she wrote him off as 'an eccentric' in need of

[210]

therapeutic treatment. ('Perhaps, poor man, when I saw him he was physically ill.') Lord Beauchamp died a lonely exile in New York in 1938.[10] His portrait, painted when he was Leader of the Liberal party in the House of Lords from 1924 to 1931, hung in the National Liberal Club but was removed on the occasion of his abrupt departure from England. It was later restored to the Club and rehung there, so it was said, at the instance of Winston Churchill.

One of the most remarkable homosexuals at the turn of the century was the first and last Lord Farquhar, whose rapid advancement in business and court circles is said to have been due to his skill in exploiting his physical charms. The fifth son of a Scottish baronet by an illegitimate daughter of Lord Reay, Horace Brand Farquhar began his career as a clerk in the East India commercial house of Forbes, Forbes & Co., and through the Forbes family was introduced to the Marlborough House set of the Prince of Wales and so to Queen Victoria, who took a fancy to him and created him successively a baronet and a peer. Previously he had been a Liberal Unionist MP and had married the wealthy widow of the banker Sir Edward Scott. He then took up banking in Scott's Bank (later absorbed in the Westminster) and with the help of the Duke of Fife, who was a partner in the bank and son-in-law of the Prince of Wales, became the Prince's financial adviser and made considerable sums of money for His Royal Highness. Like the Duke of Fife too, Farquhar was one of the founders with Cecil Rhodes of the Chartered Company of South Africa, until the complications caused by the Jameson raid necessitated their retirement.

On the Prince's accession to the throne, Farquhar was put in charge of the royal household, whose affairs he managed for some years, and he also served as a court official under George V. At the same time he became treasurer of the Conservative party and as such was responsible for the management of the party's finances. He supported the Lloyd George coalition government during the First World War and was advanced a step in the peerage. On the break-up of the coalition in 1922 he was made an earl, at the age of seventy-eight. On his refusal to hand over £20,000 in connection with the recent election to the Conservative party on the ground that the money had been subscribed expressly for the coalition, he was summarily dismissed by Bonar Law, the new Conservative leader, who had been told that Farquhar was 'so "gaga" that one does not know what to make of him.'

[211]

There can be little doubt that Farquhar gave this sum to Lloyd George and other sums for his account, as well as £40,000 from the Party Fund to a charity nominated by the King (which Farquhar had in turn received from Lord Astor), and his transactions can only be regarded as embezzlement. But he continued to be seen at court and the King received him in audience a fortnight before his death in 1923. In the past he had been a lavish entertainer at Castle Rising, his estate near Sandringham, and he had no doubt let it be known that he had not forgotten various members of the royal family in his will. Indeed, when this fantastic document was opened, it was seen that he had made the most generous bequests, among them £100,000 to Princess Arthur of Connaught and a similar sum to her son, besides substantial legacies to the King's private secretaries and others connected with the court. But when the executors came to distribute the estate, they had a disagreeable surprise. Farquhar was bankrupt. His personal fortune, if it ever existed had disappeared like the Party Fund. Perhaps it was as well that he left no heir and his titles died with him. [11]

One curious case must also be mentioned. One night in late September 1920, the thirty-eight-year-old ex-Socialist MP Victor Grayson who was homosexual (or rather bisexual) walked out of a restaurant in or off the Strand, where he had been drinking with some friends saying that he would be back in a few minutes. In fact he was never seen again by his friends or his family. His disappearance caused a sensation at the time, and there were stories that he had been murdered by Tories or Liberals or driven to suicide by the Establishment.

The son of a Yorkshire carpenter, Grayson was born in Liverpool and later trained as an apprentice engineer in Bootle. He also studied at Liverpool University and Owen's College, Manchester. At the same time he was attracted by Left-wing politics and began to speak on Labour and Socialist platforms in his native city. Indeed his eloquence was spellbinding. During this period he had a homosexual affair with a man named Henry Dawson who worked on Merseyside. As a 'Socialist Independent' at a by-election in July 1907 Grayson contested the Colne Valley constituency near Huddersfield, winning it against a Conservative and a Liberal. At first his speeches were a success. In 1908 he was suspended for referring to the Commons as a 'House of Murderers' responsible for starvation in the country and he was carried fighting and struggling out of the Commons chamber. Grayson's notoriety due to this incident led, on Bernard Shaw's initiative, to his becoming political editor of *The New Age*, a weekly preaching guild socialism, then under the editorship of a brilliant journalist A. R. Orage and running at a loss; Grayson's appointment substantially increased the journal's circulation to 22,000, so that it made a profit. Unfortunately at the same time Grayson began to drink with deleterious effects upon his health as well as his political career. His attempts to socialise Labour policy did not commend themselves to the leading members of the Labour party such as Philip Snowden, and as a result he lost the seat at Colne Valley in 1910, coming bottom of the poll. Although he continued to be associated with *The New Age*, his drinking and extravagance eventually landed him in the bankruptcy court.

By the time he married in 1912 he was a heavy drinker. His wife was a beautiful young London actress called Ruth Nightingale, whose stage name was Ruth Norreys and who had appeared with Beerbohm Tree in Arthur Pinero's comedy *Sweet Lavender*. Shortly after her marriage she joined a Shakespearean touring company which was going to New Zealand, and together she and her husband went out there to start what they hoped to be a new life, since Grayson was now a bankrupt. But the Great War suddenly changed everything. Victor joined the New Zealand Army as a private and went to the Western Front in France where he was seriously wounded and invalided back to England, while his brother Jack who served in the Grenadier Guards was killed. To add to his troubles, his wife Ruth, with whom he was deeply in love, died in giving birth to their daughter Margot Elise in February 1918. Her death was a great shock to him and he became subject to fits of acute depression. He would disappear from time to time and would reappear after a while, usually staying with his mother Mrs Elizabeth Grayson at her home in Liverpool.

The last time he saw his mother in September 1920, he was dishevelled and looked haggard, due no doubt to his drinking. Mrs Grayson thought he was not eating enough and asked him what he would like for dinner the following night. He told her that he would not be there for dinner, and on being asked why not, he told her that he was going to Hull to speak at a meeting. However, he did not go to Hull but to London where, as already noted, he was last seen drinking in a restaurant bar. One theory which has been put forward to account for his disappearance was that he had publicly threatened to expose the sale of political honours at this time, notably by an unsavoury character named Maundy Gregory (who later served a prison sentence for this offence) and that Gregory killed him, afterwards secretly disposing of Grayson's body.

Grayson's disappearance has hitherto been a mystery. Because of his war service he was entitled to a disability pension. But the New Zealand authorities, who wrote several times to his old London address in Brixton, never received any reply to their inquiries. One theory is that he was 'fed up' and left the country briefly – it was in the days before passports – and when he returned it was under another name. According to another theory he emigrated to Australia and died and was buried in Western Australia. This was confirmed by a Cabinet minister in the Western Australian Government in Perth to Tom Smith MP and the minister even offered to show the English Member his grave. But when Tom Smith subsequently wrote to the Western Australian Attorney-General, that individual informed him that he could find no proof that Grayson had ever been buried there.

Again it has been suggested that after his return from abroad Victor Grayson married a wealthy woman under his new name, settling in some part of England and dying there. This seems the most likely explanation. In 1939 Mr Sidney Campion, a journalist and civil servant who had known Grayson personally, declared that he had seen Grayson on the London Underground railway:

I was in a District Line tube train when a man who I am absolutely certain was Victor Grayson got in at Sloane Square Station.

He was prosperously dressed in morning coat and top hat and was accompanied by a smartly dressed and vivacious woman of about forty. As the train entered Westminster Station he lifted his rolled umbrella and said: 'Ah, the old Firm!' The voice was Grayson's as I remember it.

They both laughed and the woman said: 'We must look in there again some time, Victor.'

Here seemed another perfect chance to solve the mystery. Yet even this promising trail faded out: the couple left the train suddenly before Mr Campion could make up his mind to speak to them.

Grayson's homosexual letters to Henry Dawson, whom he addressed

[214]

as 'my stricken darling', were written in 1904 and 1905 and the originals are now preserved in the Museum of Labour History in London. The letters have been used by Dr David Clark, the present Labour MP for South Shields, in the biography he has written of the man who was regarded by many of the rank-and-file in the Labour movement at the time of his election to the House of Commons in 1907 as the embodiment of working-class achievement. Yet how disappointing not to say mysterious was his future. 'No man ever had greater opportunities, no man ever cast them aside more foolishly', wrote the Labour leader Philip Snowden, who succeeded him as MP for Colne Valley. 'I have seen many tragedies in the Labour and Socialist movement. I have seen none so sad as the tragedy of Victor Grayson.'

'From the letters and other evidence', Dr Clark is reported to have stated,

> I think it is clear his former homosexual tendencies, which he suppressed, had returned, though quite obviously he was bisexual. At the time many of the people he was mixing with were homosexuals. Others were rather shady, unscrupulous types. He decided he had had enough and they helped him to leave the country. Later he returned to live in various parts of England, under a different name, until he died naturally a few years later.

That may well be the solution to his mystery.[12]

2

During the Second World War only one socially prominent politician was prosecuted for alleged homosexual offences. This was Sir Paul Latham, thirty-six-year-old millionaire, Baronet, old Etonian and Conservative MP for Scarborough and Whitby, whose wife was a daughter of the Earl of Drogheda. He was tried by court martial in 1941 on charges of improper conduct with three gunners and a civilian while he was serving as an officer with the 70th Searchlight Regiment, Royal Artillery, in Sussex. There was a further charge of attempted suicide, since he had thrown himself off his motor-cycle (and as a result was seriously though not fatally injured), on learning that a letter from one of the gunners containing allegations against him had been seen by the military authorities. It was a particularly tragic case involving the ruin of a most promising career, since he had joined the army of his own accord at the beginning of the war and he could easily have been excused service in the armed forces through being an MP; he had of course now to resign his seat in the House of Commons. 'I imagine that whatever your decision is in this case,' his defending counsel told the court, 'Sir Paul's life is now pretty well damned'. In fact, he was found guilty on ten out of thirteen charges and was sentenced to be cashiered and also to two years' imprisonment, of which he served eighteen months.[13] His wife, by whom he had one son, the present Baronet, divorced him while he was still in prison. But his mother gallantly stood by him. Paul Latham told James Lees-Milne, adviser on historic buildings to the National Trust, that she 'befriended him when he was in prison, never missed writing, never reproached him, and never has done so since. He says she has always been and always will be his best friend.'

Lees-Milne, in his entertaining diaries, records two visits he made to Herstmonceaux where Latham owned the 'fairy-tale castle', originally a fifteenth-century fortified manor house and now the home of the Royal Greenwich Observatory. Lees-Milne's first visit was in 1943, a few months after Latham had been released from prison. 'He was very thin but healthier and handsomer than I remember him', wrote Lees-Milne.

He still had a frightening look of craziness in the crimped gold hair, anthropoidal head, albino eyebrows and cold blue eyes. He talked incessantly of himself and prison. He is touched that everyone on the estate is nice to him . . . He is obsessed by sex and already haunts the most dangerous places, he told me. He also enjoys repeating disobligingly things said about one. How much is true, and how much invented it is hard to say. He is a sadistic man . . . I am terribly sorry for him but would pity him far more if he were less wayward and less egocentric.

On the occasion of his second visit, three years later, Lees-Milne wrote:

27th April 1946. This afternoon I trained to Eastbourne where Paul Latham met me at the station. Just the same in appearance, like a bounding retriever puppy, hatless, his hair still yellow, clustering and curly. Complexion slightly sunburned . . . He was giggly and rather endearing. We dined with his old mother, who is staying in Eastbourne to be near him. She is a dear, ordinary old woman of seventy-nine, adoring her son. Paul is angelic to her and I have seldom seen any son treat his mother better . . . He is greatly improved. Far less hysterical and more reconciled. Less sex mad. Seems to take a far saner view of life. He will of course always be self-centred in that he at once takes it for granted that one is interested in whatever local or domestic matter is absorbing him at the moment . . .

Paul has a butler who lives out. He, Paul, pays *19s 6d* income tax and all his money is in trust, so he cannot live on his capital. It is hard for someone in his circumstances, very rich on paper with little money to spend. Went to the Castle after luncheon and walked round it. Paul has sold it to Greenwich Observatory. This was my doing for I introduced the Astronomer Royal to him three years ago when he came to ask for a house from the National Trust.

29th April. Paul says that no one has ever insulted him since he came out of prison, but I noticed that the people in the Eastbourne hotel stared at him. It gives me a perverse pleasure to be seen with him. He is always doing kindnesses and giving people lifts, and making jokes. Yet he is profoundly unhappy.

Paul Latham died in 1955, and his only son Richard, who succeeded to the baronetcy, emigrated to Canada where he married a Canadian and settled in British Columbia. Paul's sister Audrey married four times, her fourth husband being Major-General Sir Stewart Menzies, the wartime head of MI6, otherwise the British Secret Intelligence Service.

3

'Never go to a public lavatory in London', the Oxford physicist Professor Derek Jackson once warned an astonished Frenchman. 'I always pee in the street. You may be fined a few pounds for committing a nuisance, but in a public lavatory you risk two years in prison because a policeman in plain clothes says you smiled at him.'[14]

A good or rather bad example of this was provided by the case of a Labour MP, Mr William J. Field, who had been a Parliamentary Private Secretary in the second Attlee government, and belonged to many local government bodies including the Hammersmith Borough Council of which he was Leader. In January 1953 he was convicted at Bow Street magistrate's court and fined £15 for soliciting or importuning in a public place for immoral purposes, the essence of the offence being that he did so 'persistently'. He was arrested as a result of police surveillance of two West End urinals one evening between 9.25 and 10.15 p.m. According to the police evidence – and the police were unquestionably acting as *agents provocateurs* – Field stood beside or in front of various young men in these urinals, smiled at them and 'looked in the direction of their persons.' None of the people in the urinals appeared to be affected by his alleged conduct. On appealing to a Queen's Bench Divisional Court, Field's counsel argued that what his client had done did not amount to importuning within the dictionary meaning of pestering, although it might have amounted to soliciting, i.e. 'inviting'. But the Lord Chief Justice, Lord Goddard, rejected this argument. 'There is no real distinction to be drawn between persistently soliciting and persistently importuning,' he said in dismissing the appeal; 'the draftsman put in those words to make it more emphatic.' The unfortunate result was that Mr Field was obliged to resign his seat in the House of Commons and he disappeared from public life, a tragic loss.[15]

A regular witch-hunt of homosexuals went on at this time, largely inspired by the then Home Secretary, Sir David Maxwell-Fyffe, later Lord Kilmuir. The most socially conspicuous victim of the witch-hunt was twenty-seven-year-old Edward John Barrington Douglas-Scott-Montagu, third Baron Montagu of Beaulieu, an old Etonian and ex-Grenadier Guards Officer, who was best known for the vintage car museum which he had formed in the grounds of his historic Hampshire home. In this way Lord Montagu was as eccentric and unconventional as the recently convicted novelist and autobiographer Rupert Croft-Cooke, 'rejecting the class system which so many of his friends and neighbours held sacred', to quote his friend Peter Wildeblood.

His guests, both at Beaulieu and in his London flat, formed an extraordinary assortment of conflicting types: business men and

[218]

writers, Duchesses and model-girls, restaurateurs and politicians and musical comedy actresses and Guards officers and Americans wearing hand-painted ties. He was always intensely busy and often merely used to introduce his guests to each other and then disappear . . . Trivial though it may seem, this kind of behaviour enraged some people who took themselves extremely seriously and expected Lord Montagu to do the same. He made enemies, as well as friends.

Among the former could be reckoned the Hampshire County Constabulary.

Members of the local troop of boy scouts used to act as guides at Palace House, the Montagu property at Beaulieu, on the days it was open to the public. During the August bank holiday weekend in 1953, Montagu and one of his house guests, a film director named Kenneth Hume, took two of the scouts to a beach-hut he owned for a bathe. According to Montagu, the purpose of the visit was to find a camera which had been left there on a previous visit, and the bathe was only incidental. He reported the loss to the police; but when the police came to see him, they showed much more interest in him and his friend Hume than in the camera. Under questioning, the scouts now accused Montagu and Hume of having indecently assaulted them in the beach-hut. On the face of it, this story was most unlikely. Had there been any substance in it, Montagu would hardly have complained to the police in the first instance and asked them to make inquiries. What made the tale even less plausible was that he had only a week or two previously announced his engagement to a charming girl with whom he was obviously very much in love. (The engagement was subsequently broken off.)

While the police inquiries were still proceeding, Montagu went to France and from there directly to America. On learning that a warrant had been issued for his arrest, he immediately returned to England and surrendered to the authorities, at the same time handing over his passport. At his trial, which took place at Winchester assizes in December 1953, on charges of committing an unnatural offence and an indecent assault, the prosecution sought to prove that instead of flying direct from Paris to New York on 25 September, as he swore in his evidence he had done, he had returned to England for a brief visit of a couple of days and had flown to America from England on 25 September. In support of this the prosecution pointed to an entry in his

[219]

passport which seemed to indicate that he had been stamped out of Boulogne by the French passport authorities on 23 September. Montagu denied this vigorously, saying he had not been in Boulogne for several years, and on examining the passport the judge pronounced that the date had been altered, the figure '5' having apparently been changed from a '4'. The obvious inference was that the passport, which had been in the possession of the police ever since Montagu had given it up, had been tampered with to show that Montagu was a liar, and that if the jury could be convinced that he was lying about his movements, they might naturally conclude that his other evidence was not to be believed. It was never proved that the police were responsible for the passport forgery, neither was any official explanation of the forged entry ever forthcoming. As things turned out, Montagu was acquitted on the more serious charge of committing an unnatural offence, but on the lesser charge of indecent assault the jury disagreed, and the Director of Public Prosecutions decided that he and Hume should be tried again on this charge at the next sessions.

The arrests of Peter Wildeblood and Michael Pitt-Rivers took place three weeks later, their premises being searched without a warrant, as had happened with Croft-Cooke. In addition to several specific indecency charges they were also accused of conspiring with Lord Montagu to commit them. The addition of the conspiracy charge in Montagu's case was most unfair and calculated to prejudice gravely his chances of acquittal at his retrial. Peter Wildeblood, who was diplomatic correspondent of the *Daily Mail* at the time of his arrest, and Michael Pitt-Rivers, a cousin of Lord Montagu's, were specifically accused, besides conspiracy, of offences with two RAF men named Edward McNally and John Reynolds at the beach-hut near Beaulieu and also at the Pitt-Rivers estate in Dorset. Wildeblood had borrowed the beach-hut for a holiday in 1952, and there was a small party there on the first night attended by Montagu and some of his house guests from Beaulieu. The prosecution was to suggest that it developed into a Bacchanalian orgy of the most revolting character. Actually it was a rather tame affair, there being no dancing between males or anything of that kind. As a matter of fact, throughout the evening the hut was encircled by girl guides, apparently engaged in bird-watching – a fact which, as Wildeblood observed afterwards, did not suggest that anything very lascivious was taking place.

[220]

Montagu, Pitt-Rivers and Wildeblood were tried together at Winchester assizes in March 1954. The charges in respect of the boy scouts on which the jury had disagreed at Montagu's previous trial were not included in the indictment, since neither Pitt-Rivers nor Wildeblood had anything to do with these. But, of course, the extensive publicity which the previous trial had received was bound to prejudice Montagu in the eyes of the jury and in the circumstances to militate against his having a fair trial on the second occasion that he stood in the dock. The principal witnesses against the three defendants were the two airmen.

Reynolds and McNally are put forward as perverts, men of the lowest possible character [said counsel in opening the case for the prosecution], men who were corrupted, who apparently cheerfully accepted corruption, long before they met the three defendants. It is not to be laid at the door of the defendants that they were a party to this corruption at all.

These are witnesses whom we, in law, know as accomplices. They were willing parties to these unnatural offences, although, of course, they were committed under the seductive influence of lavish hospitality from these men, who were so infinitely their social superiors.

It came out in the course of the trial that the hospitality the airmen received was quite the reverse of lavish, consisting for the most part of bottles of cider and simply cooked meals on the stove in the hall of Wildeblood's Kensington flat. It also came out that Reynolds was interrogated by the police for a total of eighteen hours and that McNally had been persuaded to 'confess' on being told that Reynolds had already 'squealed'. The airmen were further shown to have been involved in twenty-four other homosexual affairs, as a result of which neither they nor any of the others were ever prosecuted. McNally had a friend named Gerry, a male nurse, whom he described as 'my husband', and a receipt produced by the defence from the Regent Palace Hotel in London showed that they had shared a room there together. 'The fact that neither of them was charged with an offence', Wildeblood afterwards wrote, 'proves, I think, conclusively that the Crown in this case was not even concerned with the administration of the law as it stood. It was simply out to put Lord Montagu behind bars.'

The Montagu trial which lasted for eight days, was so well publicised on both sides of the Atlantic that it is unnecessary to go into it in further detail here beyond emphasising the atmosphere of heavy prejudice which characterised it throughout. The conspiracy counts bore heavily on all the accused, particularly Montagu, as well as the admission by Wildeblood, frankly and honestly made under cross-examination, that he was an invert. It may be added that Sir Theobald Mathew, the Director of Public Prosecutions, took the liveliest personal interest in the case. Not only did he give the assurance that Reynolds and McNally, no matter how many offences they might admit, would never in any circumstances be prosecuted, he also took the trouble to come down from London to Winchester and be present in court when the sentences were passed after the three defendants had all been convicted – eighteen months in the case of Pitt-Rivers and Wildeblood, twelve months in the case of Lord Montagu. 'To punish a man at the age of twenty-seven for what was alleged against him at twenty-five must be a difficult task,' said Montagu's counsel in his plea for mitigation to the judge. 'If it had not been for recent events, Lord Montagu today would be a happily married man. That must be a devastating thought. He is a useful member of the House of Lords and a kindly landowner, he is faced with a bitter future.'

Fortunately for Lord Montagu his future was not so bitter as his counsel at the trial envisaged. He got married and his career prospered, particularly in the world of motoring, transport museums and historic houses. And, of course, the offence of which he was wrongly and unfairly convicted is no longer an offence today and has not been so for nearly twenty years. Lord Montagu is currently Chairman of the Historic Buildings and Monuments Commission.

4

There have been several homosexuals in Parliament in recent times, but with a few exceptions their behaviour has been discreet and they have consequently kept out of trouble. One such person was the Rt Hon. Sir James Tynte Agg Gardner, Lord of the Manor of Cheltenham, who represented Cheltenham in the House of Commons intermittently from 1874 until his death fifty-four years later. A cautious bachelor, who was knighted in 1916 and made a Privy Counsellor in 1924 shortly before he died, he lived in the luxury Queen's Hotel in his constituency, carefully avoiding any breath of scandal.

Another and better-known homosexual in English political life was the author and critic Sir Harold Nicolson, who began his career in the diplomatic service, married a lesbian, and after unsuccessfully contesting the Combined Universities as one of Oswald Mosley's New Party candidates at the 1931 Election, was eventually elected as National Labour Member for West Leicester which he represented from 1935 to 1945. He was also a Governor of the BBC. The only political office which he held was Parliamentary Secretary to the Minister of Information which he was for barely a year during the war. He would have liked to become a peer but he failed to reach the House of Lords, although he was made a KCVO for his flattering biography of King George V. 'Harold had a series of relationships with men who were his intellectual equals, but the physical element in them was very secondary', his son Nigel has written.

He was never a passionate lover. To him sex was as incidental, and about as pleasurable, as a quick visit to a picture-gallery between trains. His asexual love for [his wife] Vita in later life was balanced by affection for his men friends, by some of whom he was temporarily but never helplessly attracted. There was no moment in his life when love for a young man became such an obsession with him that it interfered with his work, and he had no affairs faintly comparable to Vita's.[17]

He once told Tom Driberg, whimsically, of an incident in a provincial hotel bedroom, where a waiter who had brought him some tea – 'a *ravishingly* beautiful youth' – lingered for a few moments and then said, awkwardly, 'Can I ask you a question please?' Harold, his hopes raised, said 'Yes, oh yes!' Instant deflation followed, according to Driberg, for the boy blurted out: 'Can you get me a job with the BBC?' While potency may fail in old age, Nicolson also told Driberg that desire does not, an axiom which Driberg found was only too true. Nicolson wrote constantly to a notorious homosexual, the late Guy Burgess, then in Moscow. 'So, in all the circumstances,' Driberg considered, 'I thought it notably courageous of Harold Nicolson to keep up this

[223]

correspondence with a man whom all the media were blackguarding as a traitor and "pervert".[18]

Harold Nicolson had two homosexual friends in particular, both remembered by a single book and both killed during the war. The first was Robert Bernays, Liberal MP for North Bristol and Harold's closest friend in the House. In 1942 he joined the army as a sapper in the Royal Engineers, became an officer, and was killed three years later, aged forty-two. His book *The Naked Fakir* was a study of the Indian leader Mahatma Gandhi. Nicolson's other friend was Christopher Hobhouse, who like him had stood as a New Party candidate at the 1931 Election, being soundly defeated and losing his deposit. Shortly afterwards he shared chambers with Nicolson at 4 King's Bench Walk in the Temple, where he wrote much of his excellent study of Charles James Fox. He later practised law mainly at the Divorce Bar, earning no less than £1,500 in his second year. After the outbreak of war he joined the Royal Marines and while stationed at Fort Cumberland, Portsmouth in August 1940 was killed by a direct hit during an enemy air raid a few days after his thirtieth birthday. He had recently got married and his wife was pregnant. 'Christopher and three fellow-officers were blown to pieces', Harold wrote in his diary at the time. 'They would not let her even attend the funeral since there was so little left. Poor girl. She is to have a baby in March and wants me to be godfather. She is left without a bean. I feel so sorry about it.'[19]

The most pronounced homosexual in recent times in the House of Commons, in which he served first as an Independent and then as a Labour Member with one small break from 1942 to 1974, was Thomas Edward Neil Driberg, Lord Bradwell. Journalist, broadcaster, gossip, drinker, high churchman, liturgist, and chairman of the Labour party, Tom Driberg's ruling passion was homosexuality. He first became known through his 'William Hickey' column in the *Daily Express* under the headline 'These Names Make News', in which with characteristic skill he regaled his readers with the fascinating trivia of society life. He later wrote biographies or biographical studies of such diverse personalities as the press magnate Lord Beaverbrook, the defector Guy Burgess, the Moral Rearmament founder Frank Buchman, and his fellow journalist Hannen Swaffer, besides an unfinished and posthumously published frank autobiography appropriately entitled *Ruling Passions*. Although he had a multitude of homosexual adventures,

Driberg was only tried once in court. That was before he became an MP, when he befriended two unemployed miners whom he met casually in the street late one night in 1935 and who asked him where they could find a lodging. He invited them home to his flat where they spent the remainder of the night and subsequently accused him of indecently assaulting them. His employer Lord Beaverbrook not only kept reports of the case out of the newspapers but he paid the costs of his trial at the Old Bailey where he was acquitted.[20]

His propensities soon became known in the House of Commons. Once, around the end of the war, Driberg accused the Foreign Secretary Anthony Eden of flirting with kings. Almost without knowing what he was saying, according to Sir Robert Bruce Lockhart, Eden retorted: 'I do not know how far the Honourable Member is an expert in flirtations or in what kind of flirtations.' Driberg went as white as a sheet as the House roared with laughter. After the debate Driberg approached Eden and said: 'That was a very neat retort you made,' while he pretended to laugh the matter off as if there were no inner meaning. Nevertheless he was considerably shaken by the incident.

Throughout his time as an MP Tom Driberg had only two brushes with the police and neither resulted in his prosecution. The first was shortly after his first election when he went to Edinburgh to speak at a by-election for Tom Wintringham, who had commanded the British battalion of the International Brigade in the Spanish Civil War and later founded the Osterley Park Training School for the Home Guard in Middlesex. (Wintringham was standing as an Independent but in the event was defeated.) One night during the election Driberg was caught with a Norwegian sailor, who had his trousers down in an air raid shelter, by a policeman who wished to take them both to the station. However, Tom produced a visiting card with his name and description as an MP and the writer of his pseudonymous column in the *Daily Express*. 'William Hickey!' said the policeman. 'Good God, man. I've read you all of my life! Every morning'. That was the end of the matter after Tom had promised that if the policeman would let him off, he would never do such a thing again. It worked. When he got back to London next day, he was able to describe the incident, almost as a joke to two friends, Harold Nicolson and Robert Boothby. One of them – Tom thought it was Boothby – subsequently recounted it to Compton Mackenzie, which gave him the idea for his novel *Thin Ice*, about the precarious life of a homosexual politician, published in 1956.

Driberg's other encounter with the police took place in a 'cottage' (homosexual jargon for a public lavatory) in 'the charmingly called Jockey's Fields' off Theobald's Road. As he wrote afterwards:

> This incident was mainly sordid because the younger of the two policemen involved acted as an *agent provocateur* – choosing, out of half-a-dozen empty stalls, to stand in the one next to me, and lying about what he was doing out at that time of night (on his way home from work in a hotel, he said). Initially there was vulgar abuse by the older policeman, but he calmed down and the matter was closed when I again used the formula that had been successful in Edinburgh – reinforcing it with an assurance that any charge would be hotly resisted, with benefit of learned counsel and the evidence of a genito-urinary specialist, if necessary in court after court, and pointing out that magistrates do not always look kindly on uncorroborated police evidence. The police like quick convictions of accused persons who have been foolish enough to accept their advice and plead guilty. They do not relish having to spend day after day in court on some piddling little case in which there is no prestige for them and the risk of an acquittal.[22]

Early in 1974 Tom Driberg retired from Parliament after thirty-two years' service, twenty-three of which he had been on the National Executive Committee of the Labour party, being Chairman in 1957–8. Yet he had never even held junior office when his party was in power. Why? 'The answer is simple,' he has written, 'both the Labour Prime Ministers with whom I served, Attlee and Wilson, knew of my reputation as a homosexual and both were deeply prejudiced puritans – though Attlee had been at a public school, Haileybury, at which homosexual practices flourished in or soon after his day.' He concluded that 'it is possible for a practising homosexual to do an adequate job in public life, but that if it is known that he is homosexual he will be subject to discrimination.'

After his retirement it might have been expected that Tom Driberg, in view of his distinguished political service, might have exchanged the green benches of the House of Commons for the red benches of the

House of Lords. But Harold Wilson, who was Prime Minister at the time, had a further grudge against Driberg because of an obituary of himself which Driberg had been asked to prepare for *The Times*. It appeared that a young friend of Driberg's managed somehow to secure a copy of the obituary, not from *The Times*, and showed it to the editor of the satirical magazine *Private Eye* which promptly printed part of it. Wilson understandably was furious and refused to nominate Driberg for the life peerage which in view of his political career he plainly deserved.[23] However, in the event the Prime Minister was persuaded to change his mind, possibly by Michael Foot, with the result that in 1975 Tom Driberg became Lord Bradwell of Bradwell juxta Mare, taking the title from his beautiful Georgian house Bradwell Lodge in Essex.

Unfortunately he did not live long to enjoy his peerage. In August 1976 he collapsed in a taxi after a heart attack, and he was taken to hospital where he died.[24] Few people recalled that he had a wife. He married Mrs Ena Mary Binfield in 1951. His old employer the *Daily Express* appropriately described the occasion as 'the most interesting marriage of the year'. And well it might.

Besides William Field, the most unfortunate homosexual case between the end of the Second World War and the change in the law in 1967 was that of forty-four-year-old Ian Harvey, MP for East Harrow and Under-Secretary for Foreign Affairs, in 1958. Harvey, a most likeable and congenial character, had had a distinguished career, first at Oxford, where he was President of the Union and then in the Royal Artillery during the war when he was Adjutant of his regiment and afterwards Brigade Major with the Second Army in Holland with the rank of Lieutenant-Colonel, having also been to the Staff College where he passed the course and became a fully fledged gunner. He was released to contest Spelthorne, a Middlesex constituency in the 1945 election. It had once been a safe Conservative seat but boundary changes had made it very vulnerable so that the Labour candidate won. Harvey was subsequently adopted by East Harrow which he won from Labour in February 1950, the same election at which I was returned for North Belfast. I had previously met him when he was chairman of the Coningsby Club of young Conservatives, when I admired his ability, of which he gave further proof in the House of Commons when he became secretary of the powerful Conservative Backbenchers 1922 Committee and then successively a junior minister at the Ministry of Supply and the

Foreign Office. I had no idea that he was homosexual, nor had any of his colleagues in the House of Commons I am fairly sure, owing to his discretion. I was interested in the homosexual problem and played a part in the formation of the Wolfenden Committee which recommended the change in the law relating to homosexual offences which after fourteen years eventually reached the statute book in 1967, and I had written extensively about it, particularly in the context of the Oscar Wilde trials.

The occasion of Ian Harvey's undoing was a dark and misty November night in 1958. He had been to a dinner at the Polish Embassy where there was a good deal to drink and had returned to the House for a division which in the event did not take place. He had himself had something to drink with the hospitable Poles but he was not drunk. It was not a cold night, and wishing for a breath of fresh air before he drove home to Richmond, he parked his car near Storey's Gate and went into St James's Park. It was just after eleven o'clock and the guardsmen of the Household Cavalry were returning to Wellington Barracks as the pubs had just closed. Making a circle of the park, he entered the Mall, which is a known place for homosexual pick-ups. As he was walking along, a guardsman in uniform passed him at a slow pace and Harvey knew what that meant. He turned and caught up with him and together they went into the Park.

Of course he should have realised from his knowledge that the park is regularly patrolled before midnight, and that he should have been on his guard and refrained from his action. Unfortunately he did not, with the result that he and the guardsman were detected by a park ranger and a policeman. They were both taken to Cannon Row police station and on the way Harvey tried to make a break for it but he was quickly overpowered. His second mistake was to give a false name at the station but, knowing he was bound to be recognised, he later revealed his true identity. This caused a certain amount of consternation, so that the officer in charge of the police contacted the House of Commons who confirmed his identity. Harvey was then put in a cell for the first time in his life and at 3.30 a.m. he was released on the understanding that he would appear at Bow Street in the morning. This he did and was formally remanded and given bail under his own recognisances until 10 December.

After discussing the matter with his solicitor, Harvey decided to

[228]

plead guilty at the police court to avoid further publicity, instead of going to the Old Bailey and fighting the case. Had he followed the latter course he might just conceivably have been acquitted by the jury, since he was not charged with a homosexual offence but merely with a breach of the park regulations. However, he decided to let the case be tried summarily and in the result was fined £5. He also paid the guardsman's fine. 'I felt it was the least I could do,' he wrote afterwards. In his plea of mitigation his counsel remarked, 'He will pay for this for the rest of his life.' There was some truth in this since he had to resign not only his Foreign Office post but also his parliamentary seat.

Ian Harvey's fall was tragic, since he might otherwise have risen to Cabinet rank and even ended up in the House of Lords like Tom Driberg, whose homosexuality was notorious but who had always managed to avoid being charged, whereas Harvey habitually behaved with the utmost discretion as an MP with the exception of one fatal night. 'Having worked to achieve all this [in political life] and then to shatter it in a single unguarded hour was a heavy blow to me,' he wrote afterwards in his frank and courageous autobiography.

Despite kindly assurances from numerous well-intentioned but misguided people that I would be back once it had all blown over, I knew that this was completely untrue. The gates were closed to me for ever and I could only remain on the outside looking in which is a terrible experience for one who has been on the inside looking out. Psychologically it carried with it the most damaging and dangerous of all conditions – deprivation. It was little consolation to be told that public memory is short and it will all soon be forgotten. That may be a truism but it is not a personal truth.

Curiously enough it has been and continues to be otherwise in the world of the theatre. While William Field and Ian Harvey had to resign from Parliament, the career of the actor Sir John Gielgud was unaffected after he had pleaded guilty to importuning in a Chelsea mews in 1953 and been fined £10, although when he was charged he had given his occupation as clerk, hoping no doubt to be unrecognised in court. However, he received a sympathetic ovation on the first occasion on which he appeared on the stage after his conviction. It was rumoured at the time that Sir John might be deprived of his knighthood, which he had recently received for his outstanding services in the theatre. But this could not legally have been done, since Sir John's offence was a misdemeanour and not a felony, an anachronistic difference dating from the time when all felonies from treason to sheep stealing were punishable by death. Incidentally the actor pleaded in mitigation that he had been drinking.[26] His lapse was soon forgotten and did him no harm, since in 1977 he was made a Companion of Honour by the Queen.

5

Since the tragedy of Ian Harvey there have been two cases of parliamentarians who have been accused of having homosexual relationships and one case in which a parliamentarian was accused of indecent assault of a homosexual character. The names of all three have been cleared, the third being acquitted of the charge brought against him at Southwark Crown Court after the jury had disagreed. The individuals in question were the life peer Lord Boothby, the former Leader of the Liberal party Jeremy Thorpe, and the Conservative MP for Leeds North-West Dr Keith Hampson, who had been Parliamentary Private Secretary to the Defence Secretary Mr Michael Heseltine. All three cases attracted considerable publicity at the time, which must have been an embarrassment to their recipients.

On 12 July 1964, the *Sunday Mirror* came out with astonishing headlines to a sensational story occupying three-quarters of the front page:

PEER AND GANGSTER: YARD INQUIRY

It was stated that the Metropolitan Police Commissioner, Sir Joseph Simpson, had ordered a top-level investigation into the alleged homosexual peer who was a 'household name', and a leading thug in the London underworld, who was involved in West End protection rackets. The investigation was said to be conducted by Detective Chief Superintendent Frederick Gerard, who was inquiring into Mayfair parties the peer and thug had been to, the peer's weekend visits to Brighton along with a number of 'prominent public men', his relationship with certain East End gangsters 'and a number of clergymen', and allegations of blackmail. Within forty-eight hours, it was added, Sir Joseph would be meeting the Home Secretary to give him details of the story.[27]

Next morning a press photographer named Bernard Black appeared at the offices of the *Sunday Mirror* and the *Daily Mirror* with a reel of photographs which he claimed were of the peer and the gangster. Later the same day, Sir Joseph Simpson denied that he had ordered any investigation, nor had he seen the Home Secretary, nor was there any witch-hunt of titled homosexuals. Finally, in the late afternoon, Bernard Black again visited the *Mirror* offices in Holborn Circus demanding the return of his pictures on the ground that the copyright in them did not belong to him. The *Mirror* refused to hand them over.

Three days later, on 16 July, the *Daily Mirror* under the headline, THE PICTURE WE DARED NOT PRINT, described how this picture in its files showed 'a well-known member of the House of Lords seated on a sofa with a gangster who leads the biggest protection racket London has ever known.' Less than a week later, on 22 July, there was an explicit follow-up in the West German magazine *Stern* which published an article entitled 'Lord Bobby in Trouble'. Seemingly unconcerned with the English law of libel, the German magazine named Lord Boothby and his relationship with Ronald Kray, a notorious homosexual and sadistic East End gangster with a country house in Suffolk. The *Stern* article was illustrated by pictures of Ronald Kray and his twin brother Reginald in boxing kit alongside an early photograph of Boothby and Winston Churchill.

Boothby consulted Arnold Goodman, later Lord Goodman and then senior partner in the firm of solicitors Goodman, Derrick & Co., also Gerald Gardiner, QC, later Lord Gardiner and Lord Chancellor. They suggested that before issuing a writ against the *Mirror* newspapers for libel, Boothby should write a detailed letter to *The Times* explaining his situation, which they were sure that the newspaper would publish since Boothby was friendly with the editor Sir William Haley. The editor agreed to print the letter which was largely drafted by Gerald Gardiner, who insisted on the insertion of a sentence which he regarded as crucial: '*I am not a homosexual.*' In the letter which ran to 500 words and which appeared on 2 August Lord Boothby related that he had been in France and on his return to England on 16 July he found Parliament, Fleet Street, and other 'informed quarters' seething with rumours that he had had a homosexual relationship with a leading thug in the London

[231]

underworld and that he had been photographed with him in a compromising position on a sofa, and other details as retailed by the *Sunday Mirror*.

Boothby went on to describe how he was once photographed 'with my full consent in my flat (which is also my office) with a gentleman who came to see me, accompanied by two friends, in order to ask me to take an active part in a business venture which seemed to me of interest and importance.' He explained how he had turned down the proposal, adding that, although he had since learned that the man he was photographed with had been guilty of a criminal offence, he emphatically had no knowledge of this at the time.[28] 'I am not a homosexual,' he continued, 'I have not been to a Mayfair party of any kind for more than twenty years. I have met the man alleged to be "King of the Underworld" only three times on business matters; and then by appointment in my flat, at his request, and in the company of other people.'

He had never been to a party in Brighton with any gangsters – still less with clergymen, he went on. Nor had anyone ever tried to blackmail him. Furthermore the police had denied making any report to the Home Secretary in connection with him. 'In short, the whole affair is a tissue of atrocious lies.' He concluded with a challenge to the *Mirror* newspapers. If either of them possessed documents or photographic evidence against him, 'let them print it and take the consequences'.

Five days later the *Daily Mirror* published an unqualified apology to Lord Boothby, and all imputations made against Lord Boothby were unreservedly withdrawn. In addition, Mr Cecil King, chairman of the International Publishing Corporation, which owned the *Mirror* group, apologised as well and paid Lord Boothby £40,000 plus his legal costs. Ronald Kray also received an apology, but no money.

Afterwards, in discussing the matter with Lord Boothby, he told me that Ronald Kray had rung him up 'out of the blue' for the initial appointment. He had no idea who Ronald Kray was. However Kray explained to him that he would like Boothby to become chairman of a construction company in Nigeria which was building a new township there, a project in which Kray was interested. Boothby said he would like to think it over, and the second time that Kray called Boothby told him that he could not take on the proposed company chairmanship because of the pressure of other work. It was on this occasion that Kray brought the photographer Bernard Black with him and asked Boothby

[232]

whether he would mind posing for some publicity photographs with him. The unsuspecting Boothby amiably agreed. Thus, as he told me, his relationship with Kray was minimal and was as described in his letter to *The Times*. The most flattering of the pictures taken by the photographer was sold by Ronald Kray for £100 to the *Daily Express* which published it on the front page on 6 August.

However, although Boothby's character was completely vindicated, it is worth mentioning that the law eventually caught up with Ronald Kray and his twin brother. Early in 1969 they were both tried for murder at the Old Bailey, found guilty, and sentenced by Mr Justice Melford Stevenson to life imprisonment, of which the judge recommended that they should serve not less than thirty years. The Kray twins were thirty-five at the time of their downfall.

6

On 4 August 1978, the forty-nine-year-old MP for North Devon Jeremy Thorpe, former Leader of the Liberal party, and a Privy Counsellor, was charged at Minehead magistrates court, along with three others, with conspiracy to murder a male model named Norman Scott, who in the face of strenuous denials by Thorpe claimed to have had a homosexual relationship with him. The other alleged co-conspirators were David Holmes, forty-eight, a former Liberal party treasurer and a close friend of Thorpe, whose best man he had been at Thorpe's first marriage to Caroline Allpass; and two business men from South Wales, Mr John Le Mesurier, forty-seven, and Mr George Deakin, forty-eight. All four defendants were remanded on bail pending a further court hearing on 12 September, a date subsequently twice postponed. Meanwhile on 1 September the Director of Public Prosecutions indicated that Thorpe was further accused of inciting Holmes to murder Scott. At the same time Jeremy Thorpe declared that he had no intention of resigning his parliamentary seat and that he intended to fulfil his political engagements. There was a question whether he should attend the Liberal Party Conference at this time. Although urged to stay away by the President, he appeared on 14 September for twenty minutes on the platform where he had a cool reception, and then departed.

The committal proceedings opened at Minehead on 20 November.

After the evidence for the prosecution had been given, Jeremy Thorpe's solicitor Sir David Napley submitted that there was no case to answer since the principal witnesses were 'inveterate liars'. These were Norman Scott, the male model who had also been a horse trainer; Peter Bessell, an investment consultant, thrice married former Liberal MP for Bodmin and a former Congregational Lay Preacher, who was then living in America; and Andrew Newton, a former airline pilot, who was alleged to have been hired to kill Scott. Similar submissions were made on behalf of the other defendants. Nevertheless the Minehead magistrates committed all four defendants for trial at the Old Bailey.[30]

Jeremy Thorpe, a man of outstanding intelligence, integrity and political ability, was the son of a Conservative MP and the grandson on his mother's side of another Tory Member. He was converted to Liberalism by his godmother Megan Lloyd George, daughter of the great Liberal leader and wartime Prime Minister. At Oxford he was elected President of the prestigious Union and was also President of the Liberal Club. Called to the Bar in 1954, he practised for a while at the Devon Sessions, while at the same time being drawn into local Liberal politics. He was adopted as the official Liberal candidate for the rural constituency of North Devon and was elected MP in 1959 after being defeated at the 1955 Election. In 1960 he befriended Norman Scott, a youth of twenty, who was working in riding stables in Oxfordshire. They became friends and Scott used to stay in Jeremy's London flat, where he met several of Jeremy's influential friends. Scott also stayed with Jeremy and Jeremy's widowed mother Mrs Ursula Thorpe at her house in Oxted. It was here, in November 1961, Scott subsequently alleged, that his homosexual relationship with Jeremy began. Later Mrs Ursula Thorpe attempted without success to stop the friendship, although she knew that Scott had canvassed for her son at the 1964 Election when Jeremy was returned for North Devon by a comfortable majority of 5,136, thus turning a marginal seat into a safe Liberal one.

Jeremy Thorpe's subsequent political fortunes may be briefly summarised. In 1965 he became Honorary Treasurer of the Liberal party, and two years later, following the loss of one Liberal seat at the 1966 Election and the consequent disenchantment with Jo Grimond's leadership, Jeremy Thorpe was chosen as party Leader, a position which he was to hold for the next nine years, throughout the Heath and Wilson governments. During this period he suffered several reverses.

Scott, who had been married and divorced, caused trouble by threatening to reveal his alleged relationship, which he did. Then in the 1970 Election the Liberals won only six seats in the Commons, while Jeremy's majority in North Devon dwindled to 369. At the same time Caroline Thorpe on her way to London after the declaration of the poll was killed in a motor accident. Also the South Africans were believed to be trying to get rid of Thorpe on account of his outspoken opposition to apartheid. Finally, in a secret straw vote among Liberal MPs following Scott's allegation, Thorpe was defeated but managed to retain the leadership through strong support from the rank-and-file Liberals in the country.[31]

Nevertheless as time passed it became clearer and clearer that Jeremy Thorpe's days as Liberal party leader were numbered, and with the trial of Andrew Newton, the ex-airline pilot in March 1976 on a charge of possessing a firearm with intent to endanger life, Jeremy Thorpe's resignation became a foregone conclusion. Newton had killed Norman Scott's Great Dane Rinka on a Devonshire moor and he tried to fire again, this time at Scott, but the gun jammed.

'Has anyone ever told you, or ever suggested to you, that you are an incorrigible liar?' Newton's counsel asked Norman Scott, who was the principal prosecution witness.

In his testimony Newton alleged that he had been blackmailed by Scott, who had secured a photograph in the nude of him which Newton had forwarded to an advertisement with an accompanying letter under the mistaken impression that the advertiser was 'a lady of leisure', but in reality was Scott, with the result that Newton paid Scott various sums of money totalling £28 between November 1974 and October 1975. Also he contradicted a statement he had made to the police in which he had mentioned Thorpe by name and he now denied emphatically that he had been hired to kill Scott and was paid by someone else to do so. 'At no time did I have any intention of harming Scott with the firearm,' he swore. 'All I wanted to do was to frighten him so much that he either gave me back the photograph and the letter or he stopped blackmailing me.'

The jury found Newton guilty on 19 March and the judge sentenced him to two years' imprisonment, which stunned Newton who was expecting a suspended sentence. But Mr Justice Lawton had no doubt that the sentence was fair. 'This was a cunningly contrived incident on

[235]

your part,' said the judge to Newton in passing sentence. 'Had it not been for the chance of the pistol jamming, and your being unable to stop it from being jammed, the consequence of this incident might have been very, very grave indeed.'[32]

16 March 1976, the date on which Newton's trial opened in Exeter was also the date of Harold Wilson's resignation as Prime Minister as well as the date on which Princess Margaret's marriage to Lord Snowdon ended. Whether these three events were anything more than a coincidence is a matter of conjecture.

Two months later, on 9 May, Jeremy Thorpe again denied Norman Scott's allegations in the *Sunday Times*, which also published some letters from Thorpe to Scott tending to support Jeremy's denial. As this move was likely to induce Scott to issue a writ for libel – which he did, though eventually he withdrew it – it has been suggested by a contemporary observer Chapman Pincher that it could only have been a last-ditch effort by Thorpe to avoid resigning the Liberal leadership. Pincher has also suggested that a speech by Harold Wilson, reported in the same issue about South African efforts to undermine the Liberal as well as the Labour party, was designed to help Thorpe.[33] If it was, it had no effect, since Thorpe resigned on the following day, giving a 'sustained Press witch-hunt' as his reason to his successor David Steel.

Some months later, a freelance journalist Barrie Penrose, who was writing a book with a freelance colleague Roger Courtiour called *The Pencourt File* about Wilson and Thorpe, asked the ex-Prime Minister whether there was any connection between the Liberal party and his resignation. 'The only connection with the Liberals is that if Jeremy had gone, let us say, in February or March [1976] . . . they would have linked my going with his. There was a double scandal. They would have said his homosexual partner [was] the Prime Minister, or something like this. And Mrs Thatcher would have said: "They're all going!" . . . I had to take Jeremy into consideration . . . If Jeremy went, it would preclude my going.' But if Jeremy did not, which left the way open for Wilson to go which he did in March 1976, Jeremy might stay and veto a Lib-Lab pact which their respective successors Steel and Callaghan favoured.[34]

In the latter part of 1977, rumours circulated implicating Peter Bessell and others in a plot to murder Scott. In the *Observer* on 23 October Penrose and Courtiour disclosed something of what Bessell had told them when they interviewed him in California a year before. 'He [Bessell] described meetings he had in late 1968 at which ways of killing Scott were discussed . . . Bessell told us that the man we must refer to as "X" suggested to him that David Holmes be instructed to kill Scott . . .' But within a few months Scott had got married and according to Bessell, all thoughts of murdering him were dropped. If Newton was to be believed, they revived eight years later. The inference plainly was that 'X' was Jeremy Thorpe.

On 27 October Jeremy Thorpe held a press conference at the National Liberal Club, at which he was accompanied by his second wife Marion, the former Countess of Harewood, whom he had married in 1973. Jeremy reminded the assembled journalists how he had first met Norman Scott. 'When he called on me at Westminster one afternoon in 1961, Scott was down on his luck and I felt sorry for him.' He went on to admit that he had had 'a close and even affectionate friendship' with the former male model, at the same time stressing that 'no sexual activity of any kind ever took place' between them. As for Andrew Newton's recent allegations, he went on, 'I do not know Mr Newton. I have had no direct or indirect communication with Mr Newton. I have made no payment to Mr Newton. I have no knowledge of any payment being made to Mr Newton and of any arrangement made by anyone to pay Mr Newton.' He would not, he said, resign his seat in Parliament.

'Have you ever had any homosexual relationships?' asked the BBC reporter Keith Graves.

'Go on,' Marion Thorpe interrupted angrily. 'Stand up and say that again.'

'That is not the major allegation,' Thorpe answered. 'The major allegation is that there was a Liberal hired to murder a man.'

'Because he was allegedly having a homosexual relationship with you,' the reporter said.

'It may be that our priorities are different,' Thorpe replied, keeping his temper. 'It has been alleged that a man was hired to murder somebody. That is a very, very serious crime.'[35]

On 20 October Chapman Pincher asked in the *Daily Express*:

Was there a big Westminster cover-up to save Jeremy Thorpe from being forced to resign the Liberal leadership? The question arises following a decision by the police to reopen the case in which Andrew

Newton, a former airline pilot, threatened the life of male model Norman Scott after shooting his dog.

If there was such a cover-up, it failed, as we have seen, since Jeremy Thorpe resigned his leadership on 10 May 1976.

However, in Thorpe's case the police were apparently determined that he should be prosecuted, despite the wishes of the Director of Public Prosecutions. So they leaked information, not to Fleet Street, but to the satirical magazine *Private Eye* which they considered was the most effective and indeed the only way of forcing the issue. The *Private Eye* story, 'The Ditto Man', which contained details of police interviews with Thorpe, was the final factor in persuading the DPP, Sir Thomas Hetherington, that a prosecution was unavoidable.[36]

The trial of Jeremy Thorpe and his three alleged co-conspirators was set to begin at the Old Bailey on 29 April 1979. However, a General Election had been announced with polling day on 4 May. Jeremy could not contest the election in North Devon unless the trial was postponed, which it was for nine days when the local Liberal constituency party made it clear that they wished Jeremy to be their official candidate. There was a further complication when the writer Auberon Waugh announced his intention of standing as a representative of the 'Dog Lovers' party, conceivably with the killing of Scott's dog Rinka in mind. Waugh's election address was partly a vilification of the Liberal candidate, and Thorpe's legal advisers were obliged to apply for an injunction restraining Waugh from distributing it on the ground that it would prejudice Thorpe's fair trial. The injunction was granted by the Court of Appeal after it had been turned down by the Divisional Court. The election duly took place and Jeremy lost the North Devon seat to the Conservative candidate by over 8,000 votes.[37] Waugh polled only 79 votes and forfeited his deposit.

The postponed trial opened before Mr Justice Cantley and a jury at the Old Bailey on 9 May. Since the proceedings swamped the pages of the newspapers for the ensuing six weeks, it is unnecessary to do more than describe them briefly here. Peter Taylor, QC, led for the prosecution and George Carman, QC, for the defence of Jeremy Thorpe. The evidence for the prosecution, which if believed by the jury, would have branded the former Liberal leader with gross homosexual activity and abuse of money given to him for party purposes, as well as

[238]

conspiracy at least to cause grievous bodily harm, was given by Scott and Newton, as well as by witnesses, notably Bessell, involved in back-stage transactions. Peter Taylor, in referring to Scott's visit to Mrs Ursula Thorpe's house at Oxted, submitted on behalf of the Crown that a night in November 1961 was 'the start of a homosexual affair which is at the root of this case.' The charges were vehemently denied by all the defendants, though Thorpe's counsel acknowledged that his client had had homosexual tendencies at one time.[38].

Jeremy Thorpe, David Holmes and John Le Mesurier, on their counsel's advice did not go into the witness-box, their respective counsel explaining to the jury that the accused had the right not to testify. Only George Deakin, the defendant least implicated, did so. In his summing up the judge called Scott a crook and a fraud, Newton a highly incompetent assassin, who was undoubtedly an accomplice if conspiracy was proved, and Bessell a humbug whose evidence should be treated with suspicion.

On 22 June, the jury, after retiring for fifty-two hours, found all four defendants not guilty. The verdict was undoubtedly right, although Mr Justice Cantley was criticised, for veering too far in Thorpe's favour in his summing-up.

On 1 October 1979, Jeremy Thorpe, whose counsel had declared at the trial that his political life and future were now irrevocably denied to him, told his constituency party in North Devon that he did not wish to be considered as their future candidate because he could not guarantee the time necessary to win back the seat for the Liberals. Although he has conspicuously faded out of British public life, Jeremy Thorpe remains chairman of the Political Committee of the United Nations Association and Vice-President of the Anti-Apartheid Movement.

7

One evening in May 1984, Dr Keith Hampson, forty-one-year-old Conservative MP for Leeds North West and Parliamentary Private Secretary to the Defence Minister Mr Michael Heseltine, found himself with some spare time on his hands, since his wife, who was a journalist, was working late and there was no need for him to return to their Chelsea home before 11 p.m. He had been working all day himself on a speech for the Minister to the Institute of Strategic Studies, and the previous night had been a particularly late one in the House of Commons. Feeling tired and in need of some relaxation, Hampson broke off his work about six o'clock and had a few drinks with friends in a pub near Conservative Central Office. Afterwards he returned to the Defence Ministry and did some further work until 9.15 p.m. He then decided to go to the West End to see a licensee of another pub off Shaftesbury Avenue and his wife, whom he knew. They were out so he left after having had one drink. 'Soho is a lively place,' he admitted afterwards, 'and I decided to stay there and fill in time.' He drove round the one way street system in his car until he found a spare parking place in Berwick Street. On getting out of the car, he saw a sign which said 'Male Review'. In fact it was a homosexual club called the Gay Theatre and he decided to go in and see what was happening there. He was asked for £5 as an entrance fee but when he hesitated, saying he was only going to stay for half-an-hour, he was admitted for £2. The place was dimly lit, rather like a cinema, but when his eyes became accustomed to the dimness, he could see a nude man dancing on the stage. After he had been there for a few minutes, he noticed two people come in, a man in an open necked shirt and a woman whom he thought was wearing a rubber trench coat. The woman interested him because, as he said afterwards, he thought she was 'a chap in drag'. Since he had drunk several glasses of beer, which were beginning to have their effect upon him, he got up from the chair on which he had been sitting opposite the stage and went upstairs to the lavatory to relieve himself.

On returning to the theatre the two individuals he had noticed were standing against the wall at the back of the auditorium, and in order to get a better view of the woman, he positioned himself beside the man with the woman on the man's other side. Bending down to look at the woman, he may have accidentally touched the man, who turned out to be a police officer, while the other individual was a woman police constable. The plain clothes policeman immediately grabbed Hampson, produced his warrant card, and asked the MP to accompany him upstairs. He agreed to do so, after which he was arrested on a charge of committing a homosexual offence, and was cautioned, to which he made no reply. He was then taken to West End Central Police station where he was formally charged with indecently assaulting the plain clothes policeman, after which he was released and allowed to go home.

Keith Hampson, a doctor of philosophy, educated at Bristol and Harvard universities, was one of Edward Heath's bright young men, being his personal assistant at the 1966 and 1970 General Elections and in his House of Commons office. After a spell of lecturing on American history at Edinburgh University, he was returned for Ripon at the 1974 Election with a majority of 16,000. Consequent upon boundary changes, he transferred to Leeds North West which he won for the Tories at the Election in May 1979 and again with a majority of over 8,500, in Margaret Thatcher's landslide victory in May 1983. Meanwhile he had been successively Parliamentary Private Secretary to the Minister of Local Government Tom King and to the Defence Minister Michael Heseltine, unpaid posts but always regarded as a sure stepping stone to political office in government. In 1975 he married Frances Einhorn, a model, who was killed in a motor accident just four months after their wedding. A few years later he married again, his second wife being Susan Cameron, a journalist working for the *Financial Times*. Following his arrest he resigned his PPS job with the Defence Minister.

Keith Hampson's trial which lasted for two days opened before Judge Gerald Butler, QC, and a jury of nine men and three women at Southwark Crown Court on 18 October 1984. Mr Roy Amlot prosecuted and the accused was defended by Mr John Mathew, QC.[39] Mrs Susan Hampson, who accompanied her husband to the court each day, gave evidence as to character. She said she had known him for two years before their marriage five years previously 'and there is a baby on the way'. She firmly denied that he had ever displayed homosexual inclinations of any sort and added that they had no homosexual friends.

Reminding her that she had been in court and heard the police evidence for the prosecution, Mr Mathew asked her why she thought her husband had gone to such a club as the Gay Theatre. 'Do you think it was out of curiosity?'

'Yes,' Mrs Hampson replied. 'Keith may have wondered what it was like.'

Five other witnesses testified as to the defendant's character, including Lord Tonypandy, former Speaker of the House of Commons, who wrote in a letter read to the court that the allegation was 'so totally out of character' that he could not understand what happened. He had found Hampson to be 'an honourable man whose word is his bond', the letter

went on, 'and it was a very great shock when I heard of his court case.'
Another character witness was Julia Langton, political correspondent
of *The Guardian*. She said she had known the accused for ten years and
had twice been on holiday with him. She was astounded by the news of
his arrest, as it was 'wholly out of character'.

The witnesses for the prosecution were Police Constable Stuart
Marshall and Woman Police Constable June Maudling. In his evidence-
in-chief PC Marshall said he had been attached to the clubs squad for
about three months when he visited the Gay Theatre on 3 May with
WPC Maudling. 'We arrived just after 10 p.m.', he said, 'and were
checking for offences under the Sexual Offences Act.' He spoke briefly
with the club's manager and then went downstairs where there was a
small stage on which a male in his early twenties was dancing naked.
The police witness went on to state that he had seen Dr Hampson leave
the auditorium and go upstairs and when he returned he stood beside
him, looked at him, and then made the alleged indecent assault, putting
his left hand at the back of his (the police officer's) right thigh, while
at the same time the accused's right hand grasped his groin area,
specifically 'my penis and testicles'.

Cross-examined by defence counsel, PC Marshall said he knew that
the club had been raided by police a number of times. Once in the
previous month, nine or ten people were arrested and men had also been
arrested for alleged indecent assaults on police officers. He added that
WPC Maudling was his 'partner' in the clubs squad and that they had
both kept observation on this club before. He denied that he had
deliberately dressed to look like a homosexual. He had worn very tight
jeans, an open-necked shirt, black jacket and training shoes. He had a
chain round his neck and his hair was brushed back.

'Obviously', Mr Mathew put it to the witness, 'the object of
you going dressed like that was to fit in with the scene in the gay
club?'

'I was in plain clothes and that is the clothes I would wear any day,'
PC Marshall replied.

'You must at least have been expecting that someone might make a
homosexual overture towards you?' counsel persisted.

'I did not expect a homosexual overture.'

'Were you hoping somebody would, so you could make an arrest?'

'No, sir.'

[242]

The witness went on to deny the suggestion that WPC Maudling had very close cropped hair and said he could not remember whether she was wearing a long trenchcoat.

'She might have given the appearance of a man dressed as a woman – a man dressed in drag?'

'No, sir,' replied the witness. Finally PC Marshall denied counsel's suggestion that he had made 'a precipitous arrest'.

When WPC Maudling went into the box, she said she had been wearing a brown-collared check patterned dress and a lady's fawn overcoat mac, which was knee-length. She added that she had been standing about three feet from PC Marshall and that Hampson had stood on the other side and looked at Marshall.

'He may have been looking at you,' remarked Mathew.

'I never saw him looking directly at me,' this witness replied. 'I saw him looking at PC Marshall'.

'A woman tends to be a little bit of a curiosity in this type of club?' counsel put it to her.

'People do look at you, yes,' WPC Maudling admitted. She added that she saw Hampson put his right hand on her colleague's thigh and move it up to his groin.

When it was his turn to testify, the defendant denied this most emphatically, although he admitted to his counsel that his left hand may have inadvertently touched the policeman's thigh.

'Did you take any action towards that police officer with any indecent thoughts in your mind?'

'No, of course not,' the witness replied.

Cross-examined by Mr Amlot for the prosecution, the witness was asked why he went to such a place at all. 'It was a sense of devilment one sometimes gets into,' he replied.

'It's possible you touched the police officer's penis?' the prosecuting counsel suggested.

'No, absolutely not,' the witness answered with renewed emphasis.

Summing-up next morning, Judge Butler reminded the jury that Dr Hampson was a man of exemplary character. 'He is an MP and a man who, at the time, was high in the affairs of government. But he appears in the dock as an ordinary citizen, subject, as all of us are, to the laws of the land.' The judge went on to recall that Dr Hampson's first wife had died in tragic circumstances and that he subsequently remarried. 'It is plainly a happy marriage,' he added. The judge continued: 'Many highly regarded and high-ranking people who know him well told you not only of his integrity and good character, but also said that to suggest that he was a homosexual, or had homosexual tendencies, was absurd and unthinkable. He has told you that he is not a homosexual.' Finally, after remarking that 'sleazy' was a fair description of the Gay Theatre with which he suggested that maybe the jury would not disagree, he told them that they should remember that 'the history of mankind is littered with debris of men who have acted more stupidly than anyone else would have thought possible at the time.'

The jury was absent for just over three hours when they were recalled by the judge who told them that he would be willing to accept a majority verdict. After retiring again for two more hours the jury returned to the court and the foreman informed the judge that there was no possibility for them to reach a verdict, either unanimously or by a majority of at least 10 to 2. After discharging the jury and telling them that it was no reflection on them that they had failed to reach a verdict, Judge Butler asked the prosecution to consider carefully whether there should be a second trial. In this event the retrial should take place as soon as possible. He added:

Although it is not a matter for me in any way, I nevertheless think it right to suggest, in all the circumstances, the prosecution might care to consider the future course of this case particularly bearing in mind the widespread and massive publicity it has attracted. I simply ask: Can the prosecution be satisfied that this defendant can have a fair retrial?

'In the usual way', Mr Amlot for the prosecution assured the judge, 'careful consideration will be given – and no doubt as soon as possible – as to whether a retrial is necessary or not in this case.'

At a brief hearing a week later, the prosecution announced that the case against Dr Hampson would be dropped following the jury's disagreement and there would be no retrial. Mr Amlot stated that the question of a retrial had received 'the most anxious consideration' by the DPP, the police, himself and ultimately the Attorney-General Sir Michael Havers. 'In the exceptional circumstances of this particular case,' Crown counsel went on, 'it has been decided that the interests of justice do not require a second trial. I therefore offer no evidence upon the indictment.'

Judge Butler concurred and said that he would direct a verdict of not guilty to be recorded. 'That, of course, has the same effect as if the defendant had been tried and acquitted,' the judge added.

Dr Hampson, who was not in court to hear the decision, later spoke of his 'relief' at the outcome of the proceedings. 'It has been a long ordeal,' he said. 'I have always maintained that I was innocent of the charge and this outcome is a vindication of my position. Susie and I hope that we can now get on with our work now that the matter is over.' Dr Hampson's constituency party executive were equally relieved, since the court's decision removed any doubts over his future continuance as an MP. 'We hope it is the end of the matter', a constituency spokesman was reported as saying, 'and doubt very much if anything more will be said.'[40]

Unfortunately it was not the end of the matter for Susan Hampson. The stress of the case against her husband and the subsequent uncertainty about the outcome – she was pregnant at the time of the trial – brought on a miscarriage and she lost the baby she was expecting in the following spring. 'Obviously emotions play a large part in pregnancy,' a friend told Nigel Dempster of the *Daily Mail* at the time. 'This is very sad for both of them.'[41]

The role of the police in this case cannot be said to reflect much credit on them, and it is difficult to resist the conclusion that they acted as *agents provocateurs* when the police officer's statement that he and his woman 'partner' were 'checking for offences under the Sexual Offences Act' is contrasted with the plain clothes he was wearing – tight blue jeans, open-necked shirt, black jacket, etc. 'Obviously,' as Dr Hampson's counsel put it to the policeman in cross-examination, 'the object of your going dressed like that was to fit in with the scene in the gay club,' although the policeman denied this and said they were the clothes he 'would wear any day'.

The use of the police as *agents provocateurs*, whether in public lavatories or in Soho homosexual clubs properly registered and licensed, is thoroughly objectionable on grounds of public policy, and although the senior officers in Scotland Yard deny it, the present writer has no doubt that they do act in this way in order to secure convictions. Even at the time of Dr Hampson's trial two men were charged with

[245]

gross indecency while in the audience at the Gay Theatre Club and each fined £60. Maybe they were lucky. The maximum penalty for an indecent assault on a male person is ten years' imprisonment, as provided by the Sexual Offences Act, 1956, section 15.

Call Girl Affairs
and Enthusiastic Amateurs

1

LEGAL and social attitudes in Britain to the oldest profession in the world, as female prostitution is often called, have varied between repression and licence, with the emphasis on the former, unlike various European countries which have endeavoured to regulate the conduct of brothels in different ways. The only serious attempt at regulation in Britain was through a series of Contagious Diseases Acts which required compulsory medical examination of prostitutes in military and naval garrison towns between 1864 and 1886. The legislation was repealed after its suspension in 1884 owing to the opposition of women's liberation leaders like Josephine Butler, Florence Nightingale and Harriet Martineau, who stressed the affront to female modesty of vaginal inspections, arguing that the state was not merely countenancing vice but actively patronising it. Yet probably never at any time in British history had prostitution been such a thriving business, from high class courtesans like Catherine Walters ('Skittles') and Laura Bell, who lived in luxury, to poor seamstresses and other garment workers who sold their bodies to eke out the miserable wages of their sweated labour. In the 1860s there were fifty thousand prostitutes known to the police, but the actual number was considerably more, indeed many more in relation to the population than today's equivalent of call girls and enthusiastic amateurs.[1]

Gladstone's interest in rescuing 'fallen women' from the dangers of their life was the subject of malicious gossip then and later. The statesman was in the habit of talking to prostitutes in the London streets, particularly at night, and sometimes of visiting them in their rooms and bringing them home and introducing them to his wife. In 1853, a young unemployed clerk named William Wilson followed Gladstone, then Chancellor of the Exchequer, on one of his nocturnal walks and witnessed his being accosted at 11.40 p.m. in Long Acre by a young woman whom he spoke to and accompanied to her lodgings in Soho. The youth addressed Gladstone by name and called him a lecher and threatened to 'expose' him unless he gave him 'a tidy sum of money' or a post in the Inland Revenue. The blackmailer trailed the irate minister to Sackville Street where Gladstone saw a policeman and gave the youth in charge. (Wilson got twelve months with hard labour, although after he had served half his sentence Gladstone asked the Home Secretary to release him as a personal favour.) Later, in 1882, after Gladstone had become Prime Minister for the second time, an Irish Conservative MP and old Etonian, Captain Arthur Loftus Tottenham, who represented County Leitrim, was leaving the Athenaeum Club where he had been dining when he saw Gladstone talking to a prostitute on the Duke of York's steps. Next night at dinner Captain Tottenham recounted what he had seen, and a lady who was present immediately wrote to the Prime Minister's private secretary Sir Edward Hamilton, presumably with the intention of warning Gladstone. After consulting Lord Rosebery, then Under-Secretary at the Home Office, Hamilton showed the lady's letter to his chief, venturing to say that in his opinion Gladstone's conduct was open to the gravest misconstruction. The Prime Minister himself replied to the lady on a postcard:

It may be true that the gentleman saw me in such conversation, but the object was not what he assumed, or, as I am afraid, hoped.

W.E.G.

The Prime Minister did not immediately heed this warning but when it was repeated four years later, reinforced by a popular Church of England Canon besides Rosebery and Hamilton, Gladstone on reflection agreed that he had been running considerable risks by his conduct and promised to abstain in future from speaking to women in the streets at night. That Gladstone's behaviour was extremely imprudent in the circumstances is beyond doubt, as also is the fact that it was inspired by his high moral code.[2] Nor was there the slightest truth in the charge publicly made by the journalist Captain Peter Wright after Gladstone's death that despite his high moral principles expressed in public, it was Gladstone's habit 'in private to pursue and possess every sort of woman.'*

The Criminal Law Amendment Act of 1885 was a milestone in the history of prostitution in Great Britain since it outlawed procuring and brothel-keeping and imposed penalties on the proprietors of brothels and their agents who lived on the earnings of prostitutes. Its object in the terms of its title was 'to make further provision for the protection of women and girls, the suppression of brothels and other purposes', and its appearance on the statute book was in great measure due to the efforts of W. T. Stead, editor of *The Pall Mall Gazette*, in exposing the evils of juvenile prostitution and white slavery. (Stead was not concerned with the notorious section 11 which made homosexual acts between consenting male adults an offence whether committed in public or *in private*: for this so-called 'Blackmailer's Charter' Stead's fellow journalist Henry Labouchere, MP, editor of *Truth*, was responsible.) The Act of 1885 did not make prostitution in itself illegal. The prostitute was still free to ply her trade and to solicit in the streets provided that her soliciting did not amount to a public nuisance and was not the subject of a complaint by the individual whom she attempted to solicit. On the other hand, the madams who owned or managed 'houses of ill fame' and their inmates were now obliged to operate very much under cover, while the courts were fairly liberal in their interpretation of what constituted a brothel.[3]

The various legislation concerning prostitution was broadly speaking consolidated in the Sexual Offences Act, 1956. Meanwhile a Departmental Committee under the chairmanship of Sir John (later Lord) Wolfenden had been appointed by the Home Secretary to consider the law and practice relating to prostitution and homosexual offences and to make recommendations for further changes in the law if considered necessary. The Committee reported in 1957 and as a result of its recommendations regarding prostitution the Street Offences Act was passed in 1959. This made it an offence carrying increased penalties for a 'common prostitute to loiter or solicit in a street or public place for the

---

* Gladstone's character was vindicated by Gladstone's two sons in the case of *Wright v. Gladstone* (1927). For details of this interesting case, see the present writer's *Their Good Names* (London, Hamish Hamilton 1970).

purpose of prostitution', although prostitution remained legal subject to this restriction. From the public point of view it was no doubt a desirable change, since the prohibition of soliciting virtually cleared the streets of prostitutes, who were a disgrace to London and other cities and towns. However, from the prostitutes' point of view the restriction was an onerous one, since henceforward they risked conviction if they frequented the streets in urban areas with the object of plying their trade. The result was the emergence of the 'call girl' accustomed to advertise her wares either in print or by introductions from nominally respectable friends.

Advertising by prostitutes was the subject of an interesting case at the Old Bailey in September 1960.[4] In this case, Frederick Charles Shaw, aged thirty-two, of Greek Street, Soho, was charged under three counts: (1) conspiracy to corrupt public morals; (2) living on the earnings of prostitution; (3) publishing an obscene magazine, viz the *Ladies' Directory*. Three issues of the directory contained the names, addresses and telephone numbers of prostitutes and in some instances their photographs in the nude as well as abbreviated expressions indicating that the women in question were prepared to indulge in sexual perversions of a sadistic or masochistic character for the satisfaction of their clients. Five prostitutes gave evidence that they had paid for the advertisements out of their earnings, varying from 25 guineas for the front cover to 2 guineas for a small notice, adding that they were useful in bringing in clients. The accused did not call any evidence in his defence nor did he go into the witness-box himself. However, he had admitted to the police that his avowed object in publishing the directory was to assist prostitutes to ply their trade, which as a result of the Street Offences Act, 1959, they were no longer able to do by soliciting in the streets. His counsel pleaded in mitigation that the defendant was genuinely concerned with finding out whether the law would take any action and had taken legal advice which unfortunately turned out wrong. Defence counsel also submitted that there was no such offence in English law as conspiracy to corrupt public morals and that there was no evidence to support the charge that Shaw had been living on the earnings of prostitution. Judge Maxwell-Turner ruled against both these submissions and in due course Shaw was convicted by the jury on all three counts and sentenced to nine months' imprisonment.

'Whether you took legal advice or sought to find out whether what you were doing was legal or not,' said the judge in passing sentence, 'you pursued a course of conduct which the jury has found corrupted and debauched public morals . . . Clearly the publication of these directories encouraged both prostitution and the practices advertised in them . . . You were clearly enriching yourself at the expense of public morals.'

Shaw thereupon appealed to the Court of Criminal Appeal which dismissed his appeal but granted the appellant leave to appeal to the House of Lords, having held that conspiracy to corrupt public morals was a common law misdemeanour. By a majority of four to one the Lords held against the appellant.[5] Thus, in spite of the solitary dissenting judgment, Shaw's case has established that the offence of conspiring to corrupt public morals is part of the law of England and that such a criminal offence was committed in the circumstances of this case. The case has also caused prostitutes to be much more discreet in their advertisements, in future tending to masquerade under such legitimate occupations as masseurs, escorts and club hostesses.

Another aspect of prostitution besides advertising must be briefly mentioned, namely 'kerb-crawling', that is motorists who cruise the streets in cars soliciting potential prostitutes. In January 1985 Miss Janet Fookes, Conservative MP for Plymouth Drake, introduced a private member's bill, outlawing kerb-crawling and imposing penalties for this offence ranging from a maximum fine of £400 for a first offence to £2,000 for a third offence.[6] Its aim, she was reported as saying, was to give greater protection to women and girls.

In every major city and town there is a small area, sometimes a larger one, where the residents are made unhappy, and where on occasions women are afraid to go out on their own. It is intolerable in a civilised society there should be no-go areas for respectable citizens.

Public attention had been drawn to kerb-crawling in December 1976 when the colourful Labour peer Lord Wigg of Dudley, who precipitated the Profumo scandal, appeared before a magistrate who decided that he had gone kerb-crawling one night in Mayfair. However, he was acquitted of insulting behaviour with which he was charged, the magistrate pointing out that kerb-crawling was not in itself illegal. (In fact Lord Wigg was not kerb-crawling at all but looking for news-vendors of the early editions of the following day's papers.)

Miss Fookes's Bill passed its second reading in the Commons but ran into trouble during the report stage when it was 'talked out' by two fellow Conservatives Mr Matthew Parris (Derbyshire West) and Mr Anthony Marlow (Northampton North), who objected to some of its provisions, Mr Parris speaking for more than an hour against it. Miss Fookes was naturally very disappointed and angered. However, the two dissident Tories had second thoughts and when the measure came up again a week later they let it pass. After being considered by the House of Lords it eventually became law later in 1985.[6]

2

The two most prominent call girls to emerge in the 1960s were Christine Keeler and Marilyn ('Mandy') Rice-Davies, who lived successively with a fashionable but somewhat dissolute osteopath named Stephen Ward, son of a Canon in the Church of England. Ward, a highly sexed man, was aged fifty when he first met the girls, who were still in their teens. He had a small London flat at 17 Wimpole Mews, W.1., and a country cottage on the Astor estate of Cliveden. He used to pick up pretty girls and seduce them, while they stayed with him in London and the country. He was a compulsive name-dropper and was in the habit of procuring girls for his influential friends. Some of these had perverted tastes and Ward was said to have arranged for whipping and other sado-masochistic performances in his flat. One of Ward's call girls, Vickie Barrett, was an adept at wielding a cane or riding whip on middle aged and elderly gentlemen, while dressed in underwear and wearing high-heeled shoes, which incidentally Ward bought for her; this exercise cost her clients £1 a stroke. Another call girl, Margaret Ricardo, admitted going to Ward's flat which was then in Bryanston Mews with a girl friend and a man, and after she arrived she had intercourse with the man and Ward did likewise with the girl at the same time in the same room, which had a two-way mirror. The four call girls – Keeler, Rice-Davies, Barrett and Ricardo – were all to give evidence for the prosecution when Ward was charged with living on the earnings of prostitution, which he was at the Old Bailey in July 1963.[7]

[252]

Five months previously Christine Keeler made the following statement, which she signed, as also did Mandy Rice-Davies by way of corroboration:

The more rich and influential people I met the more amazed I was at their private lives. Names who are household words take part in the most obscene things. One night I was invited to a dinner party at the home of a very, very rich man. After I arrived I discovered it was a rather unusual dinner party. All the guests had taken off their clothes. There were both men and women there and the men included people I would not have suspected of ever doing anything improper. There was some well-known barrister who, I am sure, would be willing to make stirring speeches in court attacking that sort of thing.

There were also some well-known actors and a politician whom I recognised. The most intriguing person, however, was a man with a black mask over his face. At first I thought this was just a party gimmick. But the truth was that this man is so well known and holds such a responsible position that he did not want to be associated with anything improper. And I can assure you that party was improper. The guests were not just ardent nudists. Even I was disgusted.

This story was retailed by newspapers in this country and also in countries abroad where it was said that a prominent public figure was the man in the mask.

'There is a great deal of evidence which satisfied me that there is a group of people who hold parties in private of a perverted nature,' wrote the Master of the Rolls Lord Denning in his report on the operation of the Security Service, which was published in September 1963.

At some of these parties, the man who serves the dinner is nearly naked except for a small square lace apron round his waist such as a waitress might wear. He wears a black mask over his head with slits for eye-holes. He cannot therefore be recognised by any of the guests. Some reports stop there and say that nothing evil takes place. It is done as a comic turn and no more. This may well be so at some of the parties. But at others I am satisfied that it is followed by perverted sex orgies: that the man in the mask is a 'slave' who is whipped: that the guests undress and indulge in sexual intercourse one with the other: and indulge in other sexual activities of a vile and revolting nature.

Stephen Ward was undoubtedly present at some of these parties, and on one occasion when there were initially more men than women Ward telephoned Christine Keeler and Mandy Rice-Davies and asked them to come, which they did towards the end of the party. It was said that the man in the mask, alleged to be a minister, wore nothing except the mask with a little card saying 'If my services don't please you, whip me.' Ward, when examined by Denning, denied that he told the two girls that the man was a minister. In fact Lord Denning found that there was much to disprove the rumour that he was. The judge saw quite a number of those who were at these parties, in particular a solicitor, who impressed him by his truthfulness, besides the host and hostess and also the man in the mask himself. 'He is now grievously ashamed of what he did,' Lord Denning stated in his Report. 'He does not bear any resemblance whatever to the minister who was the victim of rumour.'[8]

In addition to his sex obsession Ward was a gifted artist. Indeed he had been employed by the *Daily Telegraph* to go to Israel to execute drawings at the trial of the Nazi Adolf Eichmann in Jerusalem. Among Ward's patients was the editor of the *Daily Telegraph* Sir Colin Coote to whom Ward expressed the wish to visit Moscow and draw pictures of Mr Khruschev and other Soviet personalities since according to Lord Denning, Ward admired the Soviet regime and had Communist sympathies. As a result Coote introduced him to Captain Eugene Ivanov, then Assistant Naval Attaché at the Russian Embassy in London, who was also a member of GRU, the Soviet secret military intelligence directorate.

William ('Bill') Waldorf Astor succeeded his father as third Viscount Astor in 1952 when he was forty-five and inherited the Cliveden estate near Taplow in Buckinghamshire. He had previously served in the House of Commons and it was when he represented Wycombe that the present writer first met him as a fellow MP. When he was Parliamentary Private Secretary to the Home Secretary Sir Samuel Hoare before the war, he became a strong opponent of capital punishment, Hoare (later Lord Templewood) also being a convinced abolitionist. Bill Astor was a public spirited man, doing valuable work for hospitals and refugees as well as funding various educational and social charities. He also inherited a famous stud of racehorses and a 250-acre farm, both of which he managed himself. In 1950 he got to know Stephen Ward when he went to see him as a patient after a fall in the hunting field. Six years later he let an attractive cottage on the Cliveden estate to Ward at a nominal rent of £1 a year. Astor sent Ward many of his friends as patients, guaranteed his overdraft, lent him money, and introduced him to the guests who often stayed at Cliveden. Astor was three times married and liked women with whom he sometimes had extra-marital relations. These included Mandy Rice-Davies. When asked by counsel at the magistrate's court where Ward was charged with living on immoral earnings, if she was aware that Lord Astor had denied her statement that she had been to bed with him, Mandy replied: 'He would, wouldn't he?' Her reply became so celebrated as to justify its inclusion in the new edition of *The Oxford Dictionary of Quotations*.[7]

Christine Keeler came from Wraysbury between Windsor and Staines, where she spent most of her childhood in a converted railway carriage without a bath and electricity, her mother being a devout Catholic and her stepfather a man with whom she did not get on. She left home when she was about fifteen and drifted to London where she got a job at Murray's Cabaret Club as a show-girl, which involved, as she put it to Lord Denning, 'just walking about with no clothes on'. For this she was paid £8.50 a week plus £5 for sitting out with a customer, with extra if the customer bought drink or flowers. ('Of course, if you went home with them you might get £25 but that was nothing to do with the club. I only went home with the ones I fancied.') Years later when interviewed by John Mortimer she admitted that all she wanted was fun. ('Nothing serious. To me life was for having a good time.')[10] It was at the club that she met Stephen Ward who danced with her. She later went to live with him in Wimpole Mews, but surprisingly they never had sexual relations. ('I loved him but I didn't fancy him.') He took her to the cottage at Cliveden and introduced her to many men, sometimes men of rank and fashion, with whom she had sex. One such individual was said to be the slum property racketeer Peter Rachman with whom she lived for a time, although it has also been stated that they were not introduced by Ward but met by accident. Later on Ward, according to Lord Denning, introduced her to the drug Indian hemp and she became an addict. She also met two coloured men Lucky Gordon and John Edgecombe who trafficked in the drug and she lived with them.

Mandy Rice-Davies, also employed at Murray's Club, was another fun-loving girl, who also lived for a time with Stephen Ward and was taken over by Peter Rachman when he had finished with Christine. Her father was a Birmingham policeman and she came from Solihull, a few miles from Birmingham in Warwickshire. She was a pert little girl, the same age as Christine, and although Christine was rather better looking and played the major part in the subsequent dramatic scandal, it was Mandy who managed to capture the newspaper headlines with such expressions as 'Call me Lady Hamilton!' and 'He would, wouldn't he?' She had a roguish twinkle in her eyes and a smart line in repartee. Even after she had left Rachman and was living with Stephen Ward, her ex-lover according to her still paid her an allowance of £100 a week. 'My saving grace in life has always been my ability to get on with most other people,' she has written demurely.[11] These people included Stephen Ward and Lord Astor.

In the ensuing drama the weekend of 8/9 July 1961 was of crucial importance. On that weekend Lord Astor entertained a large house party at Cliveden. His guests included Mr John Profumo, then Secretary of State for War, a Privy Counsellor and a prominent member of Mr Macmillan's government, although he was not in the Cabinet. Mrs Profumo, the former actress Valerie Hobson, accompanied her husband. There was a large swimming pool near the house which Astor allowed Ward to use. On the Saturday evening, after nightfall, Astor and the other guests walked down to the pool where Ward and several girls including Christine Keeler were bathing. The host and Mr Profumo walked ahead followed by Lady Astor, Mrs Profumo and the other guests. When she heard the sound of voices Christine, who had discarded her swim suit and was bathing naked, rushed out of the pool to get it, but Ward had hidden it, so she seized a towel and used it to hide her nakedness. The incident was treated as a piece of fun and there was nothing indecent in it. When Ward and the girls got dressed, they all went up to the house and joined the party there for a while. Profumo was obviously attracted by Christine and he obtained her telephone number from Ward, who then apparently encouraged Keeler to see the War Minister on the ground that he was both distinguished and important.

[256]

Next day Ivanov came down to the cottage and in the afternoon there was another bathing session in the pool in which both Astor's and Ward's guests took part, the Minister and the Soviet attaché taking part in swimming races. That evening Ivanov drove Christine back to London, while Ward followed on later. Ivanov had a bottle of vodka in his car, from which he and Christine had several drinks before arriving at Ward's flat in Wimpole Mews. 'We got rather silly and that's when it happened', Christine said later. In other words, she let Ivanov make love to her on the floor of the flat. This was the only occasion on which this happened, she subsequently asserted. But other individuals took a contrary view, believing that she went to bed with Ivanov on a number of occasions, on one of which she also slept with John Profumo the same day. That Profumo had sex with Christine on several occasions at Ward's flat is beyond doubt. On one occasion he borrowed a car and on this occasion he took Christine to his house in Regent's Park, a visit which Christine afterwards described with some particularity.[12]

Meanwhile the Security Service (MI5) had been taking an interest in Ivanov, whom they hoped might be persuaded to defect. They knew of Ivanov's friendship with Stephen Ward, and a MI5 officer called Wagstaffe, using the cover name 'Woods' and posing as a man from the War Office, gave Ward lunch on 8 June. Ward agreed to co-operate, although the officer had some reservations about him considering him indiscreet, which was true. However, immediately after the Cliveden weekend Ward reported the presence of the War Minister at Lord Astor's house party, and 'Woods', who thought that Profumo's acquaintance with Ivanov might jeopardise the possibility of Ivanov's defection, passed the information to the Director-General Sir Roger Hollis, who agreed that the War Minister should be warned of MI5's interest in Ivanov and Ward. He asked the Cabinet Secretary Sir Norman Brook to do this. Accordingly Brook spoke to the Minister on 9 August, suggesting that Profumo should be careful in his future relations with Ivanov and Ward. Profumo replied that since the Cliveden weekend he had only met Ivanov once, for a few minutes at a reception in the Soviet Embassy for the astronaut Major Gagarin. He added that he knew Ward better, as did many others, and he thought it might be helpful if they too were warned, particularly another Minister. (Brook did warn him.) The Cabinet Secretary went on delicately to refer to another matter: 'Was it possible to do anything to persuade Ivanov to help us?' Profumo wisely and understandably declined this request, and Brook reported back to Hollis in this sense.[13]

Profumo evidently thought that the real reason for Brook's call on him was a polite way of indicating that the Minister's assignations with Christine Keeler should cease. Profumo happened to have arranged to see Christine on the following night, and he now wrote to her putting her off. However, neither Brook nor Hollis knew that Profumo was having an affair with her and they had no reason to suspect it. Profumo's letter, written on War Office stationery, was as follows:

Darling,
    In great haste because I can get no reply from your phone –
    Alas something's blown up tomorrow night and I can't therefore make it. I'm terribly sorry especially as I leave the next day for various trips and then a holiday so won't be able to see you again until some time in September. Blast it. Please take great care of yourself and don't run away.

Love J.

P.S.   I'm writing this 'cos I know you're off for the day tomorrow and I want you to know before you go if I still can't reach you by phone.

Conceivably Profumo and Keeler may have met once or twice more, but the affair had petered out by December 1961 which was the last date on which he saw her, and they did not meet again. That might have been the end of the matter had it not been for Keeler going to live at Brentford with the West Indian John Edgecombe, whom she subsequently left when she leased a flat in Great Cumberland Place. On 14 December 1962 she called at Ward's flat in Wimpole Mews where Mandy Rice-Davies was now living with Ward. Somehow Edgecombe discovered she was there and turned up in a mini-cab. When the girls refused to admit him, he pulled out a gun and fired several shots at the door. He then made off in the cab but the police caught and arrested him. This incident naturally focused the attention of the press on Christine Keeler and Stephen Ward. Christine now told several people that she had been to bed with Profumo and also Ivanov, and it looked as if the scandal might break by her either testifying at Edgecombe's trial or writing an article in a newspaper. In fact, Edgecombe's trial was postponed on account of the illness of the mini-cab driver and it did not take place until 14 March 1963, by which date Christine had left the country for a holiday in Spain unknown to the police who were consequently unable to produce her as a witness. In the event Edgecombe was convicted of possessing a firearm with intent to endanger life and sentenced to seven years' imprisonment.[14]

3

Meanwhile Christine had sold her story along with the 'Darling' letter from Profumo to the *Sunday Pictorial*, £200 paid in advance. When Ward discovered this, he was considerably worried, since he did not know what the story contained or would contain. Consequently he warned Ivanov that embarrassing revelations might result for both of them. Ivanov consequently reported this to his GRU employers in Moscow who immediately recalled him, and he left London on 29 January 1963. At the same time reports were reaching the Security Service from a reliable source about Profumo's association with Christine Keeler and that the girl had also been visited by Ivanov. However, Hollis decided that it was not within the proper scope of MI5 to enquire into these matters, since the service was not concerned with a Minister's private life, and even if Profumo was sharing a mistress with Ivanov there was no reason to suppose that information had passed from the Minister to the Assistant Naval Attaché through the girl. In any event Ivanov had now left the country, so any present risk had gone. Hollis accordingly decided that no approach should be made to anyone 'in the Ward *galère*'.

A few days later, on 4 February, Wagstaffe, the MI5 officer who had originally approached Ward as a potential agent but had later dropped him as being indiscreet and unreliable, sent a memorandum to Sir Roger Hollis:

If a scandal results from Mr Profumo's association with Christine Keeler, there is likely to be a considerable political rumpus . . . if in any subsequent inquiries we were found to have been in possession of this information about Profumo and taken no action on it, we would,

[259]

I am sure, be subject to much criticism for failing to bring it to light. I suggest that the information should be passed to the Prime Minister and you might also like to consider whether or not, before doing so, we should interview Miss Keeler.[15]

After discussing this memorandum with his deputy Graham Mitchell, Hollis repeated his conviction that the matter was outside the proper function of the Security Service and that 'no inquiries should be made by us', which meant that they should not interview Keeler. Anyhow the allegations were already known to the Prime Minister's office, Hollis added. In fact a senior newspaper executive on the *News of the World*, Mark Chapman-Walker, told Mr Macmillan's Private Secretary Tim Bligh about Keeler's deal with the rival paper the *Sunday Pictorial*, and Bligh had seen Profumo, whom he advised to see the Government Chief Whip Martin Redmayne. This Profumo immediately did along with Bligh, recounting his version of the events of the second half of 1961. He remarked that after the Cliveden weekend 'in order to get a giggle in the evening' he had subsequently gone round to Stephen Ward's flat 'to meet a few young people and have a drink before dinner.' Most of the young ladies to be found there were not the sort of people one would wish to accompany one to a constituency meeting. But his wife had many theatrical friends and he was used to relaxing in this *galère*. He had written a harmless letter to Miss Keeler which started 'Darling' and he had given her a small present of a cigarette lighter. But he strongly denied having slept with her. He also mentioned Sir Norman Brook's visit, that he had been told by the Cabinet Secretary he should see as little as possible of Ward since there was a security problem involved, and that he had heeded this warning. His lawyers, Profumo concluded, advised him to do nothing until the newspaper article or articles appeared, and take legal proceedings if they contained anything libellous.[16]

'I was satisfied with these assurances,' Mr Macmillan wrote after they had been reported to him by his Private Secretary on 4 February. 'No doubt Profumo had frequented circles in which, in my youth, it would have been thought inappropriate for a Minister to move. But times had changed, and although I had not myself much knowledge of this new social world I recognised that the distinctions which had ruled in the past no longer obtained.'[17]

Three days later, on 7 February, the head of the Special Branch at Scotland Yard reported to MI5 that the police in Marylebone had interviewed Christine Keeler on 26 January and been informed by her that there was an illicit association between herself and Profumo, that she had met Ivanov on a number of occasions, and that Stephen Ward had asked her at the time of the Cuban crisis to discover from the War Minister the date on which 'atomic secrets' were to be handed by the Americans to West Germany. A few days later Ward told the police that he had been a close friend of Ivanov, whose nickname in diplomatic circles was 'Foxface'. However, in Hollis's absence, his deputy agreed with the subordinate officer concerned that there was no security interest involved to warrant further steps being taken. 'No action on this at present,' Graham Mitchell minuted the file. 'Please keep me informed of any developments.' The Prime Minister was not informed. Nor for that matter was any other government minister.[18]

The *Sunday Pictorial* waited until after the Edgecombe trial before publishing anything on Christine Keeler. But instead of an article by her it published one by Stephen Ward on 17 March on the subject of his friendship with her but not mentioning Profumo, although Ward was reported as stating that 'Christine knew a number of distinguished men in public life.' Talk now became widespread about Profumo and Keeler, notably that the War Minister had contrived her disappearance as a witness in the Edgecombe trial.

On 21 March, a week after the Edgecombe trial, the Labour MP George Wigg, who took a particular interest in security matters, asked the Home Secretary in the House of Commons either to deny the rumours circulating about a member of the Government Front Bench or else to appoint a Select Committee to investigate them. He was supported by two Labour colleagues, Mr R. H. S. Crossman and Mrs Barbara Castle. Later the same night Profumo was summoned from his home by the Government Chief Whip and the Law Officers to draft a personal statement which it was felt he should now make to the House. The draft was approved by the Prime Minister next morning which was a Friday and the War Minister delivered the statement at the opening of business in the Commons later the same morning.

In his statement the War Minister declared that, in view of the fact that his name had been connected with Miss Keeler's disappearance, he had not seen her since December 1961, prior to which he had seen her on about half a dozen occasions in Dr Ward's flat. Nor was he in any way responsible for her absence from the Edgecombe trial. 'Miss Keeler and I were on friendly terms,' he said. 'There was no impropriety whatsoever in my acquaintanceship with Miss Keeler.' He added that he would not hesitate to issue a writ for libel and slander 'if scandalous allegations are made or repeated outside the House.'[19]

'Profumo has behaved foolishly and indiscreetly, but not wickedly,' Mr Macmillan noted in his diary the same day. 'Of course all these people move in a raffish theatrical, bohemian society, where no one really knows anyone and everyone is "darling". But Profumo does not seem to have realised that we have – in public life – to observe different standards from those prevalent today in many circles.'[20]

The Prime Minister's confidence in the War Minister was strengthened by the latter's action in issuing writs for libel against two foreign journals *Paris-Match* and the Italian *Il Tempo* and their London distributors. In the first case, the defendant retracted immediately and in the second Profumo was awarded costs and damages. Ward and Keeler both confirmed that what Profumo had said in the House of Commons was true. There the matter might have ended had it not been for anonymous letters received by the Criminal Investigation Department at Scotland Yard, alleging that Ward was living on the immoral earnings of Christine Keeler, Mandy Rice-Davies and other girls. On 1 April 1963 the Commissioner of Police, who had been consulted by the Home Secretary, decided that Ward's activities should be investigated. This decision sealed Profumo's fate. The police took statements from many of the girls, notably Christine Keeler which they signed. Keeler's dealt mainly with Ward's conduct, but in it she confessed to having had sex with the War Minister. She said he had taken her to his house in Regent's Park when his wife was away, a visit which she described in these words:

When I went to Jack Profumo's we went off the Outer Circle to a house on the left-hand side of a small road. I went up some steps into a square hall where there are two large ornamental animals, I think dogs. The dining room was on the right and the stairs are straight ahead on the right. The stairs bend to the left and on the left and on the wall is a picture of all the things that Valerie likes and dislikes, including pigeons and jewellery. Facing the top of the stairs is Jack's office, with a drinks cabinet inside. I noticed a strange telephone and he said it was a scrambler. Next door is the Profumos' bedroom with an adjoining bathroom. I think there were a lot of mirrors in the bathroom.

'I last saw Jack in December 1961,' she added. 'Stephen Ward had asked me to get information from Jack about the Americans giving the Germans the Bomb. I did not get this information because it was ridiculous and could have been made in a joke.'[21]

At first Ward was co-operative. But when his patients and friends were questioned which they were, sometimes repeatedly, he voiced his objections to a number of authorities including the Home Secretary, his local MP and Mr Harold Wilson, the Leader of the Opposition. 'Over the past few weeks I have done what I could to shield Mr Profumo from his indiscretion, about which I complained to the Security Service at the time,' Ward wrote to the Home Secretary on 19 May. 'When he made a statement in Parliament I backed it up, although I knew it to be untrue. Possibly my efforts to conceal his part and to return him a letter which Miss Keeler had sold to the *Sunday Pictorial* might make it appear that I had something to conceal myself. I have not.' Next day he wrote to Mr Wilson: 'Obviously my efforts to conceal the fact that Mr Profumo had not told the truth in Parliament have made it look as if I myself had something to hide. It is quite clear now that they must wish the facts to be known, and I shall see that they are.' Mr Wilson sent a copy of this letter to the Prime Minister. It should be added that Ward had previously seen Mr Macmillan's Private Secretary Tim Bligh in the presence of a Security Service Officer, the main object of the visit being, as Lord Denning put it in his Report, 'to get the police inquiries called off and to blackmail the Government threatening that, unless the inquiries were dropped, he would expose Mr Profumo's illicit association with Christine Keeler.'[22]

In response to further pressure by Harold Wilson, the Prime Minister sent for Hollis on 29 May and for the first time learned from him the substance of Christine Keeler's statement of 26 January to the police, as already described. Hollis added that the evidence was considered too slender to permit Ward being prosecuted under the Official Secrets Act. ('He is not known to us to have been in touch with any Russian since Ivanov's departure. The security risk that Ward now represents seems to me to be slight.') Mr Macmillan thought the story ridiculous since Profumo had no information on 'atomic secrets'. Nevertheless he did not feel that this development should be wholly disregarded. Hence he asked the Lord Chancellor Lord Dilhorne to look into the matter further and he informed Harold Wilson of his action.[23] Profumo was accordingly seen by the Chief Whip and Bligh, who told him it looked as if there would be an inquiry and that the Lord Chancellor would wish to see him; also if there was any flaw in his story it would do the Government enormous damage. It was put to him strongly that if there was anything untrue in his statement to the House, he ought to reveal it of his own accord. He again denied that he had said anything that was untrue.

On 31 May Parliament adjourned for the Whitsun recess. The Prime Minister and Lady Dorothy Macmillan went to Scotland, while Profumo and his wife left for Venice. Shortly after his arrival there Profumo, assailed no doubt by a guilty conscience, told his wife the truth. 'Oh, darling', said Valerie Profumo as soon as she heard the details, 'we must go home now just as soon as we can and face up to it.' They arrived in England on Whit Sunday. Two days later Profumo again saw the Chief Whip and the Prime Minister's Private Secretary. Without any preamble he told them, 'I have to tell you that I did sleep with Miss Keeler and my statement in that respect was untrue.' It was plain that he could not remain a member of the Government. Next day he sent a letter of resignation to the Prime Minister and its contents were communicated to Mr Macmillan in Scotland. In the circumstances this was accepted, as it was bound to be, since Profumo, despite careful warning from friends and colleagues, had deliberately lied to the House of Commons and the Law Courts. Nor did he wait on the Queen to hand over his seals of office: they were sent by messenger. He also resigned his seat in Parliament. The House of Commons later held him to have been guilty of contempt of the House. His name was removed from the list of the Privy Council. Meanwhile the *News of the World* on 9 June began the serial publication of Christine Keeler's life story, for which 'literary gem', as Mr Macmillan described it, the newspaper paid her £23,000. At the same time the *Sunday Mirror* published on its front page a photographic copy of the 'darling' letter. Profumo's disgrace was complete.[24]

4

Coming in the wake of the Vassall homosexual spy case, the Profumo affair was most embarrassing for the Government, particularly the Prime Minister, to judge by his remarks in the relevant volume of his memoirs, *At The End Of The Day*. Newspapers were markedly hostile. '*The Times* was awful . . . really nauseating', Mr Macmillan wrote in his diary on 7 July looking back. 'The "popular" Press has been one mass of life stories of spies and prostitutes, written no doubt in the office. Day after day the attacks developed, chiefly on me – old, incompetent, worn out.'[25] The Cabinet was loyal, but the public generally believed the Government to be about to break up. 'Why in God's name', Lord Beaverbrook asked the *Express* defence correspondent Chapman Pincher, 'should a great political party tear itself to rags and tatters just because a minister's fucked a woman?'[26] On 17 June the Prime Minister had to defend his conduct in a difficult debate in the House of Commons when twenty-seven Conservatives abstained in the vote, 'not only the usual malcontents,' Mr Macmillan noted, 'but a lot of worthy people, who had been swept away by the wave of emotion and indignation.' Besides Lord Lambton, the abstentionists included Sir Martin Lindsay, Mr Nigel Birch, Mr Aubrey Jones, and Miss Joan Quennell.[27] There were widespread accusations of lax security, and to allay public anxiety on this question Mr Macmillan asked Lord Denning to report on the operation of the Security Service in the light of the circumstances leading to Profumo's resignation, and the adequacy of the Service's co-operation with the police in security matters; also to consider any evidence there might be for believing that national security had been or might be endangered.

In addition to the Profumo-Ward scandal, the Prime Minister wrote:

a kind of Titus Oates atmosphere prevailed, with the wildest rumour and innuendo against the most respectable Ministers. Altogether, partly by the blackmailing statements of the 'call girls'; partly by the stories started by or given to the Press; and partly (I have no doubt) by Soviet agents exploiting the position, more than half the Cabinet were being accused of perversion, homosexuality and the like.

At the same time, as he told the Queen, although the precise role that Ward had played was not as yet known, he (the Prime Minister) had begun 'to suspect in all these wild accusations against many people, Ministers and others, something in the nature of a plot to destroy the established system.'[28] Fortunately this state of affairs did not continue for very long. There was an encouraging public reaction in the Prime Minister's favour which Mr Macmillan capped in a constituency speech in which he made it clear that he intended to hold on, doing what was best for the country and his party. Nevertheless, the situation was bound to have an adverse effect upon the Conservatives at the next General Election in the following year which in the event they lost to Labour.

The subsequent course of events may be recounted briefly but not in strict chronological order. First, Lord Denning's Report, which was published on 26 September 1963. It took its author seven weeks to hear the witnesses, about 160 in all, ranging from the Prime Minister, Profumo, Wigg, and the Director-General of the Security Service, to Stephen Ward, Christine Keeler and five other girls who knew Ward well. In addition Denning had numerous written memoranda, including the Lord Chancellor's report which was not published separately but which Denning used to a considerable extent. According to Chapman Pincher, Dilhorne believed Hollis to have been grossly at fault for keeping the Prime Minister and Home Secretary in ignorance of the facts for so long, but the Lord Chancellor was opposed to any public criticism of MI5 or its chief.[29] So also was Lord Denning, who played down Hollis's action on the ground that the Security Service was only concerned with security risks and not with a Minister's moral misbehaviour. 'Their principal interest was in Captain Ivanov, the Russian intelligence officer: and secondarily in Stephen Ward, as a close friend of his,' Lord Denning concluded. 'They took all reasonable steps to see that the interests of the country were defended. In particular they saw that Mr Profumo and another Minister were warned of Ward. They kept the Foreign Office fully informed. There is no reason to believe that there was any security leakage whatever.'[30] The Prime Minister later expressed his satisfaction that the Report, whose publication he authorised subject to some minor omissions on security grounds, 'proved an overwhelming answer to the campaign of scandal and obloquy which had raged throughout the summer.'[31]

In an interesting commentary on the Report a few days after its publication, George Wigg observed that in raising the matter as he did in the Commons he was not concerned with Profumo's morals but was thinking of only one thing – security. Naturally he was one of the witnesses who appeared before Lord Denning, but he was alarmed by the letter which he received from Denning inviting his attendance. 'As I expect you know,' Denning wrote, 'I have been entrusted by the Prime Minister with the task of inquiring into the reports which are circulating which affect the honour and integrity of public life in this country.' This was not, in fact, what his Lordship had been asked to do, though there was an aside in the Prime Minister's statement to the Commons which might seem to give him this authority. Wigg did his best to point out what he considered to be the absurdity of Denning's letter. He told him that if he was going to inquire into the honour and integrity of public life he was not going to produce a report by July, the date he hoped. Indeed Wigg thought privately that Denning would be still hard at it, even though he lived to be a hundred.

Wigg refused to answer any questions that seemed to him to be irrelevant to the issue of security. For instance, what did he think about the Duke and Duchess of Argyll and their recent divorce? Wigg replied that he was not interested in divorce cases and knew nothing about them. 'But don't you think I ought to investigate an aspect of their divorce?' Denning persisted. (This was the story of a photograph of a man minus his head which had been removed from the photograph, the man supposedly being a Minister, who allegedly paid the Duke money through an intermediary in the person of Stephen Ward to prevent himself from being cited in the divorce case.) 'My Lord, I have no views about the matter,' Wigg replied. 'It is entirely a question for you to decide.'[32]

In his commentary Wigg wrote:

A High Court Judge is not qualified to pontificate about 'the honour and integrity of public life'. The honour and integrity of public life are decided by the general attitude of a civilisation, and if Lord Denning in his Report had named names and pried into personal secrets it might have proved to be an alarming precedent. We might have been on a slope that leads to the Police State.

Not that Lord Denning has wholly resisted the temptation. There

[267]

was no need to go into all the tittle-tattle about the man in the black mask and all the rest of it. Indeed one of the questions we might ask ourselves is whether a rather prim judge is the proper person to let loose on the warm, corrupting world of prostitutes, titled parvenus, spies and procurers.

On 5 June 1963 Lucky Gordon, the West Indian with whom Christine Keeler had lived before she left him for John Edgecombe, was tried at the Old Bailey for assaulting Keeler on the previous 18 April. At his trial Keeler was a prosecution witness and gave perjured evidence, for which she was later herself prosecuted. Gordon, who strongly protested his innocence, was sentenced to three years' imprisonment. A few days later Stephen Ward was arrested and taken into custody. When he duly appeared before the Marylebone magistrate's court, he was charged under eight counts with living on the earnings of prostitution, of which the first two counts respectively concerned Christine Keeler and Mandy Rice-Davies. His trial at the Old Bailey began before Mr Justice Marshall on 22 July. Mr Mervyn Griffith Jones appeared for the prosecution and Mr James Burge for the defence.[33]

It is unnecessary to describe the trial which resulted in Ward's conviction. The proceedings were grossly unfair to the defendant, the police, who incidentally had interviewed Keeler no less than twenty-four times, giving him the impression that they were out to find him guilty at all costs. Christine Keeler, Mandy Rice-Davies, Margaret Ricardo, and Vickie Barrett all testified for the prosecution, and Miss Barrett subsequently admitted that her evidence, or a substantial part of it, was untrue. Ward was deserted by all his influential friends, including Lord Astor, and none of them came forward to testify in his defence. A year or so after the trial, when I was staying at Cliveden as the guest of the Astors, I asked Lord Astor why he had not done so. He replied that he was originally willing to do so but was persuaded by the defence as well as his own lawyer not to because it would have been too risky for him, since he would have been subject to cross-examination by the prosecution. Ward gave evidence in his own defence, and in his examination-in-chief he was asked by his counsel about his contacts with 'the secret service'. Much to MI5's embarrassment he named as his case officer 'Mr Woods of Room 393' at the War Office.[34] Luckily for the Security Service he never discovered Woods's real name. Had Ward

[268]

appealed against his conviction, it is more than likely that the Court of Criminal Appeal would have quashed the conviction on the ground of the judge misdirecting the jury. But, as will be seen, Ward did not appeal.

The only light relief in this sordid and depressing case was provided by the journalists and reporters outside the court who thought up two amusing stories about Christine Keeler. The first was the answer to the question, what newspapers did she take? 'One *Mail*, two *Mirrors*, three *Observers*, a *New Statesman* every week and any number of *Times*.' The other story which went the rounds was what Christine Keeler's doctor said to her. 'A few days on your feet and we'll soon have you back in bed!'[35]

On the morning of 31 July, before the judge had completed his summing-up and the jury had returned their verdict, Ward took an overdose of the powerful barbiturate nembutal and was admitted unconscious to the hospital in West London appropriately named St Stephen's. He was convinced that the judge's summing-up must result in his conviction which in the event it did. He never recovered consciousness and died three days later.

In his book *The Trial of Stephen Ward* (1964), the well-known author and television personality Ludovic Kennedy, who assumed that some of the unsubstantiated allegations in Lord Denning's Report were based on fresh evidence for which there had been corroboration, telephoned one of the officials who had assisted Denning in his inquiry and asked for his help on one or two points. The official was Mr Thomas Critchley, an assistant secretary in the police department of the Home Office, who had been private secretary to Mr R. A. (later Lord) Butler when he was Home Secretary. Ludovic Kennedy did not mention him by name since 'he asked me not to', but the official subsequently asserted that he spoke to Mr Kennedy on the understanding that he was not to be quoted. At all events, according to Kennedy in his book, the official told him that there had been no fresh evidence (in the sense of evidence from witnesses whom the police had not already seen) and that most of the allegations about Ward had been supplied by Christine, Mandy and other prosecution witnesses. Kennedy then asked for the source of the allegations about Ward arranging whipping parties, and he could hardly believe his ears when Mr Critchley said, 'Vickie Barrett'. Kennedy, according to himself, pointed out that these and

[269]

other allegations had not been proved at Ward's trial, to which Mr Critchley allegedly replied, 'Well, I daresay we were a bit unfair to Ward there. We were under a lot of pressure, as I expect you know, and we didn't really have time to read the report of the trial in detail.' The Home Office official was understandably indignant when this damning admission was quoted by Ludovic Kennedy and he refused either to confirm or deny it. 'The report is done and finished with and I don't want to be involved in any controversy,' was all he would say. 'I think that is also Lord Denning's view.' Nevertheless, as Ludovic Kennedy remarked in his book, following Mr Critchley's admission: 'The Denning Report has been criticised for whitewashing the living: a less attractive feature of it is that it also defames the dead.' To which Chapman Pincher has added: 'The overall effect of the Denning Report was to reduce the embarrassment factor in every possible way so that no Establishment figure was to blame. I am not saying that this was Denning's intention but it was certainly his achievement.'[36]

In December 1963 Christine Keeler pleaded guilty at the Old Bailey to having committed perjury at the Gordon trial and she was sent to prison for nine months, serving her sentence at Holloway. 'When I went into Holloway,' she recently told John Mortimer, 'I was really pleased to get a bit of peace. I was psychologically exhausted. It wasn't a very pleasant place but I met a girl there who's been a good friend to me. She works for the Labour Party.' Since then Christine has had two husbands, a labourer and a company director, 'quite a contrast'. She now lives on social security in a tower block council flat in World's End, Chelsea, with a vandalised, graffiti-stained lift. Asked whom she loved most out of all the men in her life, she replied, 'Oh, I loved Stephen. Always. I'm very loyal.'[37] Yet he was about the only one with whom she never had sex. Incidentally Ward did a drawing of her which he signed and inscribed 'To dear Christine at Cliveden.' She later sold it, and in 1984 the Trustees of the National Portrait Gallery bought it from a dealer for £1,000. 'It is a great drawing,' said Christine. 'I must see it in the gallery – I think it is going to be quite fun.'[38]

Mandy Rice-Davies has fared rather better than Christine Keeler, although she too has spent time in Holloway – but it was only nine days for a driving licence offence. Like Christine she too has been married twice. Her first husband was a steward in El Al airlines called Rafael Shaul, whom she married in 1966, afterwards being converted to the

Jewish faith. With his help she started a Chinese restaurant in Tel-Aviv, and also 'Mandy's Discotheque', which was patronised by everyone who was anyone in the former Israeli capital and by many foreign visitors. In 1968 she bore him a daughter, Dana, but to her surprise Mandy was not enough for him. 'He used to stray a bit here and there', she has recalled. 'When it started to happen I didn't do anything and I didn't say anything. Then, one day, he strayed with somebody and stayed there . . . That's when I became more open myself and started looking at men again.' She and Rafael Shaul were divorced in 1977. Meanwhile she has had at least three lovers, an Argentinian consul, a Swiss business man and a French restaurateur, Jean-Charles Lefevre, who managed the Chinese restaurant in Tel-Aviv. She eventually married Jean-Charles but her second marriage only lasted a year due, it appears, to her husband's violent jealousy. Her last lover, who wanted to marry her, was a Canadian millionaire Joe Libo. ('I called him Mr Super Money. I left Israel for him. But I was worried that the day I married Joe I would never feel free again.') The marriage was all set, but almost at the last moment Mandy turned round and took a plane to England. She now lives with her daughter Dana in an elegant North London flat, wears expensive designer clothes and impressive jewellery, reads *The Times*, rides and does needlework.

She is comfortably off with her Chinese restaurants in Tel-Aviv and Rhodes besides appearing from time to time on television and acting in a play by Tom Stoppard. She is still mistress of the flip remark. When Henry Kelly, questioning her about her past on Breakfast TV, said, 'But you were so young, you were only eighteen', Mandy replied, 'Yes, a mere babe in arms', adding quickly before her questioner could do so, 'Well, in somebody's arms!' She is friendly with her old lovers, even those she has ditched. But she and Christine Keeler rarely if ever meet. 'I knew Christine for four months,' she has said. 'Four months out of forty years, and we're stuck like Crosse and Blackwell. Mention her name and mine automatically follows. And vice versa. Which just shows how careful you have to be who you spend four months of your life with!' Nor has she any regrets about the past: 'I had a good time, I didn't get a good reputation, I didn't like the court case, but I enjoyed all the fun.'[39]

Lord Astor, who felt the effects of the Profumo-Ward affair keenly, did not survive it for long. He died suddenly in 1966 aged fifty-nine,

while on holiday in the Bahamas, which he often visited.[40] Lord
Denning is still 'pontificating' at the age of eighty-seven, while Mr
Macmillan now Earl of Stockton and aged ninety-one enthralls the
House of Lords by his speeches, although as Prime Minister nearly
a quarter of a century ago he was described as old, incompetent and
worn out. However, the individual who has really worked his passage
home is John Profumo. He has devoted his time since the scandal
to welfare work in London's East End, notably at Toynbee Hall,
for which he was created CBE in 1975. 'I'll never retire,' he was
reported as saying recently. 'I'm part of the East End furniture
now.'[41]

5

A decade after the Profumo scandal there were two more cases of call
girls which deserve comment. They concerned Lords Jellicoe and
Lambton respectively and by accident coincided, although they were
not in any way connected, a fact which was particularly unfortunate for
Lord Jellicoe.

George Patrick John Rushworth Jellicoe, second Earl Jellicoe, DSO,
MC, was the only son of the first Earl, the legendary Admiral of the
Fleet in the First World War. After a distinguished war career George
Jellicoe served in the Foreign Service and later gave up his diplomatic
career to enter politics. He filled various offices with distinction,
eventually becoming a member of the Cabinet in 1970 as Lord Privy
Seal, the Minister in charge of the Civil Service, and Leader of the
House of Lords, in Mr Heath's Government. On five or six occasions
between August 1972 and April 1973, he had 'casual affairs' with call
girls, whom he met as a result of telephoning one or other of two 'Escort
Agencies' which advertised in the *Evening Standard*. He entertained
them to a meal and any sexual intercourse took place late in the evening
in his own London flat and never elsewhere. The affairs were conducted
discreetly, there was no abnormal sexual behaviour, they involved no
criminal offence nor any risk of compromising photographs which
might be used as blackmail since they took place in his flat. Furthermore Jellicoe dealt with the agencies under an assumed name and never
spoke to the girls of anything remotely connected with his work.

Neither did he ever consciously disclose his identity, but somehow it leaked out and became the subject of gossip in the call girl and prostitution underworld. It was sheer coincidence that this gossip came to the knowledge of the police through two informants while senior members of the Heath Cabinet were considering the implications of Lord Lambton's case. In the event Lord Jellicoe was asked by Mr Heath if he knew anything about it and Norma Levy, the woman principally involved with Lambton. He denied any knowledge of or connection with the Lambton affair. However, Jellicoe was an extremely honourable man, and after thinking over the matter, he went to see Heath again next day, and told him that, although he had had nothing whatever to do with Norma Levy, he felt he should admit that he had occasionally made use of Mayfair escort agencies on lonely evenings. He offered to resign and somewhat surprisingly Mr Heath accepted his resignation, apparently taking the view that if he were asked a question about Lord Jellicoe in the House of Commons he could not give a negative answer with complete honesty.[42]

Chapman Pincher, writing a few years later in his informative book *Inside Story* (1978), commented that Heath's acceptance of Jellicoe's resignation made nonsense of the former belief that Profumo had been disgraced not because he consorted with a prostitute but because he lied to the House.

Both Lambton and Jellicoe immediately told the truth – in Jellicoe's case he volunteered it – yet they suffered the same fate. The truth was – as it has always been and still is – that if people in public life behave as other mortals they will be judged by harsher standards if they are caught out.

Some of Jellicoe's ministerial colleagues were furious about this, seeing it as an example of the inflexibility of mind which would eventually destroy Heath politically and his government with him. Wilson behaved more maturely when a married senior colleague was confronted at Westminster by a discarded mistress, hysterically threatening to give a sheaf of passionate love-letters to the newspapers unless he returned to her. She was pacified and ushered from the premises unobserved by the Press. The man, an unlikely Lothario, remains in the Cabinet.[43]

[273]

Antony Claud Frederick Lambton, Viscount Lambton, was the second son and heir of the fifth Earl of Durham, his elder brother having died in 1941. Aged fifty at this time, Lord Lambton had been MP for Berwick-on-Tweed since 1951 and was now Parliamentary Under-Secretary of State for Defence for the Royal Air Force, in effect Air Minister, which he had been for the past three years. When his father died in 1970, he disclaimed the Durham peerage since he wished to remain in the House of Commons, but he continued with the Speaker Selwyn Lloyd's assent to use the courtesy title by which he had previously been known. Tony Lambton is an able man, a wealthy landowner, a good speaker and writer, and a brilliant marksman in the shooting field. He habitually wears dark glasses, with a studied languid air which women have found attractive. He has five daughters and one son by his wife Belinda (Bindy), whose father was an army major from Devonshire.

At some date in the late spring or early summer of 1972 Lambton was given the telephone number of a 'Madam' who controlled a ring of highly priced prostitutes. Appointments with the girls who composed it were made by calling the telephone number of the 'Madam', who then communicated with the girls and collected her commission direct from them. The ring, which never advertised, catered for business men on temporary visits to London who stayed in expensive hotels, and it also had regular clients such as Lambton. One of its call girls went under the name of Norma Russell. In November 1972 she suddenly married Colin Levy, a man with a criminal record for offences of dishonesty. Lord Lambton made use of her services and those of other sexual partners whom she procured for him at her flat in Maida Vale. This was close by his London residence. His identity became known to her and he sometimes paid her by cheques signed in his own name.

In April 1973, in consequence of a domestic dispute with her husband, Norma Levy informed the police of her association with Lord Lambton, and this information was immediately passed on to MI5 to investigate whether any risk to security was involved. Although she did not intend to blackmail him, her husband, who had always been a consenting party to his wife's conduct thought he could make money not by blackmail but by selling the story to a newspaper. For this purpose he and an associate, who was also involved with Norma Levy

[274]

and also had a criminal record, attempted to take compromising cine-pictures of Lord Lambton in bed in the flat to supplement the evidence provided by the cheques which Lambton had signed. However, they lacked the necessary technical material and skill to take recognisable photographs under these conditions. On 5 May 1973, armed with the under-developed films and one of the cheques they approached the *News of the World* and offered to sell that newspaper their story for £30,000. In the ensuing days, members of the staff of the *News of the World* installed a tape recorder and photographic equipment for taking clandestine photographs through a hole in the wall of Norma Levy's bedroom. On 9 May Colin Levy used the recorder to tape a conversation between his wife and Lord Lambton about drugs, and on the following day a staff member of the *News of the World* took a series of compromising photographs. Eventually the *News of the World* decided not to buy the story, returning the tape recording and also handing Levy the negatives and prints of the compromising photographs that they had taken. On 17 May Levy and his associate took all this evidence to the *Sunday People* and offered to sell the story for £45,000. This paper took charge of all the evidence, paying Levy and his associate £750 and undertaking to pay a further £5,250 if it published a report confirming their allegations. In the event the *Sunday People* retained the material and produced it to the police, so that security was not actually endangered. But there was a risk to security by reason of the *News of the World* letting Levy and his associate have it in the first place, since potential buyers might have included undercover agents of a potentially hostile power or powers.

Norma Levy sometimes worked as a hostess in a London night-club and she told the owner's wife as well as the police that she thought the government ought to be informed of Lord Lambton's bedroom activities. This lady agreed and asked one of the club's regular customers to help. He did so by contacting James Prior, then Leader of the House of Commons and close to Edward Heath. Recalling how the Profumo case had affected Macmillan, the Prime Minister was shocked by the news which Prior gave him. It was agreed that Prior should see the night-club owner's wife in his Whitehall office in the presence of a senior civil servant. This was duly done, and the lady imparted the information which ended shortly afterwards in Lambton's public exposure, disgrace and resignation both of his government office and his parliamentary seat. (In the ensuing by-election at Berwick-on-Tweed, this hitherto safe Conservative seat was won by a Liberal.)

To allay public concern Mr Heath asked the Permanent Security Commission, of which Lord Diplock was chairman, to investigate the events leading to the resignations from the Government of Lord Lambton and Lord Jellicoe.[44] The Commission's Report was published as a Command Paper on 12 June 1973, its general conclusion being that no classified information was communicated directly or indirectly to the intelligence service of any potentially hostile power. Had Lord Jellicoe remained in office, the Commission reported that there was no security objection to his having access to secret or top-secret material. It was otherwise in the case of Lord Lambton, where the Commission would have felt compelled to recommend that he should be denied such access, had he continued the same course of conduct. 'He had admittedly on at least one occasion smoked cannabis when in the company of prostitutes at Norma Levy's flat,' the Report went on.

Recorded evidence existed of a conversation which suggested, whether correctly or not, his involvement with other drugs as well, and there was photographic evidence of sexual practices which deviated from the normal. This evidence was in the hands of criminals and up for sale. Lord Lambton was thus wide open to blackmail. These two factors, involvement in drugs and vulnerability to blackmail, would have involved him in disqualification for employment in exceptionally secret work if he had been a civil servant subject to positive vetting.

The Report continued:

In Lord Lambton's case, however, it is not the risk of blackmail that is the dominant factor in the risk. We are wholly convinced that he would never have yielded to any pressure to betray his country's secrets by fear of disclosure of what he had done, even if it had involved more serious criminal offences than those which the recorded conversation suggested. It is as inconceivable as in the case of Lord Jellicoe.

The real risk lay in his use of drugs, even though this was confined, as we are prepared to assume that it was, to cannabis. Under the

[276]

influence of this drug we consider that there would be a significant danger of his divulging, without any conscious intention of doing so, items of classified information which might be of value to a foreign intelligence service in piecing together from a number of different sources a complete picture from which conclusions dangerous to national security might be drawn.

We do not suggest that Lord Lambton would consciously commit indiscretions when in his normal state of mind; but we think that there would be a real risk that he might do so in a mood of irresponsibility induced by drugs; and, although we are satisfied that none of the prostitutes whom he actually used had any sort of connection, however remote, with any foreign intelligence service, there could be no guarantee that this would always be so if he continued in his course of conduct.

The Commissioners added that they were aware of suggestions that other ministers, besides Lord Lambton, may have been associated with the Levys. (Chapman Pincher, for instance, had given Lambton the names of two of his former colleagues who might be named by newspapers in this context. Lambton commented characteristically, 'The way things are going it will soon be clear that Heath is the only member of the government who doesn't do it.')[45] However, the Commissioners stated that they had come across no evidence worthy of credence to suggest that any minister other than Lambton was involved with Norma Levy. On the same day as the Report was published, Mr Heath announced in the House of Commons that he had accepted all its recommendations, particularly that arranging for the attention of all ministers to be 'recalled regularly to the standing instructions and guidance on security matters'. Replying to Mr Wilson, the Leader of the Opposition, the Prime Minister said that there had been no weakening of the security procedures introduced in 1964 by Mr Wilson regarding the briefing of all ministers by the Security Service. 'That continued as before and was as full as possible.'

Since then, unlike Lord Lambton, Earl Jellicoe has kept out of the newspaper gossip columns. His worth has been recognised by his appointment to various public offices including Chairman of the British Advisory Committee on Oil Pollution of the Sea, President of the London Chamber of Commerce and Industry, President of the

[277]

National Federation of Housing Societies, Governor of the Centre for Environmental Studies, Chairman of the Anglo-Hellenic League and also of the Delegacy, King's College, London, of which he is also a Fellow. He spends his time between a manor house near Marlborough in Wiltshire and a town house in Kensington. His recreation is skiing rather than patronising escort agencies.

Lord Lambton, on the other hand, still immensely rich and married to Bindy, spends the greater part of the year at his villa near Siena in Tuscany with his mistress, fifty-year-old Mrs Claire Ward, former sister-in-law of the third Earl of Dudley and mother of the actress Rachel Ward. Both his wife and his mistress were in attendance, in addition to Princess Michael of Kent, at a £10,000 champagne party given for him in May 1985 by the Marquess and Marchioness of Dufferin and Ava in their grand Holland Park home in London.[46] Tony Lambton also spends his time writing novels, his first *Elizabeth and Alexandra* based on the lives of Queen Victoria's two granddaughters, the Grand Duchess Elizabeth of Hesse and the last Russian Tsarina Alexandra (Alix) wife of the ill-fated Tsar Nicholas II, whom he suggests were not murdered by the Bolsheviks with the Tsar and the rest of his family but were exiled to Siberia. 'Elizabeth was good, but a masochist' he has reportedly said of his heroines. 'Alexandra was like Lord Byron, mad, bad and dangerous to know. She had that absolute concentration on self which is the worst quality a person can have, don't you think?' He thinks he understands women better than many other men do. 'My oldest friends are all women. This thing of men not being at ease with women is very English – it doesn't apply at all in Europe.'

Asked about the Parkinson affair and whether he had a fellow feeling for the latest victim of English middle-class morality, Lord Lambton replied: 'I felt very sorry for Parkinson. I felt sorry for him because he had full attention on him and I know what that's like. But to tell you the truth, I couldn't quite see what he had done.'[47] What Cecil Parkinson did is described in the final chapter of this book.

Meanwhile the call girl's trade still flourishes. A chartered accountant, who was recently made bankrupt, was asked by the registrar at his public examination why the sum of £15,627 was written off under the heading 'H'. He replied: 'That stands for hooker.' He went on to explain in answer to the registrar's further question that 'hooker' meant call girl or prostitute. He added that he would sometimes pay £125 for a girl. And so it goes on as it always has done.[48]

For instance, a year after Lambton's resignation, Norma Levy turned up in Miami, having entered America on an Irish passport, aptly declaring that her visit was 'for pleasure'. She was later arrested under false names on a variety of charges including prostitution, giving massage without a licence and operating an immoral escort agency. Between 1975 and 1980 she was deported four times and during that period served a year in jail for illegal entry to the US. She was eventually identified through a fingerprint check by the police in Philadelphia and again faced deportation as an illegal immigrant alien.[49]

11

The KGB Takes a Hand

1

SINCE 1954 the initials KGB have stood for the Russian abbreviation of Committee of State Security, otherwise the Soviet security service. Under a variety of different names this secret police body has functioned since Tsarist times, although it employs terror to a far lesser extent than its predecessors and unlike its existence in Stalin's time it has for over twenty years been subordinated to control by the Soviet Communist Party. Nevertheless, it has remained a relatively formidable organisation in the fields of security, intelligence, espionage and counter-espionage. Its dreaded headquarters were and still are a former insurance office in Moscow's Lubyanka Square near the Kremlin, the building being known simply as the Lubyanka. It is here that besides the confinement of state prisoners, the major Soviet secret police operations are planned and KGB agents working internally or abroad are briefed and debriefed. Blackmail is resorted to, notably in respect of sexual activities or aberrations of foreigners if they are considered to serve the KGB's purpose. The most notorious victim of Soviet blackmail in recent times was a thirty-one-year-old English admiralty clerk working in the Naval Attaché's office in the British Embassy in Moscow, William John Christopher Vassall. In 1962 it was officially stated in London that Vassall was a homosexual who had been entrapped by the KGB and had as a result of the pressure put upon him been spying for the Soviets for the past seven years. He was consequently arrested and brought to trial. Vassall did not attempt to deny what he had been doing, since in his Dolphin Square flat, when it was searched, seventeen secret and confidential

Admiralty documents were discovered together with photographic equipment.

Unlike Guy Burgess and Donald Maclean, who defected to the Soviet Union in 1951, John Vassall was no 'pampered child of the Establishment' to quote the late Dame Rebecca West. 'True, he had a grand-uncle who was a senior housemaster at Harrow, and another who taught at Repton, but the old school tie hardly stretches as far as all that.' In fact, his father was an impoverished Church of England parson, who could not afford to keep him at his grammar school beyond the age of sixteen. The elder Vassall, however, had enough influence to get his son into the Admiralty as a temporary clerk, a position made permanent after the war, during which young Vassall had served as a photographer in the RAF. Whatever his use to the Russians as a spy, he does not seem to have been particularly good at his work in the Admiralty, possibly because he devoted too much energy to his private life. A slightly effeminate manner emphasised that he was 'queer', and indeed he boasted afterwards that men had told him that he had 'come to bed' eyes. A journalist who visited his flat in Dolphin Square after his arrest was surprised by its elegance and luxurious furnishings, and by Vassall's expensive suits, perfumes, catalogues of women's corsets, and pictures of hirsute French rugby players. 'On my dressing table stood a miniature toy white poodle and other furry objects, and on my bed my favourite friend, a cuddly white cheetah,' he wrote in his life story which he sold to a Sunday newspaper at the time of his trial. 'I had a photograph specially taken in colour of me and my cheetah. I wish I had it with me now.'[1]

Amongst the locally recruited staff in the Moscow Embassy was a Polish homosexual named Sigmund Mikhailski, who had been planted there by the Russians. A report from Mikhailski to his superiors that Vassall had the makings of a potential traitor led to a series of parties culminating in a dinner at which the unfortunate Vassall, according to his subsequent confession, became drunk, removed most of his clothes, and was photographed on a couch alongside a naked Russian. Another photograph, with which his Russian hosts subsequently confronted him, showed him grinning sheepishly and holding up a pair of men's briefs. To make sure that he should not escape from their net, it was said that the Russians later interrupted Vassall again, partly undressed and in the middle of a sex act with a handsome military officer who had

[281]

likewise been planted on him, threatening him that if he did not agree to spy for them they would show the photographs to senior members of the British Embassy staff and 'would make an international incident of the matter'.

Sir William Hayter, who was the ambassador at the time, has recalled in his memoirs that Vassall was 'very amusing' in a small part in an Embassy production of Terence Rattigan's *Harlequinade*. 'I remember him dimly as an obliging little figure who was useful at tea parties,' Sir William added. 'There was no excuse for him. If he had come to me or to the Naval Attaché and told us that he was being blackmailed by the Russians he could have been sent home at once without any opposition from the Soviet authorities. One or two similar cases occurred during my time, and in none of them was there any difficulty about exit visas.'[2]

In her study of treason, Dame Rebecca West has suggested with some plausibility that Vassall's failure to disclose the blackmailing story to the Embassy was because he had become a professional spy of his own accord, and that the Russians had engineered the allegedly compromising incidents to provide him with an excuse for his treachery in the event of his being caught. However, the blackmailing story was repeated by the prosecution and judge at Vassall's trial and was subsequently accepted by the press and Parliament. This in turn gave rise to the impression that Vassall was a weak, vain creature of inferior intellect. Vain he may well have been, but otherwise this was unlikely to be the correct view of a man who for seven years had carried on an occupation demanding unremitting industry in a skilled craft conducted in clandestine conditions, an endless capacity for dissimulation, and sustained contempt for personal danger.[3]

It is significant that the Tribunal, subsequently appointed by the Home Secretary under the chairmanship of Lord Radcliffe to inquire into the circumstances of Vassall's treachery, attributed this to his homosexuality, in reporting on his Moscow appointment.

The selection of Vassall, a weak, vain, individual and a practising homosexual . . . can now be seen to be the decisive mistake in the history of this case. It exposed him to the attention of the Russian Intelligence Service in conditions in which they were most readily able to identify him for what he was and to compromise him.

This is not to say that his selection was a mistake for which there

[282]

must necessarily be blame. His weaknesses were not readily apparent and the Admirality method of selection of staff for appointment of Naval Attaché's clerks was ill-adapted for assessing strength of character and freedom from those defects which the Russians might exploit.[4]

Vassall returned to the Admiralty in 1956, after completing two years' tour of duty in Moscow, and continued to work for the Russians until his arrest in September 1962. For part of this time he acted as assistant private secretary to the Hon. T. G. D. Galbraith, MP, Civil Lord of the Admiralty and eldest son of Lord Strathclyde. The precise nature of the information which he imparted to the Russians was not revealed at his trial. The Attorney-General described it as 'of the highest importance', while the Lord Chief Justice, Lord Parker, referred to the classification of some of the documents which he passed on to his spy masters as 'Top Secret'. That his espionage work was appreciated by the Russians may be gauged from the fact that they rewarded him handsomely. Vassall's Admiralty pay was only £700 a year, whereas in a single year he paid £3,000 into his bank account. What put the authorities on to his track in the first instance did not emerge from his trial, but it is probable that it was his extravagant mode of living, frequenting expensive restaurants and night-clubs in the West End of London, that first attracted attention and led to his being watched by security service agents. At the Old Bailey he pleaded guilty and was sentenced to eighteen years by the Lord Chief Justice. 'I take the view that one of the compelling reasons for what you did was pure selfish greed,' said Lord Parker in passing sentence. Vassall disagreed with this view. 'It had been nothing of the sort,' he wrote afterwards, telling his counsel at the Radcliffe Tribunal: 'It was a trap that I could see no way of getting out of.'[5]

The discovery in Vassall's flat of several photographs of Mr Galbraith and a number of letters from him to Vassall gave rise to rumours that there was or had been a homosexual relationship between the two men. However, the contents of the letters were seen to be quite trivial and innocuous when the Prime Minister, Mr Macmillan, authorised their publication, no more intimate than one would normally expect as from a minister to a confidential clerk, who was acting as his secretary. Mr Galbraith's reputation was completely cleared by the Tribunal of

Inquiry, although the incident of the letters can hardly be said to have contributed much to the advancement of his political career.[6] Vassall's evidence before the Tribunal confirmed that of Mr Galbraith as to the nature of their relationship. Vassall was brought from prison and questioned by the Attorney-General (Sir John Hobson).

'It is plain, Vassall, that you had conceived an admiration at least for Mr Galbraith?' – 'Yes.'

'Anything more?' – 'I just liked him very much.'

'What do you think his view of you was?' – 'I think he liked me and appreciated what I did in my own way for him and for Mrs Galbraith.'

'You, of course, had met a great number of men in the course of your life?' – 'Yes.'

'And you know that we know that with many of them you have established a homosexual relationship?' – 'With some people, yes.'

'You know quite well when another man has conceived a homosexual affection or regard for you?' – 'Yes. Sometimes I did not know what it was to start with.'

'But you found out fairly quickly?' – 'Sometimes.'

'Was there anything in Mr Galbraith's attitude towards you that led you to believe that he had formed a homosexual attraction or admiration for you?' – 'Not a physical homosexual attraction, no.'

'Anything else?' – 'Not that I can think of.'

'Was there any sex of any sort discussed between you and him at any stage?' – 'No. We never discussed sexual matters.'

'Or any display of physical affection, however slight between you and him?' – 'No.'

'Are you sure of that?' – 'Yes.'[7]

The Vassall affair had the effect of drawing general attention to the 'security risk' aspect of homosexuality and incidentally to the fact that the 'risk' was very largely the result of the existing state of the law. Some Labour politicians criticised Mr Galbraith for not having cottoned on earlier to the fact of Vassall's homosexuality; but here they were really getting their own back on the Conservatives for their criticism of Mr Hector McNeil, when he was Labour Minister of State at the Foreign Office in 1951, for having so long tolerated the much more blatant homosexual Guy Burgess as his assistant private secretary. Mr Donald

Maclachlan, a former naval intelligence officer who was editor of the *Sunday Telegraph* at the time of the Vassall affair, gave as one of the reasons for official failure to detect Vassall's 'character defects' as being connected with society's growing tolerance of the homosexual character. 'To the Whitehall of 1962 he is in the category that a Jacobite was in 1745 or a Catholic in the days of the Spanish Armada: unreliable because he cannot altogether help it: a potential traitor because he has a guilty secret: a colleague with a weakness which cannot be condoned but whom it is distasteful to persecute.'[8] In the Radcliffe Report, which was published some months later, the Tribunal admitted that it knew enough about Vassall to say that 'he was already committed to homosexual practices' before he was posted to Moscow, but that the fact of Vassall's homosexual behaviour was 'a private matter, and in any event information about homosexuals in general is not collected and recorded by the Security Service'.[9] The omission, it is not unreasonable to assume, was speedily rectified.

Vassall served his prison sentence in Wormwood Scrubs, Maidstone and Durham. When he became eligible for parole, he made three applications for release on licence and was turned down each time by the Parole Board. His fourth was successful and he left prison in October 1972 after eleven years. A Roman Catholic like his mother, he sustained much comfort from the faith of this church during his imprisonment and afterwards when he composed his autobiography in a monastery. 'I bitterly regret the pain and distress I have caused my family, my innumerable friends and colleagues,' he wrote in this work which was published in 1975. 'Looking back on the ghastly position in which I found myself, I realise that although at the time I felt quite helpless, I should not have allowed myself to become entangled in the deplorable and dreadful world of espionage on behalf of a foreign power.'[10] Or, as prosecuting counsel put it in a more recent spy trial, 'nothing – and that includes blackmail – could ever justify giving away your country's secrets'.[11] For that offence Vassall paid the penalty, a severe one but more lenient than that meted out by the Russians to their national Colonel Oleg Penkovsky who was tried along with the British business man and MI6 agent Greville Wynne in Moscow in May 1963 for handing over Soviet intelligence secrets to the British and Americans. Penkovsky was sentenced to death and executed.[12] After the publication of his autobiography, and appearing on television at the same time, Vassall changed his name to that under which he now lives pseudonymously.

2

The KGB has also used heterosexual activities as a means of blackening the characters of figures in British public life and hopefully destroying them. Two individuals who have been subject to this treatment were an MP and an Ambassador in Moscow, the instruments for their exposure being respectively an Intourist employee and a chambermaid.

Commander Anthony Tosswill Courtney, OBE, was a retired officer in the Royal Navy when at the age of fifty in 1959 he was elected Conservative MP for East Harrow at the by-election caused by the resignation of Ian Harvey in the circumstances which have been described above. Courtney had spent much of his previous career in naval intelligence when among other accomplishments he had become a qualified interpreter in Russian, a language which he came to speak fluently. This had stood him in good stead when he was posted to the British Naval Mission in wartime Moscow. His wife Elizabeth *née* Stokes whom he married in 1938 had been secretary to the Defence Security Officer in Malta. During the two years Courtney spent in the Soviet Union as deputy-head of the mission, he got to know and like the country and its people, although he was conscious of his surveillance by the secret police then known as the NKVD (People's Commissariat of Internal Affairs).

Compulsorily retired from the navy with the rank of Commander in 1953, Tony Courtney entered business as an export consultant, specialising in East–West trade and registering as ETG (Eastern Trading Group) Consultancy Services. In particular he represented the Electrical and Musical Industries and the Associated British Engineering groups of companies, which involved him in visits to Moscow and contacts with the Soviet Ministry of Foreign Trade, and other government departments. As a result his business prospered, being helped to a considerable extent by his knowledge of the language and his experience of the Societ Union as a wartime ally. His business success was furthered by his election to the House of Commons, a success which he attributed largely to the excellent impression his wife had made at the candidates' selection meeting, where he had been chosen out of over a hundred applicants and a final short-list of four, which included the chairman of the constituency party. Being an MP was reflected in the higher seniority of the officials in the various Soviet ministries and departments with which he had to deal in his commercial capacity. All seemed set fair for Courtney both as an export consultant and parliamentarian.[13]

I was myself an MP at this period and I recall Courtney's appearance to take his seat in the House for the first time. 'Here comes your battleship!' shouted a Labour Member as the new MP made his way to the Clerks' table to take the oath and sign the register. 'Yes,' responded the ebullient Conservative Gerald Nabarro, 'and with a battleship's majority!' (He was to increase the majority of 2,000 to 6,000 at the General Election.) I was also present in the chamber on 8 July 1959, when Courtney made his maiden speech on the theme of Anglo-Soviet relations, in which he expressed the belief that the best hope of progress lay in the commercial field. The speech was well received by the House, although it must have been rather disconcerting for the maiden speaker when Winston Churchill walked out in the middle of it.

In March 1961 Courtney suffered an unexpected blow, when his wife to whom he had been happily married for twenty-three years, although they had no children, suddenly died as a result of a heart attack. Courtney was devastated by the loss, but he carried on with his business, attending the British Industrial Exhibition two months later in Moscow, the first to be held since the Bolshevik Revolution. Trade fairs are apt to be boring affairs and this one was no exception. Time hung heavily on Courtney's hands and he found some consolation in looking up old friends whom he had met on his previous visits. One of these was a member of the Intourist staff, Zinaida (Zina) Volkova, an attractive unmarried woman in her middle thirties with fair hair and hazel eyes, whom he had first met two years previously when he was staying in the Hotel Ukraina and she was in charge of the hotel car service for foreign visitors. They had become friends and he took her to the theatre and elsewhere, but they always met in public places. On the occasion of the Trade Fair he was staying in the old National Hotel, nearer the Kremlin than the Ukraina and more popular with the visiting foreign élite. Courtney, who gave her dinner there, had sensed that since his wife's death her attitude to him had become noticeably warmer in the knowledge that there was no wife waiting for him on his return to England.

In the course of the meal one of the invisible barriers which had kept them from becoming more intimate was drawn aside. Here is how Courtney described what happened:

> Just how it occurred I have no idea, except that it was certainly on her initiative, but it is a fact that for the first and last time in our acquaintance Zina came up to my bedroom after dinner and stayed there with me for several hours. Our affair was not a success. It was therefore not altogether surprising that on the next occasion when we met she expressed some distress at having behaved in the way she had, saying that she knew now that it was not really what I had wanted.

It never entered Courtney's head, as he subsequently admitted, that the bedroom had been 'bugged' by the KGB and that the compromising scene had been photographed by concealed cameras. Although Zina had no doubt developed a sincere affection for Anthony Courtney, it is difficult to resist the conclusion that she acted as she did on the instructions of the KGB, although she may afterwards have regretted it.[16]

In March 1962, a year after his first wife's death, Courtney married Elizabeth Lady Trefgarne, widow of the Labour peer the first Lord Trefgarne and a woman of some means, owner of a property in the Bahamas and a director of the Trefgarne family firm of machine tool manufacturers with four children ranging from eight to twenty-one, the latter being the eldest son who had succeeded to the Trefgarne peerage. Their Member's second wife was welcomed by the East Harrow Conservative Association as a charming and useful asset. Shortly after his remarriage Courtney told his wife of the incident with Zina, and the two women later met in Moscow. The second Mrs Courtney liked Zina and went so far as to write to her and invite her to spend her summer holiday with her and her husband in England, offering to pay her fare if she could get a visa. Elizabeth Courtney never received any reply to her letter.

Meanwhile Anthony Courtney made a point of intervening in House of Commons debates on security matters, pointing an accusing finger at

Victor Grayson MP. The MP who disappeared without trace.

The Earl of Birkenhead. Lord Chancellor (*below left*)

Mona Dunn, Birkenhead's young mistress. From the portrait by Sir William Orpen painted about the time Birkenhead first met Mona in 1919. (*below right*)

Christine Keeler

Rt Hon John Profumo MP

'He would, wouldn't he?'

Viscount (Bill) Astor

Mandy Rice-Davies

The osteopath Stephen Ward under arrest June 1963

Drawing of Christine Keeler at Cliveden by Stephen Ward (*below left*)

Captain Eugene Ivanov, Assistant Naval Attaché and intelligence officer at the Soviet embassy in London. Here he is seen kissing Mrs Murphy, wife of his opposite number at the US Navy Headquarters in London. (*below right*)

Zina Volkova

Commander Anthony Courtney MP

Charles Vassall outside the British
embassy in Moscow

The Hon T. G. D. Galbraith MP suspected of having had a homosexual
affair with Vassall.

Earl Jellicoe, Leader of the House of Lords outside 10 Downing Street

97 Onslow Square, London. Lord Jellicoe had a flat in this building.

Viscount Lambton MP,
Parliamentary Under-Secretary of
State for defence for the Royal Air
Force, at home in London

Norma Levy, Lord Lambton's
mistress and call girl flying home
from Spain

John Stonehouse with his wife
Barbara signing copies of *Death of an
Idealist*, December 1975.

Mr Justice Eveleigh the judge in the
Stonehouse-Buckley trial (*below left*)

Mrs Sheila Buckley (now Mrs
Stonehouse) arriving at the Old Bailey
July 1976. (*below right*)

The Rt Hon Cecil Parkinson
MP

Sara Keays (*right*) and her twin
sister Elizabeth as portrayed in
Private Eye.

the Soviet Union for the KGB's successful penetration of Britain's security. For instance, on 7 May 1963 he spoke in the debate on the Radcliffe tribunal's report on the Vassall case, pointing out that the KGB had 'forgotten more than we shall ever know about practical, efficient espionage.' He blamed Sir William Hayter for what had happened over Vassall, remarking that it was significant that nowhere in the report could he find an acceptance by the Foreign Service, the Foreign Office and the Radcliffe tribunal of the ultimate responsibility of the head of the British mission in Moscow for what went on during his tenure of office. He proceeded to refer to the 'psychological dominance' which the Soviets endeavoured to establish over members of foreign missions in Moscow. 'Individuals who are not prepared to accept this are usually removed or "framed", or find it necessary to go,' he said. 'Life is made a little too difficult for them, for in multifarious ways the Russians can bring pressure to bear on the embassy staff.' In conclusion he recommended the limiting of the members and status of the diplomatic representatives of the Communist bloc countries together with the facilities afforded to them.[17]

A few months later, in the adjournment debate, before the House rose for the summer recess in 1963, Courtney raised the specific question of diplomatic representation between the United Kingdom and the Eastern European countries in the light of recent grave security cases associated with such traitors as Vassall and Philby. He mentioned *inter alia* the glaring anomaly by which the Soviet Embassy in London employed Russian chauffeurs and other staff, while the Soviets insisted that similar staff in the British Embassy in Moscow should be Russians who naturally reported to the KGB. Our present diplomatic relationship with the Soviet Union, he said, 'called to mind a pair of dancers, a self-satisfied gentleman performing an elegant minuet, oblivious of the fact that his partner was doing the twist.' Peter Smithers, the Parliamentary Under-Secretary at the Foreign Office, admitted the discrepancy in both numbers and treatment of diplomatic missions but saw little advantage to be gained by correcting it. Publicity might be harmful to these relationships, he said, and 'the whole question of representation . . . must be handled in confidence.' Courtney described this as 'a classic exposition of the diplomatic view point of a former age.'[18]

Towards the end of the year the MP for East Harrow spoke in the

[289]

debate on the Denning Report on the Profumo affair, asking why, since Commander Ivanov was known to be an intelligence agent, the Soviet Ambassador Alexander Soldatov had not been sent for and told that his assistant naval attaché was engaged in undiplomatic activity. No official reply by the Macmillan Government was made to this query.

In February 1964 Courtney was host at a luncheon party in the House of Commons for the Soviet ambassador's wife Mme Soldatova when he spoke in Russian praising the achievement of the visiting Soviet woman astronaut Valentina Tereshkova. The ambassador's wife took the opportunity of telling Courtney that, unlike the speech he had just made, certain of his other utterances in the House were not regarded with favour by the Soviet Embassy. He was again warned shortly afterwards in similar terms by one of the Embassy secretaries at a reception. However, when he visited Moscow in May in connection with his business Courtney did not detect anything untoward or unusual in his reception there and thought little if anything more of it.

On the other hand, Courtney had to face trouble on the private domestic front where his wife Liz, who may have resented his long absences from home on political and business matters, began to show her resentment. In August 1964, when he was in Moscow and staying as usual in the National Hotel, he received a letter from her to the effect that she had decided to leave him as their marriage had not turned out to be the success she had hoped. This missive was no doubt opened and copied by the KGB before it reached Courtney's hands. Courtney telephoned her at home and persuaded her to change her mind. Since he spoke on an open line from the hotel this call was also probably monitored by the KGB. On his return to England, his normal family life was resumed and at the General Election in October Liz was a great help to her husband and worked hard for him throughout the campaign. However, the Conservatives under the leadership of Sir Alec Douglas-Home (as the present Lord Home then was) lost the election to Labour, and although Courtney succeeded in retaining the seat at East Harrow it was by a substantially reduced majority (2,259 as compared with 5,947 in 1960).

Early in the new Parliament the Member for East Harrow suffered a further domestic blow. In January and again in March 1965, Anthony Courtney, his eldest stepson Lord Trefgarne and also Alec Douglas-

Home, Leader of the Conservative Opposition, each received anonymous letters, bearing a Harrow postmark, accusing Elizabeth Courtney of having been unfaithful to her husband and adding that he 'should resign as our MP before there is a further public scandal in the Party.' Courtney immediately saw the Conservative Chief Whip Willie Whitelaw, who was helpful and sympathetic, but Whitelaw could do little except agree that Scotland Yard should be informed, although in the event the identity or identities of the anonymous letter writers were never discovered. 'Rightly or wrongly,' Courtney was to state afterwards, 'I did not tell him that there was substance in the allegations, and it was a dreadful thing to feel that my family troubles should be known to others who wished me ill.' Furthermore, this private worry adversely affected his constituency work and at the same time he began to feel that the steadfast support of the officers in the local party association which he had come to take for granted, was by no means as solid as he imagined, due in part to concern about the possible intervention of a Liberal candidate at the next Election.[19]

Nevertheless, Courtney's affairs continued to prosper both politically and commercially. In the House of Commons he became Vice-Chairman of the Conservative Navy Committee, and in March Alec Douglas-Home invited him to wind up in the debate on the Navy Estimates for 1965 which he did from the Opposition Front Bench. At the end of March he left on a business trip to the Soviet Union. For the first time he had a feeling that he might be detained by the KGB on some pretext. Hence he drafted a letter to the Labour Foreign Secretary Michael Stewart which he left with his wife to post in the event of such an unfortunate occurrence. However, the letter was never sent since the visit went off well, being one of the most successful Courtney had ever made, as he was able to set in train the project of the formation of an Anglo-Soviet trading company. Courtney's apprehension for his personal safety was dictated by a review he had recently written for the *Evening Standard* of a translation of the wartime memoirs of Admiral Golovko, who commanded the Soviet Northern Fleet. In his review Courtney had attacked the Admiral's unfounded allegations of the Royal Navy's incompetence and bad faith in safeguarding the Arctic convoys which carried supplies to the Soviet Union during the war. For this Courtney had been counter-attacked by the Soviet newspaper *Red Star* which stigmatised Courtney's review as a 'wicked libel' and accused him of attempting 'to shake the faith of foreign readers in the Soviet Union and its peaceful Leninist foreign policy.'[20]

However, all went well for Courtney on this visit. Besides business, he also looked up old friends including Zina, whom he took to a performance of Rimsky-Korsakov's opera *Sadko* at the Bolshoi. But one old friend whom he failed to see and who pretended not to know him was the ex-ballerina Lydia Manukhina whom he had known for twenty-three years; after unsuccessfully telephoning her, he tracked her down to her flat where she told him in response to his knock on the door to go away and stop bothering her, denying all knowledge of him. This could be interpreted as conveying an urgent message to Courtney that there was danger and to keep away, as he subsequently realised. Indeed he recalled what happened to a woman friend of the *Daily Telegraph* Moscow correspondent during the war, who was arrested after the correspondent's departure for England on leave as a preliminary to his being refused a re-entry visa. But at least Courtney was relieved that Lydia had come to no harm, although the incident worried him. Also unlike the *Daily Telegraph* journalist Courtney was granted a visa by the Soviet Consul-General in London for his next visit to Moscow which he had planned for 25 July 1965. In the event he did not make the visit since at the weekly meeting of the 1922 Committee of Conservative backbenchers on 22 July Sir Alec Douglas-Home announced his resignation as party leader with the result that Courtney felt that he should postpone his visit and stay in London for the election of Douglas-Home's successor. The election, which took place on 27 July, fielded three candidates, Edward Heath, Reginald Maudling and Enoch Powell. Heath was elected with 150 votes against Maudling's 133 and Powell's 15. Courtney, who had cancelled his Moscow trip, voted for Powell.

3

Two days before Parliament was due to rise for the summer recess in the first week of August, 1965, Courtney was in his London flat when the telephone rang. The caller was his Tory colleague John Tilney, who told him that something extremely important had happened and asked him to come along at once to the House and have a word with him. Ten minutes later they met in Westminster Hall. Tilney was holding a buff-coloured envelope which he put in Courtney's hands. 'Have a look at that!' Tilney said. 'Several Members have already received them.'

The envelope contained a foolscap-size of rather poor quality glossy paper with six photographs, headed by the following:

'I'm not a Profumo, But . . .'
(A story in photographs)
1959
Why not try to become an MP
to combine business with pleasure
and to conduct shady business while
'Defending public interests'?

Of the six photographs three were innocuous, two evidently obtained from election literature and the third showing Courtney in naval uniform taken by an old friend Boris Ward, who likewise had had many business dealings with the Soviet Union. The other three photographs showed Courtney in a state of undress and in two pictures accompanied by a woman or women, one of them lying sideways on a bed. The first picture showed Courtney by himself with no clothes on. In one of the other two he was portrayed seated on a bed, partly clothed, beside a fully-clothed woman whose blouse he seemed to be buttoning or unbuttoning at the back. It was difficult positively to identify the woman in this picture, but Courtney concluded that it must be Zina Volkova. In the third picture there was a woman in the background, half-clothed and reclining on a bed, full face, but a rectangular patch had been blacked out across the eyes and this was evidently designed to conceal her identity. The hair style seemed to be similar in both pictures which indicated that they were of the same person. (In fact she was Zina.) At the bottom left hand corner of the broadsheet was a reproduction of a typewritten letter from the House of Commons signed by Anthony Courtney and partly concealed by an enlarged version of his business visiting card. The letter, which was addressed to the wife of the Russian General Gromov, must have been intercepted by the KGB in Moscow, photocopied and the copy affixed to the broadsheet in such a way as to prevent identification, although a search of Courtney's filing

[293]

cabinet by his secretary revealed a carbon copy. Underneath the photographs were the ominous words, 'To be continued'.[21]

At least six copies of the broadsheet had been sent to other MPs including George Wigg, the Prime Minister's security adviser, and Merlyn Rees, Courtney's Labour opponent at the 1959 election who had since been returned for another seat.[22] Two copies had been sent to Courtney's wife, one at their London address and the other at their country house at Chobham. A copy had also been received by the news editor of the *News of the World* and one had also reached Mrs Jo Burton, Courtney's Agent in East Harrow, and in the absence of the Association Chairman, Mr Jack Shrimpton, who was on holiday, she had passed it on to the President Sir Theodore Constantine. 'Well, Anthony,' said Constantine, when they met a few days later at a garden party in Harrow Weald, 'this is a bad business. If this thing gets out and someone starts leaving copies about in the pubs you can never expect to hold the seat.'[23] To add to the Member's troubles, Elizabeth Courtney, who at first appeared inclined to stand by him and call the Soviet bluff, finally decided to leave her husband and file a petition for divorce, on the ground of his adultery with Zina Volkova some time in 1963.

On 25 August Courtney saw George Wigg in what was not a very reassuring interview. On the same day Courtney wrote to Ted Heath, now the Conservative party Leader, asking if he could come and see him to discuss a matter of some importance. He knew that Whitelaw, the Opposition Chief Whip, had already informed Heath in general terms of what had occurred, but Heath had been away and was too tied up on his return to see Courtney immediately. Meanwhile Courtney had a second meeting with George Wigg at 10 Downing Street when the Prime Minister was also present. Harold Wilson was sympathetic and assured Courtney that the affair would not be used against Courtney in the party political sense but indicated at the same time that no action was contemplated against the Russians. 'What I want to know is – who are they getting at?' Wigg remarked as Courtney was walking back with Wigg to his office. 'They are cracking the whip at someone, and I want to know who that someone is. This may be just the tip of the iceberg' – the 'someone' was almost certainly Tom Driberg who was acting as a double agent. Wigg went on to tell Courtney that the Government had been thinking of some way to show confidence in him. What would he say, Wigg asked, if they put his name forward as one of the candidates for Speaker, the position being vacant through the sudden death of Sir Harry Hylton-Foster? Courtney replied that he could hardly imagine anyone less suitable than himself for such an arduous job but that nevertheless he was grateful for the suggestion.[24]

Two days later Courtney went along with Theo Constantine to see Heath in his flat in Albany. He asked Constantine to accompany him since the Association President had seen the broadsheet and was familiar with Courtney's domestic difficulties and Courtney considered him to be a friend. Heath was waiting with Whitelaw when they arrived. Courtney repeated the full story, explaining that the compromising photographs in the broadsheet, though conceivably faked, could have been based on an actual incident in 1961. According to Courtney, the reactions of his audience were wholly unsympathetic, and afterwards Courtney felt it only right, as he put it, to record his impression of 'a complete absence of that human quality of personal involvement which to me at any rate is the mark of true leadership towards a colleague in trouble.' In the event Courtney was ushered coldly from the flat, while Constantine and the Chief Whip remained behind.[25]

During the recess Courtney's situation progressively deteriorated. Early in October his solicitor informed him that his wife was going ahead with the divorce and could be expected to use the broadsheet in evidence. Consequently it was too late for Courtney to publish his full story since the matter was *sub judice* and if he did so he would risk being adjudged guilty of contempt of court. However, he considered it safe to supply some information to the *Sunday Telegraph* which that journal published on 17 October 1965. Extracts from the article are as follows:

Information has reached Whitehall that the Russian Intelligence Service, K.G.B., intended to detain Commander Anthony Courtney, Conservative M.P. for Harrow East, on a trumped-up charge in Moscow last July. There is evidence in London that the K.G.B. has watched Cdr. Courtney during visits to Moscow on business as an Export Consultant. Secret devices, including the 'bugging' of his hotel room with cameras, have been used. But for the resignation of Sir Alec Douglas-Home as Conservative Shadow Prime Minister in July Cdr. Courtney would have gone to Moscow and walked into the hands of the K.G.B. It is believed that he would have been held incommunicado while negotiations were made for an exchange with the Krogers, or George Blake, now serving prison sentences for espionage in Britain . . .

The K.G.B.'s operation is seen in Whitehall as an attempt to eliminate a serious political opponent. This would be done by trying to discredit Cdr. Courtney in his absence from the country, destroy his career in the Commons, and to deprive him of his business which lies mainly in Russia. Soon after Parliament reassembles next week Cdr. Courtney intends to take Parliamentary action. He has given the full facts of the case to Mr Wilson and to the Government.

He has been advised not to visit the Soviet Union for the time being . . . He said to me last night: 'This unexpected action by the Russian secret police is a severe setback to my hopes of contributing towards an improvement in Anglo-Soviet relations. It amply justifies the criticisms I have made about the misuse of diplomatic immunity by the Soviet Embassy in London.'

Two days after the foregoing appeared, Courtney had a further unhappy meeting with Whitelaw and Heath in the latter's room in the House of Commons. It appeared that Heath had seen Harold Wilson and had received from the Prime Minister information which appeared to conflict in certain respects with what Courtney had told his party leader. If Courtney proceeded with his intention to make a parliamentary statement on the lines he had indicated, Heath now told him, the Government would disown him. 'How then can you expect me to give you any support?' Heath added.[26]

On 10 November, the satirical magazine *Private Eye* published an informed article on the Courtney affair. 'Terrified of anything that smacks of Profumo,' wrote the article's author, 'Heath and his lieutenant Edward du Cann are doing their damnedest to shut the fellow up.' (This was not true of du Cann, the Conservative party Chairman, whom Courtney had not seen for months.) Courtney now took counsel's opinion who advised him that the *Private Eye* article was certainly libellous but that it would be against Courtney's interest to sue the magazine in the civil courts. Counsel also advised Courtney not to make any parliamentary statement, since it could not be the full story and there would be gaps in it of which ill-wishers could take advantage. To this Courtney agreed, proposing instead to introduce a Bill under the ten-minute rule in the Commons restricting diplomatic privileges.

A week after the appearance of the *Private Eye* article, Courtney by invitation met his constituency party officers in the Chairman's house. It was the first occasion that the Member had had an opportunity of putting his case to a representative body of the local Conservative association, which he did his best to do within the limitations of the law of contempt of court. Constantine, the President, summed up the purpose of the meeting under two heads – first, to inform the Member that an election in East Harrow could not be won in present conditions with Courtney as candidate; and secondly, that Courtney should write to the chairman stating that he would not be seeking re-election. To the first, Courtney replied that this must remain a matter of opinion and that he did not necessarily share it; and secondly, that he would consider not standing at the next election, but proposed as an alternative to resign immediately and stand for re-election at the subsequent by-election. This proposal, which caused some consternation, did not commend itself to the meeting.

The officers felt they should be at liberty to discuss the matter with the Executive Council, but Courtney objected to this, since he was inhibited by the pending divorce proceedings from telling the Executive the whole story. However, when the Executive met, on 12 January 1966, it passed a resolution in their Member's absence that alternative candidates should be considered to fight the seat at the next election. Meanwhile Courtney's business had collapsed, since in view of the publicity following the *Sunday Telegraph* and other press articles, particularly in *Private Eye*, most if not all his client-firms repudiated him and withdrew their agencies. But Courtney at least had the satisfaction of introducing his Diplomatic Privileges Bill in Parliament where it was printed and had an unopposed first reading, although it was killed when it came up for its second reading and one of the Government Whips shouted the traditional 'Object'. Courtney was also relieved when, as announced in the press on 29 January, his wife withdrew her divorce petition, probably because if she had gone on with it she would have been obliged to admit her own adultery.

The remainder of the Courtney saga may be briefly recounted. At a special General Meeting of the East Harrow Conservative Association on 21 February 1966, the Executive's decision was overruled by a majority of 454 votes to 277, in the course of which a hard-working Young Conservative raised a laugh when he declared that Commander

Courtney had proved to be a good MP, and that, this being so, the Member might sleep with the entire Bolshoi Ballet as far as he was concerned. Constantine and the other officers thereupon resigned. With this renewed vote of confidence Courtney stood as the Conservative candidate at the General Election on 31 March 1966, but this time unlike 1964 it was a three-cornered contest with a Liberal splitting the Conservative vote. In the event, after two recounts, the East Harrow seat was lost to Labour by 378 votes.[27] The previous adverse press publicity had been too much for Courtney, not to mention two senior clergymen of the Harrow Council of Churches who had issued a statement in which the East Harrow constituents were asked on moral grounds not to give the Conservative candidate their support.[28]

Three months later, on 13 June 1968, Mrs Elizabeth Courtney's second divorce petition was heard and she was granted a decree *nisi*, the court exercising its discretion in respect of her own admitted adultery.

On 14 January 1967, Anthony Courtney again appeared before a Selection Committee, and on 14 March the final meeting was held at Harrow Weald County Grammar School, the scene of his former triumph. Two others besides Courtney had been chosen to attend, both of them considerably younger men. Looking round the hall with its smaller assembly than the previous occasion and lacking its solid phalanx of his middle-aged supporters, Courtney felt that the result was a foregone conclusion. It was. By a clear majority, a twenty-seven-year-old stockbroker named Hugh Dykes was chosen as the prospective Conservative candidate for East Harrow. For Courtney the decision seemed and was politically mortal. The KGB had really won.

Courtney had to begin a new career, and in 1969 he became managing director of the New English Typewriting Company. He also lectured and wrote a most readable autobiography, *Sailor in a Russian Frame*. In 1970 Mr Dykes was returned as MP for Harrow East. In 1971 Courtney married as his third wife Mrs Angela Bradford, while the former Mrs Courtney married a Mr H. C. H. Keir of Dundee in the same year. In 1981, Sir Theodore Constantine, who had strongly opposed Courtney's readoption and against whom Courtney had been awarded £200 damages and costs estimated at £3,000 in a High Court action for slander on 20 March 1968, was created a life peer for public and political services, taking the title of Lord Constantine of Stanmore.[29]

4

The son of an officer in the Royal Navy, Sir Geoffrey Harrison, KCVO, GCMG, was educated at Winchester and King's College, Cambridge. On coming down from the university, he entered the Foreign Service in 1932, serving successively before the war in Tokyo and Berlin, during the war in the Foreign Office, and afterwards as Counsellor in Brussels, Minister in Moscow, and Ambassador in Brazil and Persia, where he was awarded the Order of Homayoun (1st Class) by the Shah. After a further spell in the Foreign Office as Deputy Under-Secretary of State, he returned to Moscow as Ambassador in 1965, this being his last posting since normally he would be due to retire in three years on reaching the age of sixty when he could look forward to final promotion to the peerage.

Local embassy staff in Moscow – interpreters, drivers and domestic servants – were provided by the Soviet Diplomatic Corps Service Bureau, which expected them to report to the KGB, although some were known to have refused to work for the KGB and to spy on their employers. When Sir Geoffrey and his wife arrived in the summer of 1965, among the Russian domestic staff was a chambermaid called Galya, a buxom blonde. Galya lived outside the compound but came in every day to work in the ambassador's flat on the first floor of the British Embassy building with its fine view across the Moskva river to the Kremlin. As Sir Geoffrey's successor Sir Duncan Wilson described her, 'there was no doubt that she was one of the Russians' top drawer girls. She was noticeably in a completely different class from the rest of the domestics.'[30] At all events Galya appears to have lost little or no time in exercising her wiles on the Ambassador, to which Sir Geoffrey eventually succumbed. How long the affair lasted is unclear. According to one version it began in the summer of 1965 soon after Sir Geoffrey's arrival, although he subsequently admitted that it was a 'short affair', which presupposes that it began some time later. He has also been quoted as saying: 'She was a young attractive girl. I did not ask whether she was working for the KGB, but the assumption was that every Russian working in our embassy was a KGB employee. As a trained diplomat, it was an aberration on my part.' He admitted that the affair had been carried on after the Embassy closed for the day. By contrast the ambassador, who was not at all flamboyant, ran a 'tight ship' at the

Embassy and liked to deliver lectures to the staff on the necessity for security and secrecy.

In the latter part of 1966, the Labour Minister George Brown, who had become Foreign Secretary in the Wilson Government, arrived in Moscow for talks with the Soviet Foreign Minister Andrei Gromyko. He stayed in the British Embassy, and, as the then *Daily Telegraph* Moscow correspondent John Miller has recalled, he (Miller) joined George Brown and Sir Geoffrey in the ambassador's sitting room one evening after dinner when Galya, who was dressed in a tight little black dress and a white apron, appeared with coffee and brandy for the ambassador and his two guests. The Foreign Secretary rose to his feet and promptly gave Galya a big hug and a kiss, saying, 'That's better. I've always wanted to kiss a Russian lass.'[31]

Galya may well have been reporting to the KGB as early as this date about the ambassador's infatuation for her as well as passing on any information of likely interest to the KGB which came her way. According to the *Daily Telegraph* correspondent, he understood that the KGB let Sir Geoffrey know that they were aware of his relationship with Galya and, as they also knew the ambassador was shortly due to retire, they stepped up the pressure at the time of the Soviet invasion of Czechoslovakia in August 1968. There were hints that it would be 'advisable' for him to take a much more 'reasonable' approach to the Kremlin's tough policy towards Czech liberalisation. The ambassador's reaction was to inform the Foreign Office of his 'aberration' with the result that he was immediately recalled to London for 'consultation'. He and Lady Harrison flew back to London on 25 August 1968, five days after the Soviet and other Warsaw Pact forces had moved into Czechoslovakia and occupied Prague and the other major towns. Sir Geoffrey's recall was understandable in the circumstances and aroused no particular public interest at the time, while the real reason was not disclosed, the true facts being kept secret from all but a handful of British security officials. However, Whitehall's displeasure was apparent to those in the know, since it was believed that the ambassador, whose retirement was now announced, did not make the traditional call on the Queen to mark the occasion. He now virtually disappeared from public life, not becoming a company director or such like. Nor was he ennobled which he otherwise might have expected to be. Instead he lived quietly, presumably on his pension, in his country home near Horsham.

The ambassador's affair remained a secret to all but a few until February 1981 when it was publicly revealed for the first time by the *Sunday Times*, following a recent disclosure that the US Assistant Military Attaché in Moscow Major James Holbrook had been recalled to Washington as the result of a 'sex orgy' trap by KGB agents. 'People have asked me why I chose this moment to bring this matter into the open', Sir Geoffrey was reported as saying. 'Let me be quite clear – and I feel quite strongly about this. I did not take any initiative in its timing. I made no disclosures whatsoever, but I do know who was responsible. Someone has stabbed me in the back.' Further questioned by news reporters at the time, he said: 'Of course I have my regrets. I was warned before I went to Moscow about this sort of thing. Anyone going to the Iron Curtain countries is warned this can happen. It was a very silly thing to do. My wife knew what had occurred at the time and she stood by me.'[33]

The original disclosure of the reason for Sir Geoffrey's recall was made in confidence to a journalist about four years before the story broke in the *Sunday Times*, the information being corroborated by Harold Wilson's personal and political secretary Marcia Lady Falkender.[34] When he heard of this, Sir Geoffrey said he regarded the information as classified and that it should not have been divulged to a journalist. As for the glamorous Galya she was sacked by Sir Geoffrey's successor, whose wife described her as 'a bit of a tart, certainly not in the first flush of youth.'[35] After she had been sacked Galya applied for a job in the Australian Embassy in Moscow, but she did not get it as word about the KGB *femme fatale* had been passed round to the Australian and other missions. However, no doubt she is working appropriately for the KGB elsewhere. Nor is she likely to publish her version of her affair with the British ambassador in the Soviet press.

5

In June 1985 a significant spy trial opened at the Old Bailey before Mr Justice Stocker and a jury of seven men and five women in which seven young British servicemen – five airmen and two soldiers belonging to 9 Signal Regiment in Cyprus – pleaded not guilty to a total of twenty-

[301]

eight charges under the Official Secrets Act alleging offences during the two years between February 1982 and February 1984. According to the prosecution, the accused, who had been blackmailed after taking part in homosexual orgies, betrayed hundreds of secrets of the greatest sensitivity to a foreign power, almost certainly the Soviet Union. 'They passed on whatever they could get their hands on – some with undoubted alacrity – causing in their wake exceptional damage to the interests of this nation,' said Mr Michael Wright, QC, for the prosecution. 'The case for the Crown against all seven is that each of them betrayed his country – by systematically channelling to foreign agents, a vast quantity of highly classified secret and top secret information . . . Nothing – and that includes blackmail – could ever justify giving away your country's secrets in the way that these men undoubtedly did.' Their reward was money, drugs or sex with men or women. On his own admission the ring-leader, Senior Aircraftman Geoffrey Jones, was alone personally responsible for the passing of some two hundred top secret documents and something like eight hundred documents classified as secret or confidential.[36]

Ironically, it was the twenty-one-year-old bisexual Jones of Pontypool, Gwent, a special telegraphist like five of the six others, who caused the spy ring's downfall by his infatuation with a woman. He was due to return to Britain in February 1984 on completion of his tour of duty with the signal regiment in Cyprus. In trying to delay his departure in order to continue his association with the woman, a Filipino singer called Josie, he fell foul of routine requirements of his unit's discipline by failing to comply with clearance procedures. That blunder alerted an astute warrant officer, and during questioning Jones admitted that he had associated with Josie and that he had told her about his work. Gradually Jones's interrogators realised that they were dealing with a network of spies. The story began in February 1982 when Jones, who was depressed and short of cash, met an Arab called John in a Larnaca night-club. Jones drank with John, who told him that he was a Saudi Arabian in the fruit and vegetable business. As the evening wore on Jones became increasingly drunk and eventually accepted an offer from John to put him up for the night in his flat on the outskirts of Larnaca. There he was given cannabis to smoke and more drink and in his own words became 'pretty high'. Two Arabs then appeared and the next thing Jones knew was that they were taking off first their clothes and then his. Unknown to him Jones was photographed in the act of buggery. He spent the remainder of the night on the sofa in John's flat, and in the morning John told him that he had evidence of what had taken place, no doubt meaning photographs, and that the other two Arabs were witnesses. John then said that he wanted details of Jones's job and unless he got them he would tell Jones's superiors about what had happened in the flat. Jones, who was scared that he would be dismissed from the RAF, agreed to co-operate.

Thereafter Jones would regularly pass on classified information either direct to John at his flat or by leaving an envelope behind a lavatory cistern in the Larnaca night-club for John or one of the two other agents to collect. These were a man known as Alex, who said he was a major in the KGB, and a Cypriot named Papa Artine, who was said to have been a theatrical agent. Jones acted alone until April 1982 when John said he was not satisfied with the amount of information he was being given and told Jones to recruit other members of the signal regiment.

'Jones began to do just that,' said prosecuting counsel. 'It is a thoroughly unattractive story. According to Jones, he recruited the other defendants one by one, organising homosexual parties, persuading them to take part and thereafter threatening to expose them to their superior officers.' All the men, counsel went on, had confessed to 'indulging in what can only be described as homosexual orgies.'

These events included such practices as dressing up in women's tights, mutual masturbation, oral sex and buggery. The parties were sometimes known as balcony parties because they took place on the balcony of the barrack block in which they all lived. Sometimes they were even more graphically known as splash parties.

The Crown case against Jones, who had a fetish of dressing himself in women's tights and masturbating, said prosecuting counsel, was that 'on his own confession he formed this espionage ring and thereafter he orchestrated its operation.'

Turning to the second defendant, Adam Lightowler of Newton, Powys, counsel said he became involved in the 'splash' parties in April 1982 and in the same month was introduced by Jones to John. The latter told Lightowler that he knew all about his homosexuality and wanted

[303]

information in exchange for silence. 'It scared me,' said Lightowler later; 'I didn't want the regiment to think I was queer, so I went along with it.' Asked why he had been picked out of the ring to take over from Jones as organiser once Jones's tour of duty had come to an end, Lightowler allegedly replied: 'Of the group I was the most intelligent there.'

Christopher Payne of Brighton, the third defendant was the only married man in the ring. Regular 'splash' parties were held at his house, at which the co-accused were present, and it appeared that his wife Bernie joined in these parties and supplied various sexual favours, sometimes for money. One of the uglier aspects of the case was that the fourth defendant, Wayne Kriehn of Carshalton blackmailed Payne into allowing him to provide him (Kriehn) with sex. Kriehn had apparently discovered that Payne had taken money from the troop tuckshop to buy petrol. He threatened to expose Payne unless Bernie provided him with sex and, during 1983, Kriehn 'made regular use of her'.

Kriehn was in turn himself blackmailed by Alex. He was in bed with a Filipino girl when a Cypriot came in. 'When the guy came in,' Kriehn admitted, 'the girl got off the bed and the Cypriot buggered me. I was so placed that I couldn't do anything about it. The guy left and I finished making love to the girl.' The following week Kriehn again met Alex who identified himself as a KGB major. 'He said he had a photograph of me and the Cypriot and that my security officer would be informed if I didn't give any information.'

Gwynfor Owen, the fifth defendant, of Bangor, Gwynedd, was recruited to the ring after attending 'splash' parties in Jones's room. Jones allegedly told him that he would be in trouble if he refused. It was suggested that he might be attacked as well as being reported to his security officer.

As for Signalman Martin Tuffy of Wallasey, Merseyside, the sixth defendant, he too admitted attending 'splash' parties but he was the only one of the group who did not dress up in women's tights. 'This was not because of any sense of delicacy on his part', said counsel. He was a small man and apparently there was not a pair available. A heavy drinker, Tuffy was blackmailed into joining the spy ring after having sex with a man named Paul to whom he was introduced by Jones.

The seventh accused, Lance Corporal Anthony Glass of Stockwell, was the only one not employed as a special telegraphist. He served as a clerk, and in 1982 Jones allegedly asked him for details of confidential matters related to the unit. Glass passed them on innocently, but later Jones asked for more information and threatened to expose his initial breach of security.

The remainder of prosecuting counsel's opening speech was delivered in camera, as were most of the rest of the proceedings in this unsavoury case, which lasted for 118 days and cost the tax-payer upwards of £5 millions. An eighth defendant, Senior Aircraftsman David Hardman was discharged at the outset of the case because the judge held that he was medically unfit for the interrogation at the time, since a doctor was not present. Consequently the Crown offered no evidence against him.[37]

6

It is very questionable whether so much of the trial should have taken place in camera instead of in open court. For a start, as was subsequently disclosed, all seven accused retracted their confessions which they had made to the local RAF security police – The Provost and Security Service – specifically naming their two interrogators, Flight Sergeant Barry Mason and Sergeant Timothy Sheehan, by whom, it was alleged, they had been bullied into confessing. The defence contended that the men had been kept for more than a month in solitary confinement in cells the size of a lavatory with bare wooden boards and a mattress; that the interrogators had repeatedly shouted questions at them while standing inches from their faces; that they had been interrogated for seven hours a day with only an occasional cup of tea; that they had been threatened that their parents would also be dragged into the investigation; and that the interrogators had shone bright lights into their faces so that at least one of the airmen, Christopher Payne, had needed medical treatment for his eyes.[38]

Incidentally Christopher Payne's wife Bernadette (Bernie) was also interrogated, although she was eight months pregnant at the time. 'They took me into the room and asked me what this was about.'[39]

I told them I knew nothing. I was interrogated for about six or seven hours, then I was allowed to see Chris. He was very ill. I just

[305]

wondered how they'd done it. I told them Chris had been set up. They asked who by? I said I didn't know and they just turned round and shook their heads and finally told me I'd had sexual intercourse with one man, a defendant (Kriehn). I just broke down and cried . . . I have been branded a virtual prostitute in court. People have suggested that I slept with lots of different men and got up to many strange things. But that is not true. It was also suggested that I accepted money for sex. That was also not true.

The signals regiment was based at Ayios Nikolaos, popularly known as Ay Nik, some twenty miles from Larnaca, and it had a listening post at Troodos in the mountains. There the signalmen would sit wearing headphones linked to radios. Their task was to tune into different frequencies and monitor the messages they intercepted, usually in code, sometimes Morse, or cipher. It was these, presumably in decoded or deciphered form, that Jones was alleged to have passed 'by the bagful' to the Russians.

The prosecution admitted in the course of the trial in camera that the Crown case against the defendants was 'contaminated by half truths and shot through by utter lies'. For instance, when Jones first met the 26-year-old Arab 'John', whose real name was Mohammed Alia Al Kohezy and who was alleged to be the pivot of the spy ring, John was not in Larnaca, but 2,000 miles away in Jeddah where he was attending to his fruit-and-vegetable business. Nor was the Tsokkos 7 hotel, where John was supposed to have his flat, in existence at the time. As for the theatrical agent Papa Artine, to whom Jones and some of the others were accused of passing secrets at his office in Nicosia, the agent indignantly denied it. 'It is all nonsense,' he declared. 'These men have never been near my place.'

An important witness was the Filipino cabaret singer and leader of the pop group the Ladybirds, Josie Ighilan, who flew from Manila to London to give evidence for the defence. She denied that either she or any other member of the Ladybirds had been encouraged to mix with the accused by John. However, she admitted that Geoffrey Jones had become infatuated with her, but she did not share his infatuation until the final days of their acquaintance. 'He was young and we liked him,' she said. 'He was fun but I never slept with him; it is totally untrue to say that, although I did feel some love for him. We never had any close sexual relationship. He would bring me presents . . . toy dogs, cassettes of pop music, an RAF pendant. But he would never talk about work with us. He used to shake his finger when we asked him.' She added that after the servicemen had been arrested, she was questioned by the Cypriot police. 'They asked me about Jones and John, and all my photographs and possessions were confiscated.' The pop group was subsequently deported and split up.

Another of the Ladybirds to testify along with her husband was Ning Ning, a Singapore Chinese. She too denied that Jones was a spy, while her husband a British engineer, whom she had subsequently married, disposed of the charge that she had slept with two of the other airmen by stating on oath that at the time he married her she was a virgin.

It will be recalled that the prosecution alleged that Jones and John had indulged in a homosexual relationship. This was supported by a photograph showing John giving Jones a kiss and a hug during a party in Larnaca. The defence submitted that this was simply an act of 'horseplay' between two men relaxing together. In his summing up Mr Justice Stocker referred to this photograph and pointed out that the jury must consider the defence's explanation of the incident. The judge also pointed out that all the accused men claimed that because of the circumstances in which the interrogations were conducted and their length and multiplicity, the men ended up by saying what they thought the investigators wanted to hear. 'Some were unable to tell the truth from falsehood.'

In the event, in what was to be the longest and most expensive spy trial in English legal history, all the defendants were acquitted. The verdict, which it took the jury thirty-six hours to reach, raised a storm in the House of Commons, where Mr James Stanley, the Minister of State at the Defence Ministry, announced on 29 October that the whole matter would be investigated by a leading QC, Mr David Calcutt, former Chairman of the Bar Council, while the Prime Minister Mrs Thatcher at question time stated that the Security Commission was also examining the proceedings.

At the same time, Sir Anthony Meyer, a senior Conservative MP disclosed that in August 1984 after the servicemen had returned from Cyprus and been charged, but eight months before their trial began at the Old Bailey, he had seen one of them, Senior Aircraftman Owen who had been remanded in custody at Wormwood Scrubs. As a result of their conversation Meyer obtained Owen's release on bail and also wrote to the Defence Minister, Michael Heseltine expressing the 'deepest anxiety' over the case, particularly in view of the acquittal of another Cyprus based airman Paul Davies who had been accused of passing secrets to the Syrians through a female intermediary and had also been interrogated by the security police. Meyer had not written to the Minister demanding that the charges be dropped. 'I wasn't in a position to demand anything', he was reported as saying. 'I just had misgivings. I felt an injustice had been done in the Paul Davies case and that a follow-up was about to be perpetrated. It was a warning that the Government was going to end up with egg on its face, which is exactly what happened.'[40]

Sir Anthony added that the junior Defence Minister Lord Trefgarne had replied to him pointing out that the trial judge in the Davies case had held that the police questioning was admissible, and that it would be 'quite improper' as well as 'quite ineffective' for him or the Ministry to interfere once criminal proceedings had been launched. Of course, this was nonsense. The defendants had not yet been committed for trial, and the proceedings could have been terminated by the simple expedient of the prosecution deciding on reflection not to offer any evidence against the accused.

Meanwhile, despite the trial and acquittal of the seven signalmen, intelligence experts in Whitehall and Washington are convinced that the Cyprus base continues to be threatened by a top Soviet agent probably in the Government Communications Headquarters at Cheltenham (GCHQ) passing secret messages to Russia which have been repeated to Cyprus. Significantly in his statement to the House of Commons, Mr Stanley, the Minister of State at the Defence Ministry, announced that at the time the allegations against the servicemen were made, 'a serious breach of security appeared to have occurred and it included the loss of documents'. More than that the Minister refused to say.[41] Such was the cover-up.

One other disquieting feature about this trial was subsequently raised by Tory MP Toby Jessel in the Commons, namely the manner in which the jury had been selected, Mrs Thatcher being present in the House on this occasion. According to Mr Jessel, the eight defence counsel met on 14 April and discussed how best to use the right of peremptory challenge of potential jurors to obtain a jury 'most likely to acquit.'

[308]

Every defendant in a criminal trial is now allowed to object to three potential jurors without giving a reason, so that in this case, this amounted to 24 possible challenges. In the event, with the jury finally empannelled, defence counsel made 12 challenges against nine men and three women, respectable looking, mature, decent people. Incidentally all the men wore ties, while none of the jury – average age 24 – did, at least when they returned their verdicts – one was in a T-shirt, another in jeans, while the foreman, with tattooed arms, spoke with a rough Cockney accent. No wonder Mr Jessel declared that it was 'quite intolerable' that counsel's pre-trial meetings of the kind described above should remain legal. 'Surely it is time that the law was changed as a matter of urgency,' he said.

Mrs Thatcher intervened to say that the circumstances of counsel's pre-trial meetings were a matter for the Bar Council, while the Home Secretary was instructing the new Crown Prosecution Service in the same sense. However Mr Jessel was dismissive of both suggested remedies. He pointed out that the Crown Prosecution Service would not be set up in London until April 1986. As for the Bar Council's investigation, this, said Mr Jessel, was 'a fobbing-off ploy by the legal mafia which everyone should be able to see through – including the Home Secretary.'

The British jury system, introduced by the Normans, has long been the envy of the civilised world. Due in part to the abolition of the property qualification, which has increased the number of would-be jurors in the last dozen years from eight million to 22 million and the changing of the age limit to 18–65, it has now sunk in practice to a low ebb. In Northern Ireland juries have been abolished altogether in serious criminal trials. If the jury system comes to an end in the rest of the United Kingdom, the Cyprus spy trial must bear part of the responsibility.[42]

[309]

12

Members of Parliament
and their Private Secretaries

1

IN 1975 a Tory MP pinpointed what was in his opinion an acute shortage of a certain commodity at Westminster. That commodity was, and no doubt still is, sex. 'The truth is we don't get the opportunity,' Mr Charles Irving, forty-eight-year-old bachelor Member for genteel Cheltenham, was reported as saying. 'Most of our time is spent on the benches in the Commons rather than at home in bed. I am not a sex maniac. But I am a human being. In this job I have had a rapid turnover of women. They will not stand the hours.' Mr Irving reportedly went on:

> What do wives think when husbands come crawling in exhausted at four a.m.? It is bound to create unrest because it affects normal family life. Few people are aware of the extreme hardship on MPs who have to manage on their menial parliamentary salary; are faced with the highest divorce rate in the country, and have all-night sittings interfering with their conjugal rights. Quite frankly many of us are sex-starved. You don't expect any of the married MPs to come out publicly and admit it, but believe me it is the talk of the building.
>
> I am not afraid to say it. But by saying this I hope I don't get all the elderly widows of Cheltenham chasing me down the street asking if they can relieve my tension.

'There is obviously a lot of truth in Mr Irving's remarks,' commented Mrs Ann Winterton, mother of two sons and a daughter. 'I rarely see my husband except on Sundays.' Her husband Nicholas was, and still is, Tory MP for Macclesfield. However, Ann Winterton neatly solved her complaint by getting elected an MP herself in the 1983 General Election for Congleton, the neighbouring constituency in which she and her husband have their home. But very few MPs' wives succeed in doing this, particularly those with children. 'Families do suffer,' Molly Meacher, mother of four and wife of the Labour MP for Oldham West has remarked on the subject. 'The hours preclude normal women – by that I mean normal women who want children – from becoming MPs.' The particular circumstances make Mrs Winterton's case exceptional.[1]

Charles Irving was reported at the time as being so concerned that he was thinking of forming an MPs' union, and was consulting Clive Jenkins, the general secretary of the Association of Scientific, Technical and Managerial Staffs. But nothing seems to have come of Irving's idea. Neither does he appear to have suffered from the unwanted attentions of Cheltenham's elderly widows. The real truth of the matter is that one does not have to become an MP, but if one does, like the present writer did for close on ten years, the Member has to take the rough with the smooth, balancing the advantages of prestige and position against the late nights and other discomforts. As at present constituted, Parliament cannot get through its business without prolonged sittings. As for the salary, of which Mr Irving also complains, it was £700 a year with an extra £100 for a secretary, when the present writer was elected in 1950. In 1975 it was £4,500, and it is now £18,000 with as much again for secretarial and other expenses, including research assistants who were unheard of in my time.

Among those with whom MPs in the course of their duties have been in close and sometimes intimate contact are their private secretaries, with resulting emotional involvements. One former Member and two currently sitting Members, all former Ministers, come to mind in this context. They are respectively John Stonehouse, Nicholas Fairbairn and Cecil Parkinson.

2

Many MPs have had affairs with their private secretaries over the years. None perhaps was so bizarre as that of the Labour Member and former Minister, the Right Honourable John Stonehouse, who pretended that he had been drowned while swimming off Miami Beach, Florida, in November 1974. His private secretary and mistress Mrs Sheila Buckley was a party to his action and subsequent disappearance, evidenced by coded letters which she sent him in Australia where he was living under an assumed name or rather two assumed names and where she hoped to join him so that they could get married and begin a new life together. But things went wrong for them both, and when two years later the MP stood in the dock at the Old Bailey charged with twenty-one offences alleging fraud, forgery, conspiracy and theft, his mistress stood beside him facing six charges alleging theft and conspiracy.

John Stonehouse was born in Southampton in 1925, being the second son and youngest child of his parents, of whom his father William Mitchell Stonehouse was a Post Office engineer and local secretary of his trade union and his mother Rosina, a one-time scullery maid in the Isle of Wight, was a local Councillor (later Mayor) and President of the Southampton Co-operative Society. The family lived in a council house which they were eventually able to buy. After brief spells in elementary schools in Southampton, young John left at the age of sixteen to become assistant to the Senior Probation Officer there at a weekly wage of twenty-two shillings and sixpence. Three years later, in 1944, he joined the RAF and after he had trained as a pilot became an education officer. In 1947, with the aid of an ex-Serviceman's grant he went to the London School of Economics where he was taught by the renowned Professor Harold Laski, and became Chairman of the Labour Society, eventually graduating BSc with honours. When he was studying at the LSE he met and courted a beautiful seventeen-year-old secretary in the Fabian Society named Barbara Smith whom he married in 1948.[2]

Meanwhile Laski, who guided his students in politics as well as their studies, advised Stonehouse to put in for selection as a Labour parliamentary candidate and gave him an unsolicited letter of recommendation to the selection committee for the suburban constituency of Twickenham. In the event he was selected at the age of twenty-three and fought the 1950 General Election when he was defeated by the Conservative E. H. (later Sir Edward) Keeling, who had represented the constituency for the past fifteen years. At the General Election in the following year he was selected for Burton-on-Trent. 'It was a measure of his imagination at that time', a friend has recalled, 'that the tough brewery workers of Burton selected him even after he told them he never touched beer.' Their choice was justified by the fact that the sitting Conservative won by only 733 votes in a straight fight in which Stonehouse halved the previous Tory majority.

John Stonehouse was now launched on a political career, and after filling several jobs in the Co-operative Movement including one running a farm in Uganda with his wife, he was eventually returned as MP for Wednesbury at a by-election in February 1957 after the local Member, Mr Stanley ('Featherbed') Evans had been ousted by his constituency party for supporting the Eden Government over the Suez invasion.[3] Although he endeared himself to the Labour leader Harold Wilson and had transferred from Wednesbury to Walsall North owing to boundary changes, Stonehouse did not think he would be offered any political office when Labour won the General Election in the autumn of 1964 by a narrow majority. But to his surprise he was. 'I want you to join Roy Jenkins at the Ministry of Aviation; you were a pilot, weren't you?' the new Prime Minister said to him. 'You should do well there and I think you can get on with Roy.'[4] As Parliamentary Secretary to the Ministry of Aviation, John Stonehouse did both, notably in securing export orders for British aircraft. Transfer and promotion to other ministerial jobs followed: Under-Secretary for the Colonies; Minister of Aviation; Minister of State, Technology; Postmaster-General (he was the last to hold that office); and Minister of Posts and Communications. In 1968 at a lunch at No 10 Downing Street, when King Hussein of Jordan was the principal guest, the other guests including the Foreign Secretary Michael Stewart and the Minister of State in the Department of Technology, Wilson remarked that he had decided to recommend Stonehouse for elevation to the Privy Council, adding that the citation should be for services to export. Stonehouse was naturally delighted with his recognition, since it was unusual for a Minister not in the Cabinet to become a Privy Counsellor. He was later to recall the first Council meeting at Buckingham Palace which he attended and at which he was sworn in. Richard Crossman, the Lord President, was ten minutes late and came in without apologising to the Queen and the others present for keeping them waiting. The formal business after the swearing in consisted of a single item, a Rhodesian Order in Council, which was somewhat academic since Rhodesia had already declared its independence. The Lord President merely read out the title and the Queen said 'Approved'. The Clerk to the Council, turning to the

Queen, then stated that at the next Privy Council 'Your Majesty will be asked to approve the siting of a public lavatory in Guernsey.' Robert (now Lord) Mellish, one of the Ministers present, suggested to the Queen that she might consider refusing her approval 'and so make history'. The Queen replied with a smile that she would wait for something more important.[5]

In June 1968, the same month that Stonehouse became a Privy Counsellor, the Prime Minister transferred him to the office of Postmaster-General with a brief to reorganise the department and set up a new Post Office Corporation with a view to the Post Office ceasing to be a government department and becoming a new public authority with responsibility for running the postal, telecommunications, giro and remittance services. Stonehouse, somewhat unwisely as it turned out, had himself appointed chairman of the new board, and he attracted much unfavourable publicity for his mishandling of the two-tier postal system, the reorganisation of the London telephone directories, which had to be abandoned, and finally for precipitating the unnecessary telegraphists' strike in 1969 at a cost to the Post Office of some £2 millions. This latter affair destroyed the Prime Minister's confidence in the Post Office chief. 'Wilson never really forgave Stonehouse' a ministerial colleague later recalled. 'He felt that the Cabinet had been misled. I think Stonehouse himself came to realise Wilson's feelings.'[6] Nor were matters helped by MI5 reporting to the Prime Minister that a Czech defector, Josef Frolik, named Stonehouse as one of two Czech agents operating in Britain. In the event Stonehouse was cleared of any complicity in treacherous activities, although he had visited Czechoslovakia on a number of occasions and had been instrumental in 'twinning' Wednesbury with the Czech industrial town of Kladno. Nevertheless, the spying 'smear' did Stonehouse's reputation no good.[7]

About Christmas 1969 John Stonehouse, guessing that Labour might not win the next General Election, was instrumental in forming three companies which he could control if and when he ceased to be a minister, thus breaking the spirit but not the letter of the rules governing a minister's business interests. The companies were Connoisseurs of Claret Ltd., Export Promotion and Consultancy Services (EPACS), and Systems and Consultancy Services. Sheila Buckley was a director of these companies, with authority to sign cheques, thus keeping his place on the board warm for the minister when the time came. It did come in June 1970 at the Election which the Tories won led by Edward Heath. Thus Stonehouse's fall from political grace and his loss of office was caused by the electorate rather than the Prime Minister who lost his office like the rest of his ministerial colleagues.

Sheila Buckley, it may be added here, was a slight, petite girl with brown hair, daughter of a retired butcher named Leslie Black. She was twenty-two when in 1968 she became Stonehouse's private secretary at Westminster at a salary of £1,000 a year, the result of replying to an advertisement. She was efficient and decorative, just the right combination for the tall and handsome MP who seemed to be moving up fast in the Labour hierarchy. In 1969, when Stonehouse was Postmaster-General, she married Roger Buckley, an accountant. But the marriage was not a success and ended in divorce four years later, in March 1973, when Sheila sued her husband on the ground of his adultery. Roger Buckley afterwards blamed Stonehouse for alienating his wife's affections, asserting that the wining and dining that she enjoyed at her boss's expense was beyond his means. After her divorce Sheila moved into a flat in Petty France, which Stonehouse rented. This became their love nest, although Sheila always denied to her parents that she was having an affair with him.

In 1970 and in the immediately following years things did not work out as well as Stonehouse had hoped. Connoisseurs of Claret, the wine-importing business, went into the red, while EPACS, although it had some useful consultancy appointments and was initially quite successful, did not prove to be the money spinner that Stonehouse had hoped. However, he had another enterprise, a trading company, Global Imex, which he persuaded a Lonrho executive named Andrew Scott to join since Scott specialised in exports. At the same time, March 1972, Stonehouse augmented his income by becoming chairman at £4,800 a year of Aeromaritime Ltd., the UK subsidiary of an American group specialising in electronic defence equipment, although he had nothing to do with the day-to-day running of the company. 'We hired him for what I would call *bella figura*,' said Aeromaritime's managing director Brian James afterwards. 'He simply sat in the chair at board meetings and acted like a good chairman.'

Stonehouse's next business enterprise was to build a bank with paid up capital of £1 million. The recent independence of Bangladesh, the

former East Pakistan, offered an opportunity for Stonehouse to capital-
ise industrially, exploiting his popularity with the newly founded state
to which he had contributed prominent political support. The 'bank',
known as the British Bangladesh Trust (BBT) with Stonehouse as
unpaid chairman, was floated in November 1972, but the share issue
was considerably under-subscribed in spite of financial support from
such heavyweights as Sir Raymond Brookes of Guest Keen and Nettle-
fold, and Sir John Clark of Plessey, besides the Crown Agents for
Overseas Governments. Subscriptions from Bengali investors, of
whom there were plenty in Britain, were few and disappointing. The
under-subscription was largely due to a damaging article in the *Sunday
Times* Business News by Richard Milner and Anthony Mascheranas
alleging malpractices in recruiting support for the project, particularly
by circulating a prospectus in Bengali containing false statements such
as that the Trust had been promised full banking status by the Bank of
England within 12 to 18 months, whereas it had not; besides which
Stonehouse had not disclosed in the official prospectus that he was also
the bank's landlord via EPACS.

The BBT's beginnings, with offices at 27 Dover Street, which also
housed EPACS and Global Imex, were thus not very auspicious.
Scotland Yard immediately mounted a fraud investigation on the basis
of the *Sunday Times* article. Although the matter was reported to the
Director of Public Prosecutions, it was dropped after Stonehouse
appealed to the High Commissioner of Bangladesh, who pointed out to
the Foreign Office that the so-called prospectus in Bengali was not an
official prospectus but merely an information sheet, and if any proceedings were taken against Stonehouse it would be unjust and harmful to
relations between Britain and Bangladesh. But Stonehouse's image as a
merchant banker was dented by this inquiry. Furthermore he had
difficulties in raising the balance of the paid up capital, and he was
obliged to borrow from other banks. Then Keith White, the Trust's
General Manager, had an illness which led to his resignation after
Stonehouse, who had visited him in hospital, asked White to sign the
company register to the effect that he had attended a board meeting at
which he had not in fact been present. White then sued Stonehouse for
alleged failure to repurchase his £10,000 investment. Also the Deputy
Manager, who had come with fine references from Lloyd's Bank and
the Bank of Cyprus, turned out to be an undischarged bankrupt. In an

attempt to extricate himself from the mire, Stonehouse closed down the Bangladesh operation renaming the company London Capital Group (LCG), 'so that it could appeal to a wider public for business', while the BBT was nominally retained as 'a specialised subsidiary'. Sir Charles Forte, head of the Forte hotel group, and James Charlton former secretary of the British Aircraft Corporation, joined the LCG board.

'As the weeks and months of 1974 wore on the burdens became heavier,' Stonehouse was to recall; 'I was being squeezed into a corner from which there was no escape. Together with the worries brought on by the Bank's incredible problems I had the suspicion that my col-leagues in the House of Commons no longer respected me. Was this because the rumours had been spread that I had been the subject of fraud investigations by Scotland Yard, or because there had been tittle-tattle about my alleged spying for Czechoslovakia, or for some other reason? I shall never know; but I was wounded by it.'[8] He was also wounded by Harold Wilson dropping him from the Front Bench Opposition team in 1970 and again for passing him over for office after the General Election in February 1974, when Wilson became Prime Minister for the second time in a minority Labour government.

Meanwhile there was a damaging credit squeeze. With fringe banks collapsing in the wake of London and Counties Securities, of which Jeremy Thorpe was a director, major banks like Barclays and the National Westminster began to tighten up on personal lending. Also Labour's new Chancellor of the Exchequer, Denis Healey, used his first Budget on 26 April to stop rich entrepreneurs from setting off overdraft interest payments against their income tax liabilities. It was coin-cidentally in the same month that Stonehouse ascertained from Mrs Jean Markham, who lived in his Walsall constituency, that her husband Joseph Arthur Markham had died the previous month. In due course Stonehouse obtained a copy of Markham's passport in Markham's name, forging Markham's signature. He also procured a copy of the birth certificate of Donald Clive Mildoon who died in Walsall shortly afterwards.

Other executives in the Stonehouse companies resigned because they did not like or failed to understand the complexity of his financial dealings. Andrew Scott, the Lonrho recruit, did so at the withdrawal of £30,000 from Global Imex to shore up the Bangladesh bank, and left in February 1974. Besides Keith White, there followed Global Imex's

[317]

managing director John Collaro, the company accountant Alan Le Fort and the Bengali bank director K. B. Ahmed. Collaro simply could not understand what Stonehouse was doing. 'He never told you,' Collaro said afterwards. 'He'd sit brooding downstairs, and then come up with his latest thing. He wasn't a business man. He was a politician playing at business.' One of Stonehouse's speculative projects nominally in conjunction with Collaro, was an attempt to sell 15 million dollars worth of Romanian cement to Nigeria via New York. The deal did not come off since Stonehouse's New York brokers could not ship the consignment to Nigeria at an economic price. (Part of Stonehouse's share of the £380,000 expected profit for Global Imex was to be paid 'offshore' so as to avoid tax. On one occasion he told a fellow director: 'We have vehicles for money to be paid offshore, in Switzerland or Lichtenstein.')

On 4 November 1974, following the second General Election in eight months at which Labour were returned with an overall majority in the Commons of three, Stonehouse spoke in the debate on the Queen's Speech, attacking his own party's economic policy and offending his fellow Labour Members but pleasing the Tories. A few days later he flew to Miami, where he had an appointment with an aerospace company, which might invest in LCG. He kept the appointment after having flown to Mexico City and back using his Markham passport and an American Express credit card in Markham's name as a test exercise. In the event he then flew back to London as he considered it advisable to return to Miami with Charlton, staying with Charlton at the Fontainebleau Hotel where he had stayed before. On 20 November he went for a swim, leaving his clothes on the beach and his other possessions including his Stonehouse passport and traveller's cheques in his hotel room. When he did not return, Charlton reported his disappearance to the hotel management and it was presumed that he had been drowned.

However, John Stonehouse had not been drowned. He had faked his death and under his Markham alias had flown to Australia having previously taken out life insurance policies worth £125,000 payable directly to his wife in the event of his death. (If the amount had been made payable to his estate he realised that it would be swallowed up by his debts.) At the time of his disappearance his companies were overdrawn by £200,000 and he personally owed banks and credit companies more than £729,000. No wonder he wanted to escape to a new life under a new name with his mistress secretary.

3

Stonehouse left Miami without difficulty, flying to San Francisco on his Markham passport in new clothes which he had left at Miami airport. From San Francisco he decided not to fly direct to Sydney but go via Hawaii, which he did by economy flight to Honolulu. There he stayed at the Sheraton Hotel on Waikiki Beach from which he put through two long distance telephone calls to Sheila Buckley in the flat which he had rented for her in Hampstead.

Visiting the Bank of Hawaii, he introduced himself as Mr Lewis Jones and asked the bank officials to exchange a sum of $13,177 in pounds sterling and US dollar notes into two bank drafts made payable to Markham. This was done and when he arrived in Melbourne on 27 November Stonehouse immediately went to the Bank of New South Wales in Collins Street. Here he found that, in accordance with his instructions, the Midland Bank in London, where he had opened an account in the name of Joseph Arthur Markham, had transferred £12,000 for the credit of this alias. At the same time he handed over the two Hawaiian bank drafts which the Bank of New South Wales exchanged for a single draft; this draft Stonehouse then endorsed to the Swiss Banking Corporation in Zurich and sent off with a request to await his instructions for the return of the amount in the name of Mildoon. He had now decided to use the Mildoon alias in preference to Markham, in order, as he put it, 'to give flesh and bones to my second Australian personality.' This was to prove a fatal mistake.

Next morning, 28 November, he withdrew most of the money in the New South Wales Bank account, amounting to some 22,000 Australian dollars in $50 and $10 notes, which he put in a satchel he was carrying for the purpose. He then went to the Bank of New Zealand a few doors along in Collins Street, where he saw the manager whom he asked about interest rates and investment, saying he was an insurance broker intending to work in Australia for a year before emigrating to New Zealand. He then produced the contents of the satchel which were counted by the teller, being told at the same time that he would receive

9 per cent interest on the amount of the deposit in the name he had given – Donald Clive Mildoon.

'We are very pleased to have your account, Mr Muldoon,' said the manager whose name was David Rowland.

'No, not Muldoon,' said Stonehouse. 'Mildoon.'

'We have a leading politician in New Zealand with the name Muldoon,' the manager replied apologetically. 'That's what confused me.'

'Yes, I've heard of him,' Stonehouse remarked. 'Quite a character.' This was Robert Muldoon, Leader of the National Party and a future Prime Minister, whom Stonehouse had met on a visit to New Zealand when Muldoon was Minister of Finance and Stonehouse himself a Minister in the Wilson Government.[9]

One of the New Zealand bank clerks named King had seen Stonehouse come in and deposit his money, although he did not know the new customer's name. About 12.30 p.m. Mr King went for a lunch time walk which took him past the Bank of New South Wales. By sheer chance he saw the man with the satchel emerging. (For some reason Stonehouse had gone back to the first bank, possibly to draw out some more cash.) King then went in and learned from one of the clerks whom he knew there that the man with the satchel had had an account opened at that bank in the name of Joseph Arthur Markham. On returning to his own bank and discovering that their new customer was Donald Clive Mildoon, King reported the matter to Mr Rowland. The manager's suspicions were aroused since there had been a series of bank frauds recently in Melbourne and he thought it possible that Mildoon/ Markham was planning such a fraud. He alerted the police accordingly. At the same time Mr Rowland noticed in his bank record that 'Mr Mildoon' should be treated with extreme caution on any future visit and that he should not be allowed to have a current account on which he could draw by cheque without further identification.[10]

Having completed his banking business, Stonehouse took one of his suitcases to the Regal Hotel, a cheap establishment in the St Kilda suburb of Melbourne noted for its prostitution, massage parlours and other ephemeral delights. From there he hurried off by taxi to the Tullamarine airport where he caught the BOAC plane to Singapore with minutes to spare, his American Express card in the name of Markham being accepted without question in payment of the fare.

From Singapore he flew on via Bangkok to Copenhagen, arriving on 29 November. There he had a secret meeting with Sheila Buckley, who joined him for a few days, and to whom he had previously given £1,600 to tide her over until such time as they could settle down together in Australia. The remainder of his time in the Danish capital was mostly occupied studying the English newspaper accounts of 'the Stonehouse mystery', the general conclusion being that he had died by drowning.

Stonehouse left Copenhagen on 8 December to return to Melbourne, which he did via Moscow and Delhi (using the cheap Aeroflot line), and so on to Bangkok, Singapore and Perth, touching down two days later at Tullamarine airport. Thence he went by taxi to the St Kilda hotel where he had left his other suitcase, buying a newspaper on the way in which he saw some apartments to let in Flinders Street in the heart of the city. At his request the taxi first took him there where he found an inexpensive apartment, paid a month's rent in advance and moved in the same day. 'We are glad to have you with us, Mr Mildoon,' said the proprietor's wife. 'You will be one of our big family.'[11] On 11 December he went to the Bank of New Zealand and applied to open a current account, saying that he expected to be married shortly. However, in view of the manager's instructions he was unable to open a current account there, since he could not produce a passport in the name of Mildoon or other satisfactory proof of identification. He then went to the Commonwealth Banking Corporation which catered for migrants; here he was able to open two accounts in the name of Mildoon. He said that he had substantial amounts owing to him in Switzerland, and credence was given to his statement by the arrival at the bank of the amount of the draft which he had endorsed to the Swiss Banking Corporation in Zurich.

Unfortunately for Stonehouse, Nemesis was catching up with him. On Christmas Eve the Victoria State police, who had been watching the pseudonymous Mr Mildoon's movements as a suspected illegal immigrant, arrested him at St Kilda where he had been to the Regal Hotel to collect any mail which might have been sent to him in the name of Markham from the Bank of New South Wales. When he was searched at the police headquarters a letter from Sheila Buckley was found in one of his pockets. Under interrogation he admitted that he was John Stonehouse.

'Do you know when we first started following you we thought you

[321]

were the Earl of Lucan,' said one of the fraud squad officers. 'You were such an English gentleman and we knew Lucan was missing in England and wanted as a murder suspect.' (Lucan was being sought for having killed his children's nanny.) At the same time another officer told him: 'We got on to you because you opened two bank accounts. We had no other reason to be suspicious of you at all, and for a time we almost gave up, thinking we were on a false track, but the Lucan suspicion kept us going. And then the possibility that you were Stonehouse came through, and we sent to Interpol for a full description of you which seemed to fit.' This was supported by blown up prints of his Stonehouse passport photograph which the officer showed him.[12]

Stonehouse was taken from police headquarters to the Maribyrnong Detention Centre for illegal immigrants where he was held until he appeared in the Magistrate's Court on Boxing Day. Meanwhile he had been allowed to telephone his wife in England and she immediately flew out to Melbourne, her fare being presumably paid by Express Newspapers which had acquired her story and the right to take exclusive photographs. When he appeared in court, Stonehouse was handed a number of cables. One was from Harold Evans, the editor of the *Sunday Times* ('Glad to see that you are alive and kicking') asking for an article. The request, Stonehouse wryly remarked afterwards, had come two years and two months too late![13]

Three days later Stonehouse was released from the Detention Centre and granted provisional liberty on the ground that being a Member of a Commonwealth Parliament he was entitled to stay in Australia. For the next five weeks he moved about Victoria with his wife, staying at fourteen different addresses, hotels, motels, and for a short period in hospital where he had a mental breakdown. Throughout this time he was being vigorously pursued by news reporters. On 5 January 1975, an *Express* reporter questioned him about his disappearing act, in particular causing his wife pain by his action. 'That is my greatest regret in the whole business,' said Stonehouse. 'It was a dirty trick.' He went on:

The trouble with people back home is that they are looking for a logical reason. They don't realise my state of mind for months before I left England. I had come to the end of my tether. Business associates were blackmailing me to get their own way. Economic environment was playing havoc with my companies. Everything was going wrong.

[322]

You have no idea how I felt. In the end I just wanted to get away and become a plain human being again. All right, so it wasn't a normal thing to do. I wasn't in a normal state of mind.

He admitted that there was 'a great deal of Peter paying Paul'. In other words, attempting to bolster one company by borrowing from another, transactions which caused disputes with other directors. Particularly vulnerable, he admitted, was his Bangladesh bank, London Capital Group.[14]

On 13 January 1975, Stonehouse, who was staying with his wife in a motel in New South Wales, wrote to the Labour Leader of the House of Commons, Edward Short, asking him to put in motion the formalities required for his resignation as Member for Walsall North. He also referred to his desire to remain in Australia and to his illness. 'I have consulted a leading Australian psychiatrist with regard to my breakdown,' he added, 'and following these consultations I now appreciate that the long trauma I suffered was caused by a deep disillusionment with the state of English Society and the complete frustration of the ideals I have pursued in my political and business life.'[15]

When Stonehouse told his Australian solicitor about this letter, the solicitor strongly advised him not to tender his formal resignation, accurately predicting that if he ceased to be an MP he would not be granted migrant status and would have to leave the country. This was precisely what Mr Clyde Cameron, the Federal Minister of Labour and Immigration, indicated in a parliamentary statement in Canberra. Meanwhile the House of Commons in Westminster had appointed a Select Committee to consider Stonehouse's position and in its interim report on 19 March recommended that no action such as expulsion from the House should be taken for the time being since non-attendance was an insufficient ground for such action.

Stonehouse heaved a sigh of relief. But his peace of mind did not last long. Two days later on 21 March it was shattered by a visit from Detective-Inspector R. H. Gillespie. 'Sorry, John,' said the inspector. 'I've got some bad news for you. I have a warrant for your arrest.' The warrant was an extradition one and charged Stonehouse with fifteen offences of theft, forgery and fraud. When Stonehouse appeared in court the same day, the Australian government prosecutor stated that bail was opposed by the Chief Metropolitan Magistrate in London and should accordingly be refused. Stonehouse's solicitor caused a ripple of laughter by pointing out that Australia was no longer a British colony and that its courts were independent of directions from Bow Street 12,000 miles away or anywhere else outside Australian territory. As a result Stonehouse was released on bail by the Melbourne magistrate. Six further charges were added during the next fortnight, involving in all nearly £170,000.[16]

At the same time Sheila Buckley, who had flown out to Australia in February to be with her lover and former boss at his request, was likewise charged with six offences involving theft, fraud and conspiracy. Stonehouse, who had met her at the airport when she arrived, got his solicitor to handle her case also, since she too was arrested. Both had to report daily at the same police station in Melbourne pending the outcome of the extradition proceedings.

Barbara Stonehouse had known of her husband's affair with his secretary for some time, but she loyally stood by him, assuring newspaper reporters that he had been 'a damned good husband.' This is hardly borne out by the letters which Sheila Buckley wrote to her lover after his disappearance and which eventually became public knowledge through the press at his subsequent trial. By the end of 1973 it appears from this correspondence that she thought she was pregnant by him and that she even discussed with Mrs Stonehouse the possibility of having an abortion at a clinic. However, in the event she apparently tried to induce one herself. 'Can't get a doctor re you know,' she wrote to her lover whom she called 'My Dear Dums' on 12 December 1973. 'But it's pretty sure – think I'm going to lose it. I've dragged so many cases around – climbed hall walls – run the lot, that I feel like I'm losing it anyway.' She was mistaken since a pregnancy test which she took a month later proved negative.[17]

Both John Stonehouse and Sheila Buckley were extradited on 18 July 1975, being accompanied on the flight to England by Scotland Yard officers. For some weeks Stonehouse was kept in Brixton, the remand prison, and was repeatedly refused bail before it was eventually granted on 27 August. By this date Parliament was in recess so that he was unable to visit the House of Commons which was not in session. On 13 October, the same day as committal proceedings began in the Horseferry Road magistrate's court, he went to the Commons where he saw the Speaker Mr Selwyn Lloyd with a view to making a personal statement, stood for a few minutes at the Bar of the House, but did not take his seat, sensing a frosty reception. Mr Speaker Lloyd agreed to the personal statement but insisted on vetting it beforehand with the result that about half of it was deleted.

This much heralded personal statement was delivered a week later, on 20 October. It began with a slightly theatrical gesture when Stonehouse rose from a seat on the Opposition Conservative backbenches, explaining that he did so because he had sat there for most of his time in the House over nineteen years. As he tried to elaborate he was pulled up by the Speaker for not sticking to the agreed text and he was again interrupted when he began to launch an attack on the press. After denying allegations that he had been a CIA agent and had spied for the Czechs he went on to give the best explanation he could for his 'extraordinary and bizarre conduct', namely that he had suffered a complete mental breakdown which an Australian psychiatrist had described as psychiatric suicide. 'It took the form of a repudiation of the life of Stonehouse because that life had become intolerable to me', he went on. 'A new parallel personality took over, separate and apart from the original man who was resented and despised by the parallel personality for the ugly humbug and sham of the recent years of his public life.' In view of the facts, he hoped the House would agree that 'the Honourable Member for Walsall North had no intention of removing himself from the processes of justice as established by Parliament.'[17]

He spoke for precisely thirteen minutes to a crowded and silent House. His two daughters Jane and Julia were in the public gallery along with his mistress Sheila Buckley, but Mrs Stonehouse was not there. The statement over, Members left the chamber and John Stonehouse looked a lonely man as he followed them. Only one MP, the Conservative Michael Grylls, greeted him with a few friendly words.

Shortly afterwards, on 5 November 1975, John Stonehouse was committed for trial along with Sheila Buckley. The end of the Stonehouse drama was in sight. And what a drama! As its central figure remarked after he had been discovered in Melbourne, 'this story has everything – sex, politics, spies, big business, fraud and faked death.'

4

The trial of John Stonehouse and Sheila Buckley opened at the Old Bailey before Mr Justice Eveleigh on 27 April 1976. Mr Michael Corkery, Second Senior Prosecuting Counsel to the Crown, conducted the prosecution. Stonehouse's solicitor originally instructed Mr Richard Du Cann, QC, to defend his client, but at the last moment Stonehouse withdrew his instructions and said he would conduct his own defence, which he was entitled to do. At the outset of the proceedings, before arraignment, he tried to explain to the judge that he had done this because he considered that the prosecution was pursuing a 'largely political case' against him. This led to a sharp clash between them in which the judge told the defendant that unless he sat down he would be 'taken down' and there remain until he obeyed the directions of the court. The prisoner afterwards apologised. He pleaded not guilty to twenty-one charges of forgery, fraud, false pretences, conspiracy and theft of the proceeds of cheques, also to two further charges of making false statements to obtain legal aid. Sheila Buckley, who was defended by Lord Wigoder, QC, pleaded not guilty to five joint charges of theft and one of conspiring to defraud creditors of Export Promotions and Consultancy Services Ltd. (EPACS). The swearing in of the jury took some time owing to ten potential women jurors being challenged, four by Stonehouse, five by Sheila Buckley's counsel and one by the prosecution. Others were excused on health and personal grounds. Eventually seven men and five women were empanelled.[19] As the case proceeded, one of the women jurors became ill and the case was continued with eleven in the jury box.

'Cast out of your minds prejudice,' Mr Corkery warned the jury in opening the case for the Crown, 'cast out of your minds any political sympathies or beliefs. This is a criminal trial involving grave dishonesty, and politics don't come into it whatsoever.' Crown counsel emphasised that on the day he faked his death Stonehouse owed £375,000, much of which he had no intention of paying, such as what he owed to credit card companies. He had also, said Mr Corkery, forged two applications for birth certificates, those of Markham and Mildoon, and one for a passport in the name of Markham. As for Mrs Buckley, counsel went on, she was more than just a loyal secretary following instructions blindly. 'There is substantial evidence that she was

[326]

a willing participant.' Mr Corkery also read her coded letters to Stonehouse in Australia which had been intercepted by the police.[20] Incidentally the prosecution later withdrew the charges relating to the applications for the birth certificates after it was demonstrated that the Registry Office was legally bound to supply such certificates on request even where the applications were not signed.[20]

It is unnecessary to describe in detail this marathon trial which lasted for sixty-eight days. Stonehouse's eighty-two-year-old mother, who was living in a one bedroom flat in Southampton, wished to give evidence for her son, but he refused to allow her to do so. Neither of the two defendants chose to go into the witness-box and testify on oath. Instead they made unsworn statements from the dock which meant that they could not be subjected to cross-examination.

In his statement Stonehouse referred to his co-defendant as 'a great woman' who intuitively understood his deep psychological problem and helped 'a disoriented person' to adjust. 'The situation between Mrs Buckley and myself is that we were very close in our political work for many years,' he told the jury. 'She was doing an excellent job for me as a constituency secretary, and after her husband left her an intimate relationship grew up between us.' He did not elaborate but proceeded to explain how he developed a 'parallel personality' – that of Joseph Arthur Markham, and the relief it brought. During 1974, the year he disappeared, he said, there was a build-up of extra pressures of an intense kind. They were not ordinary business or political pressures but a combination of things of such weight that they were crushing John Stonehouse. He had been imbued with idealism but events had disillusioned him. Stonehouse was being 'destroyed by evil forces', something that could not be understood by callow people who never had ideals of their own. 'In the middle of 1974 I was drawn irresistibly to establish a second parallel personality who would give me relief from the awesome pressures on John Stonehouse, ex-Minister and Privy Counsellor.' His voice rose with emotion as he then told the jury 'how marvellous' it was for 'Joe Markham' to be able to obtain a passport openly at the Passport Office, start a bank account in Markham's name and have 'fantasies' about going to Australia. However, he did not attempt effectively to defend his acts of forgery nor the large sums of money he had allegedly obtained by deception and false pretences.[21]

[327]

Sheila Buckley's statement from the dock was more concise than her lover's, lasting forty-five minutes in contrast to his five days. She described her intimate relations with him, her suspected pregnancy by him and her visit to Australia after he had reappeared there. 'Even though I find myself in this dock as a result of those actions,' she said, 'I cannot change my mind even now. If I had the same decisions to make all over again tomorrow, I feel certain that those decisions would remain the same. My long ordeal has been, to say the very least, painful. But the safety of a man or a woman is of far greater importance than pain and humiliation. I have no regrets.' She went on to say that when she first became a director of the Stonehouse companies, it was at his request. She had 'no real say' in the running of them. They were what she would describe as 'a one man band' with Stonehouse controlling them. She added that she had no real interest in business and had always been more interested in politics.

Mrs Buckley went on to describe the telephone calls she had received from her lover after his disappearance. On the occasion of the first call from Hawaii she repeatedly asked him where he was, she said, but he would not say. She went on:

He sounded completely distraught and it was very difficult to make any sense of what he was saying. He was incoherent and I thought he sounded suicidal. He said things like 'Help me, Sheila.'

I asked him whether I should let his family know that he was alive and he said emphatically that I should not. I asked him whether this was wise, but he simply repeated that I should not. He asked me to give my word that I would not tell anyone that he was alive until he gave me permission to do so. He sounded so desperate I had no option but to give him my word.

During the second call he said he was in America which she had already assumed because of reports that he had left his passport in the hotel in Miami. 'The telephone calls were extremely confusing,' she said, 'since at all times Mr Stonehouse spoke in the third person. For instance, he referred to "John" as another person and said he had to die to get away from the pressures in England.'

The third time he telephoned she thought was in the early morning of

[328]

3 December 1974. On this occasion he said he was in Copenhagen and she agreed to join him there for a few days. 'I believed at the time that I might be pregnant, wrongly as it turned out, and that Mr Stonehouse was the father,' she continued. 'He still sounded very distraught and still spoke in the third person.'

When she arrived in Copenhagen, she found him sitting, head in hands, at the airport. 'He was completely distraught, nervous and drawn. He was not wearing any form of disguise and I could not understand why he had not been recognised as he sat there.' He explained to her, she said, that he had 'become Mr Markham.' He also asked her to write to him in Australia in the name of Mildoon, which left her 'totally confused'.

After her return to London, she said, she saw Mrs Stonehouse when the latter was being questioned by the press about Stonehouse's relations with her, Sheila Buckley. 'In anger she [Mrs Stonehouse] told me of other affairs she believed Mr Stonehouse had had with other women. I was very upset and I felt very lonely and isolated. I was the only one who knew that Mr Stonehouse was alive and I was hearing terrible things about him that challenged the whole basis of our relationship.'

Finally, after receiving a telephone call on Christmas Eve 1974 from Mrs Stonehouse who had learned that her husband was alive, Mrs Buckley said that she too agreed to go to Australia. 'Although I have been much criticised by the press for my silence when I knew Mr Stonehouse was alive after his telephone calls to me,' Mrs Buckley concluded, 'I can only say that I consider my actions at the time to be the only possible way of dealing with the situation.'[22]

The trial at the Old Bailey ended on 6 August 1976, the sixty-eighth day. Together with the committal proceedings at the magistrate's court which lasted for eighteen days, as well as the expenses of the Scotland Yard Fraud Squad who travelled more than 200,000 miles in Australia, America and Europe on Stonehouse's trail, the whole affair cost the British taxpayer an estimated £750,000. The jury were out for over sixteen hours spread over two days. Stonehouse was found guilty on thirteen counts out of twenty-one and Sheila Buckley guilty on five out of six, the sixth being the conspiracy charge to defraud the creditors of EPACS. On hearing the verdicts, Sheila Buckley began to cry, and as the judge prepared to pass sentence she was

[329]

unable to stand unaided and was allowed to remain seated in the dock.

In reply to the customary question of whether he had anything to say why sentence should not be passed upon him, Stonehouse begged the judge to bear in mind his long years of altruistic work for people in Britain and abroad, also his services to the state. 'I have lost practically everything I possess,' he added. 'I am now shattered politically and also in my private life.'

'You falsely accused other people of cant, hypocrisy and humbug', said Mr Justice Eveleigh in sentencing him, 'when you must have known all the time your defence was an embodiment of all these things . . . You didn't simply decide to disappear when oppressed by business burdens. You decided to do so in comfort. It is clear from the evidence in this case that self-interest has been well in the fore. You aimed to get rich quickly, in some way convincing yourself that you had missed your chance in the past and 1970 onwards was a chance you deserved to have. That, as I see it, is why you had so many companies. That is why you had a bank account in America into which money originally obtained in this country was subsequently diverted. You were not an unlucky business man escaping from undeserved financial problems. It all arose from your own initial devious behaviour, whatever its object may be. I don't think any penalty I can impose will make the slightest difference in the way you personally will behave in the future. But I have no reason to think there will be any repetition of these offences.'

The judge then sentenced the defendant to seven years made up as follows – six years on the cheque charges, six years concurrent for falsely obtaining travellers' cheques and airline tickets, six years concurrent on the insurance charges, five years concurrent on the charges relating to overdrafts, six months concurrent for falsely obtaining a credit card, and one year consecutive for the passport application offence. The charges of making false statements to obtain legal aid were in the circumstances withdrawn by the prosecution as were the charges concerning the birth certificate applications in the names of Markham and Mildoon.

On the other hand, Sheila Buckley received a two-year sentence suspended if she did not get into any further trouble during that period. 'I have no doubt that you were fully aware of what was going on,' the judge told her.

You have been referred to in this court as a secretary or typist. Mr Stonehouse gives a better evaluation of your assistance to him. But you are a person of good character up to now and I have no reason at all to believe that if you had not met Mr Stonehouse you would have committed any kind of criminal offence. . . . I think you were extremely unfortunate to meet this persuasive, deceitful and ambitious man. I know you won't recognise it; women in your position rarely do. Fortunately for you I recognise it. Were it not for that, you would be sentenced to imprisonment which you would be called upon to serve here and now. But I do recognise that John Stonehouse's influence must have been tremendous. One has only to see the manner in which he sought to mesmerise the jury in this court to know he could have told you anything, and while it is clear that you knew the situation, he no doubt persuaded you your duty was to go along with him.[23]

After passing sentence, the judge also declared the two defendants bankrupt. In addition Mrs Barbara Stonehouse announced her intention of divorcing her husband. 'Of course I have regrets,' she told a press reporter at the time. 'Who wouldn't have regrets? We had so many happy years together, but I cannot go over and over these things again. This time it is inevitable. We are parting.' She obtained her divorce in 1978 while her husband was still serving his sentence. Meanwhile, following his conviction, he ceased to be an MP and a member of the Privy Council.

In February 1981, after his release from prison, where he gained the maximum remission for good conduct, having served three years, John Stonehouse married Sheila Buckley. They now have a son and are living happily together in a one bedroom flat in West London where he is now writing 'thrillers', of which the first *Ralph*, was published in 1982. 'This is my new career,' he was reported as saying at the time. 'As a result of the tranquillity I have had in the past few years and extremely happy relationship with my wife, I have found a new world I never knew really existed.'[24]

5

A few days before Christmas 1981, reports appeared in the press that a girl had been found hanging on a lamp-post outside the London flat of Mr Nicholas Fairbairn, MP, the Solicitor-General for Scotland. It later emerged that the lady concerned was Miss Pamela Milne, the thirty-four-year-old daughter of a retired major-general, who was a House of Commons private secretary, having acted in this capacity for Sir Ian Gilmour, Mr Charles Morrison and latterly Mr Fairbairn, with whom she had been having a love affair. Miss Milne subsequently denied that she had tried to hang herself from a lamp-post or from anything else. 'I wouldn't have the energy to climb up a lamp-post,' she was reported as saying. However, she admitted that she had tried to take her own life in Mr Fairbairn's flat in Roupell Street, Waterloo. 'Nicky wasn't there at the time but [his daughter] Charlotte was,' she said. 'It must have been terrible for her. What is true is that I was taken to St Thomas's hospital suffering from an overdose of drugs. I took the drugs in an attempt to commit suicide.' Asked by a reporter why she had done this, she said: 'I was depressed.' Further asked if this had anything to do with her relationship with Mr Fairbairn, she allegedly replied: 'It could have been contributory.' Apparently her romance with her House of Commons boss had gone on for some years and had now come to an end. The suicide attempt took place on 26 October 1981.[25]

Nicholas Hardwick Fairbairn, aged forty-eight at this time and Tory MP for Kinross and West Perthshire, was (and still is) one of the most colourful characters in the House of Commons. Owner of Fordell Castle near Dunfermline in Fife, he describes himself in *Who's Who* as author, farmer, painter, poet, TV and radio broadcaster, journalist, dress designer (he is said to design his own clothes), landscape gardener, *bon viveur* and wit. In recent editions of this invaluable work of reference he has variously described his recreations as 'giving and forgiving', 'being sharp and blunt at the same time', and 'the cure and eradication of British tick fever'. In the current edition he lists them as 'philanthropy and philogyny', of which the latter term (coined by him from the Greek) is presumably a synonym for making love to women. He is very interested in women and sex, an interest he may well have inherited from his father, a noted psychologist who developed the theory of object relations, according to which releases of tension such as in orgasm and

[332]

sneezing, are essential to sanity. In 1962 Nicholas Fairbairn married the Hon. Elizabeth Mackay, daughter of Lord Reay, by whom he has had four daughters and a son. Their marriage was dissolved in 1979, and his friends thought that after the divorce formalities were completed he would marry Miss Milne. But this did not happen and he has since married another lady. Mrs Thatcher considered that his affair with Pamela Milne was a private one, 'though sometimes affairs break down.'

'Nick has apparently done nothing wrong,' said a Conservative parliamentary colleague at the time of the Pamela Milne incident. 'But I cannot see how he can continue in his present office. His name has become involved in a scandal and he will come under tremendous pressure to resign.' Asked if he intended to resign, Fairbairn replied: 'There is no prospect of such a thing. I would like to think that the press might have some feelings for human beings.' To do her justice the jilted Miss Milne publicly stated that, although their relationship was over, she bore Mr Fairbairn no grudge at all.

'A man needs a woman, but a woman needs to be needed,' Mr Fairbairn has stated, discoursing on his favourite subject. 'The man, therefore, must give something to her but never take from her.' Attacking Miss Janet Fookes's kerb-crawling bill, particularly the clause which makes it an offence 'for a man to solicit a woman for sexual purposes in a manner to cause her fear,' Mr Fairbairn was reported as saying: 'I must promise the Honourable Lady, who is the proposer of this bill, that I have always been attracted to her but I have never actually dared to ask her to go to bed with me. After this, I would have to say to myself, "How am I going to put it so that it is not likely to cause her fear?"' Miss Fookes was reported as having replied that she would rather sleep with a dead cod.[26]

It was in the same speech that Nicholas Fairbairn related that an encounter had occurred at Holyroodhouse in Edinburgh where Mrs Thatcher had been the guest of Lord Elgin, the Lord High Commissioner of the Church of Scotland.

A gentleman who occupied a grand office and whom out of chivalry I will not name, had taken grandly of wine and therefore as wine does allowed veritas to overcome him. So he went up to the Prime Minister, and in words I will not use said to her that he had always

[333]

fancied her, to which the Prime Minister replied: 'Quite right. You have very good taste. But I just don't think you would make it at the moment.'

Although Mr Fairbairn declined to identify Mrs Thatcher's would-be paramour, the *Daily Star* had no such inhibitions. Under the headline YOU CAD, SIR, the newspaper named the sixty-six-year-old baronet Sir Iain Moncrieffe of that Ilk as the man responsible. 'Goodness me,' said the baronet's wife. 'I thought they were calling Nicky Fairbairn a cad. All that nonsense in the papers is entirely untrue except that we were at Holyrood in 1981.' Lady Moncrieffe added that her husband had only once had the honour of being presented to Mrs Thatcher, and that the only words he spoke were: 'I don't always think much of your party, but I do support you.' To this, according to Lady Moncrieffe, Mrs Thatcher replied with a polite smile. The view in Downing Street was that it was 'extremely unlikely' that Mrs Thatcher would have made the remark attributed to her and that it was 'not her style'. There was some talk of Sir Iain suing the *Star* for libel, but any action he may have contemplated was frustrated by his sudden death.

'This is just one of those stories' was the opinion of the Conservative party chairman, Mr John Selwyn Gummer. As for feeling in Mr Fairbairn's constituency, his agent thought there had been a lot of fuss about nothing. He added, in what might be described as a masterly understatement: 'Mr Fairbairn expresses himself slightly differently to [sic] other people.'[27]

Nicholas Fairbairn did not resign over his affair with Pamela Milne and her attempted suicide. But he did resign some months later over remarks he made about a Glasgow rape case outside Parliament instead of, as he should have done first, in the House of Commons. Thus his remarks on sex eventually caught up with him. But he still sticks by the truth of his story about the Prime Minister as showing what an extraordinarily witty woman she is. ('Hers was a classically good riposte which caused amusement. It was a harmless vignette.') 'The press wants Parliament to be plastic and bland,' so he thinks. 'We are in danger of destroying individuality and personality, and there will be a triumph of the faceless. Everything which is not dull becomes scandalous.' He certainly has a point there.

6

Not so bizarre as the Stonehouse affair, though rivalling it in the amount of publicity it received, was the Parkinson affair, which unlike Stonehouse caused its central figure's political party some damage as well as reflecting unfavourably upon the Prime Minister's relevant attitude and conduct.[28] On 5 October 1983, the Right Honourable Cecil Parkinson, MP, Secretary of State for Trade and Industry with a seat in the Cabinet, and former Chairman of the Conservative party, made a statement to the press through his solicitors, in which he acknowledged that he had had a 'relationship' with his former private secretary Miss Sara Keays, aged thirty-six, and that she was expecting his child in the following January. He went on to state that he would be 'making financial provision for both mother and child.' (£100,000 was the rumoured figure.) He admitted that it had been his intention to marry Miss Keays, that he had told her of his 'wish to marry her', but that he had later changed his mind. He added: 'My wife, who has been a source of great strength and I decided to stay together and to keep our family together.' The contents of this statement, made, he said, with Miss Keays's consent, were confirmed by her London solicitors. At the same time officials at No 10 Downing Street stated that Mrs Thatcher was aware of Mr Parkinson's statement but viewed it as a private matter, adding that the question of his resignation 'does not and will not arise.'[29]

It emerged the following day that the Prime Minister had known about the 'relationship' and about Sara Keays's pregnancy at least three months earlier. Because of it apparently she had removed Mr Parkinson from the Party Chairmanship and installed the political fledgling John Selwyn Gummer in his place on the previous 14 September. Indeed she may have known about the 'relationship' for much longer, possibly as far back as April 1982, at the time of Cecil Parkinson's inclusion in the inner cabinet concerned with the Falklands war, when she may well have learned of it through the Home Secretary or the head of MI5 when Parkinson was presumably vetted for security. But there was no official confirmation or denial of this. However, Parkinson let it be known through parliamentary lobby correspondents and the like (contrary, it seems, to his agreement with his ex-mistress) that he had disclosed 'the full facts' to Mrs Thatcher after the polls had closed on 9 June in the

General Election which he was credited with having so brilliantly and successfully masterminded.

Prominent among Mrs Thatcher's critics was the Bishop of Bath and Wells, the Rt. Revd John Bickersteth, who later publicly attacked the Prime Minister for not accepting Parkinson's resignation after he had first admitted his affair with his secretary to her. 'She should be as loyal to the nation as she has been to Mr Parkinson,' said the Bishop, who was also Clerk of the Closet to the Queen.[30]

Cecil Edward Parkinson, aged fifty-two at this time, had been a clever grammar school boy with a modest family background in Lancashire, who managed to reach Cambridge where he graduated in arts, besides running for the University against Oxford. While in his mid-twenties and in the process of qualifying as a chartered accountant, he met and married Ann Mary Jarvis, whose father was a rich business man. This alliance was of considerable commercial benefit to him, since in the succeeding years, besides becoming a partner in his accountants firm, he acquired a number of company directorships, as well as founding the lucrative Parkinson Hart Securities Company. He first entered the House of Commons in 1970 at the by-election in Enfield West caused by the death of Iain Macleod, the Conservative Chancellor of the Exchequer. He quickly mounted the first step in the political ladder by becoming a Parliamentary Private Secretary, progressing to Assistant Government Whip, Minister of State for Trade, and then Chairman of the Conservative party with which he combined the offices successively of Paymaster General and Chancellor of the Duchy of Lancaster. Already a Privy Counsellor, he was promoted to the Cabinet in April 1982 following the reshuffle consequent upon the Falklands campaign, the conduct of which he helped to plan. In the new government following the Conservative victory at the polls in June 1983 Mrs Thatcher appointed him to the important Cabinet office of Secretary of State for Trade and Industry, although she already knew of his 'relationship' with Sara Keays and that he had promised to marry her when he had obtained a divorce. But for this he might well have been made Foreign Secretary instead of Sir Geoffrey Howe.

On 10 October 1983, the day before the opening of the Conservative Party Conference in Blackpool, Cecil Parkinson said in a television interview on BBC's Panorama that 'if ever I ceased to be an asset and became a liability, and the Prime Minister felt so, then of course I would leave immediately.' His words were to come true sooner than he thought. He was not present at the opening day of the Conference and so did not hear the backbencher Mr Ivor Stanbrook, MP for Orpington, denounce him as 'a self-confessed adulterer and a damned fool', who should have insisted on resigning. At the same time Mr Stanbrook condemned the party establishment's 'evident determination to pretend that nothing is wrong.' Incidentally on the same day details were disclosed of how Sara Keays narrowly missed being selected as the Conservative candidate at the Bermondsey by-election the previous February.

It was not until two days later, on the Thursday, that Parkinson made his first appearance at the Conference where he wound up the debate on free enterprise and industry. He was accompanied by his wife Ann and there was an outburst of rapturous applause when they mounted the platform along with Mrs Thatcher, although it was not exactly clear whom the applause was intended for, possibly all three. But there was no doubt about the recipient of the applause in Mr Parkinson's speech when, in an oblique reference to his adultery, he thanked the first woman he had betrayed, while making no reference to the second, an allusion described as 'deft and graceful' by the *Guardian* and 'a poignant moment' by the *Daily Telegraph*. However, even as the *Guardian* a few hours later was preparing to tell its Friday morning readers, in a page one lead story, that Cecil Parkinson had 'demonstrated he is home and dry', he was getting his come-uppance from Sara Keays.

During the night of 13/14 October Miss Keays issued a statement to *The Times* which was also immediately transmitted to the Prime Minister as well as her former lover in Blackpool. In this statement Miss Keays said *inter alia* that her baby had been conceived in a 'long-standing, loving relationship which I had allowed to continue because I believed in our eventual marriage'; that Mr Parkinson had first asked her to marry him in 1979; and that in May 1983, when she knew of her pregnancy, he changed his mind and decided that he no longer wished to marry her. At the same time she had told him that she could not deny her baby the right to the identity of its father. She went on to state that she had implored him during May and early June to inform the Prime Minister, because 'his name and mine were sufficiently linked in political circles for speculation to be inevitable,' but that he would not agree to this. However, on polling day (9 June), according to Miss

Keays, he changed his mind again and sought a reconciliation, asking her to marry him, a request which she had 'gladly accepted'; and on the same evening he told her that he had informed Mrs Thatcher of their relationship and that he would be obtaining a divorce in order to marry her. On 5 August, Miss Keays continued, Mr Parkinson had gone abroad on holiday with his wife and family, 'having reassured me of his intention to marry me', but on 1 September when Mr Parkinson met her he told her that he had once more changed his mind and that while he was abroad he had decided not to marry her after all. Meanwhile she had been asked by press reporters, on 23 August, whether it was true that she was pregnant by Mr Parkinson. Press comment, government pronouncements and 'the continued speculation about this matter' had put her in 'an impossible situation', she concluded, and she therefore felt she had 'both a public duty and a duty to my family to put the record straight.'

Cecil Parkinson saw Margaret Thatcher at 2 a.m. and told her that in his opinion Miss Keays's statement made it impossible for him to remain a member of the Government, which besides the Prime Minister and his own family would be seriously if not irretrievably damaged if he stayed. Mrs Thatcher asked him to give the matter further consideration and after several sleepless hours he returned to the Prime Minister's suite in the Imperial Hotel and offered his resignation which she accepted. Their brief talk, according to *The Times*, was said to have been distressing for both, and one of Parkinson's friends said he was 'quite broken'. He and his wife left Blackpool without more ado.

On New Year's Eve, 31 December 1983, shortly after 11 p.m. Sara Keays gave birth to a daughter at St Theresa's Hospital, Wimbledon. The baby, who was delivered by caesarian section with a spinal anaesthetic weighed 8 lb 3 oz and had brown hair like her father's. 'Sara is coping very well,' said her twin sister Elizabeth, while Cecil Parkinson was quoted as saying: 'I wish the baby peace, privacy and a happy life.' She was called Flora Elizabeth and left the hospital with her mother eleven days later. In the following March a formal maintenance order was made against the father.[31]

For the greater part of the two years following his resignation Cecil Parkinson, while remaining an MP, kept a relatively low public profile, concentrating on his business interests, incidentally collecting a dozen or so more company directorships, and except on a few occasions

Application Number Y39336

CAUTION:—It is an offence to falsify a certificate or to make or knowingly use a false certificate or a copy of a false certificate intending it to be accepted as genuine to the prejudice of any person, or to possess a certificate knowing it to be false without lawful authority.

QBX 061878

CERTIFIED COPY   OF AN ENTRY

NHS Number LBBVM 289	**BIRTH**	Entry No. **289**

Registration district   Merton

Sub-district   Merton   Administrative area   London Borough of Merton

1. Date and place of birth   CHILD
Thirty first December 1983
St. Teresas Hospital, Wimbledon

2. Name and surname	3. Sex
Flora Elisabeth KEAYS	Female

4. Name and surname   FATHER
Cecil Edward PARKINSON

5. Place of birth
Lancashire

6. Occupation
Member of Parliament

7. Name and surname   MOTHER
Sara Lavinia KEAYS

8. Place of birth
Keynsham, Avon

9.(a) Maiden surname ———	(b) Surname at marriage if different from ——— maiden surname

10. Usual address (if different from place of child's birth)   Winsbury House, Marksbury, Bath, Avon

INFORMANT

11. Name and surname (if not the mother or father) ———	12. Qualification Mother

13. Usual address (if different from that in 10 above)   ———

14. I certify that the particulars entered above are true to the best of my knowledge and belief
Sara Keays by declaration dated 31st January 1984   Signature
Statutory declaration made by Cecil Edward Parkinson on 11th Jan 1984 of informant

15. Date of registration	16. Signature of registrar
Second February 1984	J.M.Banks Registrar

17. Name given after registration, and surname

See note overleaf

CERTIFIED to be a true copy of an entry in the certified copy of a register of Births in the District above mentioned. Given at the GENERAL REGISTER OFFICE, LONDON, under the Seal of the said Office on   11th December 1985

Form A502AX Dd. 8349836 10M 1/85 Mcr.(306041)

SC

keeping out of the news and away from the media. One such occasion was in December 1984, while a guest speaker at Warwick University Conservative Association's annual dinner. The Government's plans to cut student grants with a consequent financial burden on parents were mentioned, and a lecturer in politics interrupted the guest speaker, saying: 'You should know all about being a parent!' Parkinson, who was understandably enraged by this remark, reportedly retorted: 'I don't think I owe you anything. I don't think you have the right even to speak to me, you little rat!' Parkinson's words were loudly applauded, although the lecturer subsequently denied that what he said referred to the guest speaker's affair with Sara Keays.[32]

The other occasion on which Parkinson received adverse publicity occurred in March 1985, when *Private Eye*, alluding to him in its 'Grovel' column, stated that the 'latest crush' of 'the great swordsman' was on his current House of Commons secretary Mrs Angela Mathew, who was reported as saying that work kept her so busy that she could not return to her country home in Gloucestershire at weekends so that her children had to be 'ferried up to London to see her'. Mr Parkinson described the story as 'all a pack of lies, all lies', and applied to a High Court judge in chambers for an injunction stopping the distribution of the relevant copies of *Private Eye*. The injunction was granted and upheld by the Court of Appeal with the result that the remaining 100,000 copies of the magazine which had not already been distributed appeared with a blank space where the story had been. At the same time Mr Parkinson and Mrs Mathew issued writs for libel against *Private Eye*. The publishers of the satirical magazine were said to have settled for £30,000 by way of damages besides apologising unreservedly, a relatively modest penalty in view of the fact that the magazine had an extensive readership and its profit was reputedly running at about £850,000 a year. 'Cecil Parkinson's libel action was just the kind of action *Private Eye* needed, a real blessing in disguise,' one of the magazine's directors told *The Observer* shortly afterwards. 'It was better than full page advertisements!' And a great deal cheaper, he might have added, in the light of the settlement.[33]

At the end of her first year of her second term as Prime Minister, Mrs Thatcher along with several senior Cabinet members made a point of attending the Conservative Central Office reception in honour of Cecil Parkinson, when he was presented with a blue despatch box in recogni-

[340]

tion of his work at the previous General Election. However, in August 1984, when she was asked shortly before her Cabinet reshuffle whether she intended to bring him back, she replied that she thought this would be 'a little too soon', although she made it clear that she did not rule it out 'during the lifetime of this Parliament'.[34] She also made a point of inviting Parkinson to her husband Denis's seventieth birthday party at Chequers in May 1985. Interviewed shortly afterwards on television by David Frost, she said: 'I have a great admiration for Cecil Parkinson. He had built up a business, knew how to run one, therefore can read anyone else's balance sheet, can cross-examine in a way only a person who has built up their own business can. He was a quite outstanding Minister and we miss him very much. He was also a very good communicator, very good on the media.'[35] Indeed Mrs Thatcher was several times on the record as saying how much she missed him in Cabinet. In July 1985 she gave a strong indication that she intended to reinstate him despite reservations of senior colleagues that considerable political risks were involved.[36]

However it was not to be. Although she did not change her mind until almost the last minute before her second Cabinet reshuffle in September 1985, in the event she was overruled or persuaded in a contrary sense by Viscount Whitelaw, her deputy and Leader of the Lords, and Mr John Wakeham, the Government Chief Whip, who no doubt stressed the danger of bringing back Parkinson at a time when the Conservative Party image needed distinct improvement and the Tories were lagging behind Labour in the opinion polls. The decision was taken at Chequers on 1 September when the membership of the new Cabinet was finally decided, and Parkinson was left out. Immediately afterwards the Prime Minister telephoned her errant ex-colleague who was on holiday with his wife in the Bahamas and informed him of the decision 'with regret'. No doubt she was right to play safe. Had she reinstated Cecil Parkinson, it would not only have been a negation of the 'Victorian values' which she has constantly extolled in the past but would also have given offence to other senior ministers and party managers, not to mention the lords spiritual in the Upper House and the clergy generally, who believe in the observance of the Seventh Commandment even in such a permissive age as the present. For Cecil Parkinson it must have been a cruel blow, since there is unlikely to be another Cabinet reshuffle before the next General Election and he must be fated to remain indefinitely on the back

[341]

benches in the House of Commons. However, as Mr Harold Macmillan, now Earl of Stockton, remarked at the time of the Profumo affair over twenty years ago, 'we have – in public life – to observe different standards from those prevalent today in many circles.' This dictum apparently still holds good, as many people think it should.[37]

Nearly three centuries earlier the dramatist William Congreve put the following lines into the mouth of one of his characters in *The Mournful Bride*:

> Heav'n has no rage, like love to hatred turn'd,
> Nor Hell a fury, like a woman scorn'd.

At all events Sara Keays was scorned not only once but twice. Or was it more? Parkinson first asked her to marry him in 1979, changed his mind a year later, proposed again in 1981 and was accepted. After she discovered that she was pregnant in May 1983, he told her to have an abortion, which she understandably refused to do, upon which he again refused to marry her. However, he changed his mind once more on the day of the Conservative victory at the polls in June 1983 when he proposed a third time, having told Mrs Thatcher that he wished to divorce his wife and marry Sara. However, after his summer holiday with his wife Parkinson jilted her again, as we have seen. All this and much else besides are related in Sara Keays's account of the affair which she astutely arranged should be serialised in *The Mirror* during the week of the Conservative Party conference in Blackpool in October 1985, the instalments being designed to form the basis of a book entitled *A Question of Judgement* which has since been published.[38]

The serialised extracts contained a revealing exchange of letters between Sara's father Colonel Hastings Keays and the Prime Minister Mrs Thatcher. ('I am not a rat, Colonel Keays,' Parkinson allegedly told the Colonel after the Prime Minister had shown him his first letter in which he stated that Sara was pregnant by him. 'You are speaking to your future son-in-law.') Also there was the story of her selection as Conservative candidate for Bermondsey, including how her name was removed from the list of Conservative party candidates as the result of pressure from Conservative Central Office then under Parkinson's jurisdiction. There was too an embarrassing account of how Parkinson stayed one night with Sara leaving his car outside her house with

Cabinet boxes in the boot. During the night the car was stolen much to Parkinson's consternation and he had to inform the police which he did from his own London home, thus giving the false impression that the car had been stolen from there. Fortunately the car was quickly recovered, the Cabinet boxes apparently being unopened since the thieves were primarily interested in spare parts for other vehicles. Finally, there was the admission that Parkinson had talked to Sara about Cabinet discussions on the Falklands War, thereby conceivably being in breach of the Official Secrets Act.

Parkinson stayed away from the Conservative conference, having found it convenient to make a business trip to Hongkong with his wife during that week.

The *Mirror* articles certainly made more lively reading for the delegates at Blackpool who had to listen and subsequently read the cliché-ridden speeches of the ministerial leaders, despite Mrs Thatcher getting an eight-minute standing ovation for her rhetoric.

Jilly Cooper, who covered the conference for *The Mail on Sunday*, described Norman Tebbit, the new Party Chairman, as looking like the second murderer in *Macbeth* until he smiled. 'We must play as a team,' he told the delegates. 'We must revitalise every organ in the party.'

'Not Cecil's, for God's sake,' Jilly Cooper overheard one delegate mutter.[39]

The Parkinson affair has been well summed up by Marcia Falkender in her weekly column in the same journal and in the same issue:

I can reveal that in the days just after Mrs Thatcher's Falkland victory, when we are led to believe that she was still ignorant about Cecil's long running affair, she indicated to him over late-night drinks that with that second General Election victory and her 60th birthday under her belt she would make way for a new leader.

At that time her two favourites were Cecil and Norman Tebbit – with Cecil by far the apple of her eye.

Now Cecil has destroyed his political career because he was a weak man torn three ways by his wife, his mistress and the Prime Minister.

Or, as the political editor of the *Mirror* group Joe Haines has put it: 'Had she not written this book, we should have lost a fascinating revelation of low standard life in high places . . . It is not the story of a scorned

[343]

woman bent on revenge. It is the story of a woman betrayed by her lover and by her party, who is determined to put the record straight.'[40]

Sara Keays's book *A Question of Judgement* was published on 5 November 1985. Interviewed by ITN on the previous evening she said in her opinion Cecil Parkinson would be back in the Government by then if Mrs Thatcher had accepted his resignation on polling day in 1983. She went on to blame the Prime Minister for a 'very grossly unfair judgment' and for causing her a great deal of suffering. In allowing Cecil Parkinson to carry on in office after he had publicly acknowledged their love affair was in effect saying, Sara Keays declared, that 'what she had been told by my father, and what she had been told by Cecil on my account, was untrue.' Consequently she emphasised that she had the right to defend her reputation, which she had done in her statement to *The Times* and later in her book.[41]

'Nobody ever questioned his role,' she was reported as saying of her ex-lover on the day of the book's publication.

Nobody has ever said that if he didn't wish to conceive a child he should have left me alone . . . It is a very curious result of the age of the Pill that all responsibility has been transferred to the woman. The one thing that people can say that I did wrong was having an affair with a married man. It's the one charge I will accept. I broke one of society's and one of Christianity's rules in having an affair with a married man. Beyond that there's nothing I can truthfully say about my involvement with him about which I feel ashamed. Nothing whatsoever.

'If I did wrong, what about him?' she went on. 'He was the one who was married, for God's sake. He kept the thing going. I didn't. I wasn't married. Why is it always the man who is seduced and not the other way round? I didn't want to see his family hurt in any way. I never sought to harm them. I've suffered in a way thousands of women have suffered, the anguish of an unhappy love affair. Cecil Parkinson has never had to justify his behaviour. He was forgiven. My reputation was damaged for ever in the eyes of most people.'[42]

It is well known that they order these things differently in France where many married politicians have mistresses and are not subject to the restrictions prevailing in Britain. Asked about the Parkinson-Keays

[344]

affair, President Mitterand characteristically commented: 'If I had to select my Cabinet with such restrictions placed upon me, I would only have forty homosexuals left to choose from!'

As for Sara Keays, she has said: 'Once the book is out of the way, the matter will be behind me. I do not want to return to this subject.' And with that remark the affair can best be left.

7

One thread runs through the tangled web which is the subject of this work – the damaging effect upon the deceiver in British public life and society whose sexual frailties are exposed. The permissiveness which has characterised the past quarter of a century, facilitated by legislative changes in the law of divorce, abortion, homosexuality and soliciting, has lessened or removed altogether the social penalties incurred by the sexually immoral individual in Victorian times, although Members of Parliament still probably remain most at risk. Soliciting by prostitutes, whether the person solicited has complained or not, is now an offence, and this has led to the practice of call girls who advertise in the press under the cover of escort agencies or massage parlours. On the other hand, kerb-crawling has recently become a criminal offence, but it is difficult to enforce because the kerb crawler can always say he stopped to ask the way or the time, and the female at the kerbside is unlikely to contradict him unless she happens to be a policewoman in plain clothes.[43]

Some cases which might have been described have been omitted because the author has written about them in detail elsewhere. For instance, there is the Powderham Castle affair. This concerned William Beckford of Fonthill, author of the oriental tale *Vathek*, and the sixteen-year-old Hon. William Courtenay, son of the second Viscount Courtenay of Powderham and known as 'Kitty'. In October 1784 it was announced that Beckford, who had recently married, was to receive a peerage. However the news got out that Beckford, while on a visit to Powderham, had seduced Kitty, which the boy under pressure admitted. In the event Beckford did not get a peerage and fearing prosecution went abroad with his wife. Although he subsequently returned to Fonthill where he built his celebrated library, he was socially

[345]

ostracised. Meanwhile in 1811 a warrant was issued for the arrest for sodomy of Kitty who had succeeded his father as Lord Courtenay. He too fled abroad and never came back to England; he died in Paris in 1836 at the age of 66, when the Courtenay title became extinct.[44]

Again, it will be recalled that at the trial of the adulterous Queen Caroline, George IV's consort, according to Princess Lieven, Caroline threatened to reveal details of the alleged illegitimate offspring of the Royal Princesses, her sisters-in-law, of whom Sophia was the fifth and was the subject of detailed gossip to the effect that she became an unmarried mother. Her lover is supposed to have been George III's equerry General Garth, who undoubtedly did have a natural son named Thomas, who followed his father into the army and of whom Princess Sophia is said to have been the mother. But the evidence to this effect is entirely hearsay, and when she died blind like her father in 1848 Lord Lansdowne described her in the House of Lords as having 'passed a long life of virtue, charity and excellence in every position, public and private, in which she was placed.'[45]

A contemporary of the Princess was Harriette Wilson, daughter of a Swiss clockmaker in London; she has earned a place in the *Dictionary of National Biography* by reason of her scandalous (but not pornographic) memoirs. She is delicately described in the *D.N.B.* as 'a woman of fashion', but she was really a high class whore and incidentally a blackmailer. She had a mass of aristocratic lovers including three Dukes (Wellington, Leinster and Argyll), other peers of lower rank and the sons of peers including the Duke of Beaufort's (Marquess of Worcester) and Lord Melbourne's (Lord Frederick Lamb). She retired for a time to Paris where she married a swindler called William Rochfort, who treated her badly, though aiding and abetting her blackmailing communications which surprisingly she was allowed to send to her aristocratic ex-lovers through the diplomatic bag. Her charge for excising compromising references from her forthcoming memoirs was £200. This sum the Duke of Wellington refused to pay, allegedly returning her written request on which he had scrawled, 'Publish and be damned.' This is just what she did. The *Memoirs* appeared in four volumes in 1825, going into thirty editions in a year and making a considerable sum of money for her and her publisher John J. Stockdale. Her disclosures had no adverse effect upon the political career of the victor of Waterloo, since he became Prime Minister a few years later.

[346]

Among those who paid up was Queen Caroline's advocate Henry Brougham, later Lord Chancellor, who feared for his career at the Bar and the domestic trouble which would ensue if Harriette 'communicated the proofs of your infidelity to Mrs Brougham', which she threatened to do. It was to be otherwise in the reign of Queen Victoria, when no politician or public figure could avoid the dire consequences bound to follow any amorous adventures such as recounted by Harriette Wilson.

Royalty was also indirectly involved in a homosexual scandal in the person of the future King Edward VII's elder son Albert Victor, known as Prince Eddy until his elevation to the Dukedom of Clarence and Aviemore in 1890. In 1888–89 he allegedly visited a homosexual brothel in Cleveland Street, London, where another patron was Lord Arthur Somerset, a younger son of the Duke of Beaufort. Somerset fled the country to avoid arrest and never returned. But the Duke of Clarence and Aviemore, against whom there was no incriminating evidence unlike Somerset, remained in England where he became engaged to his cousin Princess May of Teck, but died of pneumonia before the marriage could take place, although the date had already been fixed and the prospective bride's trousseau delivered. Clarence's younger brother was George Duke of York, to whom Princess May in turn became engaged and whom she eventually married. The Duke of York in due course succeeded his father as George V while his wife became Queen Mary. Had Princess May married Clarence, the marriage could hardly have been fortunate, since her fiancé's health was poor and according to two surgeons he was treated for venereal disease, both syphilis and gonorrhoea, and if he had married he could have infected his wife. At all events his 'dissipated life', of which Queen Victoria complained, was essentially heterosexual in character and his reputed visit to No 19 Cleveland Street was no doubt made under a misapprehension that it was a normal whore house.[46]

Finally two cases must be briefly mentioned, each involving an element of mystery. The individuals concerned were a major-general in the British army and an archdeacon in the Church of England.

Major-General Sir Hector Macdonald, KCB, was one of the few soldiers in British military history to rise from the rank of private to that of general. The son of a Scotch crofter, Macdonald enlisted as an infantryman in the Gordon Highlanders in 1870 at the age of seventeen.

[347]

He first saw fighting nine years later in the Afghan War and as a colour-sergeant accompanied Lord Roberts on the famous march from Kabul to Kandahar. On this occasion he fought with such bravery that he earned the popular nickname of 'Fighting Mac'. At the same time Lord Roberts who led the march offered him the choice between the Victoria Cross and a commission. Macdonald chose a commission in spite of its disadvantages as regards pay and class. However, he rose rapidly from second lieutenant to lieutenant-colonel, in which rank his courage and resourcefulness during the Nile campaign earned him the thanks of Parliament and the appointment as ADC to Queen Victoria. For his services in the Boer War, when he commanded the Highland Brigade and was wounded in action, he was knighted by King Edward VII. He returned to duty in southern India, whence he was transferred to the command of the troops in Ceylon. Here disaster befell him. Nine months later, in April 1903, what the *Dictionary of National Biography* has termed 'an opprobrious accusation against him' was reported to the Governor of Ceylon.

The exact nature of the charge has never been revealed, but it almost certainly implied homosexual conduct, although it was not suggested that any troops were involved. The Governor saw Macdonald, who admitted nothing, since homosexual conduct was not an offence under the laws of Ceylon. However, Macdonald asked to be allowed to return to England and discuss the matter with the War Office authorities, to which the Governor agreed. In London Macdonald was interviewed by Lord Roberts and also had an audience with the King. What passed between them is not known, but it has been established that the King informed Roberts that he saw no reason why a court martial should not be convened in Ceylon in spite of the publicity this would entail. Macdonald was accordingly ordered to return to Ceylon and face it.

Macdonald accordingly set out by the overland route to Marseilles, where he was expected to catch the next steamer to Colombo. However he got no further than Paris, where he put up in the Hotel Regina, a high class establishment in the Place de Rivoli. There he fought his last battle – this time with himself, after he had read a statement in a newspaper of the 'grave charges' which had been made against him. He went up to his bedroom where he shot himself with a revolver – the bullet was aimed behind his right ear and killed him instantly. His body, placed in a plain coffin, was taken to London and thence to Edinburgh.

[348]

It was generally expected that he would be buried with full military honours in the county of his birth, but his widow, from whom incidentally he had been separated for several years, arranged the funeral, which took place quietly and quickly in the Dean Cemetery in Edinburgh. In 1907 a tower was erected overlooking his birthplace near Dingwall in Ross-shire. It only remains to add that the commissioners appointed in Colombo to investigate the matter unanimously and without hesitation acquitted him of any crime, attributing his suicide to false rumours spread by those who resented his humble birth and rapid promotion in the service. But the truth of the matter will probably never be known for certain.[47]

Like Sir Hector Macdonald, the Rev. John Wakeford was of humble birth, being the son of a Plymouth dockyard worker, and like Macdonald too his professional career until scandal overtook him was successful and impressive, since he was an archdeacon, a canon and preceptor of Lincoln, and widely believed to be the next bishop of this diocese. In 1920, at the age of sixty-one, he was accused of having had an illicit affair in the course of two visits to the Bull Hotel in Peterborough. At his own request he was charged before the Bishop of Lincoln in the Consistory Court where he stoutly denied the charge. He swore that he had stayed alone in the hotel on each occasion and the only woman he had spoken to was one he had met in Peterborough cathedral, where he had helped her to decipher an inscription but had never seen her before or since. The evidence for and against him was conflicting, and in the event the Court found him guilty of adultery and he was deprived of his benefices but not unfrocked as a person unworthy to remain a minister of the Church.

Archdeacon Wakeford thereupon appealed to the Judicial Committee of the Privy Council, a right long enjoyed by the clergy in non-doctrinal matters. The appeal, which began on 8 April 1921 and caused immense public interest, was heard by the Lord Chancellor the Earl of Birkenhead and two other law lords (Buckmaster and Shaw), together with four ecclesiastical assessors, who were bishops (London, Gloucester, Rochester and Ely). The appellant was represented by Sir Edward Carson, the leading advocate of the day – it was his last big case before himself becoming a law lord – while Sir Douglas Hogg, later Lord Hailsham, appeared for the respondent Bishop of Lincoln. Carson's defence was that the case against his client was a conspiracy by the hotel manager and others, including the archdeacon's brother-in-law the Rev. C. T. Moore, who was an avowed enemy. On the other hand, Mrs Wakeford supported her husband to whom she had been married for twenty-five years, and remained convinced of his innocence.

Lord Birkenhead, who was anxious to uphold the appeal, felt obliged to discount the conspiracy defence, since it would have had to be framed before the conspirators knew that Wakeford would be going to Peterborough or where he would be staying if he did. The archdeacon's only hope was to show that his signature and the woman's in the hotel register were forgeries. However, with the aid of a handwriting expert witness, Lord Birkenhead reluctantly reached the conclusion that they were genuine. His fellow judges and the assessors agreed and so the appeal was dismissed, although in delivering judgment the Lord Chancellor observed that the archdeacon's delinquency was 'lacking alike in cunning and contrivance. It is difficult indeed to associate simplicity so absolute with a course so perilous.'

After the failure of his appeal Wakeford published a pamphlet entitled *Not Peace but a Sword*, again protesting his innocence and quoting letters from various bishops under whom he had served praising his virtues. However some of this correspondence referred to an incident in 1915 when he was believed to have stayed at an hotel in Harrogate with a woman from Lincoln, an incident in which his brother-in-law's dislike of him may have originated. Continued brooding over his disgrace led to the loss of his reason and in the event he was confined to a mental asylum near Maidstone where he died on 14 February 1930. Meanwhile four bishops who felt sorry for Mrs Wakeford launched a fund amounting to £2,250 to provide her with an annuity.

To the last Mrs Wakeford was positive about her husband. 'In spite of the evidence against him,' she recalled, 'I firmly believe John Wakeford to be innocent, and whatever the world may say, no woman can live with a man, suffering for him and with him, watching him slowly losing his reason, without finding out the truth.'

The question remains, was Archdeacon Wakeford in fact guilty of breaking the seventh commandment? Alas, like the charge against General Macdonald, we shall probably never know the precise truth.[48]

Some may agree with Balthazar in Shakespeare's *Much Ado About*

[350]

Nothing that men are 'deceivers ever' and also with Mozart's librettist in *Cosi Fan Tutte* that women are the same ('So do they all'). Indeed the story of this amusing opera was reputedly based on a real-life incident which was the talk of Vienna at the time. But what of the outcome of the current theme of deceit, male and female? This has been admirably if lightheartedly expressed by Oscar Wilde in *Lady Windermere's Fan* when the author makes a socially experienced friend of Lord Windermere say that he never talks scandal. 'I wouldn't do such a stupid thing. *I* only talk gossip.'

'What is the difference between gossip and scandal?' asks Lord Windermere.

'Oh! gossip is charming!', his friend replies. 'History is merely gossip. But scandal is gossip made tedious by morality. Now, I never moralize. A man who moralizes is usually a hypocrite, and a woman who moralizes is invariably plain. There is nothing in the whole world so unbecoming to a woman as a Nonconformist conscience. And most women know it, I'm glad to say'.

In this characteristic exchange perhaps lies the essence of the tangled web which, according to Sir Walter Scott follows 'when first we practise to deceive'. That examples are not lacking in Britain among other countries this book purports to show.

Sources and Notes

1 – Aristocratic Morals in the Eighteenth Century

1. On the Castlehaven case and other homosexual cases described here, see H. Montgomery Hyde, *The Other Love* (London, 1970) 44ff. Elizabeth Chudleigh married the Hon. Augustus Hervey, later Earl of Bristol by whom she had a child, but from whom she afterwards separated. She then became the mistress of Evelyn Pierrepoint second Duke of Kingston, with whom she went through a ceremony of marriage in 1769 while her husband was still alive. Kingston died in 1773, leaving Elizabeth his fortune on condition that she remained a widow. The Duke's nephew, having discovered that she had married Lord Bristol, as her husband had become, brought a charge of bigamy against her and she was tried in the House of Lords and convicted, but she suffered no punishment. Afterwards she travelled abroad, continuing to style herself Duchess of Kingston. She died in 1788 in Paris aged 68, having led a life of extreme dissipation: see *Dictionary of National Biography* (*DNB*) IV, 298. The present author has described the Russell case in his *Carson* (1953), 164–6. In 1901 the second Earl Russell (1865–1931) was sentenced to three months' imprisonment which he duly served, but he later received a royal pardon. He died without issue and was succeeded by his brother Bertrand Russell, the philosopher.
2. See generally O. R. McGregor, *Divorce in England* (1957).
3. *id*, 10.
4. GEC *Complete Peerage*, VIII, 231.
5. *DNB*, X, 34, Henry Howard Duke of Norfolk; VII, 1114, Sir John Germain. Verelst was painting the Duchess's portrait in her apartment in Windsor Castle (of which the Duke was governor), as a pair to one of the duke, and at the end of a sitting he put his canvas and brushes in a cupboard which contained some articles of men's clothing belonging to Germain. Germain came to the artist and offered him money to say that the clothes were his

[352]

(Verelst's). Unfortunately Mrs Verelst overheard the conversation and spread the news abroad: J. M. Robinson, *The Dukes of Norfolk* (Oxford, 1982), 145–6. The Duke's portrait is now at the Norfolk family home, Arundel Castle, Sussex, and the Duchess's at Drayton House, Lowick, Northants, which she had inherited and where she lived with Germain.

6. Paul-Gabriel Bouce (ed), *Sexuality in Eighteenth-Century Britain* (Manchester, 1982), 127–8. The case of *Grosvenor v. Cumberland* for *crim. con.* was tried before Lord Mansfield, the Lord Chief Justice, in the King's Bench Division. Before her marriage Lady Grosvenor was Miss Henrietta Vernon, granddaughter of the Earl of Stafford. She is said to have first met her husband accidentally in Kensington Gardens while sheltering from the rain under a tree and he took her home in his coach. On the case, see Horace Wyndham, *Famous Trials Retold* (n.d.), 80–91. On Cumberland generally, see *DNB*, IX, 560.

7. *DNB*, XXI, 951–2. A copy of the report of the trial is in the British Library. See also Bouce, 129.

8. *The Life and Amours of Lady Ann F–l–y* (1782).

9. Bouce, 126–7. *DNB*, IV, 135–6.

10. G. Rattray Taylor, *Sex in History* (London, 1953), 189.

11. Hyde, 65–7.

12. McGregor, 13–14.

13. *DNB*, XIV, 205–6. In the codicil, Nelson described Horatia as his adopted daughter Horatia Nelson Thompson. See W. Gerin, *Horatia Nelson* (1970), *passim*.

14. *id*, VIII, 1037.

2 – The Elgins and the Marbles

1. The best biography of Elgin is by William St Clair: *Lord Elgin and the Marbles* (Oxford, 1967 and 1983). I am greatly indebted to the revised 1983 edition for many of the details in this chapter. William Nisbet assumed the name of Hamilton in addition to Nisbet on succeeding to the estates of Belhaven and Biel through his mother, born Mary Manners, who was a daughter of Lord Robert Manners and a granddaughter of the second Duke of Rutland. The estate of Dirleton was purchased in 1663 by William Nisbet's ancestor Sir John Nisbet, Lord Advocate in the reign of Charles II and a judge with the title Lord Dirleton.

2. *Sunday Times*, 22 May 1983. Miss Mercouri has recently promised that she would get the Marbles back to Greece 'in my own lifetime': *Daily Telegraph*, 18 Aug. 1985.

3. *Nisbet Letters. The Letters of Mary Nisbet of Dirleton Countess of Elgin*, ed. Nisbet Hamilton Grand (1926), 22.

4. *id*, 24.

5. *id*, 73.

6. St Clair, 86ff.

7. *Nisbet Letters*, 199.

8. *id*, 195, 197.

9. *id*, 351.

10. *id*, 240.

11. *id*, 280, 290 note.

12. Burke's *Landed Gentry*, 4th edn (1868), I, 467.

13. *The Trial of R. J. Ferguson, Esq. for Adultery with the Countess of Elgin* (1807). The trial took place in the Sheriff's Court on 22 December 1807. There is a copy of this work (20 pp) in the British Library.

14. The official MS account of the divorce proceedings which I have used is in the Scottish Record Office, Edinburgh, ref. CC8/5/29/3, pp. 1273–1473.

15. On Sir Ronald's death in 1841, Raith passed in turn to his son Colonel Robert Ferguson, MP, for Kircaldy Burghs, who assumed the additional name of Munro on inheriting the property of his grandfather Sir Hector Munro of Novar in Ross and Cromarty. Raith finally became the property of the present owner Arthur A. B. Monro-Ferguson. Mary Elgin's youngest daughter Lady Lucy Bruce married John Grant of Kilgraston, Perthshire. Their son Charles T. C. Grant of Kilgraston, who died in 1891, was Private Secretary to Sir James Brooke, first Rajah of Sarawak.

3 – From Lady Rosebery to Lord Melbourne

1. The case is fully described in the *Annual Register* (1815), Appendix to Chronicle, 283–6.

2. Marquess of Crewe, *Lord Rosebery* (London, 1931), I, 8. also *Burke's Peerage, sub* Mildmay.

3. H. Montgomery Hyde, *The Other Love* (1970), 79. *DNB*, VI, 811.

4. Roger Fulford, *The Trial of Queen Caroline* (1967), *passim*. Thea Holme, *Caroline* (1979), *passim*. H. Montgomery Hyde, *The Strange Death of Lord Castlereagh* (1959), *passim*.

5. *DNB*, VII, 1082.

6. Hyde, *Castlereagh*, 1ff, 8, 51ff.

7. *id*, 58.

8. *id*, 184ff, 190.

9. Philip Ziegler in his *Melbourne* (1976) is the first biographer to refer to this

interest. Lord David Cecil does not mention it in either of his biographies, *The Young Melbourne* (1939) and *Lord M* (1954). I am much indebted to Ziegler's work and also to the correspondence between Melbourne and Lady Branden in the Hertfordshire County Record Office (HCRO) in Hertford.

10. Ziegler, 100ff.

11. *id*, 106. Melbourne to Lady Branden, 26 Jan. 1832; 30 Nov. 1830; 9 July 1828: HCRO.

12. Melbourne to Lady Branden, 17 Jan. 1831; 8 Dec. 1831: HCRO.

13. *id*, 30 Aug., 8 March 1830: HCRO. Ziegler, 106.

14. *id*, 21 Feb. 1831: HCRO.

15. Cited Ziegler, 106.

16. Melbourne to Lady Branden, 4 March 1831; 18 Jan. 1831; 19 May 1831: HCRO.

17. *id*, 5 Nov. 1828; 18 May 1831: HCRO. Ziegler, 108.

18. Ziegler, 226ff. Alice Acland, *Caroline Norton* (1948), *passim*.

19. *The Letters of Caroline Norton to Lord Melbourne* (1974), ed. James O'Hoge and Clarke Olney, 157–8.

20. Ziegler, 232–3. Acland, 89.

21. *id*, 234. Acland, 91.

22. *id*.

23. Acland, 201–7.

24. Ziegler, 360–1.

25. Ziegler, 270. Charles Greville, *Journal*, VI, 441.

26. Ziegler, 271ff.

27. Cecil, *Melbourne* (1955), 327.

28. Cited *DNB*, IX, 115 (*sub* Lady Flora Hastings).

4 – Some Victorian Sex Scandals

1. O. R. McGregor, *Divorce in England*, 17ff. *Letters of Queen Victoria*, ed. A. C. Benson and Viscount Esher (1907), III, 378 and note.

2. Following difficulty about renewing the lease, the Clarendon was closed in 1872 and demolished to make way for shops and other smaller buildings.

3. Sir Horace Rumbold, *Recollections of a Diplomatist* (1902), 90–92.

4. These letters were printed in *The Romance of Lust* (1873–6), IV, 141ff, an erotic work compiled by the art collector and traveller William S. Potter (1805–79). The quotations which follow have been reproduced from the work by Ivan Bloch in *Sexual Life in England* (1958), 91–2.

5. *The Times*, 28 Nov., 19 Dec. 1866.

6. *DNB*, IX, 75, 357.

7. *id*, I, 1004.

8. *The Times*, 16 May 1871. A detailed account of this extraordinary case is contained in William Roughhead, *Bad Companions*, 149–83, to which the present author is indebted.

9. Charles Kingston, *Society Sensations* (1922), 213ff. Burke's *Peerage, sub.* Vivian.

10. *The Times*, 5 Aug. 1869.

11. GEC *Complete Peerage*.

12. For details see H. Montgomery Hyde, *The Cleveland Street Scandal* (1976).

13. Clodagh Anson, *Book* (1931), 124.

14. *Vanity Fair*, 5 Nov. 1870.

15. *The Times*, 25 Jan. 1879; 27 May 1924.

16. On the history of the Mordaunt case, see Kingston, 24–44. Also Philip Magnus, *King Edward the Seventh* (1964), 107–9; Kinley Roby, *The King, the Press and the People* (1975), 160ff; John Juxon, *Lewis and Lewis* (1983), 92ff.

17. The court's ruling did not become statute law in England and Wales until the Matrimonial Causes Act, 1937, which enacted that a divorce could be granted where the respondent was and had been for five years continuously under care and treatment as an insane person.

18. The period between decree *nisi* and absolute is now six weeks. Nor has an adulterer any longer to pay damages to the petitioner. Since 1969 (1977 in Scotland) the sole ground for divorce in England and Wales is the irretrievable breakdown of the marriage, established by proof of adultery, desertion, intolerable conduct or separation. The stigma of guilt has thus been largely if not entirely removed from divorce proceedings in Great Britain. There is still no divorce court in Northern Ireland or in the Irish Republic.

19. *The Times*, 27, 29 March 1884.

20. Juxon, 199.

21. *The Times*, 27, 29, 30 Nov.; 2, 3, 4, 7, 8, 9, 10, 11, 13, 14, 16, 17, 20, 21, 22 Dec. 1886.

22. *Letters of Oscar Wilde* (1922), ed. Rupert Hart-Davis, 193. On the Aylesford affair, which led to a violent quarrel between Marlborough's brother Lord Randolph Churchill and the Prince of Wales, see Georgina Battiscombe in *Society Scandals* (1977), ed. Harriet Bridgeman and Elizabeth Drury, 86–99. Lady Aylesford, who became Blandford's mistress in 1875 while her husband was touring India with the Prince of Wales, was Edith daughter of Colonel Peers Williams, MP, of Temple House, Berks; she died in 1897.

23. R. Barry O'Brien, *Lord Russell of Killowen* (1901), 206–7.

24. Juxon, 198. Marlborough's first wife, who divorced him, was Albertha Hamilton daughter of the first Duke of Abercorn. His second wife, whom he

married in 1888, was Lilian daughter of Commodore Cicero Price of the US Navy and widow of Louis Hammersley of New York. Marlborough died in 1892 and his widow then married Lord William Beresford, VC, son of the fourth Marquess of Waterford: A. L. Rowse, *The Later Churchills* (1958), *passim*.

25. Robert Hichens, *Yesterday* (1947) 203.

5 – Dilke and Parnell

1. The best biography of Dilke is by Roy Jenkins: *Sir Charles Dilke: A Victorian Tragedy* (1958). Dilke's official biography was written by his literary executrix Gertrude Tuckwell in collaboration with Stephen Gwynn: *Life of Sir Charles Dilke* (1917). Dilke's papers were deposited by Miss Tuckwell in the Manuscripts Department of the British Museum, now the British Library. See also John Juxon, *Lewis and Lewis* (1983), 194–221, and Charles Kingston, *Society Sensations* (1922), 112–26. The part played by Dilke's secretary, the French historian J. E. C. Bodley, in the Dilke affair is the subject of an interesting article by his son Major R. V. C. Bodley '(The Man Who Insulted King Edward') in the *Sunday Times*, 5 Jan. 1969.

2. Betty Askwith, *Lady Dilke* (1969), 10ff.
3. *id*, 143.
4. Leon Edel, *Henry James: The Middle Years* (1963), 106.
5. Leon Edel, *Henry James: The Conquest of London* (1962), 335.
6. Askwith, 335.
7. *id*, 155.
8. Jenkins, 232–3.
9. *id*, 235ff.
10. *id*, 261ff.
11. Edward Marjoribanks, *The Life of Sir Edward Marshall Hall* (1929), 67. Marshall Hall kept the copy of the statement which Marjoribanks found among Marshall Hall's papers and which he sent to Gertrude Tuckwell in 1931. The copy is now with the rest of the Dilke Papers in the British Library: Jenkins, 345 note.
12. Jenkins, 369.
13. The best biography of Parnell is by F. S. L. Lyons (1977), on which I have drawn extensively. See also *DNB*, XV, 322. Other biographies have been written by Jules Abels (1966), St John Ervine (1925), Henry Harrison, (1931), Joan Haslip (1936), R. Barry O'Brien (1898), William O'Brien (1926) and T. P. O'Connor (1891).
14. The house, which was built in 1779 by the amateur architect Samuel

Hayes and possibly designed by him, now belongs to the Department of Lands, Forestry Division, in the Republic of Ireland, which maintains the demesne as a centre of forestry research. The mansion has recently been restored by the Irish Board of Works.

15. Boycott was the agent for the Earl of Erne's property in County Mayo. Erne was primarily a northern landowner, his principal estate being in Fermanagh. For further details, see Joyce Marlow, *Captain Boycott and the Irish* (1977).

16. On Katharine O'Shea, who later married Parnell, see Joyce Marlow, *The Uncrowned Queen of Ireland: The Life of 'Kitty' O'Shea* (1975), to which I am considerably indebted for many of the details in the following pages. Katharine's memoirs, rigorously edited by her son Gerard, appeared in two volumes in 1914, *Charles Stewart Parnell: His Love Story and Political Life*.

17. Marlow, 221.

18. Sir Edward Clarke, *The Story of My Life* (1918), 289.

19. Marlow, 226–7.

20. Lyons, 604. Katharine Parnell died in Littlehampton, Sussex, on 15 Feb. 1921 and is buried in the municipal cemetery there. Clare, her elder surviving daughter by Parnell married a Brighton doctor, Bertram Maunsell. She died in 1911 while giving birth to her first child, a boy, Parnell's only known grandchild. The boy, who survived, grew up and served with the British Army in India where he died unmarried. Thus, so far as is known, Parnell has no surviving direct descendants: Marlow, 302.

6 – The Mr 'A' Case

1. The fullest account of Sir Hari Singh and the case in which he figured prominently with others is *The Mr 'A' Case* (1950) ed. C. E. Beechofer Roberts. See also Derek Walker-Smith, *The Life of Lord Darling* (1938), 277–86.

2. Roberts, 196.

3. *id*, 316.

4. On the trial of Hobbs, see biographies of Sir Travers Humphreys by Beechofer Roberts (1936), 195–204, and Douglas G. Brown (1960), 232–43.

5. *Hobbs* v. *Tinling* (1929), 2KB 1CA.

6. *News of the World*, 2 July 1939. The Arthurs' family seat was Glanomera, O'Brien's Bridge, County Clare.

7. *The Times*, 27 April 1961. See also Andrew Barrow, *Gossip* (1978), 23, 40, 76.

8. A. E. W. Mason based his novel *They Wouldn't be Chessmen* (1935) on Sir Hari and Captain Arthur who appears as Major Scott Carruthers, late of the Indian Army. 'That was a good idea', Mason wrote to Lady Aberconway who had helped him with revisions, 'to make Carruthers play chess with the Rajah. It might be one of the boring duties of his profession. I can easily slip it in.': Roger Lancelyn Green, *A. E. W. Mason* (1952), 212.

7 – Whose Baby? A Matter of Paternity

1. On the Russell case generally, see Eileen Hunter, *Christabel* (1973), *passim*. Also the essay by Fenton Bresler in *Society Scandals*, ed. Harriet Bridgeman and Elizabeth Drury (1977), 141–56. Also H. Montgomery Hyde, *Sir Patrick Hastings: His Life and Cases* (1960), 87–94.
2. Hunter, 61.
3. Hyde, 87–94.
4. *The Times*, 1, 2, 3, 7, 8, 9, 10, 14, 15, 16, 17 March 1923.
5. Edward Marjoribanks, *The Life of Sir Edward Marshall Hall* (1929), 426–7.
6. Hyde, 87–94.
7. *id.*
8. *id.*
9. *The Times*, 21–22 March 1924.
10. Marjoribanks, 429.
11. *The Times*, 31 May 1924. Law Reports [1924] A.C. 687.
12. *The Times*, 27 June 1924.
13. *The Times*, 30 July 1926.
14. *The Times*, 24, 25, 26, 27 Feb. 1976.
15. *The Times*, 19 Feb., 13, 28 April 1976.
16. Hunter, 183.

8 – When the Kissing Had to Stop

1. *DNB*, XXII, 109.
2. *The Times*, 3 Aug. 1875. Horace C. Wyndham, *Famous Trials Re-Told*, (N.d.) 31ff.
3. Grandfather of the present (seventh) Baronet, who lives in the Bahamas.
4. *Who Was Who 1941–1950*, p. 806.
5. *News of the World*, 6 May 1928.
6. Roland Wild and Derek Curtis-Bennett, *'Curtis'* (1937), 235ff.
7. *The Times*, 18 May 1928. In the earlier press reports Irene Savidge's

surname was incorrectly spelled 'Savage', being the name under which she was charged.

8. HMSO, *Inquiry in regard to the Interrogation of Miss Savidge*, Cmnd 3147. See also H. Montgomery Hyde, *Sir Patrick Hastings* (1960), 176ff; and *Norman Birkett* (1964), 229ff.

9. *The Times*, 3 Sept. 1933. Wild and Curtis-Bennett, 277.

10. 18 Sept. 1935. Public Record Office of Northern Ireland: D.1507/1/15. George Archer-Shee was a naval cadet who was wrongly accused of stealing a five shilling postal order from a fellow cadet: See present writer's *Carson* (1953), 263–76. The case was later dramatised by Terence Rattigan in *The Winslow Boy*.

11. D. Lloyd George, *My Darling Pussy: The Letters of Lloyd George and Frances Stevenson*, ed. A. J. P. Taylor (London, 1975), 69.

12. John Campbell, *F. E. Smith, First Earl of Birkenhead* (London, 1983), 689.

13. Lord Beaverbrook, *Courage: The Story of Sir James Dunn* (London, 1961), 106. The Orpen portrait of Mona is reproduced in colour here.

14. On Lieut.-Colonel Edmund Harry Tattersall (1897–1968) see *Who Was Who 1961–1970*, at p. 1100.

15. Beaverbrook, 112.

9 – Homosexuality

1. Montgomery Hyde (ed.), *Trials of Oscar Wilde* (1948), 236.

2. Stuart Mason, *Bibliography of Oscar Wilde* (1967), 14. A facsimile edition of *The Chameleon*, with an introduction by the present writer and an explanatory essay by Timothy d'Arch Smith was published by the Eighteen Nineties Society in London in 1978.

3. Hyde, *Trials*, 364.

4. Hyde, *The Other Love*, 147 and note (1970).

5. Hyde, *Trials*, 6. Hart-Davis (ed.), *The Letters of Oscar Wilde* (1962), 721.

6. Hyde, *The Other Love*, 137–8.

7. *id*, 148.

8. *Daily Telegraph*, 4 Dec. 1984. Edward James died in San Remo in 1984, aged 77.

9. Edward James, *Swans Reflecting Elephants*, ed. George Melly (1982), 26–8.

10. Hyde, *The Other Love*, 148–9; *DNB*, 1922–30, 390.

11. Hyde, *The Other Love*, 157–8. Robert Blake, *The Unknown Prime Minister* (1955), 497. *The Times*, 31 Aug. 1923. Farquhar's extraordinary career would

seem to entitle him to a place in the *Dictionary of National Biography*, but his name does not appear there.

12. *The Observer*, 27 Jan. 1985: article by Robin McKie. Philip Mairet, *A. R. Orage* (1936), 53. Donald McCormick, *Murder by Perfection* (1970), 23ff. Grayson's best book, which he wrote in conjunction with G. R. Stirling Taylor, was *The Problem of Parliament*, published by the New Age Press in 1909. Grayson was mistakenly convinced that the references to Sir Roger Casement's homosexual conduct in his diaries were British forgeries. On the contrary, the controversial entries were quite genuine. See H. Montgomery Hyde, *Trial of Sir Roger Casement* (1960 and 1964), *passim*.

13. Hyde, *The Other Love*, 212. James Lees-Milne, *Ancestral Voices* (1975), 203; *Caves of Ice* (1983), 42–3. Sir Paul Latham's mother, Florence Lady Latham, was the daughter of William Henry Walley of Manchester. She married Thomas, the first Baronet, in 1888, and their only son Paul was born in 1905. She died in 1950.

14. Diana Mosley, *Loved Ones* (1985), 93.

15. Hyde, *The Other Love*, 295.

16. *id*, 216–24.

17. Nigel Nicolson, *Portrait of a Marriage* (1973), 141.

18. Tom Driberg, *Ruling Passions* (1977), 234.

19. Harold Nicolson, *Diaries and Letters 1939–1945*, ed. Nigel Nicolson (1967), 110. See also Harold Nicolson's biographical Introduction to *Fox* by Christopher Hobhouse.

20. Driberg, 129ff.

21. Sir Robert Bruce Lockhart, *Diaries 1939–1965*, ed. Kenneth Young (1980), 462–3.

22. Driberg, 143–8.

23. *Sunday Express*, 17 Aug. 1975.

24. *The Times*, 13 Aug. 1976.

25. Ian Harvey, *To Fall Like Lucifer* (1971), 105ff.

26. Hyde, *The Other Love*, 296. *Evening News* (London) 21 Oct. 1953.

27. John Pearson, *The Profession of Violence. The Rise and Fall of the Kray Twins* (1972), 117ff.

28. On 5 November 1956 Ronald Kray was sentenced by the Recorder of London Sir Gerald Dodson to three years' imprisonment for causing grievous bodily harm. He served the sentence partly in Wandsworth and partly in Camp Hill prison in the Isle of Wight.

29. Pearson, 223.

30. Sir David Napley, *Not Without Prejudice* (1982), 392ff. Lewis Chester, Magnus Linklater, David May, *Jeremy Thorpe: A Secret Life* (1979), 294ff.

31. Chapman Pincher, *Inside Story* (1978), 278.

32. Barry Penrose and Roger Courtiour, *The Pencourt File* (1978), 356–69.
33. *Daily Express*, 20 Oct. 1977.
34. Penrose and Courtiour, 394.
35. *id*, 404–6.
36. Patrick Marnham, *The Private Eye Story* (1982), 193–4.
37. *Annual Register* (1978), 14–15; *id* (1979), 15.
38. *Daily Telegraph*, 10 May 1979. The fullest account of the trial is in this newspaper, intermittently to 23 June. See also Lewis Chester, etc. *op. cit.* 300ff.
39. *Daily Telegraph*, 19–20 Oct. 1984.
40. *id*, 26 Oct. 1984.
41. *Daily Mail*, 12 Dec. 1984.

10 – Call Girl Affairs

1. W. E. H. Lecky, *History of European Morals* (1913), II, 184–5.
2. Richard Deacon, *The Private Life of Mr Gladstone* (1965) 69–71, 139ff. A. L. Tottenham (1838–87) of Glenfarne Hall, Leitrim, was a retired Captain, not a Colonel. He was later MP for Winchester.
3. Kellow Chesney, *The Victorian Underworld* (1970), 329, 364.
4. *The Times*, 22 Sept. 1960: *R. v. Shaw*. All England Reports [1961], 330.
5. *Shaw v. Director of Public Prosecutions*, 2 All England Reports [1961], 446. Hyde, *History of Pornography* (1964), 198–200.
6. *Daily Telegraph*, 13 Aug. 1983, 26 Jan., 18 May, 8, 28 June, 6 July 1985. In the House of Lords, Lord Mishcon (Lab), in giving the Sexual Offences Bill an unopposed second reading on 27 June 1985, stressed the need to ensure that motorists who simply stop innocently to ask their way should not later find themselves convicted of the new crime.
7. Ludovic Kennedy, *The Trial of Stephen Ward* (1964), 62. *Oxford Dictionary of Quotations* (1980), 406.
8. *Lord Denning's Report*, Cmnd 2152 (Sept. 1963), 107–9.
9. *id*, 9.
10. *id*, 8. *Sunday Times*, 19 May 1985.
11. Auberon Waugh, 'Mandy's Story', *Telegraph Sunday Magazine*, 2 Nov. 1980.
12. Denning, 11ff, 106.
13. Nigel West, *A Matter of Trust: MI5 1945–72* (1982), 93ff.
14. Denning, 49.
15. *id*, 88.
16. *id*, 41–2.

17. Harold Macmillan, *At the End of the Day* (1973), 437, 439.
18. West, 96.
19. Denning, 61.
20. Macmillan, 439.
21. Denning, 66.
22. *id*, 67, 68.
23. Macmillan, 440–41.
24. Denning, 71–2.
25. Macmillan, 442.
26. Chapman Pincher, *Too Secret Too Long* (1984), 334.
27. Macmillan, 442. Judge Gerald Sparrow, *The Profumo Affair* (1963), 133.
28. *id*, 443, 445.
29. Chapman Pincher, 332. Dilhorne before his death expressed himself in these terms to Chapman Pincher.
30. Denning, 90.
31. Macmillan, 449.
32. George Wigg, 'Is this the End of the Affair?', *Sunday Telegraph*, 29 Sept. 1963.
33. Kennedy, 14ff.
34. West, 98.
35. Kennedy, 38, 73.
36. *id*, 250. *Daily Telegraph*, 3 April 1964. Chapman Pincher, 334.
37. *Sunday Times*, 19 May 1985.
38. *Daily Mail* (Nigel Dempster's Mail Diary), 27 April 1984. *Sunday Telegraph*, 6 May 1984.
39. Auberon Waugh, 'Mandy's Story', *Telegraph Sunday Magazine*, 2 Nov. 1980. Trudi Practor, 'Going on 40 by Mandy Rice-Davies', *Sunday Mirror*, 30 Sept. 1984.
40. *The Times*, 9 March 1966.
41. *Sunday Telegraph*, 26 May 1985.
42. The details of the Jellicoe and Lambton cases are contained in the *Security Commission Report on Security Aspects of the 'Call-girl Affair'*, Cmnd. 5368 (July 1973).
43. Chapman Pincher, 276–7. Although the identity of the ex-Labour minister is known to me, I refrain from mentioning it for obvious reasons.
44. The other members of the commission were Lord Garner, former head of the Diplomatic Service; Sir Philip Allen, former Permanent Under-Secretary at the Home Office; Lord Sinclair of Cleeve, industrialist and former President of Imperial Tobacco Co.; and General Sir Dudley Ward, former Commander-in-Chief of the British Army of the Rhine and Governor of Gibraltar.
45. Chapman Pincher, *Inside Story*, 277. Lambton was subsequently fined

£300 for drug offences at Marylebone magistrates court where he admitted that he had smoked cannabis in Norma Levy's bed.
46. *Daily Mail*, 22 May 1985.
47. Leslie Garner, *Mail on Sunday*, 19 May 1985.
48. *Daily Telegraph*, 8 June 1985.
49. *id*, 28 June 1985. *Daily Mail*, 28 June 1985.

11 – The KGB Takes a Hand

1. Rebecca West, *The Vassall Affair* (1963), 7, 9. According to Vassall he received £5000 for his life story from the *Sunday Pictorial*.
2. Sir William Hayter, *The Kremlin and the Embassy* (1966), 44.
3. Rebecca West, *The Meaning of Treason* (1963), 368.
4. *Report of the Tribunal appointed to inquire into the Vassall Case and Related Matters* (1963), Cmnd. 2009, 20. The other members of the Tribunal besides the law lord Viscount Radcliffe were Mr Justice Barry and Sir Edward Milner Holland, QC.
5. John Vassall, *Vassall: The Autobiography of a Spy* (1975), 149, 152.
6. Galbraith resigned on 8 November 1962 but was appointed Joint Parliamentary Secretary in the Ministry of Transport between 1963 and 1964. Since then he held no political office, although he remained MP for the Hillhead Division of Glasgow. He was created KBE in the New Year Honours in 1982 and died on 4 January 1982 of a brain tumour. His father, who survived him, was the first Baron Strathclyde.
7. Rebecca West, *The Vassall Affair*, 87.
8. 'Who's to Blame for Vassall?', *Sunday Telegraph* 11 Nov. 1962. The editor also wrote in this article: 'Many people have not grasped how Mr Galbraith's resignation was brought about by a whispering campaign and by the use of letters bought by the pro-Labour *Sunday Pictorial* from Vassall, the convicted spy . . . If on the strength of these letters Mr Macmillan accepted his colleague's offer to resign as evidence that Mr Galbraith was tarred, even to the smallest extent, with Vassall's treachery, he made a serious error of judgment, and snatched defeat out of the jaws of victory.' Later, in his memoirs, Mr Macmillan wrote: 'On looking back, I feel that it was a mistake on my part to accept Galbraith's offer of resignation at this stage. But he was very insistent, and did not wish to return to office until the full enquiry had been completed.' *At the End of the Day* (1973), 431–2.
9. *Report of the Tribunal*, 7–8.
10. Vassall, 193.
11. Trial of Cyprus spy ring, *Daily Telegraph*, 11 June 1985.

12. Wynne was sentenced to eight years' imprisonment, but after serving eleven months he was exchanged for the Russian agent Gordon Lonsdale held by the British. See Greville Wynne, *The Man from Moscow* (1967), and P. Deriabin (ed.) *The Penkovsky Papers* (1965).

13. Anthony Courtney, *Sailor in a Russian Frame* (1968), *passim*. I am greatly indebted to this revealing work for my account of the Courtney affair.

14. Courtney, 73.

15. *id*, 78.

16. *id*, 86–7.

17. *id*, 97–8.

18. *id*, 102. Smithers was Secretary-General of the Council of Europe from 1964 to 1969. He was knighted in 1970.

19. *id*, 117.

20. *id*, 120.

21. *id*, 130, 135–7.

22. Merlyn Rees, later a Labour minister and privy counsellor, had been returned for South Leeds in 1963.

23. Courtney, 133.

24. *id*, 149–50.

25. *id*, 150–1.

26. *id*, 171.

27. The Labour victor, Mr R. D. Roebuck, who received 17,374 votes, was a barrister and journalist. Courtney received 16,996 votes and the Liberal, Mr D. Colne, got, 4,749. Roebuck held the seat until the 1970 General Election when he was defeated by Courtney's successor Mr H. J. Dykes, who is still the Member.

28. Courtney, 208.

29. In the slander action against Constantine, Courtney alleged that at a cocktail party given by Edward du Cann at the Conservative Party Conference in 1966, Constantine told a young lecturer, Mr Anthony Thorold, who gave evidence for the plaintiff, that the underpants, which Courtney wore in the compromising photographs were of a style used by him following a rupture after his second marriage. Constantine was also alleged to have said that Courtney's claim that the incident in the National Hotel took place in 1961 was a lie. Constantine denied saying any of the things attributed to him. In his summing-up Mr Justice Hinchcliffe said it was a case of Thorold's word against Constantine's. Which was to be preferred? By their verdict for the plaintiff the jury preferred Thorold's, *The Times*, 19, 20, 21 March 1968.

30. *Daily Mail*, 24 Feb. 1981.

31. *Daily Telegraph*, 24 Feb. 1981.

32. *Sunday Times*, 22 Feb. 1981.

33. *Daily Telegraph*, 23 Feb. 1981.
34. *The Times*, 23 Feb. 1981.
35. *Daily Telegraph*, 23 Feb. 1981.
36. *id*, 11 June 1985.
37. *Daily Telegraph*, 25, 26, 28, 29 Oct. 1985.
38. *Mail on Sunday*, 27 Oct. 1985.
39. *Daily Mail*, 29 Oct. 1985.
40. *id*.
41. *Daily Telegraph*, 4 Nov. 1985.
42. *id*, 30 Oct. 1985.

12 – Members of Parliament and their Private Secretaries

1. *Daily Telegraph*, March 1975 *passim*.
2. John Stonehouse, *Death of an Idealist* (1975), 5ff.
3. *Sunday Times*, 22 Dec. 1974 (The Demise of a Super-Salesman).
4. Stonehouse, 46.
5. *id*, 78.
6. *Sunday Times*, *loc. cit.*
7. Stonehouse, 80ff.
8. *id*, 147–8.
9. *id*, 190.
10. *Daily Telegraph*, 13 Jan. 1975.
11. Stonehouse, 203–4.
12. *id*, 221.
13. *id*, 228.
14. *Daily Express*, 6 Jan. 1975.
15. *Daily Telegraph*, 20 Jan. 1975.
16. *id*, 22 March 1975. Stonehouse, 236.
17. *id*, 7 Aug. 1976.
18. *id*, 21 Oct. 1975.
19. *id*, 28 April 1976. See also John Stonehouse, *My Trial* (1976) *passim*.
20. *id*, 29 April 1976. *Sunday Telegraph; Observer*, 2 May 1976. Stonehouse, *op. cit.*, 186.
21. *id*, 8 July 1976.
22. *id*, 21 July 1976.
23. *id*, 6 Aug., 7 Aug. 1976.
24. *The Times*, 24 May 1982.
25. *id*, 22, 24, 29 Dec. 1981.
26. *Daily Telegraph*, 26 Jan. 1985. *Sunday Times* (People Notebook), 3 Feb. 1985.

27. *Sunday Telegraph; Observer*, 27 Jan. 1985.
28. On the Parkinson affair, besides contemporary newspaper reports, see Bruce Arnold, *Margaret Thatcher* (1984), 244ff.
29. *The Times*, 6 Oct. 1983.
30. *id*, 14 Oct. 1985.
31. *id*, 4, 6, 11, 13 Jan. 1985.
32. *Sunday Telegraph*, 3 Dec. 1984.
33. *Daily Mail*, 7 March; *Private Eye*, 8 March; *Sunday Times, Sunday Telegraph, Observer*, 10 March, 2 June 1985. *Private Eye* apologised in the High Court and paid Mrs Mathew 'substantial undisclosed damages', while Mr Parkinson waived his right to damages: *Daily Telegraph*, 30 July 1985.
34. *The Times*, 4 Aug. 1984.
35. *Daily Mail*, 10 June 1985.
36. *Observer*, 14 July 1985.
37. *Daily Telegraph*, 2 Sept. 1985. See also article by Paul Johnson ('Parkinson . . . and the double hypocrisy keeping him out in the cold.') *Daily Mail*, 3 Sept. 1985.
38. *The Mirror*, 7–12 Oct. 1985.
39. *The Mail on Sunday*, 13 Oct. 1985.
40. *The Mirror*, 7 Oct. 1985. Although Miss Keays received £100,000 plus from *The Mirror* for her story, it was less than the sum offered by the *News of the World* which she rejected, presumably because she considered *The Mirror* to be the more dignified journal besides being a daily and not a weekly.
41. *Daily Mail*, 5 Nov. 1985.
42. *The Daily Mirror*, 5 Nov. 1985.
43. One of the first to be prosecuted for this offence under Section 1(1) of the Sexual Offences Act which became law in July 1985 was a Crown Court judge and former Liberal parliamentary candidate, Mr Colin Hart-Leverton: *Sunday Telegraph*, 22 Dec. 1985. He was convicted and fined £200 by Wells Street magistrates court, although he protested that he had been 'framed': *Daily Mail*, 20 Feb. 1986. He successfully appealed, his conviction was quashed, and he was awarded costs against the Director of Public Prosecutions estimated at £10,000. *Daily Telegraph*, 19, 20 March 1986.
44. Hyde. *The Other Love*. 73ff.
45. 'A Study in Thoughtlessness' by Roger Fulford in *Society Scandals* (ed. Bridgeman and Drury), 51ff.
46. Hyde. *The Cleveland Street Scandal* (1976), *passim*.
47. 'The Tragedy of a Military Hero' by Anthony Livesey in *Society Scandals* (ed.) 120ff.
48. 'A Course so Perilous' by Rupert Furneaux in *Society Scandals*, 133ff.

Index